RESISTING DOMINATION

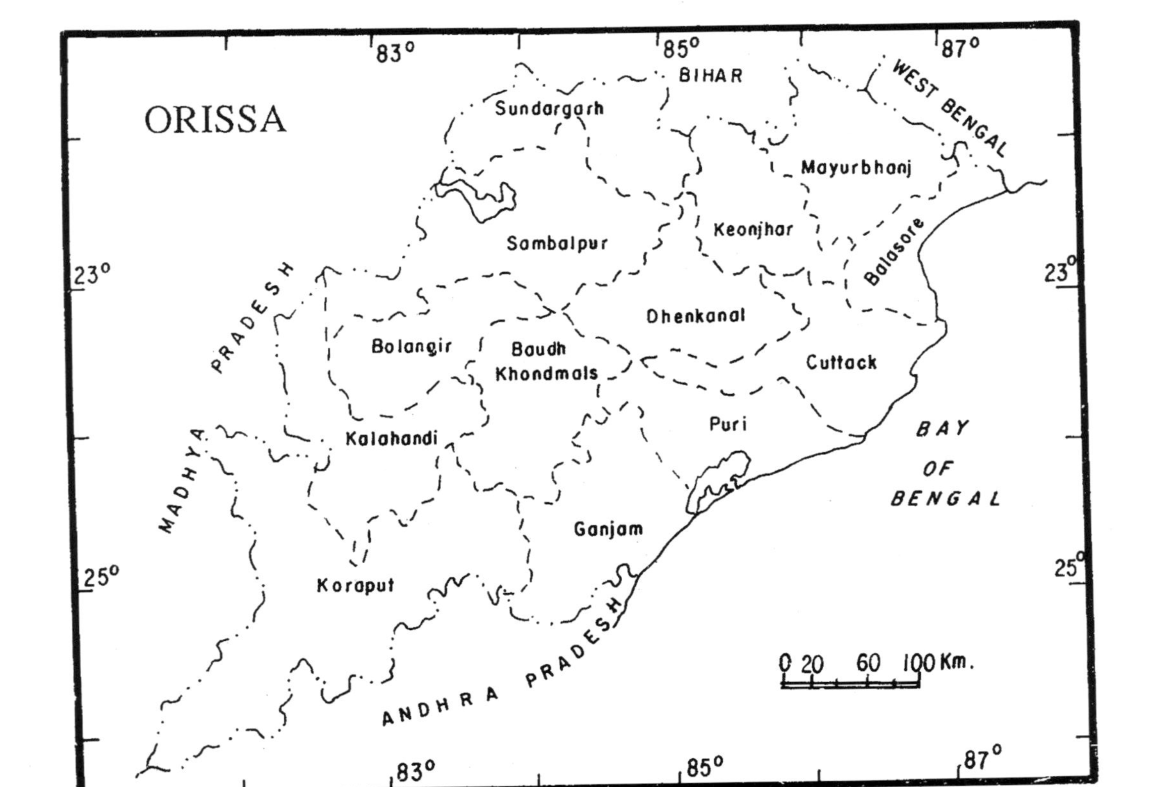
ORISSA
83°
85°
87°
23°
25°
BIHAR
WEST BENGAL
Sundargarh
Mayurbhanj
Keonjhar
Balasore
Sambalpur
Dhenkanal
Cuttack
Bolangir
Baudh Khondmals
Kalahandi
Puri
Ganjam
Koraput
MADHYA PRADESH
ANDHRA PRADESH
BAY OF BENGAL
0 20 60 100 Km.

RESISTING DOMINATION

Peasants, Tribals and the National Movement in Orissa 1920-50

BISWAMOY PATI

MANOHAR

2025

The publication of this book has been financially supported by the Indian Council of Historical Research and the responsibility for the facts stated or opinions expressed is entirely of the author and not of the Council.

First published 1993
Reprint 2021, 2022, 2023, 2025

ISBN 978-81-7304-027-6

Published by
Ajay Kumar Jain *for*
Manohar Publishers & Distributors
4753/23 Ansari Road, Daryaganj
New Delhi 110 002

Printed at
Replika Press Pvt. Ltd.

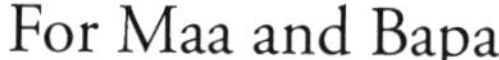

For Maa and Bapa

Abbreviations

Acc. No.	Accession Number
AICC	All India Congress Committee
AISPC	All India State Peoples' Conference
CPFLN	Confidential Police File on Laxman Naiko
HP	Home Political
IAR	Indian Annual Register
ICSSR	Indian Council of Social Science Research
IYSF	Indulal Yajnik Subject File
Mem	Member
NAI	National Archives of India
NMML	Nehru Memorial Museum and Library
NPARI	Nilgiri Praja Andolana Ra Itihas (viz. History of the Nilgiri State People Movement)
PCC	Provincial Congress Committee
REF	Report of the Joint Enquiry by the Revenue Commissioner Orissa into the Eram Firing on 28th September 1942
WWCC	Who's Who Compilation Committee

Contents

	Abbreviations	vi
	Preface	ix
I.	Changes, Crises and the Shaping of Popular Perceptions	1
II.	The Rise of the Mass Movements: Orissa, 1920-1934	60
III.	Of Movements, Compromises and Retreats: Orissa, 1936-1939	85
IV.	The Quit India Movement: The Climax of Popular Protest	142
V.	From Raj to Swaraj: The Complexities of Transition, 1943-1950	205
	Epilogue	245
	Glossary	251
	Select Bibliography	257
	Index	271
	Maps Orissa Princely States of Orissa	

Preface

The Indian national movement, which led to the freedom of the country in 1947, saw various political trends and the contribution of various classes and sections. It witnessed the broadening of popular participation from around 1920, which led to the development of three mass movements—i.e. the Non-cooperation Movement (1920-21), the Civil Disobedience Movement (1930-31) and the Quit India Movement (1942) in Orissa. Very few works discuss the development of the anti-imperialist struggle in Orissa in various phases of the mass movements. In particular the existing scholarship has largely tended to ignore the role of the peasants and tribals. Consequently, this work tries to fill this gap by examining the role of the common people and the way they related to the Indian national movement. This has been done by drawing upon a wide range of sources, including some rare material like oral evidence and folk tales to bring to life popular perception and imagination.

The study begins by exploring the nineteenth century. And while doing so, it weaves together the life and the cosmology of the peasants and tribals, highlighting the intra-regional variations and the process of colonisation. Its basic thrust is to explain how the national movement developed in an area, otherwise marked by geographical, ethnic and cultural diversities, and offers a perspective to grasp how the people of this region interacted with the anti-imperialist struggle.

Its analysis of the Non-Cooperation Movement — the first mass movement — demonstrates both the response of, as well as the tensions between, the peasants and tribals and mainstream nationalism. The Civil Disobedience Movement is discussed in a similar light, noting the shifts and the changes. These two mass movements contributed significantly in undermining the hold of colonialism. And, simultaneously the popular translations of nationalism pitted the peasants and tribals in a struggle against the internal exploiters (associated with the feudal and the colonial order) as well. Consequently, these two mass movements radicalised the anti-imperialist struggle.

And it is precisely this transition to radicalism—which got associated with the emergence of the Socialists, the Kisan Sangha (i.e. Peasant Association), the Communist Party and the Prajamandal (i.e. State Peoples') Movement which even re-cast the Congress in some ways—that has been examined in this study. It goes on to analyse how the Congress responded to electoral politics, the strong anti-imperialist and anti-feudal currents, and how it, subsequently, compromised its anti-feudal position. This study delineates the interventions of both the Kisan Sangha and the Prajamandal movement, the emergence of militant movements among the peasants and tribals of coastal Orissa and the zamindaris as well as the princely states. And, while doing so, it locates the turns and variations in the position of the Congress.

Basing itself on the background years (1940-41) this work goes on to discuss the build-up of the Quit India Movement, focusing on the new features that are visible as well as the social composition of the participants, keeping in view the complexities, tensions and the shifts, as also the popular perceptions of the Quit India Movement.

The process of decolonisation and the emergence of the new ruling class of Orissa are examined as well as how the latter related to the immediate context and its visions about the future. Also highlighted is the sweep of the peasant movement in the coastal region (leading to the share-croppers movement), a spell of the Prajamandal movement (leading to the merger of the princely states) and the way the Congress, the princes and the retreating colonial power related to these movements.

And finally the epilogue projects some of the basic features noticed. It hints at the present state of affairs, focusing on how some of the participants in the anti-imperialist movement view the past in relation to the present.

I would like to take this opportunity to thank all those whose help and cooperation made this work possible, including some who are no more like Shri Ramachandra Satpathy and many others like the 'unknown' tribal folk of Koraput and Kalahandi I had interviewed. Their faces and their word—whether it is Kausalya or Gundu Gomango—I shall never forget. Their greatest contribution was in making me think along lines I had never thought of, and making me realise how little I knew of human existence. I would also like to express my gratitude to Shri Banamali Das (Nilgiri) Shri Baishnab Pattnaik (Dhenkanal), Shri Gurucharan Pattnaik, the late Shri Sarat Pattnaik, Shri Nanda Pattnaik, the late Shri Kalindi Charan Pannigrahi, the late Shri Binode Kanungo and Shri Kishori Charan Das

Krupasindhu Misra (Ranpur) Laxmidhar Sahoo, Damodar Samantarai and Gopinath Pujari (Jeypur).

I would also like to thank the ever-helpful staff of the Orissa State Archives (Bhubaneshwar), the Board of Revenue Record Room and Library, Sahitya Samaj Library (Cuttack), The National Archives of India, the Nehru Memorial Museum and Library, the Sahitya Akademi Library, the P.C Joshi Memorial Library (New Delhi), the National Library (Calcutta), the comrades at the Cuttack Communist Party office and Ajoy Bhawan, New Delhi. I am also indebted to Amit da for his valuable comments, and suggestions.

I will always remember the encouragement I received from my parents who allowed me to do whatever I wanted. My mother's help for my research was invaluable and my brother procured material for me from various sources.

It was Indrani Sen, my friend and wife, who not only helped me through discussions and proof-reading of the drafts, but also translated many difficult poems and songs. More importantly she persuaded a lazy and difficult person like me to stick to deadlines.

I cannot end without thanking Sumit da for his support and encouragement over the years. It was he who made me believe that sailing on such uncharted seas was possible.

Biswamoy Pati

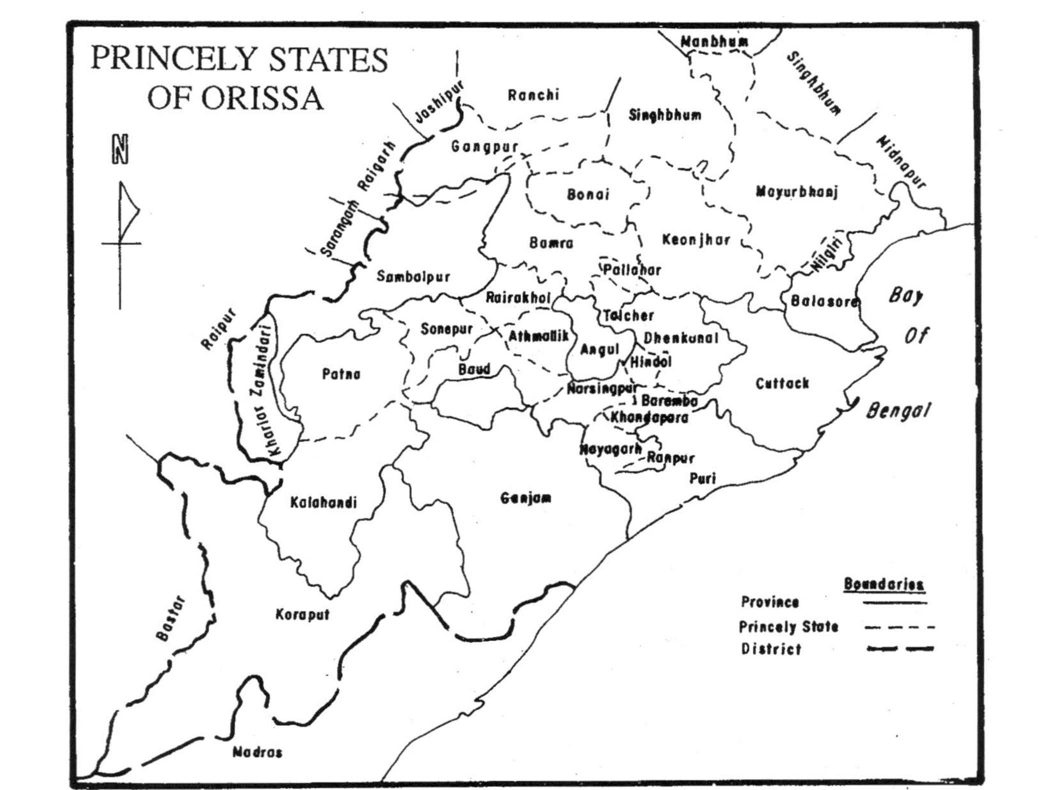
PRINCELY STATES
OF ORISSA
N
Ranchi
Singhbhum
Manbhum
Singhbhum
Midnapur
Joshipur
Gangpur
Raigarh
Bonai
Mayurbhanj
Sarangarh
Bamra
Keonjhar
Nilgiri
Sambalpur
Pallahar
Balasore
Bay
Of
Bengal
Raipur
Rairakhol
Talcher
Sonepur
Athmallik
Dhenkunal
Angul
Hindol
Khariar Zamindari
Patna
Baud
Narsingpur
Baramba
Khandapara
Cuttack
Nayagarh
Ranpur
Puri
Kalahandi
Ganjam
Bastar
Koraput
Madras
Boundaries
Province
Princely State
District

Chapter 1

Changes, Crises and the Shaping of Popular Perceptions

In order to grasp the complexities of the national movement in Orissa it is necessary to examine its background. Based on the colonisation of Orissa and the agrarian interventions in the nineteenth century, this chapter goes on to locate their implications on a wide-range of areas—from ecology and demography to the lives of the peasants and tribals. The explorations are delineated against the canvas of the cosmology of the peasants and tribals, and how they located themselves in relation to the various processes at work. The main thrust is to focus on the various levels of interaction, keeping in mind the highly complex interplay involving both the Hinduisation of tribals and the opposite process (i.e. the absorption from popular cults by Hinduism). What is discussed here are the developments which led to the narrowing down of the gulf between the tribals and the non-tribals, and thereby between the coastal region and the western interior, and, finally, between the common people and the middle class intellectuals.

I

'Most of us do not even know where Orissa is....[1] For most of us it is a mere geographical expression'.[2] These words of Gandhi are yet to become irrelevant. Travelling in trains one frequently has to explain that Orissa is not Puri and Jagannatha, and that it is a spread-out state having as many as thirteen districts touching West Bengal, Bihar, Madhya Pradesh and Andhra Pradesh. This lack of knowledge about Orissa is not something that comes out of discussions with only outsiders. The self-knowledge of the people of this province is amazingly vague. For example, a person of coastal Orissa (comprising Cuttack, Puri and Balasore) assumes that the language spoken in this tract is the real Oriya and this area is the centre of Oriya culture. He might not be even aware of the processes of interactions which have shaped the language and the culture in this tract. Or, to put it in a different way, there might be unpleasant debates if one were to mention that some of the remotest tribes of the province—i.e. the Bondas of Koraput district — speak a language which sounds like the seminal variant of Oriya spoken in the coastal region today[3] or even if we say that Jagannatha was a tribal deity which had been stolen from the Savara tribals.[4]

This paucity of knowledge, then, subsumes different aspects of Orissa including the history of the national movement. The few works that exist concentrate on the role of the local/national leaders with peripheral references to peasant and tribal participation or which study things in isolation.[5] No serious attempt has been made so far to look at the perceptions and attitudes of the peasants and tribals,[6] their culture, world-views and how they were to change in the phase of colonialism; how they were to look at different things happening around them, including themselves, in the course of the national movement and how they related to it: that is to say, an approach that seeks to look at things in their totality.

The effort here is to look at the whole province from 1920 to 1936 and then to concentrate on certain specific areas: the coastal tract (comprising the districts of Cuttack, Puri and Balasore), the five princely states of Dhenkanal, Talcher, Nilgiri, Ranpur and Gangpur[7] and the Jeypore estate. The choice of there areas is based on certain important considerations. The availability of material has been one of the major reasons.[8] The study of these areas gives us a clue to things since they had different land systems, cultural patterns and a noticeable variation in the magnitude of the national movement. Consequently, they are quite representative of the diversity that characterises the region.

While discussing the background the existing intra-regional variations need to be delineated. The coastal tract comprising Cuttack, Puri and Balasore is composed of the fertile plain. This is an area where the process of cultivation was more developed in contrast to the hilly and forested western interior. This obviously indicates the close links between the geographical/ecological system and the development of agriculture. Thus while the system of regular cultivation dominated the coastal region, 'shifting' cultivation co-existed with it in the interior. The latter, variously known as *dahi*, *jhum* and *podu*, involved burning a portion of the forest and fencing it. Given the tribal perception that the iron plough would hurt 'mother earth' tribals used either hoes or wooden ploughs[9] to loosen the soil, sowed the seeds and left. They returned only when it was time to harvest the crops. This method continues to exist event today.[10]

As for sources, these include official and non-official accounts and reports, newspapers, private papers, folk literature, personal interviews a host of secondary source material ranging from the work of historians and social anthropologists to biographical accounts, and also Oriya literature. However, certain problems and ambiguities of the sources are worth mentioning. Thus a classic example is the following table[11], showing the average life expectancy, which reveals that the 'Hinduised' tribals lived longer that the 'non-Hinduised' tribals:

Year : 1911

Tribe	Animistic		Hindu	
	Male	Female	Male	Female
Kandha	39	37	43	44
Munda	44	53	50	55
Santhal	37	57	55	42

This is obviously the subjective creation of an official's mind. Terms like 'animism' do not really mean anything. How the official could reach such a conclusion is surprising.

This ignorance displayed by colonial officials, unfortunately, occasionally colours the perceptions of some historians who use these sources unquestioningly, thereby implicitly accepting their value systems. As a result, the politics of language in colonial terminology is overlooked. The most common example is the term 'criminal tribe' used to define certain tribal groups since it fails to explain various complexities behind their so-called 'criminal' activities. Equally another misnomer is the use of the word 'attack' to describe popular protests and actions against exploiters. Similarly misleading is the labelling of *lathi*-carrying tribals as 'armed'. What is overlooked here is that it is as common for a tribal to carry a *lathi* as for an official or a historian to carry a briefcase.

Again there are certain problems of depending on oral evidence. Besides the obvious overemphasis on the role of the interviewees, there is the problem of distortion and subjectivity which need to be cross-checked with the available empirical evidence. Moreover, the gap between the tribal interviewees and the present author was another problem, given the differences in the language, understanding and perspective. One can perhaps illustrate this by citing an example. For many tribals *raija* meant *swaraj* which was associated with a host of complexities such as restoration of independence in their region from the oppressive officials of the forest department, excise department and the estate, moneylenders as well as the British. Another problem was that many of the interviewees related to time in a different way, which implied an intermingling of the past with the present.[12]

II

The Pre-Colonial Legacy, Colonial Interventions and the Social Structure

Orissa witnessed an Afghan invasion in 1568 and the Afghans ruled for a brief spell (1568-1578). The Afghans were replaced by the Mughals who held sway over Orissa from 1578 to 1751. Then came the Marathas who controlled Orissa from 1751 to 1803 when the British arrived on the scene. We have to wait for researchers to probe medieval Orissa futher. However, certain things are clear. Going by the number of temples built in this phase we can perhaps say that the medieval Orissan economy did produce a substantial surplus. Besides certain changes came into the structure of medieval Orissan economy leading to its feudalisation. Its manifestations, as the existing evidence shows, included the intermediaries and superior landlords and at the other end the reduction of peasants and artisans to the position of semi-serfs.[13]

By the time of the Mughals, Orissa was divided into two parts: the Mughalbandhi area, which comprised the coastal districts, and the *garjat* area which consisted of the princely rulers. This division was based on the geographical and ecological divisions (i.e. the coastal plain and the hilly region, which was heavily forested). Whereas the Mughals collected taxes in cash through their *subahdars* in the coastal tract, they taxed the princes in the *garjat* region. Land ownership rights were unspecified and customary laws determined rights and dues.[14]

The decline of the central authority of the Mughals saw an increase in the power and privileges of the landlords, who began claiming ownership of land.[15] During the latter part of the Mughal rule and during the period of the Marathas, the machinery of surplus extraction became more effective, resulting in the decline of the economy. Perhaps this can be a clue to explain the decline of the traditional maritime activity as well as salt manufacture.

The British conquered Cuttack, Puri and Balasore which were under the Marathas, in 1803. Shortly afterwards this tract saw attempts by the British to introduce land revenue settlements. Among the early settlements were those of 1805 and 1837. The systematisation of this was finally achieved through the *Settlement* of 1897 and a *Revision Settlement* of 1927.[16] In the nineteenth century the land settlements resulted in the dispossession of old owners, the resumption of many non-revenue paying *jagirs* and revenue maximisation. The land revenue demand increased from Rs. 10,89,000 in 1805 to Rs.21,02,900 in the 1897 *Settlement* for the three coastal districts of Cuttack, Puri and Balasore.[17] Out of an area of 83,000 square miles which comprised British Orissa in the 1920's, 12,000 square miles was temporarily-settled, 66,000 square miles was permanently-settled and 5,000 square miles were directly administered.[18]

At this point let us try to explore the development of the landholding pattern and the social stratification. We can begin by discussing the temporarily-settled estates of Cuttack, Puri and Balasore. At the top were the zamindars who had land rights and who paid fixed amounts directly to the government. These zamindars came mostly from upper castes such as Brahmins, Karanas (or Bengali Kayasthas) and Khandayats. For example, the 1897 *Settlement Report* notes that Balasore zamindars were composed of 27 per cent Brahmins, 22 per cent Karanas and Kayasthas and 28 per cent Khandayats. These zamindars were a privileged lot, who among other things, had special rights over forests and fisheries and could make profits from areas where cultivation was newly introduced. They also had the right to grant leases and create intermediary tenures.

Below them were the sub-proprietory tenure-holders who were mostly Khandayats. These people were the traditional sword-wielders and their importance originated from this phenomenon. They held hereditary tenures and were not disturbed as long as they paid the rent (which they were supposed to collect) to zamindars. They were paid a percentage for the collection of rent which varied according to the class of these sub-proprietors. It seems that they enjoyed certain privileges and status in the village and held sway over the agrarian and social structure.

Then there were the holders of *lakhiraj* grants, resumed revenue-free tenures (*bazyaftidars*) and service *jagirdars* who held rent-free lands. This category was mainly composed of Khandayats and Karanas as well as people of different castes, who pursued their caste profession.

The raiyats, mostly Khandayats and Chasas were of two categories: *thani* (resident) and *pahi* (non-resident) tenures. However, since 1859, both were treated at par and any person who held land in a village for twelve years or more became a 'settled' raiyat and paid taxes in cash.

Those who paid rents for their homesteads and had no arable lands were called *chandandars*. They were composed of people who followed their caste professions and held homestead land. Some *chandandars* were also landless labourers.

Next came the under-tenants who held lands included within the tenure or holding of a tenant. The under-raiyats paid in cash or kind. If they paid in kind they were to opt either for the *dhulibhag* system which meant a 50 per cent payment of the yield in grain or the *sanja* system. This was a contract for a fixed amount before the harvest.

At the bottom were the daily labourers. Almost every cultivator owning more than five acres of land employed them. They were mostly untouchables (like Bauris) and tribals (i.e. Savaras) and had no lands. They were of two types: *haliyas* and *muliyas*. The former bound themselves for sums of money taken as loans from their employers, and had to toil till the debt was repaid. Normally, their families stayed with them and occasionally found employment in the fields in the busy seasons and were engaged as food and fuel gatherers from the woods at other times. The *muliyas* were casual labourers who were paid mainly in kind (2 1/2 to 3 seers of rice a day) and very rarely in cash (5 *annas* a day).[19]

The coastal belt also had permanently-settled estates like Kanika and Aul. Let us try to reconstruct the landholding pattern and the social structure of Kanika. The estate had the zamindar at the top who paid a fixed amount (about Rs. 20,407/-) annually to the British government. The amount that had to be collected by him was not fixed. Originally, the *mustagirs* helped in the collection of revenue but they were relieved of their duties and lost their privileges in the 1889-94 *Settlement*. The zamindar made the customary land grants to Brahmins, village and estate servants which were rent-free (14.6% of total holdings). The raiyati tenures were of three categories: *thani*, *pahi*, *chandna*. The fact that they amounted to 84.4 per cent of total holdings indicates that Kanika's peasant economy was based on it. The holders were Kshatriyas, who were the zamindar's kinsmen, Khandayats, Rajputs, Karanas and Padhans. The Khandayats were large in number and very influential in the estate, given their earlier military status. These raiyats got their lands cultivated by others, but also cultivated portions of it themselves. People engaged in their caste professions (i.e. Khandayats, Telis, Keutas, Carpenters) had homesteads.

Kanika also had share-croppers who included the Lodha tribals working on the half-produce system. The agricultural labourers were of three types: (a) the permanent labourers who worked for the whole year and received about Rs. 15/-; (b) the permanent labourers who were employed for 3 to 6 months during the cultivation season and were paid between Rs. 3/- and Rs. 6/-, and were supplied with food, lodging and clothing worth Rs. 1-8-0; (c) and finally, there were occasional daily labourers who were paid 3 1/4 seers of paddy and, if they worked at one place for six months, were given another 5 maunds of paddy. The agricultural labourers came mostly from among Kandaras and Bauris. It appears from the 1889-94 *Settlement* that they were not absolutely landless and were engaged in cultivation.

Kanika had some tribals like Savaras and low castes like Kelas who depended exclusively on the forests. The Lodhas and low castes like Chamars depended on the forests and were also cultivators.[20]

We can now examine the five princely states in order to grasp the agrarian and social structure that had emerged. Around 1804 the state of Dhenkanal had an agreement with the British. In 1849 it had its first revenue settlement. The assessment prior to this was based on the number of ploughs and hoes owned by a cultivator. The gross rental (land) of the state increased from Rs.63,316 in 1846 to Rs. 2,39,347 in 1923. Interestingly, the *peshkush* paid by the state to the government was only Rs. 5,099.

Coming to the question of stratification we find that at the top was the government followed by the Raja. This state had no zamindars. The dominant section of the state comprised people holding *khanja* and *lakhiraj* tenures as well as holders of *brahmottar, debottar* and *paikan jagir* lands. These were held mostly by Brahmins and Kshatriyas. Rarely did they cultivate their own lands but got others to do it for them. The state depended on the *sarbarkars* to collect land revenue and other cesses as well as help in the administration. They got commissions of 12.8 per cent for the land revenue and 6.4 per cent for the forest cess. Their posts were hereditary but they could be removed by the state.

The *raiyati* tenures comprised *thani, pahi, chandna* and *paikali*. While the first three were along similar lines, as in the temporarily- settled tract, the *paikali* tenures, which were originally tax-free, came to be taxed from the 1923 *Settlement*. These *paikali* tenures were held by Paikas. The *thani* raiyats were mostly Chasas, the largest caste group in the state.

There were some raiyats who held lands of occupancy raiyats. These raiyats were purely tenants-at-will and had no occupancy rights.

Some tribals (like Savaras, Gonds and Kandhas) and some out-castes (like Panas, Bauris and Dombs) held lands which they were not supposed to sell to non-tribals and upper castes respectively.

At the bottom were the agricultural labourers, mostly Panas and most probably some tribals. These agricultural labourers were called *haliyas* and they were recruited around the month of March for one year. They were paid a loan in cash and paddy by their employers. Besides, they were also paid 3 *manas* of paddy per day and given a small plot of land (about 1/4th of an acre) or something in kind in lieu of the plot. The women agricultural labourers—*kamtunis* —were not given these plots of land.[21]

The next state, that we shall examine, is Talcher which had a treaty with the British government in 1848. The state paid a tribute of about Rs.1040/-. Table 1, however, offers us some insights into the rise of the revenue demand of the state over the years:

Table I

Year	Total land revenue (appx)
1846	Rs. 21,290/-
1890	Rs. 48,777/-
1913	Rs. 58,971/-

As in Dhenkanal, the British and the Raja were at the top. There were no zamindars in the state and, as in Dhenkanal, the land grants were held by the dominant castes. The *sarbarkars* collected the land revenue as well as other levies and run the administration. Their position was similar to their Dhenkanal counterparts.

The *raiyati* tenures comprised the *thani, pahi* and *chandna*, as in other parts of the province. The Chasas, who were the agricultural caste, constituted nearly 37 per cent of the state's population. The majority of the raiyats were 'average' (middle peasants) and very few were well-to-do ('rich' peasants). Most of the agricultural work was done by the members of the peasant family themselves.

There were a few under-raiyats and some of them had raiyats under them who were tanants-at-will. Their rents were paid in cash or kind (*sanja/bhag*).

The agricultural labourers were composed of Panas and some tribals like Savaras, Gonds and Kandhas. Male agricultural labourers were paid 4 *annas* and females were paid one *anna* per working day. Some of the Panas were settling down as peasants with small plots ('poor' peasants).

Finally, the state had some workers who worked in the coal mines and the railways and came mostly from the de-peasantised section of the state's population and people from outside. These sectors became important in the twentieth century.[22]

The Ranpur state had almost the same agrarian structure as the two other states mentioned earlier. The only significant difference, perhaps, was the appointment of a *Dewan* by the Raja, who was supposed to be 'helping' him in the administration. The first *Settlement* of 1877-79 was followed by the 1880-81 *Settlement* which expected the peasants to pay three-fourth of the assessed *jama* in cash and the remaining one-fourth in kind. This was followed by the 1899 *Settlement* which abolished the system of grain rent and saw the intervention of the colonial government in a big way leading to the appointment of a *Dewan*. This implied an obvious undermining of the Raja's authority.

The state had no zamindars and the land grants were roughly similar to those of Dhenkanal and Talcher. There existed a set of *khanjadars* who were of the Kshatriya caste, and who were descendants of the Raja's family. Their *khanjas* (land grants) were privileged enclaves where they wielded power and authority. They collected taxes through their agents and paid one fourth of this to the Raja. The *sarbarkars* under them were paid a commission of 5 per cent and some of the *khanjadars* performed this role.

The *raiyati* tenures were of similar categories and the raiyats were mostly Chasas. The raiyats of *khanjadars*, however, had no permanent rights over their lands—they could not sell their lands. There is no evidence of the under-raiyat's caste composition and perhaps, they had no rights and could be ejected. It is possible that some tribals like Lodhas, Kandhas and Savaras held some of these tenures.

The agricultural labourers were composed chiefly of Panas although other outcastes like Dombs, Chamars, Bauris and Hadis, perhaps, also performed this role. Some tribals were agricultural labourers.[23]

The chief of Nilgiri had, in 1809, agreed to pay an annual tribute of Rs. 2108 to the British government. The proceeds of land revenue increased five fold between 1850 and 1920. In social stratification the structure of Nilgiri was almost similar to the other states we have studied. There was a marked absence of big landlords. The state had a similar pattern of land grants and the *raiyati* tenures. The sub-tenants had the same position. There were some *jagirs* held by tribals in exchange for which they were expected to contribute unpaid labour to the state. These tribals were mostly Bhumij, Bhuyans, Kols and Santhals. The agricultural labour force of the state comprised these tribals and Panas. Their wages were mostly in kind.[24]

Gangpur, however, had a structure quite different from all the states we have discussed so far. Gangpur got the *sanad* from the British government in 1827. The relations between the colonial government and the Chief was regulated by the *sanad* granted in 1889 and renewed in 1905. In 1905 this state was transferred from the Central Provinces to Orissa and a Political Agent was appointed to assist the Chief. The state paid Rs.10,000 to the colonial government. The land revenue of the state can be judged from Table II

Table II

Name of area Land under the Chief	Land revenue demand before the 1929-36 settlement (appx) Rs.	Land Revenue demand after the settlement (appx) Rs.	% age increase (appx)
Khalsa	110,257	149,861	36
Zamindaris:			
Nagra	27,116	38,538	42
Hemgir	11,371	18,786	65
Sargipalli	4,691	6,962	48
Sarapgarh	1,855	2,583	39
Hatibari	5,889	8,956	52
Total	Rs.161,179	Rs.225,686	(avg) 47%

The Raja of Gangpur had the Khalsa land directly under him. These were originally leased out to *gountias* for five years in lieu of cash. These *gountias* had taken over villages reclaimed by the tribals, and it appears that they were mostly the affluent section of the tribals. However, by the 1890's the preference for such leases was given to Agharias and Telis (non-tribals) of Sambalpur. The *gountias* enjoyed privileges in terms of lands (*bhogra*) and there were no limits on collections from the peasants. Also there were the customary land grants as in any other state.

The state had five zamindaris—Nagra, Hemgir, Sargipalli, Sarapgarh and Hathibari. These were privileged landed elements, who did not have to encounter problems like the 'sunset law'. They paid *tekauli* to the Chief which amounted to only 5 per cent of the amount collected by them and this was raised to 10 per cent in the 1936 *Settlement*. The zamindars had various privileges and enjoyed a number of rights. They were originally Bhuyans but distinguished themselves from their tribesmen by calling themselves

Khandayat Bhuyans.

Below them were the *ganjhus* or village headmen whose ancestors had cleared the forests, and, who were the patriarchal heads of families. The fact that most of them were Bhuyans implies the possibility that they had received land grants. There were two main kinds of *ganjhus* : *khuntkalti* and *thica*. These headmen were the intermediaries between the zamindars and the tenants. They were given 45 per cent of the collection as their commission and enjoyed some privileges in land. Below them were sub-*ganjhus* and *sikmi gountias* who assisted the head-*ganjhus*.

The Chief also had three *parganadars* under him: Raiboga, Erga and Daldali. Raiboga paid 50 per cent of the collection to the Chief and the latter decided the amount Erga and Daldali had to pay. These *parganadars* had a large number of villages under them; they had absolute rights like the zamindars and enjoyed rent-free lands. They either collected taxes directly or took the services of *gountias*. The evidence that we have is extremely meagre but we can deduce that these *parganadars* were also tribals.

There was no distinction between the *thani* and *pahi* raiyats. There were *chandna* raiyats as well. The Agharias were the chief cultivators of the state. They had occupancy rights but could be removed by the *gountias/ganjhus* for their failure to pay rents. Some peasants who tilled the *bhogra/nijchas* lands were tenants-at-will, as were those under-raiyats who held lands of others.

The agricultural labourers came mostly from the tribal population and were composed of Mundas, Bhuyans, Oraons, Gandas and Kisans. Their wages varied from three *annas* per day for males to two *annas* for females. Some of the tribals resorted to rice cultivation. It is interesting to note that as late as 1911 we have evidence of Karuwas, who were food-gatherers and hunters. They bartered off forest products for food.[25]

The Jeypore zamindari was under the Maharaja of Jeypore. This permanently-settled estate was quite different from its coastal counterparts. The estate had entered into an agreement with the British government in 1802, according to which it paid a *peshkush* of Rs.16,000/- annually. The British government seems to have taken some time before deciding to intervene in its affairs. From 1863 the estate had an Assistant Agent and an Assistant Superintendent of Police, and the British government assumed direct administration of the estate, although there was no village establishment maintained by the government. The estate had some major land grants but from 1863 onwards most of them had been gradually taken over for direct administration by the estate. The estate had some privileged tenures. It was primarily under the *mustajari* system. The *mustajars* were village headmen who collected taxes. Their relations with both the estate and the tenants were customary. They enjoyed some privileges and rights as a result of their role and were considered to be practically masters of their villages. There is also an evidence of 'common lands' in parts of the estate. These 'common lands' were collectively worked upon, although the presence of *mustajars* does suggest differentiation. What needs to be emphasised is the notion of 'collective existence'. When a couple was to have a baby they were given foodgrain, and they left till they could come back to work again.

The Raiyatwari system was in vogue in some parts of the estate. In these tracts the estate kept registers of raiyats, their holdings and the amount they had to pay as rent. This was collected by *amins* or a villager (revenue *naiko*) appointed by the estate. The *mustajars* and *naikos* were mostly tribals.

The tenants of the estate were mostly tribals such as Kandhas, Bhattras, Parojas, Savaras, Koyas, Gonds, Bhumiyas, Gadabas, Jatapus and Didayi. They were settled agriculturists as well as 'shifting' cultivators. The settled tenants had occupancy rights granted by the Madras Estates Land Act (1908), but in practice they could be dispossesed by the *amins, mustajars* and *naikos*.

The settled tenants were assessed either on the 'seed capacity' of the land or on the number of ploughs and hoes they owned. In some areas rents were collected in cash and in some others, in kind. It was obviously difficult to tax the 'shifting cultivators', given the inaccessibility of the forests and the nature of the cultivation. However, when taxed, the assessment was based on the number of ploughs and hoes owned by them.

The tenants of the zamindaris as well as the holders of privileged tenures sometimes sub-let lands on the 'sharing system'. In any case this was a rare practice. It seems that these sub-tenants had no rights or privileges.

The agricultural labourers were composed mainly of tribals and outcastes who were paid in grain (1 1/2 *kunchums* or 3 1/2 kilograms of paddy) or 3 to 4 *annas* per day in the 1940's. Then there were the *goti* labourers who were bound to those who gave them credits. They had to work till the money and the interest was repaid.[26]

While discussing the agrarian system one should refer to the *khas* lands which were directly under the government. Some of the leading estates which came under this category were Khurda (in the Puri district) and Banki (in the Cuttack district). The structure was marked by the absence of a well formed-class of landlords; the *sarbarkars*, as commission agents, looked after the management of the villages with or without any hereditary rights or *jagir* lands. They received a commission which varied from 10 to 20 per cent of the assets of the village. Given their important role and affluence, the *sarbarkars* were to wield considerable influence. The land grants and the *raiyati* tenures as well as the broad caste pattern remained the same.[27]

Finally, there was the Sambalpur area which was acquired by the British in 1818. It was a *garjat* area. However in 1861 it was attached to the Central Provinces. Attempts to have regular settlements were initiated in 1864 and completed in 1870. The settlement was made with village headmen known as *malguzars*.[28] The post of these headmen became hereditary. This settlement was in line with the Mahalwari settlement. Sambalpur was united with Orissa in 1905.

III

Popular Perceptions

The association we have made between the agarian structure and caste should not be regarded as something fixed. Our generalisations, based partly on empirical evidence and on the present-day pattern of land holding, are intended to be flexible in order to accommodate shifts and changes in caste-agrarian structure relationships. One can perhaps refer here to plans of the colonial administration to start Pana Settlements in the *garjats* in order to 'prevent' Panas from committing 'crime', or land grants made to some Panas by the rajas to secure their services. These obviously created a differentiation within this caste, most Panas being landless agricultural labourers.[29] The case of those Brahmins who became agriculturists (*haliya* Brahmins) can be mentioned here.[30] This could either indicate a process of proletarianisation of an erstwhile landowning section or an attempt by poor non-Brahmins to seek acceptance as Brahmins. Likewise there was a differentiation among tribals as seen in the Gangpur state or Jeypur.

The problems of caste and its linkages with the agrarian structure should not be taken as fixed or absolute because of another problem. Recent research conducted on early medieval Orissa on caste evolution shows how the four-fold varna society developed late in Orissa and when it did develop there were certain differences in the form it took as compared to North India. This was due to the presence of a preponderently tribal population and the geographical variations in the region. As a result, the land grants to Brahmins and the extension of agriculture implied the conversion of most of the tribes into Sudras, which converged with the process of their peasantisation. Alongside, their chiefs were absorbed as Kshatriyas into the *varna* system. This implied the absence of any rigid polarisation. The classic four-fold *varna* system continued to remain largely notional as in practice the two-tier structure with the numerous intermediary occupational castes constituted the functional reality. Consequently, one witnesses the evolution of two clearly identifiable *varnas* based on their functions—the Brahmins and the Sudras. The Vaishyas surfaced only occasionally in times of trade and the Kshatriyas never had local roots. The rise of Kshatriyas/Karanas was a feature associated with the emergence of feudalism.[31]

Keeping this picture in mind, we can focus on certain changes visible in the nineteenth century. One obvious change was the straining of class/caste relations and a sharpening of polarisation absent in the earlier epoch. The other feature was the importance of the Kshatriya caste in the colonial period. This resulted out of two developments. One was associated with the classification strategies of the British. This process saw the assumption of Kshatriya status by the ruling chiefs and the landed sections and their recognition by the colonial administration to mark them out as the 'rulers' which evoked the classic *varna* system, with Kshatriyas as rulers. The second was the emergence of a relatively affluent agriculturist caste (Chasas) as well as Milkmen (Gaudas) who claimed Khandayat (Sword-wielding) and Kshatriya status respectively. The former, also claimed Karana status.

Some tentative generalisations can be formulaled now. The colonisation of Orissa created the basis for certain major interventions, especially in the coastal region. Here one can refer to the limited degree of infrastructural interventions (i.e. the construction of a canal system), the commercialisation of agriculture, expansion of markets, growth in commodity production, extension of agricultural space and the monetisation of the rural economy. These features, howsoever limited, strengthened the pre-existing variation between the coast and the interior. Nevertheless, the development of capitalism remained confined to the coastal region due to the backwardness of the hinterland, the absence of an infrastructure for capitalism and the re-investment of accumulation along parasitic channels like moneylending.[32]

One of the most important effects of the land settlement was the growth of a money-economy, characterised by cash rents, wages[33] and land becoming a saleable commodity. Although the process was uneven, moneylenders developed in different parts of Orissa. The desire for freedom from the economic burdens, eg. the rent demands and meeting price fluctuations at the market place, ironically pushed the peasants and tribals into bondage at the hands of the moneylenders who controlled their destiny so completely that even Lord Jagannatha or the tribal gods proved to be helpless.[34] At the turn of the century for example, 80 per cent of the rural population in the temporarily-settled areas were 'more or less permanently indebted to the mahajan, proprietory tenure-holder or zamindar.'[35] This, together with the fact that the interest rates charged by the moneylenders varied from 18 3/4 per cent to 75 per cent and that by the 1920's the Orissa cultivators paid one and a half crore of rupees a year as interest demonstrate the importance moneylending assumed as well as the problem of indebtedness. This had other implications such as landlessness which resulted out of mortgages of peasants' holdings for non-repayment of loans. Although moneylending attracted different castes in Orissa, it was dominated by the Brahmins. What seems to have developed was a credit mechanism which linked rice merchants to the peasants who were advanced cash loans against future repayments with rice.[36] The situation was perhaps even more oppressive in the princely states. The agriculturist was 'kept going' through loans. Many were born, lived and died in debt.[37]

The settlements created a land market. Its formation was a result of three sets of circumstances: the insistence on the part of the government on the sale of defaulting zamindar's estate as a device towards ensuring the security of its revenue; the inability of many zamindars to cope with the increased revenue burden; and the willingness of various moneyed persons to transfer a part of their fortunes to the purchase of estates. In Orissa the situation was worse for the landlords because of its limited agricultural resources and the failure of any enhancement in the production of paddy. The change to a silver currency system was also a contributing factor.[38]

In this situation the Bengali *amlas* who had been 'imported' to Cuttack manoeuvred auction sales and secured estates for themselves and wealthy absentees in Cuttack as well as Calcutta. This meant the dispossession of local landlords; absentees replaced them. This led to the system of intermediaries who managed the estates, and sub-infeudation.

The land settlements reinforced the class as well as the caste structure and together with other factors led to a marked social differentiation among the peasantry. The landlords came mostly from the upper castes—Brahmins, Karanas and Kshatriyas—and the cultivators were composed chiefly of Chasas and Khandayats and, in some areas, from amongst tribals who held land rights which were not uniform.[39] Some professional castes (i.e. weavers, salt-makers and oilmen) were also engaged in cultivation as a subsidiary occupation and an inversion of this pattern took place as one moves into the twentieth century. A reference can be made to the class of agricultural labourers, composed of outcastes (i.e. Panas, Bauris and Kandaras) and tribals.

The following table[40] outlines the landholding pattern of the 1940's:

Table III

Percentage of families with different sizes of landholding (in acres): Orissa

Less than 2	2-5	5-10	10 and above
50	27	13	10

Most of the landholdings were small and land was concentrated in the hands of about 10 per cent of the families.

While discussing this premise the emergence of 'rich' peasants (especially in the coastal belt) must be highlighted. The promulgation of tenancy laws and marginal attempts to improve agriculture, irrigation and communication, the availability of cheap labour and facilities offered by the commercialisation of crops such as sugarcane and betel leaf, and the grain trade contributed significantly to the emergence of 'rich' peasants. The following table[41] which shows the sale of proprietory tenures over a decade (1880-1890) illustrates the prosperity of the 'rich' peasants:

Table IV

Profession of Purchasers

District	Average yearly number of registered sale of the whole or portion of proprietory tenures	Traders and money-lenders	Zamindars	Tenure holders	Raiyats	Others
Cuttack	2095	112	358	1128	118	379
Puri	380	48	15	228	103	52
Balasore	221	10	51	84	37	39
Total	2696	170	424	1440	258	470

The evidence suggests that by the 1866 famine this strata of 'rich' peasants had emerged in coastal Orissa. This section 'had nothing to do with' the moneylenders and 'carried grain to the market'.[42] In some areas like Khurda this strata of the peasantry took over the lands of the poorer peasants through profitable contract of mortgage. The social differentiation that resulted saw this affluent section at one end of the social pole and the depeasantised proletariat, the ruined artisans and manufacturers at the other.[43]

The emergence of the 'rich' peasants did have certain implications for the caste structure. We do come across attempts at upward mobility, especially among the Chasas (cultivators) of Puri, who sought to claim the status of Khandayats, and also seek recognition as Karanas. In some cases upper caste pracrices like sati were also emulated.[44] Some contemporary comments on this phenomenon are worth mentioning: 'Money works in these cases as a mighty leveller of sub-castes. If a member of a lower sub-caste acquires money, power or authority, he marries into the immediately higher sub-caste and gradually gets amalgamated into it'. And again: 'A man of power and pelf can shut the mouth of the caste people with gold and break the social rules with impunity'.[45]

The following table[46] throws light on this subject.

Table V

	Variation in actual proportionate strength of certain castes for the Orissa Division and Orissa States	*Population of Orissa (including the princely states)*	
Castes	% Variation 1901-1931	1901	1931
Chasa	+2.0	4,982,142	5,306,142
Gaura	+22.7		
Khandayat	+45.4	(% increase 6.5%)	
Karana	+2.1		

The above table shows that the agricultural Chasa caste sought upward mobility and that this was an all-Orissa phenomenon.[47] It was reflected in the marginal increase of the Chasas (only 2%) and the very large increase of the Khandayats (45.4% — the largest for any caste). Although some Khandayats aspired for Karana status, their mobility was restricted.[48] The marginal increase of the Karanas (2.1%) and a reference to the unsuccessful attempts by Khandayats to become Karanas, reinforce our position.

The table also indicates an increase in the population of the Gauras (22.7%). In Cuttack and Balasore the Gauras sought to get themselves recognised as the Yadubansi Kshatriyas, assumed the sacred thread and refused to work as palanquin bearers.[49] Although no empirical evidence is available, we can, perhaps, locate this as a reflection of their prosperity in agriculture, and the fact that their caste profession had not received any serious setback as that of the salt-makers or the weavers.

While discussing the differentiation and changes taking place in the caste structure we can add that natural calamities like floods and famines also contributed to it. The 1866 Famine which wiped off nearly one-third of the population of Cuttack, Puri and Balasore illustrates this point. What we come across is the emergence of a new caste — Chatra-khia consisting of people who had accepted relief (Chatra) during the Famine and had been excommunicated as a result.[50]

One also comes across a rigidification of caste norms. There was also an upsurge of caste courts to try caste offences and excommunicate offenders. Interestingly, we come across one Barhai Patak Sabha composed of several high caste people, including Brahmins, which dealt with low caste cases. In Balasore low caste cases were dealt with by a person appointed by landlords. The caste *kutchery* was formally abolished in the districts of Cuttack, Puri and Balasore by 1911. However, these were retained with full vigour in the princely states to preserve the *status-quo*.[51]

Certain changes were noticeable within tribal society. The land settlement and the money economy developed simultaneously with the process of peasantisation of tribals. It also meant differentiation within tribal society. In fact, the *naikos* and *ganjhus* symbolised this phenomenon. These headmen were important because they collected taxes and provided leadership. Most of them were more affluent than their fellow villagers and the land settlements had provided them with some privileges.[52] This differentiation led to the emergence of these headmen as the 'internal' exploiters within tribal society.[53]

This phase also saw the continuation of the process of 'Hinduisation' of tribals. A few observations can be made here. This process was not an isolated and a one-way affair; rather it was dialectical. Thus, there is evidence of high caste beliefs being influenced by tribal beliefs. This point can be illustrated by referring to a local peculiarity among the Brahmins of the Jeypur estate. When a Brahmin was about to die prayers were made and a cow was gifted away so that the spirit could pass out of the body easily. The spirit was supposed to escape through the nine orifices of the body. It was felt that the spirit would pass out through the anus in case the person was 'bad'.[54]

This process dates back to the evolution of the Jagannatha cult.[55] What was new was the rapidity and the all-embracing characteristic of this process of Hinduisation, given its linkage with the development of the market economy and the peasantisation of tribals. In fact, some of the remotest tribes of Orissa were affected by this process.

This process of Hinduisation perhaps touched the affluent initially and then the others were affected by it.[56] This affected certain tribes like the Gonds and Binjhals of Sambalpur.[57] Finally, while discussing the process of Hinduisation we can mention how this also created the basis for communal tension in some pockets of coastal Orissa. One can perhaps refer here to Bhadrak in the Balasore district, where the landlords were Hindus and the Muslims were mostly agricultural labourers. In such a situation strained class relation tended to often create communal tension—a feature that became pronounced especially in the twentieth century.

Hinduisation led to the acceptance of symbols ranging from gods and goddesses to the sacred thread by some tribals like, for example, the Gonds of Sambalpur.[58] One interesting feature is that on certain occasions popular beliefs located these symbols as things 'bought' from the transmission points of Hindu society, like the big zamindars. This point can be illustrated by citing the case of the Ranas of Jeypur estate, who wore the sacred thread and believed that they had bought the right to do so from the Maharaja of Jeypur.[59] What deserves emphasis is the significance of this language of exchange, which was applied to the sacred realm. Given the rarity of exchange a high value seems to have been attached to things obtained through it.

The adoption of symbols also included cremation of the dead instead of burying them. In fact there is ample evidence which shows that the well-to-do tribals cremated the dead.[60]

Hinduisation also meant the adoption of rituals like purification at death or birth. The fear of alien contact also necessitated purification. Here one can cite the example of released prisoners or people who came back from Assam who were supposed to be accompanied by evil spirits and had to seek purification.[61] The medium of purification, as in the case of the Pengo Parojas of Jeypur, included among other things, Jagannath's *mahaprasad* of Puri.[62] Although purificatory rites did exist among the tribals in some form or the other, what was perhaps new was the entry of *mahaprasad* into tribal cultures in remote parts of Orissa.

The adoption of symbols and rituals often involved the recruitment of Brahmin priests. In fact, some tribals like the Puri Kandhas, elevated the status of some 'low Brahmins' among the low caste Hindus, by employing them. Hinduisation also crept into dietary habits and one comes across some tribals, like Mundas, giving up eating beef.[63]

The emulation/internalisation of the social practices of Hinduism is quite fascinating. The outcastes of Hindu society were regarded as outcastes by the tribals and simultaneously, Brahmins looked upon in the way Brahmins looked at outcastes. Consequently, the outcastes were kept out of the domain of marriage or acceptance of food and the process also saw a 'distancing' from the Brahmins in the sense that food was not accepted from them.[64] As a result, the supremacy of the Brahmins was more or less rejected even while 'Brahminical' mores were being taken over.

The census data for 1891-1941 period shows a decline in the tribal population, even though there are no serious reasons to explain this phenomenon. Although we have to wait for researchers to probe things and establish the links, the apparent decline of the tribal population can be taken as an index to the magnitude of this process of Hinduisation. The following tables will demonstrate this trend.

Table VI

Princely state[65]	*Variation of tribal Population*	*Variation of total Population*	
	1881-1891	1881	1891
Nilgiri	– 4356	50,972	56,198
Dhenkanal	– 70305	208,316	238,285
Ranpur	– 2093	36,539	40,115

Table VII
Sambalpur[66]

Year	*Population of those returned as 'animists'*	*Variation in total population*
1881	46,652	554,165
1891	29,353	618,825
1901	38,935	638,992
1911	—	744,193

1921	8,285	798,466
1931	3,184	880,945

Table VIII

District/State[67]	*Persons professing tribal religion* 1921-1931	*Variation in the total population* 1921	1931
Nilgiri	– 4169	65,222	68,594
Dhenkanal	– 4497	233,691	284,326

Table IX

Tribe[68]	*Net variation 1891-1931*	*Variation in total population* 1891	1931
Gond			
Nilgiri	– 4685	56,198	68,594
Dhenkanal	– 488	238,285	284,326
Gangpur	– 3558	191,440	356,674
Ho			
Dhenkanal	– 120	-	-
Gangpur	– 10,920	-	-
Kandha			
Puri	– 333	944,998	1,035,154
Talcher	– 525	52,674	69,702
Dhenkanal	– 273	-	-
Ranpur	– 12	40,115	7,711
Savara			
Dhenkanal	– 764	-	-

Table X

	Variations in the population of some tribes in the Koraput district: 1931-1941[69]	*Variations in the total population of the Koraput district*	
		1931	1941
Savara	–4807	9,49,652	11,27,862
Jatapu	–37,961		

Two qualifications regarding the tables can be made. Firstly we have focused only on the question of the decline of the tribal population. Secondly, this feature was uneven and in many areas the tribal population had increased. The link we seek to establish between this decline of the tribal population and the process of Hinduisation is also indirectly referred to in the case of some tribals. We can cite here the example of the Kandhas of Ranpur who preferred to be recognised as 'Oriya Kandhas'.[70]

A context that bred insecurity and undermined the identity and self-confidence of the tribals also made them turn to Christianity. This came to be expressed in different ways but the reason for accepting Christianity, as perceived by the Oraons, perhaps articulates this phenomenon quite well. Thus they felt that Christianity protected them from witches and *bhoots*, who were powerless *vis-a-vis* this system.[71]

What should be mentioned here is that the process of Hinduisation was not complete. One comes across the coexistence of Hindu gods and goddesses and tribal deities and the participation in Hindu as well as tribal festivals. This pattern was also similar in the case of the converts to Christianity. Very often they observed certain customs and beliefs which were antithetical to the basic tenets of Christianity, participated in tribal festivals, and, on being asked to which group they belonged, named the tribe and not the Christian connection.[72]

It will now be appropriate to say a few things about the way popular perceptions located Brahmins. This can be illustrated by citing some folk tales.

A Savara folk tale illustrates this point:

> There used to be one hundred Brahmins in the whole world at one time. They were so miserly that they used wine instead of oil to light their lamp. One day the wife of a poor Brahmin derided her husband

with the comment that unlike the other rich Brahmins he had neither lamp nor wine. The poor Brahmin, however, asserted that he was so powerful that if he took sixty steps outside his village the whole world would be turned into water. As the Brahmin walked the sixty steps his wife took no notice of the apparent boast. Immediately the whole world was covered with water and the ninety-nine Brahmins and his own wife were drowned. He himself turned into a *Kittung* (god) and lived like a burning flame on the branches of a tree.[73]

Here is a folk tale of the Santhals:

A long time ago a Brahmin came from the west. He did not eat and sat motionless in an old bamboo hut for three to four days. The villagers were quite impressed with him and offered him milk. One day the Brahmin asked to be supplied with coolies so that he could rebuild the hut. When at the end of the day the coolies asked for their wages the Brahmin wrapped himself in his clothes and recited some mantras and coins fell from his body.[74]

These folk tales reflect a complex picture. Thus the Brahmins were simultaneously looked upon with awe, respect and hatred: a result perhaps of their combining religious, philosophical and material domination. Perhaps other upper castes like Kshatriyas and Karanas were also looked upon in a more or less similar fashion.

We can reconstruct the way the untouchables perceived the high castes by referring to some religious movements among them. The Satnami religion was popularised among the Chamars of Sambalpur around 1820-1830 by a Chamar named Ghasidas. Their chief target was the caste system which was abolished along with idol worship. All were equal, except the family of Ghasidas, who assumed hereditary priesthood and its privileges. His successor Balakdas wore the sacred thread for which he was murdered by the Brahmins.[75]

The interaction with upper castes was also conditioned by a desire to enter temples. Thus, in 1881 some outcaste followers of Mahima Dharma (which had most probably originated in the princely state of Dhenkanal) marched to Puri in an abortive attempt to enter the Jagannatha temple. Contemporary newspapers (which expressed the shock of the upper castes) described it as an attempt of these people to remove the idols and burn them in accordance with a 'divine command'.[76] However, what needs to be emphasised is that this action reflected the outcastes yearning to go to the presence of Lord Jagannatha. With this was connected the perception of how the 'Lord' had been usurped by the Brahmins and hence the attempt to reassert a lost right.

Consequently, the untouchables seem to have perceived the Brahmins and high castes in a way similar to the tribals. The Brahmins and upper castes were simultaneously looked upon with awe, respect, fear and hatred —a feature also noticed by a present-day researcher[77] while constructing an untouchable's life history.

The theme of exploitation can be examind here. It can be identified as having an 'internal' and an 'external' form. However, it should be clarified that there were links as well as interactions between them. To begin with, let us examine how the 'internal' forms of exploitation changed with the colonisation of Orissa and for this purpose certain specific issues like recruitment of labour, the role of forced labourers and forced procurement of provisions, activities such as granting of loans and the imposition of cesses can be taken up. In other words, those features which had existed prior to the advent of colonialism. The changes taking place are worth mentioning. For example, the recruitment of labour came to be associated with a credit mechanism. Consequently, the *gotis* of Jeypur estate or the *haliyas* of the coastal region,[78] for example, took advances in money and worked for the person who gave them the advance till the loan and the interest on it was repaid. This reduced them to serfs. Coming to forced labourers, we find that they came to play an important role in profit-making enterprises. Similarly, the forced supply of provisions got linked to the highly profitable grain trade. Money-lending was being monopolised by the landlords so that peasants had to pay high interests and take loans only from them.[79]

Then there was the question of *tikkus*—taxes—which assumed alarming proportions. From Balasore (1890's) we get an evidence of a peasant reporting how his landlord expected *tikkus* in cash for a host of reasons which ranged from customary features like the birth of a son or the marriage of a daughter to a *tar* (telegraph) tax.[80] Thus, what seems to have happened is the monetisation of customary dues and the imposition of new burdens by an exploitative structure of the feudal, landed sections and colonialism.

New taxes meant to 'make profits' out of forests and pastures were looked upon as a feature which undermined traditional rights. Popular perceptions located how these were first 'stolen' from the people, who were then expected to pay taxes for using them.

Of course, the *tar* tax had certain other implications. Although the colonial government set up the telegraph, the landlord, as the peasants reported, levied the tax.[81] Consequently, popular perceptions perhaps established an association between the 'internal' exploiters and colonialism, howsoever weak it might have been initially. Moreover, a social historian cannot miss noting how the *tar* — a symbol of science and progress — was actually associated with oppression in the coastal tract. Thus the *tar* was, perhaps, identified as a symbol of both the zamindar and the alien colonial government.

The 'external' dimensions had certain elements: the maritime trade (Sadhaba tradition), the cotton-weaving and salt-manufacturing 'industries', which underwent changes. Orissa's Sadhaba tradition testifies to a flourishing maritime trade with South-east Asia. This had declined by the eighteenth century itself and with the colonisation of the province, recovery was not possible. Traces of it remained in popular festivals like Bali Jatra (which is associated with setting off on trading missions to Bali and Java) and folk tales like Tapoi (which is a touching tale of a girl who had seven brothers who were maritime traders, and whose sisters-in-law harassed her when the brothers had gone off on an overseas trading mission).

Orissa had a rather flourishing textile 'industry' and this was a prized item in Europe.[82] Phakirmohan Senapati mentions about the *pala* (sail) manufacturing industry of Balasore and from his estimates it appears that a large number of people were engaged in this profession.[83] After the conquest of Orissa in 1803 the Company thought of stepping up their investments in textile production in the coastal belt of Balasore, Bhadrak and Jaipur. The Company's average income from the export of Orissa's textile commodities steadily increased from Rs. 2,000 in the first year to Rs. 56,052 in the course of the first 10 years. Nevertheless in the course of the first half of the nineteenth century the cotton industry had declined.[84]

By the end of the nineteenth century traces of the textile industry survived in official records or the nostalgic writings of Phakirmohan. His 'Cha Mana Atha Guntha', for example, deals with the declining weaver community represented by Bhagia and Saria. [85]

Salt-manufacturing was another 'industry' quite important in the coastal region. The company imported salt from Orissa at an average rate of 68,269 maunds per annum during the period of 10 years prior to its conquest. Once the Company introduced salt monopoly in Bengal the Orissa salt began to be smuggled into Bengal. In 1804 salt monopoly was introduced in Orissa. This proved very profitable since the net revenue reaped from this sector was around Rs.1,04,894 by June 1805. The production was increased from year to year and it become a very important commodity to be exported to the Calcutta market. However, the focus was so much on exporting salt that there was a scarcity of salt within Orissa and its price went up.

The situation became worse in the course of the second half of the nineteenth century when Liverpool salt began to be dumped into Orissa. It was sent over in the ballasts of ships which meant that there was no expense incurred in its transportation. It was better in quality and cheaper than the salt manufactured in coastal Orissa. This rang the death-knell of a long-standing local industry.[86]

The collapse of the traditional 'industries' had grave implications for some castes like Tantis (weavers) and Khadals (salt-makers)[87] who had been associated with these 'industries'. Numerically, some of these castes were quite prominent. The following table gives us an idea about the Tanti population in the three districts of Cuttack, Puri and Balasore in 1891.[88]

Table XI

District	Total Population	Tanti Population
Cuttack	1,937,671	59363
Puri	944,998	15695
Balasore	994,625	56767

These castes depended primarily on their caste professions and only secondarily on agriculture. The crisis perhaps pushed them towards agriculture. And this was the pattern for most of the traditional 'industrial' castes. However, given the crisis in agriculture and the increasing pressure on land, this change hardly solved their problems.

In the coastal region salt production had been an alternative source of livelihood during bad harvests. The monopoly of salt production eliminated this possibility.

While discussing the theme of 'external' exploitation we can now refer to a new concept introduced by colonialism: the excise tax system. The idea was to make profits out of commodities such as liquor, opium and *bhang* as well as impose duties on *hatas*.

Of all these, the drive to make profits out of liquor had serious implications for the tribals. This can be only grasped by outlining the role of liquor in tribal society. For the tribals it was almost a part of life.[89] Evidence of the folk tradition of the Juangs, Bondas, Gonds and Savaras, for example, clearly reflects that it was Mahaprabhu who had given liquor to human beings and the Bondas feel that Mahaprabhu had taught them to distil it as well.[90] Liquor was linked to tribal religion in an intimate way. This becomes clear if one looks at liquor offerings made to the gods, some of whom were supposed to be great drunkards themselves. It is also offered at the time of epidemics to some goddesses like Dharma Pinnu, the small-pox goddess, by the Kuttia Kandhas.[91]

This can also be illustrated through a discovery during field work of the author. A Kandha had walked into the Mathili police station (in the ex-zamindari of Jeypur) with his son's head in a sack. He confessed to murdering his son who had climbed the *salapa* tree, from which the man got his supply of liquor. On the face of it this action might seem irrational. However, for the Kandha the *salapa* tree, from which he obtained his liquor, was his wife. The man had murdered his son as he had 'outraged' his own mother.[92]

Liquor is a source of amusement as well. The following folk tale, of the Bhuyans of Dhenkanal, about the discovery of rice beer demonstrates this point:

> Boram Buddha took a pot of rice and went to make a plough in the forest. He found a lot of *pitaru* roots which he took home to eat. As there was some other roots mixed with *pitaru,* he held the two types of roots separately. Accidentally, the other root fell into the pot of rice but Boram Buddha did not notice this. He forgot about the rice for some days.
>
> When he went home his wife noticed that he was not eating anything and thought that some girl must have been feeding him. When she spotted him eating *pitaru* root she got angry and through magic made them bitter.
>
> When Boram Buddha went into the forest again he collected the roots but they tasted bitter. He remembered the rice and finding it dry in the pot he poured water over it and drank it. Very soon he got drunk. He made a tambourine (*changu*) and went home dancing and drumming. When the old woman found out the secret of his merriment she also drank rice beer, got drunk and danced to his drumming.[93]

Liquor plays an important role as a relaxant. The hard work and a desire to get a respite from it, socialising, festivals, mourning at deaths contribute to its importance. It is also significant to mention that some tribals like the Gonds of Koraput district felt that liquor was very important since on having it one becomes fearless.[94] Popular perceptions also located liquor as an antidote to malaria.[95] And finally, liquor is also an important source of food for the tribal folk.[96]

Among the non-tribals it is worth mentioning that liquor distillation had been the source of livelihood of the Sundhi caste. The Sundhis were scattered in different parts of the province.[97]

The colonisation of Orissa led to a drive to make profits out of the liquor trade. The contract supply system was introduced in 1905. This system was introduced in 1905. This system prohibited local manufacture and liquor contracts were made with certain distillers and it was sold through retail vendors. These vendors would bid for the license at auctions, and most of them were moneyed people. By the 1930's the system of auctioning had been given up and the retail vendors paid fixed fees to the government.[98] Nevertheless, the fact that the vendors represented the affluent section of the rural society remained a consistent feature.[99]

Ganja and opium were also sold in a similar way. The profit from the sales of these were considerable as the following table[100] shows :

Table XII

	1906-7	1911-12	1926-27	1930-31
		(Amount in Rupees)		
Cuttack				
Total revenue (opium, *bhang*, *ganja* and liquor)		4,17,312		9,84,969
Retail price				
Country spirit		7.10.6 (per gallon)		
Opium		50 (per seer)		
Ganja		22.8.0 -do-		
Bhang		15 -do-		
Puri				
Revenue from				
Country spirit	24,000		60,000	
Ganja	66,000		1,29,000	
Opium	1,07,000		3,71,000	

The excise system was extended to the *hatas*. The *hatas* were vital centres of amusement as in any pre-industrial society, and the excise duties did appear to be an inhibiting device. [101]

Another feature was the drive to impose restrictions on forests. This was especially something that affected the tribals since forests were intrinsically connected with their existence. But most importantly, forests symbolised freedom. The deep association with forests can be demonstrated through the following Didayi folk tale which deals with the origin of trees:

> When the earth sank beneath the flood, trees and animals were destroyed. Then Rumrok made a new world and created all creatures. However, there were no trees and the people found it very uncomfortable because of the lack of shade and the world did not look nice.
>
> Rumrok pondered over the problem of the absence of shade, wood for homes and fires and finally found a solution. He took dirt from his body and rubbed it. Three kinds of seed came out and he put them aside carefully. He piled up rocks to make a mountain and spread the soil above it. Then he planted the seeds and three trees were born. He carefully guarded and nourished them and when they flowered and bore fruits Rumrok showed them to Sukro Didayi, telling him to use the wood for building and firewood.[102]

This folk tale signifies that the forests have serious religious, aesthetic and existential significance for the tribals. However, the day-to-day interaction with the forests was based on 'shifting' cultivation, hunting and food-gathering. Of these 'shifting' cultivation, also known as *podu* or *jhoom*, was a very important facet. The Oraons attached both economic and religious significance to this. For the Juangs the selection of a patch in the forest, the felling of trees and the distribution of land interlinked the social, religious and economic aspects of life. Since most of the tribal cultivators were very poor and the lands available to them were located at inaccessible and forested parts and since 'shifting' cultivation matched their implements, this was the easiest method of cultivation.[103]

The forests were also to provide a source of amusement and relaxation. The tribals' interest in hunting and the dependence on trees like *mohwa* and *salapa* for their liquor illustrate this point.

This dependence on forests was not an exclusively tribal phenomenon. Some outcastes like Dombs and Chamars also depended on the forests for their existence. The Dombs made baskets, whereas the Chamars made hide and skin products. We can also refer to Gaudas (a numerically strong caste in coastal Orissa) who depended on the forests as pasturage zones for their cattle.[104]

This dependance on forests underwent changes from the 1880's. The idea was to make profits out of forests and forest products. Forests were demarcated and various restrictions were imposed to prevent any interaction with forests. Coupled with this, leases were issued to contractors on forest products like timber, lac, hides and *kendu* and *tendu* leaves.[105] This process also involved the creation of a system of cesses for using forests and fines for violating forest rules.

How did popular perceptions relate to these changes? A common feeling was that traditional means of relaxation and rights over the forests were being 'stolen' away. Worse still, after being 'stolen' away the access to these depended on the payment of duties, cesses and fines. As a result, one's freedom to which a lot of importance was attached and which had been existing for generations, was being lost. Since the concept of 'profit' motive came before the material conditions existed and that too in a sudden and superimposed fashion, it created a sense of confusion, deprivation and anger at all those who were responsible for the changes.

How the popular perceptions to diseases was to undergo changes is examined next. The concepts differed between the tribals and non- tribals in many ways but some commonalties did exist.

In the tribal perception gods were behind illness and disease. The following folk tale of the Kuttia Kandhas illustrates this:[106]

> When the sun began to go round the earth he was disgusted to see men relieving themselves in the early mornings. One day he decided to punish them since they insulted him by pointing their organs at his face although he gave them light. The next day he climbed into the sky with a flower. When he saw Jagat Kandha relieving himself he threw the flower on him and said, 'Go and become syphillis, the scorpion disease'. Fifteen days later Jagat Kandha fell ill and the sun god was very pleased. He said to the disease, 'Become a fly and go into the bellies of many men'.

Consequently, illness and disease was linked to the displeasure of gods.

Another common belief was that gods sent diseases because the earth was getting overcrowded by human beings. The Didayis, for example, felt that *mapru* (god) sent epidemics to earth in order to prevent it from being overpopulated.[107]

Another variant of this belief was that hungry gods sent down diseases in order to obtain offering from devotees. The following Didayi folk tale reflects this:[108]

> For twelve years gods went hungry, without anyone taking notice of them. At last in despair they went to Rumrok, the supreme god, and complained that they had nothing to eat or drink, since they were born twelve years ago. Rumrok asked them to visit a Didayi in a particular village and to torment his children by giving one fever, another fits, a third dysentery and the others itches. He assured that the Didayi would soon give them all that they wanted to eat. The gods found the Didayi family large, happy and prosperous and at peace. However, very soon all of them fell ill. The Didayi was terrified and he appealed to Rumrok to help him. Rumrok said that gods were responsible for the illness in his family, and asked the Didayi to make offerings to the local godlings.

Some tribals felt that diseases were caused by the ghosts of gods. The Gadba, for example, linked leprosy to the *duma* (ghost) of a god. Finally, some like the Mundas believed that insanity was caused by one's own *bhoot* (spirit) which struck when offended.[109]

The similarity between tribal and non-tribal perception in associating evil spirits, the evil eye, sorcery and witchcraft with illness and diseases is interesting. Among the non-tribals in the coastal region, however, smallpox was associated with the goddess Sitala and the local goddesses, or *thakuranis*, as they were called.[110]

How did the people of a pre-industrial society respond to diseases? Our evidence shows a number of traditional roots and leaves which were used as medicines. Besides, one comes across attempts to propitiate gods, goddesses as well as local deities and the ghosts of ancestors. This was done through offerings of food and drinks. The non-tribals concentrated primarily on offering food whereas for the tribals the liquor component was more important. We are also told about the immunological characteristics inherent among the tribes of the Jeypur estate, especially to malaria and smallpox.[111]

In the coastal region we get interesting accounts of the practice of hoodwinking of the spirits. This was commonly practised to protect children from their attacks, especially when parents had already lost children. The child was sent round the village in a 'dust-pan' or dressed in rags or in clothes begged from friends. In the case of a boy, he was put into girl's clothes and called by a girl's name; or the child was given an opprobrious or deprecatory name, in order to make the spirits believe that he or she was of no value and not worth attacking.[112]

In this region we also have evidence of primitive methods of innoculation by hereditary Mastan Brahmins. The innoculation was performed on children. Along with the innoculation, offerings were made to Sitala since she had supposedly possessed the child.[113]

Did the popular perceptions to diseases remain unaltered? It seems on the contrary. The different process at work we have outlined along with some specific features led to certain changes. This latter aspect needs clarification. Among the specific points, mention must be made of large-scale intervention in the states and zamindaris in 'improving' health standards and the linking -up of vaccinations with 'profit' motive, especially in the states.[114] And it was perhaps the reinforcement of the exploitative dimension that aroused suspicion, hatred and fear of the 'modern' hospital. The following Ho song illustrates this:[115]

> In Oriya they call it *daktarakhana*
> In Hindi *haspatal*
> Whatever its name, it really means death.

Keeping this perspective in mind we can outline some changes in the popular perceptions of diseases. For one, in some tribal areas diseases came to be increasingly associated with non-tribals. Here one can cite the example of the Kuttia Kandhas. They came to associate smallpox with *Dharma-pinnu*, who was worshipped at all agricultural festivals. What is interesting is the way the Kuttia Kandhas came to relate to smallpox as an Oriya goddess living in the lap of luxury. Ceremonies were performed in her honour just before the sowing of the hill clearings. The invocations at her special ceremony were made in Oriya and the offerings were not the normal millet and rice beer but milk, ghee, rice and *mohwa* liquor.[116] The goddess *Mata*, for the Didayis, also represented a similar change in perception.[117]

The way in which Assam got associated with illness symbolised the pains and sufferings of all those who went to work in that far-off place. According to a belief among the Savaras, the god of wind (Ringesum) blew pieces of bones of those who died in Assam to their villages. These took the form of whirlwinds which blew off house-tops, and anyone encountering them would fall ill.

There are indications linking illness and diseases to the symbols of colonialism. The Savaras, for example regarded the 'aeroplane god' as responsible for constipation. In fact, the Savaras created a new god—*Sahibosum* and his consort. *Sahibosum* was their Sahib God. He was not a European but a touring official who went around like a forest guard or a policeman and carried cholera with him. They carved wooden images in his honour and placed them at the peripheral regions of their villages to keep him out or at least to divert his attention. He was worshipped and sacrifices were offered to him.[118]

The context also led to an increasing subordination of/violence against women. This ranged from discriminatory wages[119] to lower fees for innoculation against smallpox.[120] This also meant a greater participation in work outside their domestic surrounding. Of course, this was uneven and had links with the caste structure as the following table shows.[121]

Table XIII

Caste/tribe		*No. of female workers per 100 males*
Brahmin	(Orissa)	9
Karana	-do-	10
Khandayat	-do-	11
Chasa	-do-	13
Gauda		55
Bauri		80
Hari	(Orissa States)	79
Pana	(Orissa and Chota Nagpur Plateau)	55
Gond	(Orissa States)	63
Santhal	(Bihar, Orissa, Chota Nagpur plateau; Orissa States and the Santhal Pargannas)	87

Consequently, we find that outcaste and tribal women participated more in activities outside their homes than upper caste women. The area of work centered around cultivation, agricultural labour and trade. Certain changes in the case of tribal women were significant. A man's wealth and status came to be associated with the number of wives he had.[122] We also come across the phenomenon of female infanticide among the hill tribes in the nineteenth century. Daughters proved to be a very expensive commodity to the tribals, whose customs now came to be penetrated by the uncertainties and commercial values of a market economy. Consequently, they destroyed their infants (females) by leaving them in the jungle ravines immediately after birth. In fact, there were many villages without a single female child. There are references to the practice of 'witch-hunting' in tribal society from the Koraput district. When a woman was suspected of being a witch her front teeth were knocked out and her mouth filled with filth. She was then beaten with sticks of the castor oil plant. If she did not cry out, then it was believed that she was a witch.[123] These features appear to be striking, given the often romanticised importance attached to women in tribal society.

There are also references to *sati* in the princely states, the zamindaris as well as the coastal region. Women had to pay the price of the ruler's or zamindar's zeal to draw legitimacy from the Rajput tradition. In the coastal belt it was more broad-based and was a fallout of the dominant castes' (Brahmins/Karanas) desire to conform to their caste or class status, whereas others (especially Chasas/Khandayats as well as Telis and Banias) who had risen economically, demonstrated their superiority and their links with upper caste norms by harping on it. Although the reasons were different, the victims were ultimately women.[124]

From the coastal region we get evidence from the *Census Report* of 1931, which indicates a sharp increase of insanity among women, especially in Balasore.[125] Although we do not know whether this was because such cases came to be reported more frequently and/or because of an increase in the ostracisation of women, one cannot miss the links between this phenomenon and the context.

The violence perpetrated on children was, of course, devastating. The crisis and the absence of the women folk from their homes led to the administration of opium to children to 'take care' of them in the absence of their parents. This was a universal phenomenon in the coastal region.[126] Among the tribals, there was an alarming increase in human sacrifices, especially among the Kandhas. For them turmeric was of great commercial value. The acute crisis and the uncertainties of the market economy forced them to resort to human sacrifices to please the goddess *Tari*, so that a good harvest could be reaped.[127]

As the conditions of the peasants and tribals worsened, they sought to cope with the situation through protests and migrations. In the first place, we hear of 'criminal' tribes and castes. Here one can refer to the Panas and the Dombs who had a 'tradition' of 'crime'. For example, we are told about the 'criminal' activities of the landless Panas,[128] and of the Dombs of Jeypur estate who were 'cattle lifters' and operated as 'dacoits' on the Koraput-Jeypur road.[129] However, even some colonial officials saw links between their crime and their poverty.[130]

The nature of crime under colonialism also underwent changes. In addition to the earlier type of crime against customary laws settled locally, there now developed crimes against property. This change implied an increase in the interaction between the peasants and tribals and the colonial judicial structure. Although the bourgeois concept of crime was not comprehensible to the local agencies or the offenders themselves on many occasions, what is worth stressing is the broad acceptance gained by the new structure of justice. This process was slow and it marked the psychological inroads made by colonialism. This point can be illustrated by pointing to the phenomenon of the tribal arriving at the police station with the head of the landlord/moneylender who had violated tribal morality. Although death was the normal answer to such violation, the tribal, realising that he had committed a crime in terms of the colonial judicial system, sometimes chose to surrender to it.[131]

However, the colonial judicial system was marked by intra-regional variations. The coastal belt experienced intensive judicial intervention, leading to a greater awareness of the new judicial structure among the peasants and tribals here. In contrast, in the princely states the colonial presence coexisted with authoritarian despots. So, although theoretically under the British, in these interior tracts the chiefs framed the laws. Thus one of the chiefs of Dhenkanal placed the seat of the judge at his feet, where the judge had to sit with folded hands. This was meant to signify that the chief was above law.[132] We also get evidence of 'night courts' run by drunken officials which were aimed at terrorising the peasants and tribals.[133]

Talking more specifically, we can refer to the 'violations' of forest laws, the 'illicit' manufacture of liquor[134] and salt and diversion of canal water to the fields,[135] as examples of new types of 'crime'. The erosion of traditional rights, coupled with a justification of cheating the officials who cheated the peasants and tribals, provided the rationale for such action.[136] It needs to be also added that jail-going was seen as the solution to one major problem of life: food. Thus, during the 1866 Famine many people 'indulged' in 'crimes' to get into jails[137] which ensured a steady supply of food. These were not seen as symptoms of crisis or protest. The approach was to punish and discipline all those who were involved through the police, laws, fines and prisons.

Of course, there were also new types of crime without the protest dimension. Here one can cite the example of a common crime in the coastal belt, which was to forcibly take a person's thumb impression on a blank paper. The intention was to convert this into a legal document which could be used contrary to the wishes or knowledge of the person whose thumb impression had been taken.[138]

Besides the 'everyday form of struggle' against adversaries, protest also took the form of rebellion. Most of the nineteenth century rebellions followed a consistent pattern. Local chieftains or tenure holders led these primarily to reassert or safeguard their position which had been threatened with the advent of the British. Thus, the risings of Parliakhemedi (1799-1814), Ghumsar (1835-36) or Angul (1846-47) show how the existing economic discontent among the tribals was sought to be channelised against the British. The case was similar when we consider the Paika Rebellion (1817) or the rising of Surendra Sai. The *paikas*, it should not be forgotten, were holders of privileged rentfree tenures, and when threatened with dispossession, they rallied together different sections of the crisis-ridden peasantry and rebelled against the British. Surendra Sai's rising was an attempt made during the 1857 Rebellion to take back Sambalpur using local discontent. Although these risings had an anti-imperialist content and challenged the British, they were led by the propertied classes who wanted to maintain their privileged position.[139]

We also come across rebellions against internal exploiters. Here the militancy of the Kandhas of Kalyansingpur of the Jeypur zamindari can be cited. Kalyansingpur was a service-tenure granted by the Maharaja of Jeypur. In 1884 the holder of the grant, Krishna Deo, died without a male successor and the Jeypur Maharaja wanted to resume the grant. At Krishna Deo's advice his widowed wife, Nila Debi, had adopted a son named Gopinath. The Kandhas of Kalyansingpur supported Gopinath's sucession as his father had pointed him out as the successor before his death and also because Dolapati, Nila Debi's Manager, was a tyrant.

The situation reached a climax when on the Dussehra Day thousands of Kandhas demanded that Gopinath should play the role of the Raja. When the Rani refused, they broke into the fort and carried off the boy. Gopinath was taken to Jeypur escorted by three hundred Kandhas to represent to the Maharaja. The boy was given an allowance and sent to study at a college at Vizagapatnam. In early 1885 a party of Kandhas marched to Vizagapatnam with the intention of getting back Gopinath and installing him as the Raja of Kalyansingpur. They were pacified only when the Agent sent his own nominee to manage the estate and removed Dolapati.[140]

Around the turn of the century, we also get evidence of *melis* (organised peasant demonstrations) from parts of coastal Orissa, like the Kanika zamindari. Although led by 'rich' peasants who belonged to the Khandayat caste, these *melis* reflected the collective resistance of the peasants to the increasing economic pressures imposed by the zamindars.[141]

We also get references to popular protests in the princely states. We can cite here the case of a Raja of Nilgiri who was pulled down from his elephant by angry peasants in the 1880's.[142] Besides revealing that the conflict between the peasants and their local (immediate) exploiter could take a volatile form, it also reflects how the popular level could conceptualise this sort of an action, despite generations of servility.

The result of all the problems we have discussed also led to landlessness and migrations. The following folk poem articulates the problems and miseries involved in this process:[143]

This little finger said,
'Mother, I'm hungry.'
The next finger asked,
'How can we get food?'
The middle finger said,
'We'll borrow.'
The index finger said,
'How can we pay it back?'
The big thumb said,
'We'll eat, drink and leave the country.'

The process of migration was uneven. For example, in the three coastal districts of Cuttack, Puri and Balasore this trend originated by the end of the nineteenth century. In contrast this process began from around the 1920's in the interior areas of the province, for instance the Jeypur zamindari. What we also come across is intra-provincial migration. Our evidence shows migrations and population movement within the three coastal districts, as well as migrations from these areas to the princely states. Whereas the coastal region attracted agricultural labourers and workers in some industrial sectors, the states offered extensive areas of cheap, cultivable land for uprooted peasants.[144] In some states like Talcher the prospects for employment improved with coal-mining. Those who moved out of the province went over to Bihar, Bengal, Assam and Rangoon. The following tables give us some insight into the pattern of migration.

Table XIV[145]

1891		
District or Orissa State	*No. of immigrants from the coastal districts and the Orissa States*	*No. of immigrants from the three coastal districts*
Cuttack	24,198	
Puri	28,930	
Balasore	25,525	
Talcher		383
Dhenkanal		1 6174
Nilgiri		9990
Ranpur		5090

Table XV[146]

Year	*From Cuttack to Calcutta, Hoogly, Howrah and 24 Purganna*	*From Bihar and Orissa to Bengal*	*From Cuttack to Assam*	*From Balasore to Assam*	*From Sambalpur to Assam*	*From Orissa to Assam*
1901	40.000	-	-	-	-	-
1911	64,000	-	27,000	2,000	-	-
1915-16	-	-	-	-	-	32,000
1918-20	-	-	-	-	-	51,000
1931	-	One out of every thirty born in Bihar and Orissa was in Bengal	-	-	9,390	-

Let us at this point try to reconstruct the process of legitimisation and social control and how it was to undergo changes in the phase of colonial rule. We can begin with the cult of Jagannatha which had reinforced social legitimisation and control prior to the advent of colonialism. This cult had its origin around the eighth century A.D. Experts in the field mention that it was a tribal cult (Savara) which had been Hinduised—a fact corroborated by folk tales. Some of its rituals, indeed, are distinctly tribal and we also come across hereditary Savara cooks and priests in the Puri temple.[147]

This cult was an important component of legitimisation. The Rajas of Puri ruled in the name of Jagannatha, and some of their names were inspired by Jagannatha. These Rajas were looked upon as 'moving' Vishnus (*chalanta* Vishnu). In the pre-capitalist structure anyone who possessed Puri and the Jagannatha temple was the legitimate *gajapati* and Raja of Orissa. Consequently, there developed an intimate connection between the cult and kingship. So much so that if the tributary chiefs deceived the Puri Raja or violated the social order it was regarded as a rebellion against Jagannatha. Conversely, any service to the deity's Viceroy (Puri Raja) equalled service to Jagannatha — Orissa's over-lord.[148] The magnitude of the cult was visible throughout Orissa. For example, most of the big landlords or the tributary chiefs modelled their capitals on Puri—recreating in them a Jagannatha temple, a *badadanda* ('big street') in front of it and the annual Rathajatra. The tributary chiefs also secured legitimacy by associating themselves in some way or the other with Jagannatha or the Puri Raja—a phenomenon that developed during the eighteenth and nineteenth centuries.[149]

The most fascinating aspect of this cult was that it subsumed both 'high' or 'low' religions which came into contact with it.[150] And this process not only strengthened the cult but also its role in the process of social legitimisation and control. This can be grasped if we narrate some folk tales or religious rituals.

The Gaudas or pastoralists formed an important caste in Orissa. The following folk tale of Manika Gauduni (milkmaid) illustrates the way this caste, along with untouchables, got linked to the cult and how the Rajas of Puri secured legitimacy:

> Purosottam Deb, the Raja of Puri, wanted to marry Padmabati, the Princess of Kanchi, renowned for her beauty. But the King of Kanchi, the Princess's father, changed his mind when he learnt that on the Rathajatra day Purosattam Deb swept the floor with a broom—for the King did not want to marry off his daughter to a 'sweeper'.
>
> When the Purosattam Deb discovered this, he was furious and invaded Kanchi but unfortunately lost the battle. He then decided to attack Kanchi once more and this time sought the divine assistance of Lord Jagannatha, who in a dream promised to help him. And it came to pass that in advance of Purosattam and his troops, Lord Jagannatha and Balabhadra, disguised as military

> officers and each riding a black and white horse, began their march towards Kanchi. On the way, feeling thirsty they decided to have some curd from Manika, a milkmaid. Not having any money to pay for the curd Jagannatha gave his diamond ring and asked Manika to exchange it for money with the Puri Raja. Manika waited and when Purosattam came along she narrated the incident showing him the ring. Recognising the ring and overwhelmed by the grace of the Lord, Purosattam Deb advanced into battle. He was crowned with success and the hand of the beautiful Padmabati.[151]

The act of *chera-pahara* (sweeping the floor) on the Rathajatra day marks an inversion of roles: the Raja for the moment became a 'sweeper', identifiable as an untouchable in terms of caste. This act contributed uniquely to legitimise his rule and his existence among the untouchables and the downtrodden. Popular perceptions located him as someone who was powerless before Lord Jagannatha; as someone who performed the menial role of untouchables.

Another folk tale, 'Siri Chandaluni' (an untouchable woman) deals with Laxmi leaving the temple to stay in the house of Siri, one of her very ardent devotees who was not allowed into the temple. She did this in response to being admonished by her husband Jagannatha who had acted on the advice of Balabhadra, his brother, for paying too much of attention to Siri. Once Laxmi left the temple, food, wealth and prosperity disappeared. Very soon Jagannatha and Balabhadra realised their mistake and apologised to Laxmi who agreed to return.[152]

These myths which are associated with protest contributed at one level to strengthen the process of legitimisation and control. Their survival for centuries demonstrate this phenomenon. However, the implications were complex; at another level we discover that the poor outcast internalised the myth of a city (Puri) on the far eastern shore where both high and low ate together. Even though he spent his life outside the village limits, and his shadow, cast accidentally, 'defiled' and angered men of high caste, this myth gave him sustenance and a meaning to his existence.[153]

Among the tribals the cult was maintained and reinforced through the special roles in the cult assigned to some tribals. Here one can cite the example of the Savaras. The folk tale tradition located Jagannatha as a Savara deity who had been stolen from them by an emissary of King Indradyumna. The traditional role of the Savaras as priests and cooks of Jagannatha, among other things, contributed to their integration to the cult.[154]

Similarly, a folk tale among the Binjhals of Sambalpur traces their ancestry to twelve brothers who were the sons of Vindyabasini. One day while hunting in the forest they let off arrows which flew to the door of Lord Jagannatha and got stuck. No one could pull these out and the Puri Raja was impressed when these brothers pulled them out effortlessly, after which he granted them estates. Moreover, there is a lot of similarity between the Navakalevara—when the old idols of the three deities are disposed off and new ones are installed—and the process of renewal among tribal gods in western Orissa.[155]

However, it will be incorrect to say that the cult of Jagannatha was the only means through which legitimacy and social control was achieved. We can illustrate some other means through certain examples. One of the rulers of Nilgiri, Utareswar (1564-1610 A.D.), appears to have come into contact with the Bhuyans and he added the title of Bhuyan Mahaparta to his name to signify that he had leadership over them. Similarly, according to a custom, the Majhis of Sargipalli, who were Bhuyans, used to apply vermillion on the forehead of the Rajas of Gangpur at the time of their installation, symbolising the acceptance of their rule by the Bhuyan tribals.[156]

The system of legitimacy and social control that developed in the colonial phase was built on the foundations of the 'old', which has been already discussed. The 'old' was never shaken off and it coexisted with the new. Only the emphasis shifted from religion, myths and mysticism to bourgeois laws. The concept of 'crime' and 'punishment' based on a legal system, the notion of jails for offenders and the 'concern' for the peasantry, measures like famine relief, remission of taxes, loans, construction of irrigation and communication system and the enactment of tenancy legislation—all formed part of this drive. However, the pattern was very uneven and far from being complete. It affected only the temporarily-settled areas of Cuttack, Puri and Balasore. The states and big landlords adopted only those measures which suited them.[157] The way in which the tributary chiefs remodelled their structure reflects a similar process in which the 'old' and the 'new' were blended.[158]

The 'new' system created a lot of confusion. This can be examined by looking at some concepts of the Kandhas. For the Kandhas stolen property (normally theft of agricultural produce or wrongful occupation) had to be returned or its equivalent had to be paid. The first time the offender was given a lenient treatment and he did not have to pay any penalty. Any repetition was not dealt with as an offence against property or the individual sufferer but as a wrong against the whole society. This could not be compensated and the offender was expelled from the tribe. However, the offender's family could not be left to starve and were, thus, given the right over one half of the crops of the field attached as compensation.

The system of land tenure was very simple: each man tilled his own land and the concept of a landlord did not exist. The right to the soil was based on the priority of cultivation by the individual. Transferring property was equally uncomplicated. The seller expressed his intention to the headman, not to obtain sanction, but to publicise his intention. He took the buyer to the field along with five others, delivered a handful of the soil to the purchaser and publicly received a part of the price.

A strong sense of morality ensured truthfulness and honesty. They believed that lies would bring destruction to them. Besides, hot oil, boiling water or heated iron were used as the self-inflicted ordeal to prove one's innocence.[159]

Given these features, we can imagine the confusion that gripped the peasants and tribals in the midst of colonial 'laws' which were alien and incomprehensible to them. Popular perceptions did not completely accept the 'new' and an element of doubt and suspicion remained.[160] This was because of the nature of the 'new' itself which in colonial India meant a series of crises for the peasants and tribals. The following Oraon magic spell, meant to exorcise evil spirits, demonstrates an identification of evil with symbols of colonialism:

Pull father, pull, pull,
Pull the *bhuts* to whom,
Vows were by our fathers made.
Pull father, pull, pull,
Pull the *bhuts* to whom,
Vows were by our grandfathers,
and great-grandfathers made.
Pull father, pull, pull,
Pull the steam boat.
Pull father pull, pull,
Pull the railway train.
Pull father, pull, pull,
Pull the bicycle.
Pull father, pull.[161]

While discussing popular culture we should also refer to the tradition of the *jatra* and the *Jogi* singers in the coastal region. The former normally touched upon themes associated with religion but on occasions also highlighted economic issues and tensions affecting rural society. The evidence for the 1930's indicates this quite clearly.[162] The *Jogi* singers were wanderers and although their songs were often veiled in a religious garb they also dealt with problems and tensions of rural society.[163] Consequently the *jatra* tradition and the *Jogi* singers were extremely powerful transmission points in rural coastal Orissa as well as in some of the princely states.

But how were people brought together in the countryside? As expected, this was necessary at times of resisting their exploiters. The common call for solidarity came from drumbeats. Among the Santhals a rope with a knot was circulated; each time it changed hands, the issue and the plan of action was mentioned.[164] In coastal Orissa blasts from conch-shells and *hulahuli* (ululation) brought people together.

Another point that needs special mention is the question of leadership. Traditionally, the peasants and tribals of the coastal area as well as the interior region were led by headmen or village chiefs. Occasionally they also accepted leaders from outside like saints and 'holy' men.

This takes us to the next aspect: popular perceptions of the state. The state remained a remote, abstract and rather blurred entity consisting of things both imaginary and real: religion and myths, rajas, zamindars and officials (forest and revenue), the Queens/Kings of England and the white man.[165]

Of course, their day-to-day activities brought them into contact with the state: forest officials who 'fined' them for no comprehensible reason, the officials who enforced anti-infanticide laws, extracted forced labour or levied excise duties, the police constables who descended on their villages twice or thrice a year to rape and plunder, or the *sahukars* who grabbed their property. Nevertheless, it is quite improbable that in the nineteenth century the peasants and tribals perceived these functionaries clearly as representatives of the state. The structure of legitimisation created a belief that the rajas, zamindars or the Kings and Queens of England were just and were above wrongdoing. These limitations imposed by history on peasant consciousness could be transcended only in the late nineteenth and twentieth century.

One noticeable feature is a difference in the levels of perception between those who were in the temporarily-settled tract and those who belonged to the interior areas like the princely states or the Jeypur estate.

The people of the states had virtually no taste of the 'reformatory' measures such as those in the coastal tract. For the coastal folk, the states were derogatorily known as *garjats*, where *garjatias* lived. These *garjats* were the *andharuamulaks* ('dark zones') where the rajas could do anything they wanted.[166] Given the absolute power of the states it is possible that popular perceptions could locate the existence of the state epitomised by the raja, his *durbar* and his life. However, colonialism was a visible phenomenon in some of the British administered states, being present in the form of the *dewans* appointed by the colonial government or the troops sent to maintain law and order. This situation was more or less similar in some of the interior estates like Jeypur.

In the coastal region popular perceptions were clearer in relating to the state and colonialism. The large-scale interventions by the colonial government from 1866 onwards contributed significantly to this process. Consequently, the British component of the state in a structure which included landlords, officials and moneylenders left a distinct mark upon popular perceptions.

We can round off our discussion by trying to explain some common elements in perceptions between tribals and peasants. Perhaps no other factor contributed so heavily to this process as colonialism itself: the land settlements, growth of a money-economy, and the peasantisation/Hinduisation of tribals. One major consequence was the end of the isolated existence of the tribals as well as the peasants.

Certain clues to this premise are offered in the philosophies of existence of both peasants and tribals.[167] In the tribal world view existence was located in the 'present', in this world. The Hindu perception, which influenced the peasants, located it in the future in the 'other world'. However, the interaction with colonialism led to a growing awareness of a 'present' which was viewed as oppressive and harassing in contrast to a prosperous and happier past. For a peasant of the coastal belt the past spelled freedom to manufacture salt, for a tribal it was a prosperous world free of landlords, taxes, forest and liquor laws. Consequently, this nostalgic backward glance at the past made them view the 'present' as a confusing phase which undermined one's freedom and identity. This also made them dream of a future devoid of the problems of the 'present', when things would once again be as they were. Sometimes this process took the form of an apocalyptic vision.

Commonalities also existed in various other spheres. For one, there was a tremendous faith and belief in saviours from above. This meant that both admired and respected any source of authority and drew inspiration from priests, rajas, zamindars, even the British Kings, Queens, officials[168] or the leaders of the Congress in the twentieth century. Similarly, the concepts of 'good' and 'evil' and a strong sense of justice were shared by both peasants and tribals. These were important components in their judgement of the British, rajas, zamindars, moneylenders and officials.

Again, given the context, both viewed modern things with suspicion, hatred and fear. Developments ranging from schools and railways to steam boats and the telegraph were associated, after all, with dispossession, forced labour and oppressive cesses.

And finally, popular religion also bred certain commonalties. Each village in the coastal region as well as the interior had a deity. The concept that gods and goddesses lived almost like humans was common to both peasants and tribals. Moreover, as discussed, the cult of Jagannatha, which synthesised 'high' and 'low' religions was itself an embodiment of popular religion. Consequently, the process of Hinduisation simultaneously linked and gave an identity to both.[169]

IV

The World of the Intellectual

We can round off our discussion by examining the cosmology of the Oriya intellectuals. Needless to say, the Oriya intellectuals were as much a product of the context as were the peasants and tribals. What was perhaps different was their link with feudalism and colonialism[170] which conditioned their material existence and their perception. While the former implied a clinging-on to tradition, the latter necessitated the acceptance of colonial rule as just and beneficial—an illusion that survived till the 1920's. These features, in turn, explain many of the conflicts and ambiguities that affected the Oriya intellectuals. Thus, their world view was shaped by what was inherited, along with what was absorbed due to exposure to the middle-class tradition of the west, given their interaction with colonialism. This process reflected the absence of a break from the past[171] and left the Oriya intellectuals caught between two worlds. Their world view continued to have elements of feudalism and religious moorings and was coloured by a nostalgia for the past which had been disturbed by colonialism. Consequently, the backward-looking element contained the seeds of a future critique of colonialism.

While studying the mind of the Oriya intellectuals one can also mention certain 'threats' which it perceived. One was in the form of a religio-cultural threat posed by imperialism, given the activities of the Christian missionaries. This was especially sharp in the years following the 1866 Famine. There are references from contemporary Oriya newspapers which suggest how the conversions, especially of children, provoked a section of the intelligentsia to raise their voice.[172] Another such issue was the idea of the colonial administration to ban the Rathajatra at Puri.[173]

This religio-cultural threat, given the revivalist atmosphere, led to the increasing Hinduisation, in the revivalist sense, of the Oriya intellectuals by the twentieth century. Here one can refer to the hue and cry reported in the Oriya newspapers following the shifting of a beef stall in Cuttack city in 1920.[174]

This religio-cultural 'threat' of imperialism had another dimension: the 'threat' posed by English education which was alien and foreign to the Oriya identity. Phakirmohan Senapati's 'Dakamunshi' ('Postmaster') illustrates this. 'Dakamunshi' is a touching story of a father who had struggled very hard to educate his son Gopala and make him a postmaster. But when Gopala became a postmaster he looked down upon his father and severed links with him because he wore dirty clothes and did not know English.[175]

The other cultural 'threat' which they perceived was from the Bengalis. This centred around the emergence of Bengali landlords in coastal Orissa and the preponderance of Bengalis in the administration—features which coincided with the colonisation of the region. This 'threat' climaxed with a book by Kantichandra Bhattacharya entitled *Oriya Ekti Swadhin Bhasa Noen* ('Oriya Is Not An Independent Language') in 1870.[176] This prompted the Oriya intellectuals to turn towards the language of the masses and appropriate it in order to prove the independent existence of Oriya. With this began the process which narrowed the gulf between town and country and between the intellectuals and the common people.[177]

The exposure to the middle class tradition and humanitarianism of the West also implied condemning the exploitative rajas and zamindars. The focus was on their wasteful expenditure, excessive rent demands and the lack of initiatives to promote education.[178] This also made the Oriya intellectuals focus on the plight of the peasants, who were occasionally even urged to 'rise' and 'fight' especially in the princely states.[179] However, in the nineteenth century the illusions they nurtured about British rule prevented the Oriya intellectuals from questioning colonialism, although we get references to criticism directed against police torture in British Orissa.[180]

The intellectuals also began to question superstitious beliefs. In 1870 we get a reference to a letter written to *Utkala Putra* by a person of Jagatsingpur who had described the miracles of the local *thakurani* (goddess). The editor remarked sarcastically about how in the nineteenth century also the *thakurani* could excercise a serious influence.[181] However, the intellectuals remained cut off from the peasants and tribals and could not really understand them. This co-existed with a condemnatory attitude towards all those who worked with their hands. These complexities can be, perhaps, illustrated by citing the way the Oriya intellectuals responded to the temple-entry movement of certain outcastes, influenced by the Mahima Dharma, cited earlier. This reaction also illustrates the Oriya intellectual's obsession with their high caste status which had to be preserved. This implied looking at society hierarchically and opposing anything that threatened to dislocate it. Consequently, this kept alive the gap between the intellectuals who were mostly from upper castes i.e. Brahmins and Karanas, and the low castes and untouchables.

Certain socio-reform initiatives existed among Brahmins. Given the specificity of the *varna* system in Orissa, this can be seen as an attempt to maintain their landowning class and caste status. We can refer in this context to the Utkal Brahmin Samiti established in 1899. This was a congregation of landed elements, some of whom were English-educated. Forty-seven out of two hundred and seventeen patrons who contributed to it in 1906 were non- Brahmins.[182] Consequently, this body accepted some non-Brahmins who sought upward mobility.

In the twentieth century this trend developed with people like Gopabandhu Das taking up issues such as the reform of Brahmin society, women's education and championing primary and scientific education.[183] These broadened the scope of the socio-reform movement, and by taking up issues outside the structure of caste, Gopabandhu and some other intellectuals could gain some amount of popularity especially in the coastal tract.

The Utkala Sabha founded in 1878 attracted several Oriya intellectuals. Its first Secretary was Gopal Chandra Dutta. Its activities remained confined to the promotion of Oriya language and literature.[184] It sent four representatives to the Congress session in 1886 and thereafter delegates from Orissa regularly attended the Congress sessions.[185]

In 1903 the Utkala Union Conference, also known as Utkala Sammilani, was established. Championed by middle class intellectuals and certain feudal chiefs it continued to nurture illusions about British rule. By this time there was an attempt to focus on the amalgamation of Orissa. Nevertheless, the Utkala Sammilani remained confined to the coastal tract.[186]

It was the Swadeshi Movement (1905-08) which charged the Oriya intellectuals. It aroused them to stress on *swadeshi* which manifested itself in an attempt to revive the traditional 'industries' and promote domestic manufactures. People like Madhusudan Das were associated with this trend.[187] This coexisted with the drive to promote national education and assumed a concrete shape with the foundation of the Satyabadi Institution (1913) at Sakhigopal in Puri by Gopabandhu Das.

Ideologically, the Swadeshi Movement undermined illusions about colonialism nurtured by the Oriya intellectuals. This led to the questioning of colonial exploitation. One can refer here to Gopanbandhu Das who grasped that the traditional salt-manufacturing industry had received a blow[188] with the advent of colonialism. The famine of 1919-20 and the failure to seek redress through the constitutional apparatus furthered this process of realisation.

This questioning along with all-India developments[189] precipitated a shift away from the rajas and zamindars as well. By 1920 a dominant section of Oriya intellectuals had decided to join the Congress. With this partial break from colonialism and the feudal world the intellectuals were to turn towards the masses. And the complexities of this interaction were to determine the path that the national movement took in Orissa.

Notes

1. *Gujerati Navajivan*, 9.5.1920.
2. *Young India*, 12.5.1920.
3. This was discovered in the course of the author's field work.
4. As we shall see later there are many reasons for accepting this view.
5. For example, H.K. Mahtab, *et.al* (eds.), *History of the Freedom Movement in Orissa*, 5 vols., Cuttack, 1957.
6. We are obviously referring here to the tribal peasantry.
7. Orissa had as many as 24 princely states, excluding Singhbhum and Kharsuan which merged with Bihar.
8. While conducting the interviews the present author found a common feeling expressed by most of the interviewees that it was high time someone studied the peasant movements of Orissa; many of them talked about 'young scholars' who had begun looking in the direction but changed their projects since they faced problems about sources.
9. For example, this was discovered among the Kandhas of the Koraput district while conducting the field work. This has been discussed in 'Perceptions in a Changing Society: A Note on Koraput (Orissa)' in the *Economic and the Political Weekly*, 5 May 1990.
10. This method continues to exist in most of the western parts of the province.
11. L.S.S. O'Malley, *Census of India, 1911, vol. v, Bengal, Bihar and Orissa and Sikkim Part I Report* (Calcutta, 1913) p. 274.
12. Pati, 'Perceptions in a Changing Society, ', *op.cit.*
13. Bhairabi Prasad Sahu, 'Orissa Society: Past Trends and Present Manifestations'; paper presented at a seminar on 'State Specific Caste-Class Situation in India' TDSS Pune, 27-30 December 1987 (unpublished), see fn. 63.
14. Manoranjan Mohanty, 'Social Roots of Backwardness in Orissa (A Study of Class, Caste and Power), *Social Science Probings*, June 1984, p.191.
15. Krushnachandra Jena, *Land Revenue Administration in Orissa During the Nineteenth Century* (New Delhi, 1968), p. 33.
16. See, for example, S.L. Maddox, *Final Report on the Survey and Settlement of the Province of Orissa (Temporarily Settled Areas) vol.I 1890-1900* (hereafter *Maddox Report*); W.W. Dalziel, *Final Report on the Revision Settlement of Orissa 1922-1932* (Patna, 1934).
17. *Maddox Report, pp.* .201, 298, 392.
18. *Report of the Bihar and Orissa Provincial Banking Enquiry Committee 1929-30, pp.* (Patna, 1930), p.11.
19. *Maddox Report, vol.I*, pp. 136; 170-76; 235-36; *vol.II*, p. 384, Sakti Prasad Padhi, 'Property in Land, Land Market and Tenancy Relations in the Colonial Period: A Review of Theoretical Categories and Study of a Zamindari District', paper presented at the Seminar on Commercialisation in Indian Agriculture, Trivandrum 23-25 November, 1981 (unpublished)

pp.86-7. In the late nineteenth century the loan paid to the *haliyas* varied from Rs. 3 to Rs.10 a year; it hardly needs to be added that the system reduced them to serfs. Wages of daily labourers varied from 2 3/4 *annas* to 3 *annas* a day and was between 2 to 2 1/2 seers of rice when paid in kind; wages of women labourers were lower; *Maddox Report*, p.136.

20. S.S.Hossein, *The Completion of Report and Settlement for Kanika Ward's Estate (District Cuttack) 1889-94* (Cuttack, 1895) pp.4; 20-3; 28-9; 43-4.
21. *Final Report on the Settlement of the Dhenkanal Feudatory State Orissa 1923-24, Vol.I*, (Berhampur, 1966), pp.11-14; 24-8; 40. *Memoranda on the Indian States 1930* (Calcutta, 1931) pp.222, 223 gives us the figures of the *peshkush*.
22. *Report on the Land Revenue Settlement 1911-1912 Talcher State* (Cuttack, 1963), pp.13; 21-2; 31-5; 43; and *Completion Report of the Talcher State Revision Settlement Season 1928-29* (Cuttack,?), pp.13-14; 19.
23. G.N. Singh, *Final Report on the Original Survey and Settlement Operations of the Ranpur Ex-State Area in the District of Puri 1943-1952* (Berhampur, 1963), pp.10; 32-33; 61-71. In *ibid* p. 57 it is mentioned that the land revenue had gone up by 40.5% over the 1899 *Settlement*.
24. *Final Report on the Nilgiri Settlement 1917-22* (Berhampur, 1922), pp.1; 34-41; 51. Interview: Banamali Das (Nilgiri, May, 1982) who pointed to the absence of 'big' landlordism in the state and characterised it as a 'small' peasant economy.
25. Indrabilas Mukherjee, *Final Report on the Land Revenue Settlement of the Gangpur State 1929-1936* (Berhampur, 1938), pp.13; 17-19; 29-33; 41-46; and R.K. Ramdhyani, *Report on the Land Tenures and the Revenue System of the Orissa and Chattisgarh States Vol. III The Individual States* (Berhampur,?), pp. 43-44; 82-90. There were 907 *ganjhus* and *gountias* in the state; 19% of them were Bhuyans and 15% were Agharias. Besides upper castes (Brahmins and Kshatriyas) there were low/outcaste *ganjhus* and *gountias*; Mukherjee *op.cit.*, pp.18-19. *Memoranda on....., op.cit.*, pp. 222-23 mentions the amount paid by the state to the British.
26. N.C. Behuria, *Final Report on the Major Settlement Operation in Koraput District 1938-64* (Cuttack, ?), pp. 53-74; *Report on Land Administration in the District of Ganjam and Koraput 1938-39* (Cuttack, 1940), pp.7, 9; *Report of the Partially Excluded Areas Enquiry Committee Orissa 1940* (Cuttack, 1940), pp. 17-18; 43; 171; R.C.S. Bell, *Orissa District Gazetteers: Koraput* (Cuttack, 1945) pp.114-15; interview: Damodar Samantarai (Jeypur, June 1981), who directed my attention to the 'common lands'. For details of the exploitative system see Biswamoy Pati, 'Storm over Malkangiri: A Note on Laxman Naiko's Revolt, 1942' in Gyanendra Pandey (ed.) *The Indian Nation in 1942* (Calcutta, 1988).
27. For details see *Report on the Khurda Settlement of 1897-98* (Cuttack,?), especially pp.131-75; 193-299; *Final Report on the Resettlement Operation of Banki Government Estate* (Cuttack), especially pp.24-9.
28. H.K. Mahtab, *History of Orissa vol. II* (Cuttack, 1960), p. 445.

29. R. Clarke, 'Panas of Orissa' in M. Kennedy, *The Criminal Classes in India,* (1907; reprinted, Delhi 1985), Appendix pp.324-29 talked of a plan to start a Pana settlement at Angul, giving the Panas 'good' lands and loans, which would be written off. In the princely states like Talcher rent-free lands were given to Panas, who worked as *chowkidars; Report on the Land Revenue Settlement 1911-1912 Talcher State, op.cit.*, p. 13; Ramdhyani, *op.cit.*, p. 284.
30. We get references of *haliya* Brahmins from coastal Orissa.
31. B.P. Sahu, *op.cit.*
32. Sanjib K. Raut, 'Rural Stratification in Coastal Orissa (1866- 1900), *Social Science Probings*; March 1986, pp. 140; 143-148.
33. *Report of the Congress Agrarian Reforms Committee AICC* (Madras, 1945), pp. 140-141 outlined that the average rent per acre paid by tenants varied between Rs.8 to Rs. 2.12 *annas* and the sub-tenant paid about two-fifths of the gross produce; the daily cash wages ranged between Re.1 to Rs.1.8 *annas* for men and 8 *annas* for women or 4 seers of paddy per day.
34. The idea of bribing tribal gods to survive this crisis led to the evolution of rituals and poems. Here one can cite the example of the Kandhas whose poem, recited by the village priest as the first stab is inflicted on the sacrifical object, went thus:

    . . . Let there be no collective loss,
    Let no tigers prowl;
    The gods need so many bribes,
    So many offerings....

    Cited by Sitakanta Mahapatra, *The Awakened Wind: The Oral Poetry of the Indian Tribes* (New Delhi, 1983) pp.51-52; this poem also illustrates the proliferation of capitalism into remote tribal areas.
35. *Maddox Report I*, p.126.
36. *Report ... Provincial Banking Enquiry Committee, op.cit.*, pp. 27, 32, 34; 63; the following table cited in p. 52, *ibid* shows the extent of peasant's land mortgaged:

District	Year	% age of raiyati land mortagaged	% age mortgaged to moneylender
Balasore	1924	.84	.12
Puri	1926	.15	.02
Cuttack	1927	.60	.07

37. Ramdhyani, *op.cit., vol I*, pp.97-8.
38. Binoy Bhusan Chaudhari, 'Land Market in Eastern India 1793-1940' in *Indian Economic and Social History Review* ,vol.12, 1975 (in two parts); his focus is on the coastal districts of Cuttack, Puri and Balasore. Binoy Bhusan Chaudhuri, 'Eastern India' in Dharma Kumar (ed.) *The Cambridge*

Economic History of India vol.II c.1757-c.1970 (New Delhi, 1984), p.109 states that between 1804 and 1818, 51.6% of the old proprietors were eliminated in Orissa. Phakirmohan's, 'Cha Mana Atha Guntha' reflects on the new landlords in the coastal belt during the nineteenth century.

39. Thus, there is a clear variation between the coastal region where Tenancy Laws were promulgated and the other areas in the interior where they were vague and abstract.
40. *Report... Congress Agrarian Reforms Committee AICC, op.cit.*, p.14.
41. *Maddox Report I*, p. 201.
42. *Report of the Commission Appointed to Enquire into the Famine of Bengal and Orissa 1866, vol.I*, statement no. 52 cited by Raut, *op.cit.*, p.143.
43. Manoranjan Mohanty, *op.cit.*, p.185 seems to locate the ascendancy of the Chasas in the electoral process and as a result he sees this as a post-1947 phenomenon. However, this process originated around the end of the nineteenth century itself.
45. W.G. Lacey, *Census of India, 1931*, vol.VII, *Bihar and Orissa Part I-Report* (Patna, 1933), p. 267.
46. *Ibid.*, p. 278; and *Vol. VII Part II Tables*, p. 5.
47. N. Senapati and P. Tripathy (eds.) *Orissa District Gazetteers: Dhenkanal* (Cuttack, 1972), noted the same trend; the Chasas claimed the status of Khandayats and adopted the sacred thread; p.96. Similarly, N. Senapati and N.K. Sahu (eds.) *Orissa District Gazetteers: Mayurbhanj* (Cuttack, 1967), refer to the Chasas giving up ploughing and assuming the Karana title Mahanty; p.110.
48. Lacey,...*op.cit.*, *Part I*, p. 276.
49. *Ibid.*, 267.
50. L.S.S.O' Malley, *Bihar and Orissa District Gazetteers: Cuttack* (Patna, 1933), p.60.
51. L.S.S.O' Malley, *Census of India 1911, vol.V, Bengal, Bihar and Orissa and Sikkim, Part I, Report* (Calcutta, 1913) p.454, 477; W.W. Hunter, *Statistical Account of Puri and Orissa Tributary States, vol.XIX* (Delhi, 1976, reprint), p. 286, refers to the maintenance of caste differences within the Dhenkanal state jail. L.S.S.O, 'Malley, *Bihar and Orissa District Gazetteers: Sambalpur* (Patna, 1932), p. 93 refers to the excommunication of Jharua Brahmins since they started ploughing.
52. This has been disussed earlier.
53. Sitakanta Mahapatra, 'The Insider Diku: Boundary Rules and Marginal Man in Santhal Society' in P.C. Mahapatra and D. Panda (eds.); *Tribal Problems of Tomorrow* (Bhubneshwar, 1980), ppp.2-3, points to this problem as a result of, among other things, the growth of a market economy and differentiation in terms of wealth.
54. Nilamani Senapati and N.K. Sahu (eds.), *Orissa District Gazetteers: Koraput* (Cuttack, 1966), p.115; the normal belief of the Hindus, it should be noted, is that the spirit escaped through the top of the skull.

55. This can be traced back to c. 7th-8th A.D.
56. Given the state of things it is possible that the headmen were the first people to get Hinduised.
57. Nilamani Senapati and B. Mohanty (eds.), *Orissa District Gazetteers: Sambalpur* (Cuttack, 1971), p.117-18, refers to Gond zamindars of Sambalpur wearing the sacred thread and the advanced Binjhals claiming Rajput status. O'Malley,...*Sambalpur, op.cit.*, p.70, refers to the invention of new legends by the Gonds of Sambalpur in order to bring themselves within the framework of Hinduism.
58. Senapati and Mohanty,...*Sambalpur, op.cit.*, p.117.
59. Senapati and Sahu,...*Koraput op.cit.*, p.110.
60. O'Malley,...*Sambalpur*, op.cit., p.91, refers to 'rich' Binjhals being burnt.
61. K.N.Thusu, *Pengo Parojas of Koraput* (Calcutta, 1977), pp.14-15; Verrier Elwin, *Bondo Highlander* (Bombay, 1950), p. 262; V.Elwin, *The Religion of an Indian Tribe* (Bombay, 1955), p.490.
62. Thusu, *op.cit.*, p.15.
63. O'Malley, *Census...1911...,op.cit.*, p.235; E.T. Dalton, *Descriptive Ethnology of Bengal* (Calcutta, 1872), p.199.
64. U.Guha, M.K.A. Siddiqui and P.R.G. Mathur, *The Didayi: A Forgotton Tribe of Orissa* (Delhi, 1968), p.93. O'Malley,...*Sambalpur, op.cit.*, p. 90 refers to Binjhals not accepting food from the 'highest' Brahmins.
65. This table is based on C.J.O'Donnel, *Census of the Lower Provinces of Bengal 1891: The Provincial Tables* (Calcutta, 1893) pp.101-03; Lacey...*Census...1931* Part II *op.cit.*, p.4.
66. This table is based on O'Malley,...*Sambalpur, op.cit.*, p.218; Lacey...*Census...1931*, Part II, *op.cit.*, p.4.
67. This table is based on Lacey...*Census...1931*, Part I, *op.cit.*, pp.254-55 and *Part II*, p. 4.
68. This table is based on *ibid.*, Part II, pp. 4; 146147; 149-50; 159-60.
69. R.C.S. Bell, *Census of India, 1941. vol.XI, Orissa Tables* (Simla, 1942) pp.7; 27.
70. Singh,...*Settlement...Ranpur...,op.cit.*, p.10.
71. Dalton, *op.cit.*, p. 247.
72. Senapati and Sahu,...*Koraput, op.cit.*, pp.121;-22.
73. K.B. Das and L.K. Mahapatra, *Folklore of Orissa* (New Delhi, 1979), pp.74-75.
74. C.H. Bompas, *Folklore of the Santhal Parganas* (London, 1909), p. 306.
75. O'Malley,...*Sambalpur, op.cit.*, pp.64-5.
76. *Utkala Dipika* 12.3.1881; 26.3.1881. One can only add here that this event took place on 1 March 1881; in the clash one member of the Mahima Dharma was brutally killed by the Puri Pandas; another 15 people were imprisoned for 3 months.
77. J.M. Freeman, *Untouchable: An Indian Life History* (London, 1979), p. 384.

78. We have already referred to *gotis* and *haliyas*.
79. Without going into details, one can refer to Ramdhyani, *vol. I, op.cit.*, Mahtab et.al, The Report of the Enquiry Committee: Orissa States 1937 (Cuttack, 1939), to get a picture of this dimension. Obviously this problem was very pronounced in the princely states.
80. John Beames, *Memoirs of a Bengal Civilian* (? 1896; New Delhi, 1984; reprint), p. 213.
81. *Ibid.*
82. Letter from C. Becger, Collector of Customs, Balasore to A. Stirling, Secretary to Commissioner, cited by K.C. Jena *Socio-Economic Condition of Orissa During the Nineteenth Century* (New Delhi, 1978), p. 125.
83. Phakirmohan Senapati, *Autobiography* (Oriya; Cuttack, 1969), pp.20- 22.
84. B.S. Das, 'Decline of Balasore and Textile Industry in Orissa' in the *Quarterly Review of Historical Studies*, no. I, 1978-79, p. 40.
85. This appeared in *Utkala Sahitya* (1897); for the summary of the story see Mayadhar Mansingh, *A History of Oriya Literature* (New Delhi, 1962), p. 180.
86. Commissioner of Excise, Bengal to Board of Revenue, cited by J.K. Samal, *Orissa Under the British Crown* (New Delhi, 1977), p. 121. Senapati, *op.cit.*, pp.22-4 mentions the flourishing salt manufacturing 'industry' of Balasore.
87. Hossein, *op.cit.*, pp.20-3.
88. O'Donnel, *Census...1891, op.cit.*, pp.352; 354-56; 358; 372-73.
89. See, for example, Hemanta Das, 'Adivasi Samajare Madyapanara Bhumika' (Oriya) in *Adivasi,* October 1977-January 1978, p. 46.
90. Verrier Elwin, *The Religion..., op.cit.*, p.186; and *Tribal Myths of Orissa* (Bombay, 1954), pp.187-89; 195-96; Das and Mahapatra, *op.cit.*, p. 67.
91. V.Elwin, *The Religion...,op.cit.*, p.186; H.Das, *op.cit.*, p. 47; N.A.Watts. *The Half Clad Tribes of Eastern India* (Bombay, 1970) p. 65.
92. I was told about this at the Mathili police station (Koraput district) by the policemen.
93. Das and Mahapatra, *op.cit.*, pp. 67-8.
94. V Elwin, *Tribal Myths..., op.cit.*, pp.187-88.
95. I have heard this from many of the people I had interviewed in the Koraput district. See also G. Ramdas in *Orissa Legislative Assembly Proceedings 1946 vol.II* (Cuttack, 1946-47), p.271, where he mentions how he had heard from his grandfather that intoxicants were the only antidote to malaria.
96. H. Das, *op.cit.*, p. 47.
97. W.W. Hunter, *A Statistical Account of Bengal: Puri and Orissa Tributary States vol.xix* (Delhi, 1976; reprint), pp.182-214.
98. O'Malley,...*Gazetteers; Puri, op.cit.*, p. 250.
99. Nilamani Senapati and D.C. Kumar, *Orissa District Gazetteers: Kalahandi* (Cuttack, 1980), p.87, refers to Sundhis who combined liquor business with moneylending. This particular feature matches with that of South

Gujarat; see, for example, David Hardiman, 'From Custom to Crime: The Politics of Drinking in Colonial South Gujerat' in Ranajit Guha (ed.), *Subaltern Studies IV* (New Delhi, 1985).

100. This table is based on O'Malley,...*Gazetteers: Cuttack, op.cit.*, p. 201 and...*Gazetteers*: *Puri*; *op.cit.*, p. 248.

101. Even some, like Elwin, could not grasp the importance of the market place for the tribals. In his *Bondo Highlanders* (Bombay, 1950), p.252, he writes: 'I have never been able to understand the attraction of walking eight or ten miles to obtain' liquor from the *hatas* since this was available at home. He thought that it was due to the 'lure of the stolen fruit'.

102. Elwin, *Tribal Myths...*, *op.cit.*, pp.491-92. We should perhaps add here that most tribal deities are made of wood.

103. Kulamani Mahapatra and Kiranbala Debi, 'Shifting Cultivation in Orissa' in *Adivasi*, vol. XIV, no.4, pp.18-19.

104. Gaudas, it should be noted, were not outcastes.

105. Ramdhyani, *vol.I*, *op.cit.*, p. 33; Behuria, *op.cit.*, p. 6.

106. Elwin, *Tribal Myths...*, *op.cit.*, pp.491-92.

107. U. Guha, *op.cit.*, p. 224.

108. Elwin, *Tribal Myths...*, *op.cit.*, pp.485-86.

109. *Ibid*, p.487; S.C. Roy, *Mundas and their Country* (Bombay, 1970) p.279.

110. It is interesting to note how the Hindu goddess entered the tribals world. Thus, the Kuttia Kandhas identified small pox with the Hindu goddess Dharma-pinnu.

111. Senapati and Sahu,...*Gazetteers: Koraput, op.cit.*, p. 374.

112. L.S.S.O'Malley, *Popular Hinduism*: *Religion of the Masses* (New York, 1970), p. 138.

113. O'Malley,...*Gazetteers*: *Cuttack*, *op.cit.*, pp.69-71, gives details about this method of innoculation. The profession of the innoculators was hereditary among the Mastan Brahmins who were found in the coastal belt.

114. L.E.B. Cobden-Ramsey, *Bengal Gazetteers*: *Feudatory States of Orissa* (New Delhi, 1982; reprint), p.70; this reflects a very significant 'knowledge-power' theme.

115. Sitakanta Mahapatra, *The Awakened Wind: The Oral Poetry of the Indian Tribes* (New Delhi, 1983), p. 225.

116. N.A. Watts, *op.cit.*, p. 65.

117. Uma Guha, *op.cit.*, .p. 186.

118. Verrier Elwin, *The Religion...op.cit.*, pp.121; 180-81; 397-440. The aeroplane god was known as *Ringesum* or *Ringeboi*. This god was associated with the god of cholera, hernia and cattle diseases. Elwin, p. 440, refers to some Savaras seeing air raids in Assam during the Second World War and an air crash in the Savara belt of Ganjam; perhaps all these things led to the creation of the 'aeroplane god'.

119. We have seen this while discussing the land structure.

120. O'Malley,...*Gazetteers*: *Cuttack, op.cit.*, pp.69-71; since the life of boys

was considered more precious, the fees for innoculating them was higher than for girls.

121. O'Malley, *Census...1911, op.cit.*, pp.577-80.
122. For example, N.A.Watts, *op.cit.*, p.25 refers to polygamy as a status symbol among Savaras. Our surmise is that this process had originated at an earlier period but became more pronounced, given the development of a market society, in the colonial phase.
123. *History of the Rise and Progress of the Operations for the Suppression of Human Sacrifices and Female Infanticide Correspondence, 1836-1854*(?) p. 47. Behuria, *Settlement, op.cit.*, p. 29
124. *Appendix A* and *B, op.cit.*, The following table based on *ibid* gives us an idea about the caste of the 29 *sati* victims in the 1815-1829 period:

Brahmins	Karanas	Chasas/Khandayats	Bania	Teli	Unidentified
13	6	3	2	1	1	3

125. Lacey,...*1931, Part I, op.cit.*, p. 170.
126. Dalziel,....*Report..Revision Settlement...,op.cit.*, p. 8; J.N. Mahapatra, *Orissa in 1936-37 to 1938-39* (Cuttack, 1941), p. 106, mentions how this problem affected every district. Some empiricists like Gorachand Pattnaik, *The Famine and Some Aspects of British Economic Policy in Orissa* (Cuttack, 1980), p. 211, point to the increase in opium consumption to demonstrate prosperity.
127. Dalton, *op.cit.*, pp.277-8.
128. Clarke in M.Kennedy, *op.cit.*, pp.324-29. The Panas were generally looked upon as a criminal outcaste group in the whole province.
129. Senapati and Sahu,...*Gazetteers: Koraput, op.cit.*, p. 315.
130. Clarke, *op.cit.*,
131. In fact, Bhagabati Charan's 'Shikar' (written in 1936) and Gopinath Mohanty's *Paraja* (written in 1943) deal with this sort of a theme.
132. Sadasiba Pradhan, *Agrarian and Political Movements: States of Orissa 1931 to 1949* (New Delhi, 1986), fn. 81, p.66.
133. The 'night courts' were there in every state; see, for example Ramchandra Ram *Sangramee* (Oriya; Cuttack, 1986), pp.100-01.
134. The 'violations' of forest laws and the 'illicit' manufacture of liquor was mostly confined to the tribal areas.
135. John Beames, *Memoirs..., op.cit.*, pp.211-12, mentions how the villagers in coastal Orissa were harassed by incessant police visits aimed to prevent the 'illicit' manufacture of salt. As he puts it: 'The Police, who are practically powerless against professional smugglers, used to display great keenness and energy in arresting some poor helpless widow whom they caught boiling a little brine.... This woman was dragged fifty to sixty miles, to Balasore to be produced before a magistrate.' This, perhaps, aptly illustrates how the salt 'laws' were oppressive and were therefore hated in

the coastal belt. *Utkala Putra*, August 1870, contains a reference to a person who had been imprisoned for diverting canal water to his fields at Jobra (Cuttack).

136. F.G. Bailey, 'The Peasant View of the Bad Life' in Theodor Shanin (ed.), *Peasants and Peasant Societies* (London, 1984), p. 301, also observes how peasants justified cheating government agencies which cheated them.
137. W.W. Hunter, *A Statistical Account of Bengal vol. XVIII: District of Cuttack and Balasore* (Delhi, 1976; reprint), p. 211; Gorachand Pattnaik, op.cit., p. 56.
138. O'Malley,...*Gazetteers: Cuttack, op.cit.*, p. 204.
139. For details see, Mahtab *et.al* (eds.) *History..., vol.I, op.cit.*, P.K. Mishra, 'Freedom Struggle in Orissa' in M.N. Das (ed.) *Sidelights on the History and Culture of Orissa* (Cuttack, 1977)
140. Behuria, *op.cit.*, pp.66-7.
141. Hossein,...*Settlement...Kanika...,op.cit.*, pp.65-6.
142. Nilgiri Praja Andolana Compilation Committee, *Nilgiri Praja Andolanara Itihas* (Oriya; Balasore, 1982), p. 32,
143. Prafulla Mohanty, *Indian Village Tales* (London, 1975), p. 21.
144. O'Malley, *Census...1911, op.cit.* p. 171.
145. Based on O'Donnel, *Census...1891, op.cit.*, pp.101-03; 160-63.
146. This table is based on O'Malley, *Census...1911, op.cit.*, p.183; P.C. Tallents, *Census of India 1921, vol.VII, Bihar and Orissa, Part I Report* (Patna, 1923) p. 113; Lacey, *Census...1931, op.cit.*, p.111; and O'Malley,...*Gazetteers: Sambalpur, op.cit.*, p. 59.
147. See, for example, A. Eschmann, 'Prototypes of the Navakalavara Ritual and their Relation to the Jagannatha Cult', in M.N.Das (ed.), *Sidelights..., op.cit.*
148. In *ibid*, see Gopinath Mohapatra, 'Jagannatha, During the Reign of the Gangas and Suryas', p. 412; and M.P.Das, 'Jagannatha and Kingship', pp.415-16.
149. Herman Kulke, 'Rathas and Rajas' in *The Journal of Orissan History*, July, 1980 feels that this development took place in the 18th-19th centuries. This phenomenon becomes clear if one has a cursory glance at the Settlement Reports of the various princely states or the zamindaris or visited them today.
150. For example, Jagannatha is worshipped by Buddhists since according to a popular belief a tooth of the Buddha is inside the idol of Jagannatha.
151. See Das and Mahapatra, *op.cit.*, p. 149-150 for the story.
152. What cannot be missed is the gender angle of this folk tale.
153. Hunter,...*Statistical...Puri and Orissa...States*, pp.42-3.
154. Elwin, *The Religion..., op.cit.*, p.182.
155. Senapati and Mohanty,...*Sambalpur, op.cit.*, p.117; Eschmann in M.N.Das (ed.), *op.cit.*, p. 400.
156. ...*Report..Nilgiri Settlement..., op.cit.*, p. 41; Indrabilas Mukherjee, *op.cit.*,

p. 3.

157. For example, the concept of rent remission which was there in the coastal region did not exist in the states. The only remission granted were when revenue could not be collected by coercive methods or when land was abandoned or surrendered; Ramdhyani, vol.I, *op.cit.*, p. 97.

158. For example, most of the princely states had different departments, viz. judicial, legislative and executive which were under the members of the royal household.

159. Hunter, *op.cit.*, pp.222-23.

160. Here our position differs from that of Neeladri Bhattacharya, 'Colonial State and Agrarian Society' in Sabyasachi Bhattacharya and Romila Thapar (eds.), *Situating Indian History For Sarvapalli Gopal* (New Delhi, 1986), p.141. who focuses on the 'faith' of the peasantry in the colonial government as a result of such policies.

161. Cited by K.P. Bahadur, *Caste, Tribe and Culture of India: vol.III, Bengal Bihar and Orissa* (Delhi, 1977), p. 93; the form of this poem has been altered since the translation had been very unimaginative.

162. One can refer here to the poet and singer Banchanidhi Mohanty whose theatre group (modelled along the *jatra* tradition) toured rural Orissa, including some of the princely states, like Dhenkanal. They focused on the theme of exploitation as well; for details see Manindra Mohanty, *Jatiya Kabi Banchanidhi* (Oriya; Balasore, 1987).

163. Thus, when in 1928 the angry peasants of Balanga (Puri district) murdered Banamali Pati, a hated intermediary appointed by the zamindar to collect taxes, a booklet of songs appeared, which perhaps spread details of this event in the coastal region. The role of the *Jogi* singers in this process needs to be emphasised; interview: Bina Devi (Cuttack, December 1988).

164. Interview: Banamali Das (Nilgiri, May 1982), who referred to this method among the Santhals of Nilgiri in the 1930 's and 1940 's. Swapan Dasgupta, 'Adivasi Politics in Midnapur, c.1760-1924' in Ranajit Guha (ed.) *Subaltern Studies IV* (New Delhi, 1985), p.133, cites evidence of similar methods among the Santhals of Midnapur in the early 1920s.

165. Perhaps the Sahibosums of the Savaras, examined earlier, express this.

166. *Garjatia* was a derogative term; similarly the term 'Dhenkanalia' was a term of rebuke for the people of Dhenkanal, since they had to bear the oppression of the despotic chiefs. Of course, in the interior tracts the term 'Cuttacki', used as a term to describe people from the plains, expressed fear, suspicion, awe and hatred simultaneously.

167. Sometimes tribals are even denied a philosophy of existence. For example, as Mahtab puts it: 'I use the word tribes as it is used to denote those sections of the people...who have...(no) philosophy of life...'. Cited in Mahapatra and Panda (eds.), *Tribal Problems, op.cit.*, p.14.

168. This respect for authority took interesting forms. For example, Dalton, *op.cit.*, p.190, refers to names such as Doctor, Major and Captain among

Ho children. Elwin, *Tribal Myths...*, *op.cit.*, pp.565-66, cites a Kandha folk tale according to which their Jam Deota taught them to offer flowers and bananas to government officials.

169. O'Malley, *Popular Hinduism...*, *op.cit.*, pp.95; 122; 139; A. Escmhann, 'Hinduisation of Tribal Deities in Orissa', in A.Eschmann et.al (eds.), *The Cult of Jagannath and the Regional Tradition of Orissa* (New Delhi, 1978), p.79.
170. One can illustrate this point by citing the example of Phakirmohan Senapati whose career as a *dewan* in the princely states linked him to the structures of colonialism and feudalism.
171. See, for example, Sumit Sarkar, 'Rammohan Roy and the Break with the Past' in V.C. Joshi (ed.) *Rammohan Roy and the Process of Modernisation in India* (Delhi; 1975) to grasp this dimension.
172. *Utkala Dipika*, 9.2.1867; 23.2.1867.
173. *Ibid*, 18.4.1874.
174. *Ibid*, 24.1.1920. I use Hinduisation here in a revivalist sense.
175. See Phakirmohan Senapati. *Granthabali* (Oriya; Cuttack, 1962) for the story.
176. *Utakala Dipika*, 26.2.1870; 3.9.1870. The author taught at a school in Balasore.
177. Phakirmohan's 'Chha Mana Atha Guntha' (published in a serialised form in the columns of the monthly magazine *Utkala Sahitya* in 1897) reflects a departure from 'Sadhu Bhasa', with the author using plebian Oriya.
178. *Utkala Putra* , June, 1870; 3 November, 1873; Samyabadi Pausa 1295.
179. *Ibid*, 3 November 1873.
180. *Ibid*, June 1870, mentioned how a peasant had been beaten to death by the police at Kanika.
181. *Utkala Dipika*, 15 October 1870.
182. *Utkala Brahmin Samitira Sastha Barshika Bibarani* (Oriya; Puri, 1906), p.17-25.
183. See R.K. Barik, 'Gopabandhu and the National Movement in Orissa' in *Social Scientist*, May 1978, pp.47-8. In a speech to the Utkala Brahmin Samiti in 1921 Gopabandhu hinted how the Samiti should make itself socially relevant; cited by S.N. Das, *Utkalamani Gopabandhu Das* (Oriya; Cuttack, 1975), p. 407.
184. For details see Biswamoy Pati, 'Reviewing the Emergence of the Orissa Province' in *The Quarterly Review of Historical Studies*, October-December, 1984.
185. For details see K.M. Patra, 'Growth of National Consciousness and Freedom Movement in Orissa', *Indian Historical Review*, July 1985-January 1986.
186. *Ibid*; Pati, 'Reviewing...', *op.cit.*
187. Pati, 'Reviewing...', thus, Madhusudan Das conceived of the idea of establishing the Utkala Tannery, organising exhibitions of local crafts (i.e.

handloom and tanners) during the annual conferences of the Utkala Sammilani.

188. See for example, Gopabandhu Das's speech in the Bihar and Orissa legislative council, 13 March 1919, on the salt industry in Orissa; cited in Gopabandhu Centenary Celebration Committee, *Gopabandhu, the Legislator* (Cuttack, 1977), pp.54-74.

189. Here one can refer to the 1920 Nagpur session of the Congress where a resolution was passed which accepted the formation of Provincial Congress Committee on a linguistic basis, and the launching of the Non-Cooperation Movement — the first mass movement.

Chapter II

The Rise of Mass Movements: Orissa, 1920-1934

Between 1903 and 1920 the Utkala Sammilani was the most important political organisation in Orissa. Formed under the aegis of Madhusudan Das, it represented the hopes and aspirations of the middle class and some landed elements, i.e. princely state rulers and zamindars. Its form of politics resembled that of the Moderates and its primary objective was to attempt unification of Orissa, parts of which were with Bihar, Bengal, the Madras Presidency and the Central Provinces. In 1905 Sambalpur (which had been a part of the Central Provinces since 1895) was united with Orissa. Further, on 1 April 1912, the province of Bihar and Orissa was created. These measures were based on political and administrative considerations—not due to any pressure on the colonial administration by the Sammilani.

By 1920, the Sammilani came to be identified with the hopes and aspirations of the Congress because of certain factors. In 1920 the Congress at the Nagpur session accepted a resolution for the formation of Provincial Congress Committees on linguistic basis. The famine of 1919-20 and the failure to get relief through constitutional means, opened the eyes of people like Gopabandhu Das, who were pushed towards the rising tide of nationalism. They felt that the Sammilani had remained isolated from the people. As Gopanbandhu put it: 'The sole objective of the Utkala Sammilani so far had been to unify Orissa. For the last seventeen years all the resolutions had been passed for achieving this goal. As a result, the Sammilani had little relevance to the common man.' The situation changed by 1920 and as Gopabandhu felt, 'Orissa could aspire to achieve unification only through national independence.'[1] Such slogans as *Bande Mataram* and *Bharat Mata Ki Jai* were raised at the Chakradharpur session of the Sammilani[2] (December 1921), and they ushered a new era of mass politics in Orissa.

The launching of the Non-Cooperation Movement prepared the ground for the political integration of Orissa — which had been dominated by the Moderate-type, Utkala Sammilani which aimed at linguistic unification — with Indian nationalism. We explore here the Non-Cooperation Movement and the Civil Disobedience Movement, unravelling the various facets of these two mass movements and focus on the complexities associated with the interaction of popular pressures and Indian nationalism, highlighting how the Congress and Gandhi were shaping, as well as being shaped at the popular level. Our attempt is to also delineate the popular perceptions of Indian nationalism and the way the peasants and tribals of Orissa related to Indian nationalism, often translating/transforming the codes of their leaders on the basis of their own world-views and experiences.

I

The Non-Cooperation Interlude (1920-22)

This chapter begins with an examination of the Non-Cooperation Movement in Orissa and the popular responses which interacted and converged with it. The basic effort of the Provincial Congress Committee (PCC) was to harness all potential enclaves of discontent within Orissa and politicize them. Since there did not exist any organized movement from below, the task of the PCC was to attempt at organizing it from above.

Gandhi's visit to the province on the eve of the Non-Cooperation Movement proved important. It served to stimulate the Congress workers, and kindled new hopes among the urban intelligentsia, many of whom had remained 'aloof from the movement ... and condemned it'.[3] Gandhi was struck by the poverty of the province and wrote: 'I was prepared to see skeletons in Orissa but not to the extent I did. I had seen terrible pictures but the reality was too terrible'. He was impressed by Gopabandhu whom he described as 'a selfless worker'.[4]

A preliminary examination of the Non-Cooperation Movement in Orissa suggests that Kanika was an area of militant peasant involvement. Kanika had a rich legacy of peasant struggles. A common feature in the nineteenth century was a number of *melis* or organised demonstrations led by the *mustagirs* who were the traditional leaders of the peasantry. They belonged to dominant castes and were comparatively affluent. Nevertheless, the *melis* led by them aimed at resisting increased tax demands, and were organised almost at every revision settlement and had the broad support of the peasantry.

During the *1889-94 Settlement*, the *khas* system was introduced, which wiped out the privileges of the *mustagirs*. Soon after, in 1906 there was a *meli* led by ex-*mustagirs* like Dinabandhu Khandaitrai (who was also prominent in the 1921-22 phase).[5] the introduction of the *khas* system broadened the basis of the post-1894 *melis* for it included the *mustagirs* who had been thrown into the ranks of the other cultivators. It consolidated itself during the 1921-22 movement.

It was against this background that the Non-Cooperation Movement started in Orissa. In July or August 1921 it spread to Kanika and Aul (a neighbouring estate). The Raja of Kanika condemned the Non- Cooperation Movement and '...congratulated his peasants for remaining uninfluenced by the agitators...'. Complaints appeared in Oriya newspapers such as *Samaj, Utkala Dipika* and *Seba* that the Raja of Kanika opposed the Non-Cooperation Movement.[6] On 5 August 1921, Rama Das Babaji, an upcountry youth who was brought up on charity by the feudatory chief of Athgarh, delivered a speech at Aul and urged the peasants not to recognise the Court of Wards. He criticised the Raja of Kanika and described him as the '...creature of the satanic sarkar... (who was) opposed to the Non-Cooperation Movement in the interests of the sarkar'.[7] After this he went to Kanika, he was followed by the Raja's men wherever he went. Although people were asked not to talk to the *non-cooperators*, they had been so brutally exploited that this order hardly produced any impact on them.[8] Rama Das made emotional speeches and since he was 'in the garb of a sadhu he commanded great influence among the masses.'[9] There seems to have been a great deal of similarity between him and Baba Ramachandra, who operated in the Awadh area around this time.[10] The anti-imperialist dimension of the PCC came to be reflected when the students of Kanika High School decided to boycott their institution and attempted to disrupt it.[11] A *swaraj* ashram was established and a *swaraj jagyan* was held. A *swaraj* flag was hoisted on a tree which came to be called Gandhibrata. Bhagirati Mahapatra (Secretary, PCC) and Jadumani Mangaraj (another Congress worker) visited the estate to intensify the struggle and strengthen the Congress organisation. On 21 September 1921, Rama Das was arrested. Mangaraj delivered a fiery speech on the same day and predicted that the Raja of Kanika would soon face the consequences of the action.[12] Chakradhar Behera, a young militant of the estate, initiated a secret campaign, urging people not to give any false testimony against Das.[13]

The organisation of the peasant was strengthened through the support of such persons as Ananda Chandra Jena and Joyram Rai. Both were teachers who had been dismissed from their jobs. Jena was also a cultivator who paid a rent of Rs. 2 a year; he was the author of *Dukhini Kanika*. Other activists included Upendra Subudhira (who was a *potdar* of the Raja, but had resigned to participate in the *meli*),[14] Bisuni Madhual (who was a small cultivator and was a Khandayat by caste; although he had a piece of land, he also worked on the land of Dinabandhu Khandaitrai, [15] which suggests that he belonged to the less affluent section of the peasantry), and Basu Sethi (a landless person who pursued his caste profession of washerman).[16] These people along with Madhusudan Pattanaik (a PCC worker) worked actively among the peasants, and were responsible for the formation of several *sabhas* in different centres. A large number of peasants were enrolled as four-*anna* members, and came to be directly linked to these organisations.[17]

In such a situation , the peasants of Kanika entered the most militant phase of their struggle which lasted from January to April 1922. Initially, this phase was to converge with the Non-Cooperation Movement, and the PCC concentrated on linking the people of the estate to the all-India struggle, on the basis of the existing dispute between the Raja and the people. In January 1922, Joyram Rai and Madhusudan Pattanaik organised a meeting at Ayetan *hata* against payment of the *chaukidari* tax and the increase of taxes in 1914 imposed by the Superintendent of Kanika, Indramani Mohanty.[18]

Another meeting was organised by the PCC at the Ayetan *hata* soon after this. It was here that the first call was given by the PCC in the estate for the non-payment of rent and the *chaukidari* tax. It was also resolved that in case the authorities retaliated by auctioning land and property of the people (because of their participation in the *meli*), no one would bid for them. To prevent further trouble at Ayetan, Section 144 was promulgated in the estate, and six policemen were posted at Ayetan *hata*. Another meeting was held at Meghpur. These meetings 'instigated' the people to become militant. In places such as Jorela some individuals who had sided with the Raja were 'intimidated' by Achutanand Naik and Srikar Mohanty.[19]

By the end of January 1922, *gramya sabhas* and *circle sabhas* had been set up at Ayetan. This effort was backed by Dinabandhu Khandaitrai (who, as already mentioned, was a prominent figure during the 1906 *meli*).[20] Very soon, about four thousand people of over a hundred villages combined to form a *meli*. A regular council with office-bearers was established at Meghpur[21] to co-ordinate the agitation. Although one cannot ignore the PCC's initial stimulus, these *sabhas* were created (as observed by some of its workers) by the exploited peasants themselves.[22] With this, the *no-rent* dimension of the Non-Cooperation Movement came to be implemented by the peasants in practice. Since they came to believe that once *swaraj* would be attained, no one would have to pay rent,[23] it was logical for them to move closer to the PCC.

In February 1922 the *meli* became very strong. Those who were inclined to pay rents to the zamindar were boycotted and 'intimidated'. Besides, the peasants and tribals made inroads into the jungles and violated forest laws. Funds were collected to aid the struggle. Failing to seek redress from the Raja a petition was submitted to the Collector signed by about five thousand people. In February and March, the Collector and the Commissioner conducted inquiries,[24] but the condition of the peasants did not improve in any way.

It is striking that although in a meeting at Khurda around 10 February 1922, Gopabandhu had asked the two thousand people present there not to stop the payment of rents and jungle taxes[25] (which was in line with the position taken by the PCC), and the Non-Cooperation Movement had been called off by the Congress on 12 February 1922, and the PCC instructed its workers in Kendrapada sub-division not to meddle with the Kanika affairs and to '...expedite the payment...(of rents)',[26] the militant peasants continued their struggle. This reinforces the point already made that the peasant organisations were established by the peasants themselves.

By April 1922, the Raja lost his patience. He had already made overtures to secure the support of the colonial administration to suppress the *meli* once and for all. The opportunity for direct intervention came on 18 April 1922, when a 'crowd' of about four hundred people assaulted four peons who had gone to serve notices on certain judgement debtors. When the Inspector of Police of Kanika tried to arrest them, he was 'mobbed' by them and the prisoners were rescued.[27] After this the Superintendent of Police, Srikrishna Mahapatra, advanced to Kanika and joined the Commissioner who was camping there. The police force settled down between Jorela and Meghpur beside a pond. On 23 April around 11 a.m. about a thousand people arrived there. The police 'expected' an attack and opened fire on them, killing three persons and injuring about a hundred and forty-four persons. Among these who died were Basu Sethi and Bisuni Madhual. Sethi was leading the people on the eventful day.[28]

The PCC had retreated by this time. A reign of terror was unleashed to silence the rebellious peasants. Houses were looted and men mercilessly beaten up. The passive support of the womenfolk for the unrest becomes clear if we look at the widespread attempts made by the police to dishonour them; many of them delivered prematurely due to assaults on them. Numerous activists were arrested; they were tried in the Raja's house and were forced to admit that they were guilty. Nearly a hundred and fifty of them were tied with ropes and made to walk from the Cuttack region of the estate to the Balasore region (i.e. Chandbali and Bhadrak) and then taken back.[29]

Besides adopting these methods of terrorising the peasantry, the Raja imposed a collective fine of Rs.10,000. He was also armed with the power to collect rent by the certificate procedure by the colonial administration[30] which meant that many people who had not paid their taxes were ejected and forced to leave the estate.[31] Many affluent peasants owning between three hundred to three thousand *manas* of land were pauperised.[32] These were fatal blows which brought about the tragic collapse of the movement. By the end of April 1922 people started paying rent, not to the Raja but at the Kendrapada subdivision office. Some comparatively affluent and prominent cultivators like Sadananda Samantarai (of the village Badatailagrama) and Raghunath Samantarai (of the village Tarasha) who had supported the *meli* changed sides.[33] Thus, along with the desertion of the PCC, the unity of the peasants (which had served to strengthen their struggle) got undermined. A booklet *Dukhini Kanika*, written by Ananda Chandra Jena, who had become extremely disillusioned symbolised the decline of the *meli*. Jena wrote:

> Kanika is our mother and her lord is our father;
> We will never forsake our father; we will always lie at his feet.
> We will not mind, if he insult us,
> Again and again we will lie at his feet,
> and urge him to remove our grievances.[34]

A typical feature was to appeal to the 'Lord of India' for help. As Jena put it:

> To get out of this (trouble),
> Let us invoke the aid of the Lord of India.[35]

This was repeated fourteen times in the booklet and was in sharp contrast to the attitude of the Santhals of Mayurbhanj, a princely state of Orissa, who had risen against the princely state between 1916 and 1918 and had looked for help from Germany, the enemy of the British during the First World War.[36] Rumours floated in Kanika that Gandhi's army was on its way from Ranchi to help the movement.[37] It indicated a desperate attempt to keep the struggle alive and to inspire militancy. However, the hostile posture of the PCC at this juncture seems to be quite striking. A day before the firing, it had announced that its aim was to build good relations between the tenant and the landlord.[38]

The Raja and the colonial administration further strengthened the apparatus of coercion in July and August when batches of policemen were sent to Kanika.[39] However, by this time the *meli* had been crushed. It may be added here that the Balasore region of the estate remained comparatively passive. This was because the discontent of the peasant could not get any organisational support. It is surprising that the PCC leaders like H.K. Mahtab had reached a compromise with the authorities and the colonial administration to keep themselves out of the Balasore[40] region of the estate. Moreover, the different steps taken to terrorise the people of the estate had produced some effects.

In Balasore there was a no-rent campaign in 1922 supported by the PCC. This emphasises the point that the lack of proper organizational support left the Balasore portion of Kanika comparatively passive. The *no-rent* campaign in Balasore was against the attempt to introduce a new land settlement.[41]

Perhaps the most striking example of the PCC's attempt to keep the Non-Cooperation Movement within bounds is provided by its actions in Bhadrak. The peasants of the area stopped payment of rents during this phase. Interestingly, through the mediation of Banchanidhi Mohanty, a Congress worker, the landlords did not institute rent suits against the peasants. Instead, they filed lists of their dues from tenants at the Congress office. The PCC assumed the charge of rent collection after the Bardoli retreat.[42]

The Non-Cooperation Movement evoked a favourable response in the Puri area also. On 16 October 1921 a meeting, well attended by peasants, was held at Khandagiri and addressed by Gopabandhu himself. It called for, among other things, the appointment of a committee to safeguard the rights of the *sarbarkars* and another committee to remedy the strict forest rules.[43] The *sarbarkars* were government intermediaries who collected taxes from the peasants. They belonged to the category of peasants who were denied full land rights. The second point becomes significant when one considers the violation of forest rules which converged with the Non-Cooperation Movement. Around this time, 'in the form of direct action ... a number of men ... entered (the forests of Khurda) in broad daylight ... and cut away a number of trees'.[44]

As the Non-Cooperation Movement gathered momentum, the colonial administration sought to disrupt meetings. When on 3 February 1922 a Congress meeting was organised near Khurda town, the people were warned by drumbeats that they would be arrested if they attended it. Besides constables and *chowkidars*, 'drunken' *mehtars* (outcastes) were placed on all the roads leading to the venue of the meeting. However, this move failed since more than two thousand people attended this meeting, which was addressed by Gopabandhu Das.[45] This, perhaps, reflects how the Non-Cooperation Movement undermined the barriers of caste, which were sought to be imposed by the colonial administration in its anxiety to counter the anti-imperialist struggle.

In Puri there were also attempts to prevent the export of rice by sea. Moreover, a temporary police station at a fair was also burnt down. This opposition to the police—who symbolised colonial power—seems to have been an essential component of the Non-Cooperation Movement in Puri.[46]

In the Sambalpur tract the Non-Cooperation Movement affected Bargarh, Jharsuguda, Talpatia, and Rampalla, etc. In two camps settlement operations faced passive resistance, but the matter did not take a serious turn.[47] One also comes across instances of *hartals*, demonstrations, *hata* 'looting', and boycott of foreign goods in parts of Cuttack, Jagatsingpur and Puri.[48]

In Ganjam attempts were made by Gopabandhu to mobilise support for the Non-Cooperation Movement.[49] Efforts were made to recruit volunteers from educated sections and a daily newspaper was established for this purpose. There was also the fear of a *no-rent* agitation touching this area.[50]

The response of the peasants and tribals in two of the princely states was impressive insofar as their anti-feudal aspirations converged with the Non-Cooperation Movement. A meeting was organised in Keonjhar in May 1921 to rally them against *bethi* (forced labour) and *rasad* (forced supplies). On 17 May 1921, a *bandh* was organised along with *sankirtans* to attract the attention of the people. This was supported by some local shopkeepers. The state authorities, keen on suppressing the movement, responded by making arrests and enforcing Section 144. This agitated the Bhuyan tribals, and about 500 of them *gheraoed* the Superintendent's bungalow and demanded the release of the prisoners.[51] However, the arrested people were tried and sentenced to imprisonment, and the movement gradually subsided.

Similarly, attempts to revise rents in the state of Dhenkanal led to an agitation among the peasants. The forest rules, which had just been revised, were an obvious source of irritation. Dhenkanal being one of the most oppressive states, the authorities responded very sharply and arrested four leaders, stifling the movement.[52] Significantly, in this state the exploited people rose independently of the PCC, which virtually remained out of Dhenkanal during the Non-Cooperation Movement.

The Koraput tract also witnessed some forms of protest during this phase, when the Congress had not made any inroads. The Rampa rebellion of Alluri Sitaram Raju evoked considerable response in this tract. It reflected the popular aspirations of the tribals of this tract who were weighed down by *bethi* and were opposed to the strict forest rules.[53] Among those who actively participated in this rebellion were the Koyas. There are references to Raju's presence at Malkangiri and Padua Taluk and the Jeypore Zamindar's support to the operations directed against Raju.[54] Although not probed by historians, Raju's uprising had a profound impact on the tribals of this area. Laxman Naiko, who was to organise a powerful tribal revolt (1942), was influenced by the Rampa Rebellion.[55] It was in this phase that Laxman came in contact with a Koya youth, Ramachandra Kutia, who had joined the movement, and learnt to use the gun.[56] He came to understand the problems of the tribals as he moved about in the area. Laxman's subsequent interest in astronomy and 'medicine' explains his contact with the Rampa rebellion, and his understanding that this could help him strike roots among the hill people.[57]

Popular protest thus converged with the Non-Cooperation Movement. Following its withdrawal disappeared the fears of the colonial administration that in 'certain areas the peasants have been affected, particularly in parts of ... Orissa.'[58] However, popular protests continued in spite of desertion by the PCC.[59] The Non-Cooperation Movement clearly brought out the contrast between the politics of the Congress and the growth of mass movements in relation to local grievances.

The collapse of the Non-Cooperation Movement opened cracks within the PCC. Thus, by December 1925 the Sambalpur District Congress Committee had resolved to sever links with the PCC.[60] Gandhi's visits to Orissa in 1925 and 1927 should be seen as attempts to keep the PCC united. Moreover, once the Non-Cooperation Movement collapsed popular enthusiasm was sought to be diverted towards what come to be called the 'constructive programme'.[61] The revival of the Utkal Union Conference in March 1923 'after an interlude of two years'[62] was also aimed at diverting the mass enthusiasm.

II

The Civil Disobedience Movement in Orissa (1930-34)

We can now focus on the Civil Disobedience Movement. The period immediately preceding the Civil Disobedience Movement in Orissa saw the floods of 1927 which ravaged Balasore. Moreover, there were two major uprisings at Bamra and Nilgiri in 1928.[63] These were, in fact, symptoms of the existing discontent among the people. In 1928, the Meefar Settlement increased the already heavy land rent in Bamra. About 4,000 people tried to seek redress from the Political Agent at Sambalpur. Failing in the attempt, they organised a no-rent campaign. The movement was suppressed by the imprisonment of its leaders. Among those who led the movement were some village headmen, four of whom were removed from their posts. Around 1928 a cess *(abwab)* was imposed on the peasants in connection with the marriage ceremony of the princess of the state. This agitated the people who rose against the state authorities. Attempts to circulate the accounts of oppression through a pamphlet worsened the state of affairs. About 2,000 peasants were compelled to leave the state and go over to Balasore, where the damages brought about by the floods of 1927 had already left the peasants in a state of crisis. All these factors, led to a striking response to the Civil Disobedience Movement in Balasore.

The linking up of the Civil Disobedience Movement with the salt issue was bound to evoke a sharp response, especially from the coastal districts where colonialism, by establishing its monopoly over the salt manufacturing industry, had struck a deathblow to a traditional source of livelihood. Moreover, the 'world depression' aggravated the situation; for example, the price of rice was 8-9 seers a rupee during 1928-29.[64] The salt issue appealed to the popular mind as is reflected in the folk tales associated with salt.[65]

The salt issue had already been taken up by Gopabandhu Das and Mahtab. The former had focused on this in the Bihar and Orissa Legislative Assembly,[66] and the latter had suggested the idea of a salt *satyagraha* to Gandhi when he was at Balasore prior to the Civil Disobedience Movement.[67] This suggestion was obviously based on a realistic observation of the extremely adverse impact of the imposition of salt monopoly on the people of coastal Orissa in general and Balasore in particular. Attempts are made to exaggerate the role played by some individuals like Mahtab in actually preparing Balasore for the salt *satyagraha*.[68] However, the table[69] given below shows that whatever the importance attached to the 'achievements' of these individuals, their attempt was a mere reflection of such violations made by the people of Balasore.[70]

TABLE

Cases of Violation of Salt Laws

Year	*Cuttack*	*Balasore*	*Puri*
1927-28	83	150	46
1928-29	40	55	46
1929-30	30	31	23
1930-31	6	87	27

On 16 March 1930 the PCC met at Balasore to plan its line of action. It decided to break the salt laws and Gopabandhu Choudhary was given the charge of organizing it. The first batch of 21 volunteers led by him proceeded from the Swaraj Ashram at Cuttack to Inchudi on 6 April 1930, the day Gandhi broke the salt laws at Dandi. Very soon a large number of volunteers in several batches reached Balasore from Cuttack, Puri, Ganjam, Sambalpur, Baripada and other parts of Orissa.[71] The local people participated in the salt *satyagraha*, and at least in six centres near Inchudi[72] the preparation of contraband salt continued vigorously. Very soon the Civil Disobedience Movement gathered momentum and the Balasore peasantry responded enthusiastically. On the one hand the people in Balasore actively sympathised with the Congress-led violation of the salt laws; on the other, one comes across 'attacks' on the propertied classes and a *no-rent* campaign. Both reflected, in terms of totality, the same process. The villagers who sympathised with the Congress workers and/or broke the salt laws, as well as those who refused to pay the *chaukidari* tax, or resorted to more aggressive methods, responded to the Civil Disobedience Movement along identical lines.

This point needs some elaboration. For example, in some areas like Iram the people participated in the Civil Disobedience Movement by violating salt laws. A procession of 2,500 people which violated the salt laws included 700 women. Women processionists were also beaten at Iram. Even children ran off with handfuls of raw salt leaving the policemen on duty helpless. The people also participated in processions which hummed nationalist songs and blew conch-shells. The villagers used to supply food to the Congress workers, some of whom had come from Bihar and Madras.[73] This trend took a dramatic turn in May 1930 when about 600 villagers from the surrounding villages of Inchudi carried nine maunds of contraband salt to Balasore town and sold it, even as the police stood by helplessly. Only one person was arrested; he had offered salt to the Superintendent of Police.[74] The cases of violation of the salt laws throw considerable light on the question of popular participation. On some occasions police camps were raided and there were encounters with the police who attempted to disperse processions of salt 'makers'.[75]

As this trend slowed down with the advent of the monsoon in June 1930,[76] the militancy of the peasants came to be reflected in a different form. There occurred, for example, 'attacks' on *chaukidars* and the police, when the latter made attempts to arrest those who had refused to pay the *chaukidari* tax at Srijang.[77] In one case about 700 people 'attacked' a police party (July 1930) which was 'sent to make arrests in connection with the collection of *chaukidari* tax'.[78] The conflict seems to have originated with Bhagirathi Das (the *chaukidari* President) not issuing receipts to more than half the people who had paid the *chaukidari* tax. The villagers retaliated by stopping the payment of *chaukidari* tax and expressing that they would not pay till they were served receipts.[79] Some pro-government shopkeepers were threatened with the death of their eldest sons, while *chaukidars* were refused water, had their crops destroyed, and were threatened with arson and boycott. Such responses were sought to be suppressed through repression and punitive fines on some villages, like Srijang.[80] The police looted the houses of even some affluent people. This 'outbreak of violence' and the lack of 'sufficiently trained workers' made the PCC suspend the no-tax campaign.[81]

Collective forms of protest also surfaced when attempts were made to attach property. On 2 July 1930, the Sub Deputy Magistrate with 44 constables (15 of whom were armed) went over to Khersai to carry out the attachment of property. The following day, half a mile from the *thana*, conch-shells began to be blown and villagers followed the police party, the crowd growing larger every moment. When the police party reached Khersai, there were nearly 2,000 people shouting at and 'threatening' the police party. As the crowd grew more 'excited' and came within a range of 20 yards of the police, four rounds of buckshots were fired, which dispersed the crowd, permitting the police to proceed towards the *thana*.[82]

During the Civil Disobedience Movement an arbitration court was established in one area of Cuttack and several arbitration *panchayats* were organised in Balasore.[83] This form of protest sought to boycott the existing government institutions. In Cuttack and Puri a noticeable feature of the

Civil Disobedience Movement was the participation of women.[84] With the help of hundreds of women from the surrounding villages of Cuttack, Rama Devi and Malati Devi (PCC volunteers) violated the salt laws.[85] There was a similar response when the Rani of Kujang and the ex-Rani of Paradeep inspired women, with the help of PCC volunteers, to participate in the salt *satyagraha*.[86] The Superintendent of Police of Puri mentions male as well as female volunteers moving in procession, armed with 'daggers and lathis with the ostensible object of exhibiting themselves as fighting men'.[87]

Another facet of the Civil Disobedience Movement in Orissa was the forest *satyagraha*, which came to assume considerable momentum in Puri. It was admitted in 1929 that 'there is continued pressure and agitation for increased liberty to use both the protected and reserved forests'.[88] The glorified Paikas came to assume the role of forest officers under the Indian Forest Act, which empowered them to arrest offenders without warrants, seize property and accept charge of confiscated property when the offender was not known. Arrangements were also made to reward them when they detected offences.[89] New powers, vested with the Sub-Divisional Officer of Khurda in 1932 to grant rewards in forest cases, also point to the intensity of the forest *satyagraha* in the Puri area. Since similar powers were granted in the Sadar Sub-Division of Angul,[90] and the colonial administration was forced to open up a section of the reserved forests in 1933,[91] a considerable response to this movement in Angul can be assumed. So also in the Sambalpur division. Thus, in the Kolabira zamindari timber and firewood 'which used to be sold by the zamindar (was) being stolen by the tenants'.[92] The colonial administration viewed the question of forest *satyagraha* quite seriously.[93]

In the Koraput and Ganjam tract popular protest, which converged with the Civil Disobedience Movement, developed out of the ruthless exploitation of the tribals, perpetuated by a system of *kumutis*, *muttahdars*, *bethi*, stringent forest laws, and so on. Although the Congress had not struck roots in Koraput, a small batch of *satyagrahis* participated in the salt campaign in Koraput 'under the leadership of Radhakrushna Biswas Roy'.[94] The militancy exhibited by them is indeed striking. At Jeypur a huge meeting of 5000 people who waited for the arrival of PCC leaders were lathicharged for an hour.[95] The Savaras of Gunpur launched a no-rent struggle around 1929-30 and the authorities had to yield to their pressure by allowing them not to pay rents for a year.[96]

Further west, the Kandhas too launched a no-rent campaign and stopped payment of *kists*. On one occasion the Kandhas of Kalyansingpur attacked a police party which had attempted to serve them with warrants for refusing to pay *kists* to the Maharaja of Jeypore.[97] Narasingh Sahu of Jeypore organised the Kandhas in the Bissemcuttack *taluk*. Kudipi village and its neighbourhood were the centre of his activities. He organized a 'procession and demonstration of hill ryots' (i.e. Kandhas). The Deputy Tehsildar issued an order prohibiting meetings and speeches. When the Sub-Inspector attempted to serve this order, Narasingh waved a Congress flag defiantly and said that he took orders only from 'his Government—presumably meaning Mr. Gandhi'. When he announced his intention of returning with a party of propagandists, an Agency warrant was issued for his arrest after which he left for Parvatipur. He reappeared in the Jeypore Agency and attempted to 'organise further seditious propaganda', although he stated that he 'merely kept a *khaddar* shop and preached about growing cotton'. Arrangements were made to isolate him from the inhabitants of this tribal tract.[98]

Equally interesting were the attempts made to grab *inam* lands held by affluent *muttahdars*. For example, Subudhi Patro of Luhagudi, who was actively involved with the Kandhas, occupied Gangadhara Patro's *inam* lands. The latter made various efforts to eject him with the help of the administration. Since there was a possibility that Subudhi would pit the Kandhas against Gangadhara Patro in a similar agitation, arrangements were made to deport him from the Agency.[99]

There were considerable 'disturbances' in the Narainapatana *muttah* of the Parvatipur Agency as well. In the autumn of 1931, Kabi Sri Hari Das, a Paika claiming superhuman powers, commenced preaching rebellion in the Parvatipur Agency of the Vizagapatnam district.[100] He was arrested but escaped and returned to Narainapatana around May or June 1931. In June an abortive attempt was made to arrest him. Very soon Sri Hari Das rallied a number of hillmen, receiving considerable support from Konkoda Domboru Naiko, Jaising Lakhono Naiko, Balarama Sondhi, Kadraka Chachri Bisamjji and two other leading men from village Garidi. 'Preparations for a minor rebellion were well in hand by September 1932 when drastic steps were taken to restore Government authority in the muttah'. Das, Domboru and Lakhono were arrested and their 'lieutenants from Garidi village escaped...to Orissa'. It was considered dangerous to keep these prisoners in Koraput jail and they were transferred out.[101] Only in 1936 were they released.

The position of the Congress was better in Ganjam. During the Salt *satyagraha* a notice had been given for 'raiding' the salt factory at Huma, following which a number of Congress volunteers were arrested.[102] Of the

3000 people present there were about 1000 women. Picketing was organized against foreign goods, resulting in further arrests. On 15 January 1932, there was a demonstration in sympathy with two arrested picketers, leading to a clash with the police, who opened fire killing one person and injuring two others.[103] The Utkal Swarajya Ashram at Berhampur was quite active, and it was one of the first places (along with the *khadi* store at Vizagapatnam) to be issued with a notification, on 16 January 1932, which banned it.[104]

There were 'disturbances' in some of the princely states as well. Around 1930, a new settlement was enforced in Boudh which raised the land revenue by 400 per cent. About 2,000 people attempted to meet the ruler and seek redress. Since they were not allowed to meet him by the state officials, about 27 Kandhas proceeded to Sambalpur to get relief from the Political Agent. On their return they were cruelly beaten and imprisoned.[105] Tension also existed in Talcher, Dhenkanal and Kanika,[106] though there was no organized opposition. The PCC did not take up the issues of the peasantry in these states and the intensity of exploitation and repression stifled every source of opposition during 1929-1934.

After the Gandhi-Irwin Pact in March 1931 the Civil Disobedience Movement gradually declined. However, echoes of popular hopes and aspirations continued to be heard. Thus, released prisoners were received by large 'crowds' in Cuttack. In Balasore, Raj Krishna Bose told a 'crowd' of about 2,000 people that either the government would be destroyed or they would be destroyed. He also hinted at the formation of a parallel government. Excise shops in Balasore continued to be picketed. In Sambalpur, L.N. Misra, a PCC activist who had been released, took out a procession and addressed a meeting accusing the Viceroy of deceiving Gandhi, who had however won.[107]

At this point we can look at the prevalent rumours. During the movement itself there had been a spurt of 'false rumours calculated to increase excitement and unrest and encourage ... non-payment of taxes'.[108] After the Pact the general belief in Balasore was that the Congress had been victorious. 'The constables of the additional police at Srijang were approached by certain persons who told them that the Congress had triumphed. Why did they not leave Srijang as the preparation of salt was now permissible?' A similar trend could be perceived in Puri, where the truce was looked upon as a victory for Gandhi and meetings were held to celebrate it.[109]

After the decline of the Civil Disobedience Movement, the political emphasis initially shifted to the 'agitation in connection with the Orissa boundary and the rumoured exclusion of Parliakhemedi'.[110] The All Party Conference at Cuttack on 2 May 1931, decided 'to initiate propaganda measures for the realisation of a separate Orissa province'.[111] Gandhi, during his *padajatra* in Orissa (1934), sought to win over the people to his constructive programme. In fact, the 'anti-untouchability propaganda ... (was) undertaken more as a means of keeping Congress leaders before the public eye than anything else'.[112] All these features along with the unveiling of Gopabandhu's statue at Badadanda, Puri, by Gandhi, were aimed at diverting popular struggle and enthusiasm.

III

Conclusion

The two movements studied here are important landmarks when one tries to study the peasant and tribal participation in the national movement in Orissa. Although in many cases the popular struggles which converged with these movements were to develop under the leadership of the PCC, their growing militancy and enthusiasm cannot go unnoticed. The legacy of these two movements pitted the peasants and tribals not only against colonialism but also in a bitter struggle against feudalism, in spite of the PCC's conscious attempt to dilute, disrupt and divert the anti-feudal struggle. The basic thrust was to keep the two movements within bounds; even the PCC's 'radicalism', insofar as it boycotted government institutions and created parallel ones, was designed to achieve this goal.

The transformation of the nationalist ideology[113] through these movements should be stressed: the concept of *swaraj*, its interaction with the popular level and its changed interpretation indicate this process. Thus, for the Kanika peasant (during the Non-Cooperation Movement) *swaraj* was associated with the end of exploitation and oppressive taxes. In the Koraput region (during the Civil Disobedience Movement) it got identified with the liquidation of strict forest laws which would enable the tribal folk to reassert their lost rights over the forests. Similarly, the Balasore peasants sought to achieve *swaraj* through producing salt and refusing to pay the *chaukidari* tax. A transformation of crowd behaviour[114] is also discernible in some cases. Thus, although the salt *satyagraha* in Balasore began as a symbolic struggle centered around salt, it gradually moved in the direction of more militant methods.

Between the two movements the influence of the PCC increased horizontally,[115] especially in the coastal tract where it became a more coherently organised force. This was precisely because of the realisation of the importance of spreading in order to create a stronger base for the national movement. The experience gained by the PCC over the years, coupled with its propaganda, also served to spread its influence. However, the impact of the Depression was extremely important, since it affected a broad section of the people. The salt *satyagraha* during the Civil Disobedience Movement, as well as the violation of forest laws, contributed significantly to this process. These features, simultaneously, undermined the hegemony of colonialism.

However, the control of the PCC was not uniform and complete. Even during the salt *satyagraha* in Balasore the PCC could not keep popular responses confined to the symbolic struggle centered around salt. Moreover, violence as a form of protest also emerged in this context, reflecting the collective opposition to the *chaukidari* tax and the attachment of property. Besides, *hata* looting—although it can be explained in simplistic terms—had a serious basis, and one cannot ignore its resemblance with similar incidents in pre-industrial Europe or the Madras Presidency around 1918.[116] What needs to be emphasised is that violence was antithetical to the nationalist ideology, and it indicated the weakness of the hold of the PCC. Besides, could the PCC call off the movements?[117] Our evidence for the Non-Cooperation Movement does not support such an assertion. And, although there was a lull after the Gandhi-Irwin Pact, the response was not uniform, and when a renewed attempt was made to start the movement it hardly received any response, thereby indicating a gradual decline in popular enthusiasm.

Another discernible feature is the existence of millenarian or messianic traits in the movements. Although a variation can be perceived and it is clearer in the tribal areas, the role of Rama Das Babaji in the Kanika peasants' struggle suggests that a generalization on this can be misleading. However, certain features like the grabbing of *inam* lands from the privileged *muttahdars* remained confined to tribal areas where the Congress had no hold.

Rumours form another fascinating aspect. These developed when efforts were made (a) to intensify struggles; (b) to prevent movements from collapsing; or (c) to assert victory. During the Kanika peasants' struggle rumours of the arrival of Gandhi's army from Ranchi were aimed at intensifying the movement and preventing it from collapsing at the onslaught of repression. Rumours floating in Balasore and Puri after the Gandhi-Irwin Pact sought to assert victory.

The participation of women is another noteworthy feature. This trend developed during the salt *satyagraha* and remained confined to the coastal region. Women remained primarly involved with the symbolic aspect of violating the salt laws for which they received encouragement from within their families.[118] They participated in large numbers and were led by women from outside who belonged to dominant castes or had a feudal background. These factors, along with the fact that such action did not question the social order and was by and large peaceful, gave the womenfolk the necessary social legitimacy for participation. The positive aspect was the mobilisation of women for the anti-imperialist struggle. However, the prescribed channels and the nature of this process, while it took women out of their domestic environment, dampened the possibilities of fighting male domination and oppression.

Notes

1. *Samaj*, 29.1.1921.
2. Cited by S.N. Das, *Utkalamani Gopabandhu Das* (Oriya; Cuttack, 1975), p. 310.
3. *Report on Administration, Bihar and Orissa -1920-21* (Patna, 1923), p. 1.
4. *Young India*, 13.4.1921, in 'Extracts from *Young India* and *Harijan*', collected by the National Committee for the Gandhi Centenary (1921-1984), Private Papers Section, Nehru Memorial Museum and Library (NMML), New Delhi.
5. This part is based on The Government Report on the 'Kanika Disturbances', cited by McPherson in the *Bihar and Orissa Legislative Assembly Proceedings*, vol.V, 15 August, 1922, (Patna, 1922) pp. 1023-24.
6. *Ibid.*
7. *Ibid.* Rama Das Babaji is described as an *agraduta*, or forerunner of the Congress in Acc. No.54, p. 10, Orissa State Archives, Bhubaneshwar.
8. This is based on an anonymous letter to *Samaj* 6.8.1922.
9. McPherson, pp. 1023-24.
10. S.K. Mittal and Kapil Kumar, 'Baba Ramchandra and the Peasant Upsurge in Oudh', *Social Scientist*, no.71, 1978.
11. This feature was obviously confined to urban or semi-urban areas, and affected those who had received some education. This trend was associated with a zeal to encourage the growth of national education and was linked to the Non-Cooperation Movement in Orissa. It was observed in the Home Political file no. 303/1921: 'In September, acts of incendiarism directed against schools were reported from Orissa'; National Archives, New Delhi.
12. McPherson, *op.cit.*, pp.1023-24.
13. Muralidhar Mullick, *Biplabi Chakradhar* (Oriya; Cuttack, 1972), p.13.
14. Based on ...*Legislative Assembly Proceedings*, *op.cit.*, pp. 1023-24; 1048.
15. Mahtab, *Sadhanara Pathe* (Oriya; Cuttack, 1972), p. 61-2 mentions that Khandaitrai owned a lot of land; correspondence with Prafulla Das (Raj Kanika) helped in cross-checking this point.
16. Correspondence: Prafulla Das, for details of Basu and Bisuni.
17. McPherson, pp.1023-24; Prafulla Das, *Bharatara Sasastra Mukti Sangram* (Oriya; Raj Kanika, 1980) reproduces a part of Lambodhar Mahapatra's (a contemporary observer's) diary, which also refers to the recruitment of four-*anna* members; p. 341.
18. *Ibid.* p. 242. A number of prominent persons like Sadananda Samantarai Mahapatra (village-Badataila), Raghunath Samantarai (village-Tarasa Mauza), Punyanand Routroy, Sadananda Rasikrai (village-Bartani) and Lambodhar Mahapatra (village-Gobang) were invited to this meeting.
19. *Ibid.*
20. McPherson, pp. 1023-24.
21. *Ibid.*

22. This is clear from a letter to the *Utkala Dipika*, 13.5.1922, by some PCC men.
23. McPherson, p. 1023-24.
24. *Proceedings*, pp.1007 and 1021.
25. Reported by *Samaj*, 11.2.1922.
26. *Searchlight*, 19.2.1922. The brackets contain my addition.
27. McPherson, pp. 1023-24.
28. Based on Sibaram Das, 'Kanikara Sahid Basu-Bisuni', *Samaj*, 23.4.1981.
29. This part is based on *ibid* and Mahtab and De (eds.) *History of the Freedom Movement in Orissa*, Vol.3 (Cuttack, 1957), p. 68. Mullick, *op.cit.*, pp. 20-23, mentions details of repression in this phase.
30. *Proceedings, op.cit.*, p.1010.
31. Binode Kanungo, *Utkalamani Gopabandhu* (Oriya; Cuttack, 1976), p. 122; Mahtab, *Sadhanara...*, *op.cit.*, p. 61-2; Mahtab refers to how affluent peasants like Khandaitrai and Ashwini Kumar Palei were compelled to leave Kanika.
32. Acc. No. 54, *op.cit.*, p. 13.
33. Correspondence: Prafulla Das.
34. Translated and cited by Mahapatra, in *Proceedings*, *op.cit.*, p. 1011.
35. *Ibid.* The brackets contain my addition.
36. Mentioned by Gyanendra Pandey in a paper presented at a Seminar on 'Peasant Unrest' (unpublished), at the Bombay session of the Indian History Congress, 1980.
37. *Proceedings, op.cit.*, p. 1020. G. Rude, 'The Pre-Industrial Crowd' in *Paris and London in the Eighteenth Century: Studies in Popular Protest* (London, 1974) refers to popular actions in the name of a distant superior or king.
38. *Samaj*, 13.5.1922.
39. Mahapatra, in *Proceedings, op.cit.*, p. 1010.
40. Mahtab and De (eds.), *op.cit.*, p.68; Mahtab had promised the Superintendent of Police, Balasore that he would not enter the Balasore region of Kanika.
41. Mahtab, *Dasabarsara Orissa* (Oriya; Cuttack, 1977), p. 58.
42. Mahtab, *Sadhanara...*, *op.cit.*, p. 49.
43. *Utakala Dipika*, 16 Oct. 1921.
44. Mentioned by Godavaris Misra and Prananath Pattnaik, *Report of the Khurda Forest Enquiry Committee* (Cuttack, 1938), p. 19. The fact that after the Chauri Chaura incident Gopabandhu asked the people not to stop the payment of jungle taxes at a meeting in Khurda (*Samaj*, 11 February 1922) validates the point that the forest *satyagraha* dimension had a considerable impact on the peasants and the forest dwellers of this area.
45. *Searchlight*, 22.2.1922.
46. HP file no. 18/2/1922.
47. Nilamani Senapati and Bhabakrushna Mohanty, *Gazetteer of India; Orissa:*

Sambalpur (Cuttack, 1971), p. 79; HP file no.18/1/1921.

48. HP file no. 441/1922.
49. S.S. De, *Who's Who of Freedom Fighters in Orissa (Koraput, Ganjam and Baud-Phulbani Districts)* (Cuttack, 1969), p. iv.
50. HP file no. 18/2/1922.
51. S.N.Das, *Utkalamani Gopabandhu* (Oriya; Cuttack, 1975), p. 409; B. Kanungo, *op.cit.*, p.102.
52. See Radhanath Rath, *The History of the Freedom Movement in Orissa States* (Cuttack,1964), p. 17.
53. For example, around 1940 anyone who violated forest rules was to pay one rupee and give a hen to the forest guard; interview with Gopinath Pujari, Mathili 40 kms west of Malkangiri (Jeypur, 1981).
54. M.Venkatarangaiya (ed.), *The Freedom Struggle in Andhra Pradesh*, Vol.III, (Hyderabad, 1965), pp. 382, 387-89.
55. Laxman Naiko was not a Koya; he was a Bhuyan.
56. Dasarathi Nanda, *Saheed Laxman Naik* (Oriya; Berhampur, 1977), p. 33.
57. Sumit Sarkar, 'Primitive Rebellion and Modern Nationalism: A Note on Forest Satyagraha in the Non-Cooperation and Civil Disobedience Movements', *Proceedings, Indian History Congress* (Bhubaneshwar, 1977), p. 516, mentions that Raju wandered among the tribals claiming astrological and 'medicinal' powers. This obviously enabled him to move closer to the hill people.
58. Cited in R.P. Dutt, *India Today* (Calcutta, 1970), p. 350.
59. Thus, *Samaj* (11 February 1922) carried a report of a Congress meeting at Khurda which was presided over by one of Orissa's 'father-figure—Gopabandhu Das. At this meeting Gopabandhu asked the 2,000 people present not to stop payment of rent and jungle taxes.
60. AICC Private Papers, NMML, files 16/64/1925; G-82/1929.
61. See Gopabandhu Choudhary, *Gandhi and Utkal* (Ahmedabad, 1969), especially, pp. 17-28, to get an idea of how this was propagated during these visits to Orissa in 1925 and 1927.
62. P.K. Misra, *The Political History of Orissa: 1900-1936* (New Delhi, 1979), p. 152.
63. These have been mentioned by Radhanath Rath, *History of the ..., op. cit;* and Mahtab and De (eds.), *op.cit.*
64. The Report of the Revenue Commissioner to the Bihar and Orissa Revenue Board (Patna) on 'The Situation with Regard to Rural Indebtedness', Revenue, file M/1-37-34, Board of Revenue (Cuttack). This Report includes Cuttack, Puri, Balasore, Sambalpur, Angul, and Khondmals. The price mentioned is based on the average price of rice in these districts.
65. See Chapter I. According to the folk tale 'Kadake Mari Kadake Tari', a king asked his daughters how much they loved him. Some said they loved him as much as gold, silver, diamond, etc. But the youngest daughter told her father that she loved him as much as salt, for which she was banished

from the kingdom. As time passed the king's fate changed and he lost his kingdom. While wandering through the forests he was received by a kind lady who served him a meal. But the food seemed tasteless. When he told this to the lady, she put some salt in the food and the king ate with great relish. Suddenly, he realised the importance of salt and how he had unjustly banished his youngest daughter. As tears rolled down his cheeks the kind lady revealed her identity: she was the king's youngest daughter.

To give another example, a riddle among the Savaras goes thus: 'What is that without which the king's curry also tastes bad? ...Salt'; cited in Laxminarayan Sahu, *The Hill Tribes of Jeypore* (? 1942).

66. See the *Bihar and Orissa Legislative Assembly Proceedings*, 13 Sept. 1919.
67. Mahtab and De (eds.), *op.cit.*, Vol. 3, p. 85.
68. *Ibid.* Balasore was the most 'disturbed' district during this phase.
69. 'The Report on the Administration of the Salt Department in Bihar and Orissa during the Years 1927-28; 1928-29; 1929-30; 1930-31', Cuttack, 1929-32.
70. The number of violations was 150 in 1927-28 in Balasore and, in fact, went down during the initial phase of the Civil Disobedience Movement. The same trend can be seen in the case of Puri and Cuttack as well. This can be taken up to illustrate in a very simple and unsophisticated way the limitations of the theory that people can be only organised effectively from above.
71. *Samaj*, 16 April 1930.
72. According to Mahtab, *Sadhanara*..., p. 129, Inchudi occupied the second place as regards responses during the salt *satyagraha*, the first being the place where Gandhi himself led the movement.
73. AICC Private Papers, file no. 24/1930; Sudhakar Das, *Swadhinata Sangramara Bhumi Iram* (Oriya; Cuttack 1977), pp. 8-9.
74. *Samaj*, 14 May 1930.
75. See, for example, 'Instances of Congress Violence in Connection with the Conduct of Civil Disobedience Campaign in Bihar and Orissa', Home Political, file 14/18/1931, N.A.I. There is a reference to an attack on the police camp at Atilabad (Balasore) and attempts by the police to disperse of salt 'makers' (May 1930).
76. With the advent of the monsoon it became difficult to produce contraband salt.
77. Home Political, file 14/18/1931, N.A.I.
78. Home Political, file 18/8/1930. N.A.I. This attack is represented as 'deliberate and preconcerted ... and a direct attempt to prevent the collection of chaukidari tax'.
79. AICC file no.24/1930.
80. Mahtab and De (eds.), *op.cit.*, Vol.3, p. 90, refers to the imposition of a fine of Rs.6,000 on the villagers of Srijang in September 1930. It is stated in the *Utkala Dipika* (6 September 1930) that this took place when an 'infuriated

mob' manhandled a police party on 12 July 1930.

81. AICC file no. 24/1930.
82. *Indian Annual Register* (July-December), 1930; Vol. II, 3rd July.
83. Home Political, files 18/11/1930 and 252/3/30.
84. Mahtab and De (eds.), *op.cit.*, Vol.3, p. 4. Home Political, file 18/1/1932, N.A.I. refers to the participation of women in Balasore.
85. *Samaj*, 23 April 1930.
86. K.M. Patra, *Orissa Legislature and the Freedom Struggle: 1912- 1947*, (New Delhi, 1979), p. 75; Mahtab and De (eds.), *op.cit.*, Vol.3, p. 91. The participation of the Rani of Kujang and the ex-Rani of Paradeep reflects the character of the PCC which was anything but anti-feudal.
87. Mahtab and De (eds.) *op.cit.*, Vol .5, p. 15. The reference is most probably to female volunteer corps.
88. L.S.S.O' Malley, *Bihar and Orissa District Gazetteers—Puri* (Patna, 1929), p.161.
89. 'Forest Offences in Puri Division', Revenue File F/1-3/32, letter from Commissioner, Orissa, to Collector, Puri, 19 Jan. 1932. Board of Revenue (Cuttack).
90. 'Proposal to Vest S.D.O. Khurda with Powers to Grant Rewards in Forest Cases', 15 Sept.1935, Revenue File M/1-46/32, Board of Revenue, Cuttack.
91. 'Disforestation of some portion out of the protected forests in the District of Angul', Revenue File F/1-6/33, Board of Revenue, Cuttack.
92. 'Working scheme prepared by the zamindar of Kolabira for his zamindari forests', Revenue File F/1-3/33, Board of Revenue, Cuttack; letter from Deputy Commissioner, Sambalpur, to Commissioner, Orissa Division, Cuttack.
93. A confidential meeting of the leading government officials was arranged to meet the violation of forest laws in Sambalpur. This is evident from a letter of the District Forest Officer, dated 2 June 1930, cited in Mahtab and De (eds.), op.cit., Vol. 5, p. 3.
94. S.S. De, *Who's Who*, p.1. Biswas Roy was a clerk employed in the Jeypore Agency, who resigned around this time to take part in the Civil Disobedience Movement.
95. AICC file no. T11/1931.
96. Interviews with Nilakantha Gomango and Gundu Gomango (Savaras) of village Kuchindi; (December, 1981). The former was about 18-20 years old during this phase.
97. 'Attack on a party of Police by Khonds of Kalyansinghpur in connection with the execution of distraint warrants against them for refusing payment of *kists* to the Maharaja of Jeypore', Home Political, file F5/41/31. Unfortunately, although this file has been referred to in the index, it has not been transferred to the National Archives.
98. Based on Home Political, file 36/VI/1930, National Archives, New Delhi.
99. *Ibid.* Subudhi Patro was at the bottom of a rising among the Kandhas

shortly before this.

100. R.C.S. Bell, *Orissa District Gazetteers —Koraput* (Cuttack, 1945), p. 36.
101. Home Political, file, 44/55/1936, N.A.I.
102. S.S. De, *op.cit.*, p. iv.
103. 'Answer to David Grenfell's Question No. 22, dated February 1932', Home Political, file F81/1932. N.A.I.
104. 'Reports from Provinces for the Civil Disobedience Movement', file 106/P35/1935-36, Private Papers, NMML.
105. Mahtab, Pattnaik and Mehta (eds.), *Report of the Enquiry Committee: Orissa States* (Cuttack, 1939), pp.6-7.
106. Rath, *op.cit.*, p. 16, mentions an agitation in Talcher in 1932 against increased rents; W.W. Dalziel, *Final Report on the Revision Settlement of Orissa: 1922-1932* (Cuttack, 1933), p.126, refers to existence of tension in Kanika. *Note*: Kanika was an estate.
107. 'Alleged breaches of the Settlement of 5th March 1931 in Bihar and Orissa', Home Political, file 35/5/1931, N.A.I.
108. 'Government Review of Movement', *Indian Annual Register*, 1930 (July-December), p. 151.
109. Home Political, file 18/4/1933, N.A.I.
110. Home Political, file 18/4/1933, N.A.I.
111. P.K. Mishra, *op.cit.*, pp. 182-83. The province of Orissa came into being on 1 April, 1936. This was a timely concession to the Oriya middle class, and it also aimed at strengthening the links with the landed aristocracy, some of whom had been active in the Utkala Sammilani. Besides, it served to reinforce the 'divide and rule' policy of the Raj. Sindh was a 'grant' to the Muslims and Orissa to the Hindus.
112. Home Political, file 18/6/1933, N.A.I.
113. Here I have drawn inspiration from George Rude, *Paris and London in the Eighteenth Century: Studies in Popular Protest*, (London, 1974). Rude points out how political motives, though originally derived from outside, 'were given a particular twist in the course of their assimilation by the small masters, craftsmen and wage-earners who adopted them, as it were, to their own social and political needs. This is particularly striking in the case of *sans cullotes* in Paris who gave new meaning to the ideas of 'equality', 'liberty' and 'sovereignty' which were quite unacceptable to their Jacobin teachers'. *Ibid*, pp.32-3.
114. Rude, *ibid*, shows how '...one type of crowd is liable, by the intrusion of the unexpected or of forces outside itself to be converted into another' (p. 4), and how, '...by his position outside' the crowd, the leader was always in danger of losing his control over a protracted period, or of seeing his ideas adopted to purposes other than those he had intended' (p. 248).
115. Gyanendra Pandey, *Ascendancy of the Congress in Uttar Pradesh: A Study in Imperfect Mobilisation* (Delhi, 1978), thinks likewise.
116. See, for example, Georges Lefebvre, 'Revolutionary Crowds', in Jeffrey

Kaplow (ed.). *New Perspectives on the French Revolution*, (New York, 1965), pp.173-90; Rude, *op.cit.*, E.P. Thompson, 'The Moral Economy of the English Crowd in the Eighteenth Century', *Past and Present*, No. 50, Feb. 1971; and David Arnold, 'Looting, Grain Riots and Government Policy in South India, 1918' *Past and Present*, No. 84, Aug. 1979.

117. David Hardiman, *Peasant Nationalists of Gujerat: Kheda District 1917-1934* (New Delhi, 1981) p. 246 mentions how Gandhi's 'orders' in 1922/1932 were 'obeyed' by the peasants.

118. In many cases women, accompanied by their brothers, reported to the PCC offices to work as *satyagrahis*; see, for example, an interview with Malati Choudhury published in *Sabitri*, August 1961; on occasions we get references to 'richly' dressed ladies attending meetings where salt laws were violated; one can cite the example of Huma (Ganjam) here; AICC Private Papers, file 24/1930.

Chapter III

Of Movements, Compromises and Retreats: Orissa, 1936-1939

In the phase following the Civil Disobedience Movement in Orissa, out of the disappointment with its withdrawal, there emerged a Socialist trend, as well as a realisation among the youthful Socialists, of the need to have a fighting front for the peasants. The stage was, thus, set for the birth of the Kisan Sangha (1935).

The province of Orissa was born on 1 April 1936. It was in this context that the colonial government decided to implement the 1935 Act and hold the elections in 1937 in order to create legislatures in the provinces, including Orissa. The election was preceded by hectic election campaigns, with the Congress and the zamindars wooing the electorate. Under pressure from the Kisan Sangha the Provincial Congress Committee incorporated the abolition of the zamindari system in its election manifesto. This paved the way for the Kisan Sangha to play a crucial role in the election campaign of the Congress. It was this interaction that enhanced the prestige of both the Congress and the Kisan Sangha and stirred the countryside.

The elections led to the victory of the Congress and the installation of the first Congress ministry in Orissa. At the same time the peasant movement attained new heights. The strong militancy of the peasant movement led to a struggle between the 'left' and the 'right' wings of the Congress over the Kisan Sangha's relationship with the Congress. Whereas the 'right' wing advocated a total merger of the Kisan Sangha with the Congress, the 'left' wing upheld that the Kisan Sangha should maintain its independent identity as a fighting front of the peasants, and also maintain close links with the Congress. This tussle contributed significantly to the birth of the Communist Party in Orissa (1938).

The post-election phase also saw a shift in the Congress' position. It toned down its radical thrust, compromised its anti-feudal position and became more accommodating to the landlords. This produced a considerable impact on the peasant movement—although the process was not uniform.

And, finally, this chapter also highlights the anti-feudal upsurge in the princely states. While focusing on the popular movements, it delineates how the Congress took a backseat (following its policy of 'non-intervention') but emerged to precipitate a compromise and assume the leadership of the state peoples' struggle.

I

Radicalisation, Legislative Politics and the 'Brakes': The State of the Peasant Movement in Coastal Orissa and the Jeypur Estate

The post-Civil Disobedience period was marked by a political lull. The Gandhian alternatives of Harijan uplift and village reconstruction coupled with Gandhi's visit to Orissa were hardly sufficient to fill the vacuum. Many young activists of the Congress were disillusioned with the Gandhian retreats.[1] People like Nabakrushna Chaudhary, Surendranath Dwivedy, Bhagabati Charan Pannigrahi, Prananath Pattnaik and Gour Charan Das got together and formed the Utkal Samyavadi Karmi Sangha (Utkal Socialist Workers Association) in 1933.[2]

In a context in which the Congress work had slowed down and the Communist Party had not yet been organised, the destiny of the peasant movement passed on to the hands of the Congress Socialists. May Day was observed at Cuttack from 1933 and Sarathi, their newspaper, began circulating from around the end of the same year.[3] The floods of 1933 which had ravaged the districts of Cuttack and Puri provided the immediate context to the Socialists for working amidst the peasantry. The efforts of Mahtab to form a Krushak Sangha merged with that of the Socialists.[4] This attempt remained confined to the three coastal districts of Cuttack, Puri and Balasore although some spontaneous peasant movements did exist in other parts as well.

When it came to methods of working, the Socialists tried to use their newspaper *Sarathi*, (launched in 1933), to reach the peasantry and asked the readers to send letters stating their grievances, responses to which seldom came in.[5] Even though Mahtab wrote about 'the necessity of a social revolution',[6] the heart of the countryside was yet to be touched.[7]

The situation improved marginally after the first conference was held in February 1934. The focus shifted to establishing some camps in the districts of Cuttack and Puri and taking up day-to-day issues of the peasants arising from their interaction with landlords, moneylenders and the police.[8] The hegemony of the established order was extremely strong. The peasant regarded the landlords as god's representatives, and viewed their own existence within the framework of god's will and fate. Although the two mass movements (the Non-Cooperation and the Civil Disobedience Movements) had weekened the hold of the zamindars and the colonial administration, the sight of a petty official could, on occasions, disrupt a discussion with peasants.[9] Nevertheless, significant changes were taking place. The exposure to the peasants and tribals during the two mass movements and the sense of frustration and disillusionment with Gandhian politics narrowed down the gulf between the intellectual and the peasant. The camps and *Sarathi* epitomised this phenomenon. Consequently, the ideological background to work with the peasants was prepared.[10]

It was against this background that the Utkala Kisan Sangha was born in 1935. This gave a new thrust to and offered new possibilities for the peasant movement in Orissa. Mohanlal Gautam presided over its first conference at Cuttack in which a resolution was put forward for the abolition of the zamindari system. Although opposed by most of the leaders, the resolution was passed and the kisan delegates stoutly supported it.[11]

The Utkala Kisan Sangha welcomed people of all shades, so much so that even Mandhata Gorachand Pattnaik, who was a spokesman of the landed elements and was a retained lawyer of some big zamindars, found a place in it. Mahtab became its President and Malati Chaudhury its Secretary. Intensive work was launched in the three coastal districts of Cuttack, Balasore and Puri. The initial successes of the Kisan Sangha had a very positive impact on the rural folk by weakening the hold of the established order on them and kisan committees sprang up in different villages.[12]

The province of Orissa was formed in April 1936. When the All India Kisan Sabha had its first conference at Lucknow (11 April 1936), Orissa was represented by Mahtab, Lingaraj Misra, Nabakrushna Chaudhury, Bhagirathi Mahapatra and Surendranath Dwivedy.[13] Swami Sahajanand Saraswati was elected as the President. In a speech he argued that there was no possibility of a compromise between the landlords and the peasants except by dispossession of the landlords. Ram Manohar Lohia criticised the Gandhian policy of defending the landlords *vis-a-vis* peasants. Sohan

Singh Josh pleaded for combining the struggle for zamindari abolition with the struggle against imperialism.[14]

These developments were encouraging for the peasant movement in Orissa. The PCC, especially the youthful Socialists spread the message of the Kisan Sangha in some of the remotest corners of the province.[15] The Kisan Sabha exposed zamindar-government collusion and attracted many rural Congressmen. As Surendranath Dwivedy puts it, for the first time there was a clear realisation among the peasants that the government was on the side of the zamindars.[16] Although it is not possible to determine how widespread this realisation was, one can perhaps associate the coastal tract with his observation.

Some features stand out quiet clearly when various issues discussed in the meetings in the countryside (April to June 1936) are analysed. We do observe a contrast between the meetings of the Kisan Sangha and the PCC. The Kisan Sangha, like the PCC, urged the necessity of strengthening the anti-imperialist struggle. But it went beyond this goal by stressing the need for anti-feudal struggle as well. A section of the PCC (the Socialists) was identified with this trend. This was the 'left' wing of the PCC which was shaping, and was being shaped by, the Kisan Sangha. In contrast the PCC meetings harped only on the anti-imperialist theme and clung to the Gandhian programmes of *khadi*, village reconstruction, Harijan uplift and prohibition. This section was also active in the Kisan Sangha. This was the PCC 'right' wing and its representatives were individuals like Nilakantha Das, Godavaris Misra and Acharya Hari Har Das. However, there were some common elements in the position of both the wings *vis-a-vis* the Kisan Sangha. Both sought an amendment of the tenancy laws, the reduction of land and water taxes, enquiries into the conditions of the peasants and the promotion of primary education. Moreover, some individuals like Mahtab were associated with both the wings and were visible from the platforms of the PCC as well as the Kisan Sangha. Between April and June 1936 we observe a thinning down of the dividing line between the PCC and the Kisan Sangha. Nevertheless, the contrast between the 'left' and the 'right' wing continued.[17] Consequently, the peasant movement played a significant role in this sort of a polarisation within the PCC.

By June 1936 when the PCC woke up for the elections (scheduled for January 1937)[18], the Kisan Sangha's base among the peasants and tribals was sought to be explored. Analysing the innumerable meetings of this period (from June 1936 to January 1937) we can perceive that the Kisan Sangha's meetings merged with the PCC's election meetings and an unprecedented militancy of the 'right' wing. Its phraseology tended to veer towards anti-feudalism but it maintained its distinct character. For example, although prominent 'right' wing PCC elements like Nilakantha Das criticised the zamindars for high-rent demands they did not advocate zamindari abolition. In this phase some individuals like Mahtab got closely identified with the 'left' wing. As for the 'left' wing, it linked up the question of the 'dark zones' — princely states — with the elections.[19]

The observance of the All India Kisan Day (1 September 1936) in different parts of the province and the inauguration of the election campaign by the PCC (13 September 1936)[20] symbolised the fusion that had apparently taken place for the moment between the struggle against imperialism and feudalism. Some prominent leaders associated with local peasant struggles became the Congress candidates. For example, Chakradhar Behera, one of the heroes of the Kanika peasants' struggle, was the PCC's candidate against that of the zamindari. It is interesting to note that Biswanath Das who fought and won as a Congress candidate and became Orissa's first Prime Minister was, initially, unwilling to fight as a Congress candidate. He had been active in the Zamindari Ryot Sabha of Ganjam and wanted to be the Sabha's candidate against the Khallikote zamindar.[21] Consequently, in many cases the elections gave the PCC an opportunity to link itself to 'local' struggles and thereby strengthen its base among the peasants and tribals.

One of the most remarkable achievements of the peasant movement and the Kisan Sangha was to make the PCC accept its basic position regarding the abolition of the zamindari system, a complete remission of rents and taxes for all whose annual income was less than Rs. 250 and a debt moratorium for five years.[22] Under pressure from the Kisan Sangha the PCC was forced to release a radical supplementary election manifesto which incorporated these points. As Ranga put it: 'Orissa peasants are alone in the happy position of having made their PCC promise the abolition of the zamindari system.'[23] How does one explain this uniqueness? As discussed earlier, the formation of the PCC in Orissa (1920) had coincided with a break with the feudal elements (zamindars and rajas) who had patronised the Utkala Sammilani. This process had been reinforced by two mass movements (Non-Cooperation and Civil Disobedience). Consequently, the links between the PCC and the zamindari interests had been weakened.

It is a recognised fact that the PCC's election campaign spread like wild fire because it linked the struggle against the twin contradictions of imperialism and feudalism in its election campaign and because its chief opponents were the landed sections, represented by the National Party and the United Party. The election issues raised by the PCC were interpreted in terms of the specificity of the problems faced by the peasants and tribals and all these features led to the radicalisation of both the PCC and its peasant and tribal following.

The activities of the PCC as well as the Kisan Sangha caused serious concern among the landed elements. This spurred them into action and led to the formation of the National Party and the United Party in 1936. Although this development can be seen as a move to contest the elections, the deeper implications did relate to 'work for *swaraj* in a constitutional way, with India as an integral part of the British empire'. Their professed political philosophy of 'order' was, according to them, intended to replace that of 'chaos'[24] which was located in the politics of the PCC and the Kisan Sangha.

The visit of Nehru to Orissa in November 1936 in the 'Indian Summer of his leftism'[25] was an important event. In his speeches Nehru launched an attack on colonialism and feudalism[26] which inspired the peasant masses. Nehru's visit to Jagannatha's temple prior to his Puri meeting[27] was aimed to secure legitimacy and reflected the importance the Congress attached to the old order in its attempt to establish a 'new' order. For the peasants of coastal Orissa the fact that even Nehru accepted them and stood by them was of vital importance. Consequently, the invisible aspect of Nehru's visit was perhaps more important than his actual visit or his meetings.

The second session of the Utkal Provincial Kisan Conference was held in Puri (15 November 1936) soon after the visit of Nehru. Swami Sahajanand presided over this session which was attended by about three thousand delegates. Lokanath Misra (the president of the Reception Committee) outlined the position of the Kisan Sangha through his frontal attack on landlordism and by calling for its abolition. This was followed by Sahajanand's speech and a resolution which incorporated the social and economic demands of the Kisan Sangha regarding zamindari abolition, the transfer of the land to the tiller, a boycott of the Government in case it declared War and the formation of peasant's defence committees to guard against the oppression of zamindars.[28]

This conference stirred the peasants. A day after the conference a number of peasants visited the Sub-Divisional Officer of Puri and made various demands like the removal of the salt tax, strengthening of certain embankments and stopping the oppression of certain zamindars.[29] This act symbolised simultaneously the hopes the Kisan Conference had generated, the legitimacy enjoyed by colonial rule and a desire to seek redressal from the colonial authorities in order to settle disputes with the immediate exploiters—something so typical of peasant consciousness.

Coming more specifically to the election campaign, the PCC did tap the *hatas* and the *melas*—the traditionally important transmission points where the 'country' and the 'city' interacted. Besides speeches, the *Samaj* and the *Lokamata* carried its message to the interiors of the province. The PCC also devised the technique of appealing through symbols like grindstones or a mouse in a trap. Perhaps the grindstones symbolised colonial and feudal exploitation and the mouse in a trap expressed the wretched plight of the helpless Indians. These must have produced a considerable impact on the rural folk who could easily identify themselves with these symbols.[30]

The PCC also popularised its message through *vote geeti* which were sung by *kirtan* parties. In some areas *sadhus* held in high esteem also championed the cause of the PCC. Popular perceptions located the Congress candidates as the true representatives of Lord Jagannatha who had entered the politics of Orissa's first election. For example, a Congress candidate who had chosen blue as his colour was believed to have done so at the instance of Jagannatha, whose symbol, the Chakra, was of the same colour. Pictures of Hindu gods and goddesses also appeared on the election posters. Besides the association with yellow (which was the colour of the Congress) symbolised a link with Hinduism. It was looked upon as an 'auspicious' colour and red—the colour of the opponents—was viewed as the blood of the people.[31]

Thus the 'good'/'evil' dialectic of peasant rationality seems to have been a very vital component which shaped popular perceptions. Consequently, the PCC's association with Jagannatha was not perceived as an endorsement of the old order. The ballot box reached the peasants as the 'poor man's box' or the 'Gandhi's box' and the voters bowed to it while casting their vote.[32] The invisible legitimacy of the Mahatma weighed heavily on the popular mind. In some areas petitions to Gandhi were discovered in the ballot boxes.[33] Besides, the PCC also emerged as the saviour from above. There are references to peasants meeting Congress workers after voting in order to secure a record that would entitle them to rent-remission.[34]

The electioneering techniques of the opponents were centred around monetary incentives and appealing to the imagination of the rural folk from the 'heavens' using aeroplanes. The landed elements distributed Jagannatha's *mahaprasad* after meetings and the 'earthly incarnation' of the Lord—the Puri Raja—distributed it in order to secure the support of the Kanika voters. The obvious motive was to secure a sort of pledge from the voters. However, the hegemony of the old order seemed to be crumbling. The voters bowed to the *mahaprasad* but dropped their ballot paper in the Congress box, bowed again and walked out.[35] Adequate apologies were thus made to the Lord. Although popular perceptions accepted the 'new' by apologising to the 'old', even then this indicated an undermining of age-old beliefs and values.

Since the election forecasts had predicted an inevitable Congress defeat, the election results in which the PCC won 36 out of the 40 seats it had contested surprised everyone, including the PCC leaders themselves.[36] For the 'right' wing the radicalisation of the PCC was consternating.[37] The All India Kisan Conference projected this as an eye-opener to all those who were opposed to it.[38] For the peasants and tribals the electoral victory of the PCC meant the dawning of a 'new age'. Their hopes and imagination had been fired by the PCC and in some areas they stopped paying their taxes in order to assert the PCC's victory which they saw as their own. Gandhi was located as their Maharaja who would 'let them off all their taxes'. There was a marked enthusiasm to get recruited as Congress members.[39]

The post-election context made the landed sections extremely insecure. The varied responses ranged from panic at the radical agrarian programme of the PCC, trying to pre-empt a Congress ministry formation, retaliating against the peasants and tribals for their pro-Congress sympathies to harbouring ideas about 'making terms with the Congress'. The insecurity was primarily due to the radical agrarian programme of the PCC which was seen to be linked with its victory.[40] Of course, the colonial administration had grasped that the pre-election promises could never be implemented.[41]

Given the position adopted by the Congress High Command, the PCC refused acceptance of office and on 1 April 1937 a minority ministry headed by the Maharaja of Parliakhemedi assumed office. Its programme gives us a clue to the way in which the landed elements responded to popular pressures which, to them, had assumed spectral proportions. Among the key features the programme aimed to improve the co-operation between the tenants and the landlords; at ameliorating the conditions of the peasants; tackling the problem of rural indebtedness through 'debt conciliation' and recognising (through legislation) free transfers of holdings. The ideological foundations of the old order was sought to be strengthened by 'improving' the 'religious' and 'moral' life of the people.[42] Consequently, this programme was projected as an alternative to the PCC's radical agrarian programme and sought to reinforce the hegemony of the old order.

As for the peasant movement, the Kisan Sangha maintained its political thrust. In some areas of the Cuttack district Muslims began attending Kisan Sangha meetings.[43] Around May 1937 we get references to a very 'tense' situation resulting from peasant militancy in the province.[44] In Puri a powerful anti-*mohunt* movement developed.[45]

The PCC struck roots in some interior parts of the province, like the Jeypur zamindari, where Congress MLA's were making enquiries into forest grievances, forced labour and customary dues. Some of these meetings were very well attended considering that they attracted as many as 5,000 people on occasions.[46]

It was against this backdrop that a bitter struggle developed between the 'left' and the 'right' wing of the PCC centered on the relationship between the Congress and the Kisan Sangha. Nilakantha Das, who opened an offensive against both the 'left' wing and the Kisan Sangha, questioned the very need for an independent organisation of the peasants in a conference of the highly militant Puri Kisan Sangha. As the President he moved a resolution which proposed that the Kisan Sangha should be a part of the Congress organisation and should exist within the Congress. Thus only four-*anna* Congress members could become members of the Kisan Sangha. The obvious aim was to keep the Kisan Sangha under the control of the Congress. When put to vote, the 'left' wing failed to prevent this resolution from being passed. In an audience of about 5000 people this resolution was passed by a majority of about 100. This controversy raised its head in Orissa for the first time.[47] It symbolised the fear of the 'right' wing which came face to face with a powerful peasant movement. Even some individuals like Mahatab were eyesores to the PCC 'right' wing for their association with the Kisan Sangha.[48] The PCC 'right' wing adopted a more cautious approach, concentrating primarily on the recruitment for the PCC, the Gandhian programme and occasionally directed its attention to the allegations against the landlords, the moneylenders and the police and the 'probability' of rent reduction if the Congress formed a ministry.[49]

As for the 'left' wing, it was quite vocal in stating its position that the Kisan Sangha had its own specificity and hence could not merge with the PCC. What needs to be emphasised is that although the 'left' wing was not opposed to the idea of Congress membership, it was opposed to the merger of the Kisan Sangha with PCC. In fact, they brought in a resolution for collective affiliation of Kisan workers, youth and student organisations.[50] As articulated by the All India Kisan Conference the Kisan Sabha 'was a class organisation of the masses'. The importance of linking-up the struggle for independence with the struggle of the peasants was emphasised. As Sahajanand put it this would, instead of embarrassing the Congress, strengthen it as well as the freedom struggle.[51]

The Kisan Sangha in Orissa managed to withstand the 'right' wing offensive. It continued to expand and absorb some organisations which aimed to solve peasant grievances constitutionally.[52] Our evidence indicates that the three coastal districts of Cuttack, Puri and Balasore had emerged as the bastions of the Kisan Sangha.[53] There was an increase in the tension between the peasants and the landlords (after the elections in January 1937) in the three coastal districts.[54] Consequently, what the official reports missed out was the political intervention of the Kisan Sangha, with a radicalised PCC prior to the elections. This had shaken the foundations of the structure of social control which was partly imposed by the landlords on the peasants and partly self-imposed by the peasants themselves. The peasants had been stirred to such a level that they had transcended the fear of the landlords, the moneylenders and the police and had voted for the Congress, violating pledges secured on the *mahaprasad*.[55] After this they had started asserting themselves.

The Kisan Sangha appealed to the Congress landlords to set the ideal of renunciation and sacrifice. It expected them to demonstrate their sympathies with the downtrodden peasants by surrendering their property which could be managed by a trustee appointed by the Kisan Sangha.[56] This particular tendency reflected the utopian moorings of the peasant movement and its interaction with Gandhian politics.

The case was somewhat similar in the Jeypur zamindari. In the absence of the Kisan Sangha it was the PCC which had fired the imagination of the peasant and tribals. They stopped paying rents. This meant that the estate ran into arrears in rent collection.[57]

By the first week of July 1937, the Congress High Command had accepted the idea of ministry formation in the provinces where the Congress had an absolute majority. In Orissa the minority ministry resigned and the Congress ministry assumed office on 19 July 1937. This event was celebrated throughout the province. It was seen as a prelude to the emancipation of the peasants and tribals, with a substantial reduction in taxes and land revenue, a considerable curtailment in the powers and the privileges enjoyed by the zamindars, with a proportionate increase in their own rights.[58] Nehru's statement that the peasants could organise their own committees[59] and Biswanath Das' assurance that his Cabinet would strive its utmost to redress the grievances of the peasants[60] restored as well as legitimised the belief in the dawning of a 'new age' which had been anticipated for quite some time and which had been interrupted by the 'evil' zamindars.

The installation of the first popular ministry converged with even greater enthusiasm to spread the message of the Congress into the remotest corners of the province. The PCC wasted no time in consolidating itself in the absence of the Kisan Sangha in the Jeypur zamindari where it had been an abstract force prior to 1936. A 'Gandhi *gomasta*' was put in charge of 25 villages throughout the estate so as to note and redress popular grievances.[61]

Of course, the popularity of the PCC as well as the Kisan Sangha made this effort relatively easy in the three coastal districts of Cuttack, Puri and Balasore. The new thrust focused on looking at the policemen without suspicion and fear since, after all, they were under the control of the Congress Ministry.[62] This reflected a serious effort to re-establish the authority of the disciplining apparatus which had been severely undermined. However, the symptoms of the PCC's retreat from its electoral promises was grasped by the Kisan Sangha. It was critical of the ministry when it issued orders to stay decrees for collections of rents and taxes only till the end of December instead of a total moratorium on all debts and dues for five years.[63]

The Kisan Day celebrations of 1 September 1937 symbolised the culmination of a year of bitter struggles and hopes which had given the peasants an identity and had radicalised them. Nearly twenty thousand peasants marched to Cuttack from different parts of the province, electrifying the countryside. A mile and a half long procession of peasants with the national and the red flags with the hammer and sickle, shouting slogans like 'Down with Imperialism' and 'Abolish Landlordism', marched through the streets of Cuttack and met the Premier.[64]

Pranakrishna Padhiary who chaired the meeting pointed to the fact that the Ministers could not do much because of the limitations imposed by the New Constitution and appealed to the gathering to be prepared for a countrywide revolution against British imperialism and capitalism. And, finally, he exhorted the audience to stop the *Suniya Vethi* to the landlords on the New Year's day—October 1937. Gouranga Chandra Das, the Secretary of the Cuttack District Kisan Sangha, read the memorial which demanded a fifty per cent reduction of rents, moratorium on debts, a permanent solution of the problems faced due to floods and immediate measures to stop zamindari oppression.[65]

Malati Chaudhary (who was the Secretary of the Utkal Kisan Sangha) moved a resolution which advocated that every peasant should be a member of the Sangha as well as the Congress in order to make it stronger. The next resolution appealed to the ministers to appoint a committee to enquire into and publicise the grievances of the peasantry.[66] As for the Premier, he agreed to the principle that the peasants should be the owners of the land they tilled and have full rights over the produce of the trees and the ponds. He also promised to punish illegal exactions by law. To some the Premier seemed very non-committal.[67]

An analysis of the speeches shows that the leaders seemed to have highlighted the anti-imperialist position while toning down the anti-feudal aspect. Instead, the focus was on the symptoms of feudal exploitation. This significant omission is understandable, given the linkages of the Kisan Sangha with the PCC. After all, a popular ministry had to be given time to act. The problem inherent in this sort of a position, of course, was that since the Congress ministry was in power it would solve all the problems. It was this illusion that developed in due course.

The Kisan Day rally coincided with hundreds of other meetings held on the same day in different parts of the province and was a part of a broad campaign.[68] After this two major developments took place. The PCC and the Kisan Sangha conducted extensive enquiries regarding peasant grievances. Besides, after returning from the rally the peasants of the three coastal districts stopped paying the *Suniya Vethi*. The Kisan Day rally had provided the necessary sanction and legitimacy. They became more conscious of their rights and began resisting the customary illegal exactions of the landlords.[69]

In the legislature, September 1937 was quite crucial as the debates indicated the shape of things to come. Biswanath Das had set the perspective of the ministry by clearly denying any plans to impose a tax on agricultural incomes, and asking the landed sections 'not to be led by the cries of the Socialists'. However, there was an expectation among the PCC MLAs, as is evident from the discussions on the budget. For example, Sarala Devi regretted the absence of any reference to remission of rents and water rates. She had expected the Ministry to take a bold position and tax the landlords. Sadasiv Tripathy felt disappointed due to the low priority given to the 'excluded areas' (Koraput and Ganjam). Chakradhara Behera voiced the sentiments of the Kanika peasants by calling for an abolition of the permanent settlement and by criticising the levies and oppression faced by the peasants. Of course, the Socialists Prananath Pattnaik and Mohan Das severely criticised the budget because it did not contain any provisions for the poor.[70]

In this session two major tenancy bills were introduced in the Legislature: the Madras Estates Land (Orissa Amendment) Bill, 1937 and the Orissa Tenancy Amendment Bill, 1937. The Madras Estates Land (Orissa Amendment) Bill, 1937, was applicable to the area which had come to Orissa in 1936 from the Madras Presidency especially Ganjam. The rent collected in this area was very high since it was calculated on the basis of half the gross produce of the land. This was much higher than the adjoining areas of the province. Consequently, the Bill aimed at rationalising the rent structure by reducing it to the rent prevailing in the nearest raiatwari areas in the province with similar conditions. It was referred to the Select Committee. Before it was brought back to the House, the PCC made an abortive attempt for a compromise with the landlords of south Orissa by offering some concessions. The Bill was finally passed on 5 February 1938. The Governor refused to give his assent to it in May 1938 and it was reserved for the Viceroy's assent.[71]

The way the Congress High Command responded to the Bill after it was passed gives us an insight into how the implications were grasped, perhaps after it was passed and the pressure exerted by the landed sections. Patel wanted the Premier to have a discussion with the zamindars, although it would be 'awkward' for Das, and try to formulate a reasonable basis for rent reduction as compared to the Bill. Das was advised to utilise the pressure of the peasant movement while discussing with the landlords and point out to them that the PCC's credibility was necessary in order to prevent peasants from joining rival kisan organisations.[72]

The Bill could not be implemented since the Viceroy refused to give his assent to it. The PCC was in no mood to force a ministerial crisis over the issue.[73] The Kisan Sangha wanted the ministry to resign in case the Bill was not passed by 1 June 1938 and lead the peasants in a Civil Disobedience Movement.[74] However, the 'unpreparedness' of the Congress to force a ministerial crisis on this issue[75] and a shift to a pro-landlord position prevented such a development.

The Orissa Tenancy Amendment Bill, 1937 was introduced on 25 September 1937. It sought to abolish the mutation fee (something which had been already outlined in the programme of the minority ministry), give rights to the tenants over trees standing on their holdings, reduce interest rates from 12 1/2 percent to 6 per cent on rent arrears and restrain illegal levies of the zamindars.[76]

The landed sections responded to it with serious panic. They smelled 'Leninism' in the Bill. The Premier harped on the pressure of the peasant movement while pointing out that unless these small things were done the landlords would be scrapped as a class.[77] Outside the Legislature, the landlords got together and expressed their anger at the Bill and prayed to the Government not to pass it. They also pledged to fight the evil of socialism.[78]

By the time the Bill was finalised, a retreat was already visible. Thus the Congress Ministry agreed to an amendment which stated that in case the rights of the landlords over trees were recorded in the settlement or had been established in Civil Courts, the peasants had to pay a compensation to the landlords to secure this right. The Congress also backed out from its position regarding the mutation fees by agreeing to abolish it in degrees.[79] Besides, as pointed out by the Kisan Sangha, the Bill had nothing to offer regarding the rights of thousands of non-occupancy tenants.[80]

This Bill was passed by the Assembly on 3 May 1938. The Governor declined to make any announcement and finally gave his assent on 31 August 1938—a day before the massive Kisan Day rally at Jenapur, in Cuttack. The mighty preparations for the rally had been closely watched.[81] The peasants saw it as a victory and grasped the meaning of their strength.

At the rally attended by more than 20,000 peasants, Nabakrushna Chaudhury and Malati Chaudhury explained the issues—although 'their' representatives passed the Bill, the representatives of British imperialism had blocked it for such a long time.[82]

The Congress ministry also introduced the Orissa Moneylenders Bill on 25 July 1938. It laid down the provision that the moneylenders had to get registered in order to carry out their practice. It sought to prevent moneylenders from realising interests in excess to the amount that had been advanced, with a right to open up old accounts from 1 April 1936, for the purpose of calculations. The Bill introduced the principle of simple interest rates, not exceeding 9 per cent in case of a secured loan and 12 per cent in case of an unsecured loan. Finally, it provided for some penalties for moneylenders for illegal extortions, like cancellations of registration certificates given to them.[83] It may be noted here that the Kisan Sangha had demanded 6 per cent interest on secured loans and 9 per cent for unsecured loans.[84] The Governor gave his assent to this Bill on 30 June 1939.

What can be observed is a marked shift in the attitude of the PCC and the landed elements *vis-a-vis* each other by the end of 1937 itself.[85] The landed elements talked of *satyagraha* against the proposals of the Ministry and met the ministers to seek redressal of their grievances.[86] Some of them suggested measures to decrease the burdens on the peasantry.[87] There are references to some of them becoming Congressmen along with local workers trying to recruit the rural poor forcibly as members of the

Congress and using the legal apparatus to achieve this.[88] Rajendra Prasad's suggestion to have Nilakantha Das as the chairman of a committee to enquire into peasant grievances symbolised the position of the Congress High Command and thereby the shift at the all-India level.[89]

In fact, Rajendra Prasad emerged as a 'saviour' for the landed interests of Orissa as well as their 'right' wing defenders within the PCC. Some landlords expressed their happiness at his success in bringing about a compromise with the landed elements in Bihar.[90] Nanda Kishore Das, the Deputy Speaker of the Orissa Legislative Assembly, went a step further. He congratulated Prasad for taking a bold stand against the Kisan Sabha and thanked him for showing the way to the Orissa PCC to deal with the Kisan problem. He asserted that, 'may you be the saviour of Orissa as you have been of Bihar'.[91]

Consequently, by the end of 1937, the election promises to reduce rents had been thrown into the dustbin of history through the intervention of the Congress High Command. At the instance of Rajendra Prasad, the Premier withdrew amendments for rent reduction. As felt by Biswanath Das, the peasants were expected to pay such high rents which they could never pay.[92] Along with this was the emphasis that although the Ministry and the PCC would solve the problems of the peasants, they in turn had to pay their legal dues to the zamindars and *mahajans* since non-payment of dues was not on the agenda. Another emphasis was to crush the 'middlemen' before anything else.[93] There is also evidence of moves to demobilise peasants who had risen against the landlords and *mohunts* of Puri by prominent PCC 'right' wingers like Nilakantha Das and Godavaris Misra.[94] Besides, by the end of November 1937 the Puri landlords issued orders to their agents to collect arrears of rent before February 1938. This symbolised a sign of victory for the landlords since the PCC had not been able to introduce remission or suspension of rents as provided in the election manifesto.[95] In fact, what is interesting is that the National Party started asking the PCC to implement its election promises.[96]

The Kisan Sangha attempted to meet the challenge. It articulated its positions regarding some burning issues of the day. It attacked the paternalism of the landlords who opined that the abolition of the mutation fees would have harmful effects on the peasants. It expected laws to be framed for a six months imprisonment term for those landlords who levied illegal dues. It mentioned how the election had fired the imagination of the peasants and they wanted the PCC to fulfil its promises after the election. However, in this changed context it noted how the PCC 'right' wing had joined the landlords in attacking the 'violence' of the Kisan Sangha since there was a fear that it threatened their class interests. The Sangha spelt out the dilemma of those within the PCC (the 'left' wing) who were trying to cut the very tree under which they had taken shelter.[97]

As the gulf between the PCC and the landed elements narrowed down, the peasant movement got dampened. Our evidence indicates how the PCC, in fact, prevented the Kisan Sangha from developing in certain areas. Thus, as we have clearly seen in the Jeypur zamindari, the PCC took up popular grievances like *bethi* and illegal dues and mobilized the peasants and tribals from the outset.[98] Another consequence of this shift was the intensification of anti-imperialist politics in some government estates like Angul where the colonial government was bitterly criticised for popular grievances. The Premier visited Angul and urged for meetings with the peasants and tribals to understand their problems. [99]

However, there are instances of tension between the PCC 'right' wing and the 'left' wing (as well as the Kisan Sangha). A meeting at Darpan (October 1937), for example, opened with a garlanding of the police officials present—an attempt to re-establish their authority. The gathering of 5,000 peasants and tribals were asked not to fear the police since they would not harass them anymore as they were under the control of the peasants. However, they were warned that if they harassed the police then they would be sent to prison. Despite this, the resolution at this meeting called for the abolition of the zamindari system and forced labour (from Savaras, Ranas and the Bauris), recognising the peasants' rights over their lands, trees and forests and also expressed 'no-confidence' in the zamindar of Madhupur who was going against those on whose votes he had been elected.[100]

Similarly, in a meeting of the Mahanga peasants (28 November 1937) Krishna Chandra Naik criticised the Ministers as capitalists who would do nothing for the labouring people. He also bitterly criticised the landed elements. A local zamindar protested against these statements to Rajkrishna Bose, who stopped the speaker.[101]

However, we find evidence of struggles and the radical temper which, of course, tended to get localised in certain areas. Here mention must be made of Sukinda (Cuttack district), an oppressive zamindari. The peasants and tribals of this estate had responded to the Kisan Day rally and had stopped paying the new year's gift to the zamindar. Led by Phani Pal, a Kisan Sangha activist, 200 of them had marched to the Sub-Divisional Officer at Jajpur and had presented him with a memorandum complaining against *bethi* and the oppression of the estate officials. Landlessness was a major problem of the tribals, mostly Kols, and they wanted to clear portions of the forests. In spite of repeated petitioning this was not allowed by the landlord who had been 'making profits' out of the forests. Early in 1938, in a few days nearly one lakh trees were felled and although some tribals and their leader were arrested, a hundred acres of land had been cleared for cultivation.[102] The PCC 'right' wing viewed this as something 'unheard of', and in its anxiety to blame the Kisan Sangha and the 'left' wing (especially the Socialists)[103] it failed to identify this as a feature of popular protest which had been inspired by Gandhian nationalism.

We also have evidence of the Kisan Sangha's activities in Khurda and in some estates like Madhupur, Patia and Pachikote. The focus continued to be on the traditional demands of the Sangha. The need to have a separate organisation of the peasants and their unity with the working class was also stressed. The Kisan Sangha called for intensifying the struggle against imperialism, criticised the pro-landlord position of the PCC and called for its democratisation.[104]

This militancy, of course, coexisted with a disillusionment among the PCC 'left' wing activists.[105] It was out of this situation that the *Krushak* (organ of the Kisan Sangha) and the Communist Party were born in 1938.

As for 1938, it is interesting to observe how the context shaped the political positions of Kisan Sangha activists as well as the PCC. This can be illustrated by taking up the example of Mahtab who had been President of the Kishan Sangha. Mahtab's association with the Sangha had been an eyesore for the PCC 'right' wing and he had been looked upon with suspicion.[106] His position changed and after stating that there was nothing like a kisan or Socialist 'menace' in Orissa in January 1938,[107] he started talking about the troubles faced by the landlords because of the non-payment of rents by peasants, by February 1938. He advocated amendments to the Tenancy Act to ensure rent-collection and was a signatory to a petition submitted by the Bhadrak landlords to the Balasore magistrate, which identified the Socialists as being at the root of this problem.[108] Moreover, he also advised peasants to compromise with landlords.[109]

The annual conference of the Gandhi Seval Dal at Delang (Puri) in March 1938, where the top leadership of the Congress including the Mahatma were present, both legitimised and reinforced this retreat and reflected ts development, at the all-India level. Mahtab was elected to the Working Committee of the Congress and Gopabandhu Chaudhury who replaced him as the President of the PCC assumed office by expressing his desire to revive orthodox Congress ideology and oust the kisan and Socialist elements from the PCC.[110] This signalled the triumph of the PCC 'right' wing.

In 1938 the euphoria with the popular ministry tended to decline. The PCC, now clearly dominated by the 'right' wing, linked the local grievances of the peasants and tribals to colonial exploitation. The anti-feudal aspect was increasingly toned down.

The Kisan Sangha tried to keep up the pressure in this hostile environment. The Debt Cancellation Day was observed along with the Gandhi Seva Dal conference at Delang. Nearly 30,000 copies of a leaflet which outlined its position were distributed here. This leaflet combined its attack against imperialism and the internal exploiters while projecting the specificity of the peasant movement. The PCC's attacks on the Sangha, the arrests of some of its activists, and the effort to isolate it seem to have made this draft miss out a very significant point—the link between the Sangha and the Congress which was not spelt out. This omission was particularly relevant since Patel (who was present at the Gandhi Seva Dal conference at Delang) was questioning the necessity of the Sangha and propagating that it would weaken the Congress.[111]

Nevertheless, in this phase we do witness peasant militancy. In some areas (Kujang and Madhupur) peasant committees were formed covering a large number of villages to defend the rights of the peasants. There are interesting references to popular forms of 'stealing' fish from the landlords' tanks as well as confrontations with, and social boycott of zamindars.[112] Our evidence also indicates a 'friction' between peasants and landlords in Kanika, Dhamnagar (Balasore), Malipara (Puri), Sukinda, Madhupur, Darpan, Aul and Pachikote (Cuttack). The issues centered around grazing and forest rights. The peasants of the three districts had developed a sense of their rights as a result of their struggles and they refused to submit to demands for illegal exactions.[113]

Nevertheless, the sweep of the peasant movement got dampened by the retreat of the Congress. The 'violence' of the Kisan Sangha became an oft-repeated theme of the PCC leadership.[114] Besides, the Kisan Sangha's activities and slogans were openly criticised at meetings.[115] What developed was a notion that the popular ministry would set things right and in fact, the PCC consistently emphasised this point, which served as a vital component to hegemonise the peasants and tribals. This also implied a certain degree of dampening of the anti- imperialist struggle.[116]

With the development of the popular struggles in the princely state, the Kisan Sangha as well as the PCC 'left'-wing shifted its focus to the 'dark zones'.[117] In the absence of a democratic organisational structure in which the leaders were nominated by the top leadership, the Kisan Sangha came to be controlled by pacifists. In fact after the Kisan Day celebrations

September 1938 the work of the Sangha came to virtual standstill and its primary concern was recruitment for the PCC.[118]

Thus, there was a decline in the spirit of the peasant movement, an effort to restrain it, and an attempt by the landed sections to reassert themselves.[119] The landed sections tried to re-establish their rights on common lands, forests, pastures and tanks[120]—areas where their authority has been seriously undermined in the preceding period.

In the Jeypur zamindari the PCC leaders like Radhamohan Sahu took up popular grievances like the tax on headloads taken to *hatas*, standardisation of weights and measures and demanded free supply of agricultural implements to the peasants and tribals.[121] This reflected a shift from the earlier anti-feudal demands like the abolition of *bethi* and the forcible supply of provisions to the zamindari and government officials. Such campaigns coexisted with intensive recruitment drives, closely associated with rumours. Around July 1938 peasants and tribals of the estate believed that the'Mahatma' would visit the zamindari and those who did not produce Congress tickets would suffer from ailments.[122] Gandhi was deified and worshipped in Congress offices—which were like temples — in some areas.[123] Enthusiasm was also aroused through promises by the PCC 'that when Swaraj (would come) there would be no rents and taxes and no forest laws'.[124]

The tribal folk welcomed the Congress by taking forcible possession of land and in one instance the Congress flag was planted on such land and the local sub-inspector who arrested the accused persons and removed the flag was attacked with an axe.[125] Efforts were made to replace *gandas* (village *chowkidars* appointed by the villagers) by Congress members.[126] The following table shows the area of *podu* cultivation:

Year	Acreage
1934-35	3294.20
1935-36	3552.40
1936-37	3706.92
1937-38	4658.80
1938-39	3510.21

It indicates a sudden spurt in the 1937-38 phase, which can be perhaps cited as a rough index of popular enthusiasm to reassert lost rights. The violations of forest laws were not only confined to the estate or Malkangiri but also affected the Kọndgaon *tehsil* of the adjoining Bastar state. In early

June 1938 several thousand *harra* trees were cut down by the villagers in imitation of the tenants of the Jeypur estate.[127]

It was in this situation that a shift took place in the PCC's position. In November 1938 a rousing welcome was given to Congress leaders like Gopabandhu Chaudhury (President PCC), Godavaris Misra and Dibakar Pattnaik (Members of the Legislative Assembly). Among those who received them were Bidyadhar Singh Deo (the nephew of the Jeypur Maharaja) who had contested the 1937 elections against the Congress and had lost. The Jubaka Sangha was established under his leadership although the President and Secretary of the Sangha were Congress members. He also became the President of the Harijan movement.[128] Interestingly, Singh Deo indulged in intellectual pursuits and studied *goti* and *bethi* on which he wrote two papers. He appreciated the 'liberal attitude' of the estate *vis-a-vis* the *gotis* and felt that it should be discontinued 'as far as practicable'.[129]

This shift also implied a serious move to 'remould' the new Congress recruits in line with its politics. A training camp was opened at Nuaput (about five miles from Jeypur) in November 1938 to achieve this purpose. This was attended by around 300 to 400 people. Godavaris Misra and Gopabandhu Chaudhury organised it. At this camp the people were trained in spinning, scouting and village service. They were also taught farming, animal husbandry and the need for prohibition of liquor. These people served to link Koraput to the Congress and among them were prominent activists of the future like Laxman Naiko.[130]

The reconstruction of things becomes very difficult, given the paucity of evidence, but the PCC's campaign seem to have had intimate links with a complex process which included Hinduisation as well as a social-reformist trend. The process of Hinduisation was not new, given the perspective we have outlined earlier. What was perhaps new was its linkages with the Congress. This becomes visible if one takes into account the deification and ritualised worshipping of the 'Mahatma', the establishment of Congress *ashrams*, the stress upon vegetarianism and abstinence from liquor—features quite alien to the tribal world. These were distinctly associated with both Hinduism and the Congress and were emulated to gain a certain degree of respect and recognition from both. Of course, the phenomenon of social reformism was relatively new. This possibly arose out of a genuine concern over drinking which was an 'evil' in tribal society, leading to the ruin of many families. These points explain a marked tendency among the tribal supporters of the PCC (including prominent activists like Laxman Naiko) for giving up hunting and eating meat[131] as well as the campaigns against liquor.

By the beginning of 1939 the shift climaxed with Nilakantha Das being elected as the President and Godavaris Misra as the Secretary of the PCC. Besides indicating the all-India implication in clearest terms, this meant that the PCC and the Ministry came to be under the absolute control of the PCC 'right' wing. An all-out effort was initiated to combat the radicalisation that had taken place and counter the 'menace' of the Kisan Sangha. Training camps and *ashrams* were established for this purpose; Kisan Sangha workers were restrained through colonial laws, now controlled by the Congress ministry. There are references to peasants being warned to follow 'Gandhian' and 'constitutional' methods and serious moves to counter the ideological hold of the Socialists.[132] The abolition of landlordism became a feature quite remote.[133]

These pulls and pressures adversely affected the already demobilised Kisan Sangha. In a hastily called and thinly attended meeting of the Sangha on 27 February 1939, Phani Pal, a prominent Kisan Sangha leader, was removed from the Sangha thereby indicating a split within the 'left' wing and the Kisan Sangha. The resolution for his removal was proposed by Nabakrushna Chaudhury and Malati Chaudhury seconded it. These individuals were associated with the birth of both the Socialist Party and the Kisan Sangha. Pranakrushna Padhiary, the President of the Sangha adjourned the meeting *sine-die* after this.[134] No elections of the Sangha took place in 1939 and Orissa was not represented at the Gaya session of the All India Kisan Sabha.[135]

The demobilised Kisan Sangha left the field clear for the PCC 'right' wing to hegemonise the peasant movement. The PCC replaced struggle with negotiated settlement at the village level. Primary Congress Committees were instructed to act accordingly. Fines and social boycott were imposed on people who led struggles for raising the wages of agricultural labourers, by the Primary Congress Committees.[136]

As for the Jeypur estate, we witness a rather volatile situation which the PCC found difficult to control. The tribals were showing signs of restlessness at the loss of traditional rights and refused to get 'remoulded'. They translated their perceptions into practice. Our evidence indicates the collections of funds to set up Congress *ashrams* and the appointment of village officials superseding those appointed by the Maharaja of Jeypur. Timber was 'illegally' taken for the purpose of building these *ashrams*. Rumours circulated, perhaps to legitimise such actions, that the district police would be prosecuted and the magistrate removed by the Chief Minister of Orissa, presumably because they tried to prevent such activities.[137]

The seriousness of the situation can be judged by the tours of both Nilakantha Das and Biswanath Das in order to assess the situation. Biswanath Das made it quite clear that the laws of the land had to be obeyed and only the minister—not the people—could change laws. Such moves did apparently restrain popular militancy.[138] However, the situation remained volatile.

By July 1939 the situation in Cuttack and Puri had been seriously affected due to floods. The crisis became extremely grave due to an unprecedented price rise which ranged from 15 per cent to 100 per cent. The outbreak of the War and large-scale hoardings (leading to the disappearance of grain from the market) precipitated this crisis. In some parts of the coastal tract the Socialists and the Communists tried to build a movement. This included an attempt to reactivate the Kisan Sangha which was in a deplorable state. Prananath Pattnaik became its Secretary and pressure was put on the PCC for intensifying its struggle for *swaraj*.[139] We witness an activisation of the peasant movement after a somewhat lean period. For example, there was an increase in the total number of suits filed (123,929 in 1937-38 to 128,710 in 1938-39) as a result of non-payment of rents, especially in Cuttack and Balasore. Peasant militancy developed in some estates like Sukinda, Madhupur, Kalkala, Pachikote, Balarampur, Chausathipara and Aul in Cuttack, Kanika in Balasore and parts of Gop, Balianta, Kakatpur and the Ekrajat estate in Puri. These were centred on non-payment of rents by peasants, damaging landlords' property and trespassing on their lands. The peasants stopped *abwabs*. The 'position' and 'status' of landlords was no longer 'enviable' or 'coveted' as it had been in the past and many expressed the desire that the management of their estates be taken over from their hands.[140] Simultaneously, a decrease in the authority of the colonial structure was also indicated.[141] The problem of price rise and hoarding also affected the Jeypur estate. We get references to appeals to colonial authorities for grain, coexisting with Congress *gomastas* leading the 'looting' of a granary.[142] The latter phenomenon indicated pressures which the PCC could not control.

There seems to have been some links between the decline of the peasant movement and that of PCC recruitment in the 1938-39 period. There was a fall in Cuttack (from 58,875 in 1937-38 to 35,474 in 1938-39) and Koraput (from 50,048 in 1937-38 to 26,9000 in 1938-39); as for the whole province the figures revealed a decline (from 1,96,948 to 1,19,517 between 1937-38 and 1938-39).[143] Whereas the Kisan Sangha membership for 1938-39 stood at 20,000 for the province the membership of the

Sangha in the princely states stood at 30,000,[144] thereby indicating that the peasant movement had percolated into these 'dark zones'.

By November 1939 the anti-war position of the Congress led to the resignation of the ministry in Orissa. With this the colonial administration launched an offensive against the Kisan Sangha. Its offices were raided and its activists arrested in an attempt to smother it.[145] The PCC's emphasis now shifted to the possibility of a mass movement in the future.[146]

II

The Princely States

We can now shift our attention to the princely states: the 'dark zones' of Orissa. In these enclaves of feudalism the rajas, officials and the police could do anything and get away with it. The terrorised people could do nothing more than accepting it as their fate or the 'natural order of things'. Although there had been some movements in the states, the overall situation had remained almost unaltered. The people continued to be overburdened with every conceivable form of exploitation which included very high rent demands, forced labour, gifts and provisions, forced dues (which had become 'customary'), a monopoly system on essential commodities (*pana*, hides and oil etc.) which meant very high prices when it came to buying and very low prices when it came to selling, no rights on trees, forests, pastures and tanks and interference in social and religious matters. We also come across deaths in *shikar* expeditions, human sacrifices and sexual exploitation of women and young boys in the most perverted and unimaginable ways. Everything was legitimised through the much-feared night-courts.[147]

In 1934 Gandhi had declared that he favoured 'non-interference' in the princely states. Implying thereby that the 'dark-zones' should continue to remain dark, he had maintained that this was a 'wise' and 'sound' policy and he was convinced that interference could only damage the cause of the people of the states. The 'Mahatma' had hoped that the princes would become the 'real trustees of the people' and that this would resolve their problems.[148] How does one explain this attitude of 'non-interference'? Any simple formula of 'feudal links' of the Congress will not do, especially because upto this point of time the rajas were firm opponents of the Congress. One reason could be that the 'Mahatma' was hesitant to launch movements in the princely states where the Congress organisation was too weak to exercise any control over mass movements. Moreover, in these areas the sheer intensity of exploitation and the lack of any rights made non-violent struggles very difficult. Thus, although we have sketched peasant and tribal militancy prior to the ministry period, these were spontaneous and isolated. The oppressed in the princely states had drawn inspiration from the Congress as well as Gandhi and we have already cited evidence of the states' people participating in the Civil Disobedience Movement although the Congress had been ambivalent and had advocated passivity.

Consequently, although the All India States People's Conference (hereafter AISPC) had been formed in December 1927 and the Orissa States People's Conference had been established in June 1931 nothing much had happened and these 'dark zones' had remained isolated from the nationalist movement. However, the anti-imperialist and the anti-feudal struggles in the province, the formation of the Socialist Party, the Kisan Sangha and *Krushak*, the 1937 elections and the installation of the Congress ministry and the creation of the Communist Party were factors which inspired the people. Although the Congress (and the PCC's) position remained unaltered the PCC's 'left' wing had drifted towards the states during the 1937 election campaign. The question was how long could the PCC and the Congressmen within the states continue as silent spectators?[149]

It was in this context that in June 1937 the Orissa States People's Conference had its second session at Cuttack, which was presided over by P. Sitaramayya. He drew the attention of the gathering to the 'dark zones' and expressed the desire of the Congress to 'harness the immense latent powers of the masses in the states'. The resolutions that were passed focused on issues like responsible government, the right of the states' people (rights over their land and citizenship rights), the abolition of feudal practices (like *bethi* and *rasad*) and the setting-up of an enquiry committee to look into their grievances.[150] What was observed at this session was that the presence of some state police officers in Cuttack itself was enough to scare away several delegates.[151]

The states' people had attended some of the PCC election meetings as well as those organised by the Krushak Sangha earlier. However, the massive Kisan Day rally of 1 September 1937 must have raised their hopes and enthusiasm even higher. They began looking upon the Congress government as their government also and looked upon the 'Mahatma' as their saviour.[152] However, it was the formation of the Prajamandal and the struggles which ended the isolation of the states' people and linked them with Indian nationalism. These struggles took the PCC, the Congress High

Command and the colonial administration by surprise and implied various shifts and turns in their positions.

Another feature that needs to be emphasised is the growth of new social forces in the states, which played a vital role in this process. In the first place we come across a youthful intelligentsia (for example, Banamali Das of Nilgiri, Baishnab Pattnaik of Dhenkanal, Pabitramohan Pradhan of Talcher and Banamali Ram of Ranpur).[153] The sheer exposure to the world outside through the process of education and information about the state of things outside the 'dark zones' had raised the consciousness of these people. They had begun to view their existence in relation to the 'other side' and had begun to question the 'natural order of things' as well as visualise possibilities of a change. Another feature was the growth of a relatively affluent section of the peasantry and commercial interests[154] which were linked to the growth and development of a money economy. Whereas at one level they felt alienated from the state authorities who throttled their existence through policies which prevented their growth, at the other level their exposure to the outside world led to the development of a higher level of consciousness which reinforced the existing alienation. They also began to question the established order.

It was against this background that militant struggles developed in the states of Orissa. Nilgiri was a trend-setter not only because it had the first Prajamandal but also because it launched the first blow to the authoritarian structure represented by the feudal chiefs. Around August 1937 we have evidence of a leaflet entitled 'Get United' circulated in the state. It asked the readers to open their eyes and take a look at the Orissa province. It emphasised the necessity of collective action which was projected as the weapon through which the people of the province had managed to check the violence of the police and the zamindars. This was projected as an alternative before the people of Nilgiri. It asked the state's people how long they would tolerate the exploitation and the violence perpetuated by the state and stressed that unity alone was their liberator. This leaflet reflected the development of an organisation, especially in southern Nilgiri. Among the people associated with this trend were tribal agricultural labourers.[155]

Interestingly, the spark that set off the extremely powerful Nilgiri peoples' struggle was associated with Gandhian social reform—Harijan uplift. Drawing inspiration from the Gandhian ideals of Harijan uplift some young men of Ajodhya had started an annual dinner from about 1932 in which people of different castes—both 'high' and 'low' (untouchables) — sat down and ate together. Villagers used to contribute towards this dinner and the number of people attending this seems to have increased and in 1937 it was about 2,000. Some Congressman of the state like Kailash Chandra Mohanty addressed the people.[156]

Around November 1937 the state decided to intervene since it saw in this 'common dinner' a serious challenge to the *status quo*, which was based on a fundamental principle that all humans could never be equal. It was especially seen as subversive since some of the leaders like Kailash Chandra Mohanty and Hadibandhu Raj were Congressmen. Keen on preserving the *status quo*, which served to keep the people divided, the state authorities served notices asking the sponsors of the 'common dinner' to explain why they should not be excommunicated.[157]

Around May 1938 the state authorities decided to curb this tendency and issued two regulations imposing restrictions on associations and meetings. Since the voice of protest was seen an 'external' phenomenon the *Krushak* was banned. The *durbar* arrested Pranabandhu Agasti, an important activist of the Prajamandal. Besides, young student activists of the Balasore Students' Federation who were conducting anti-illiteracy campaigns were also arrested. This news spread throughout the state like wild fire.

It was in this context that the Prajamandal was established and its office was located at Gadiamal (in Balasore). Its first task was to apply for recognition by the Raja and seek permission to hold meetings to discuss grievances of the people. On 11 June 1938 the Working Committee of the Orissa State Peoples' Conference met at Balasore where it was decided that in case the Raja refused to recognise the Prajamandal and give permission for meetings and grant the 'right of citizenship', these would be made the minimum demands to start a Civil Disobedience Movement. Although the PCC maintained its position of 'non-interference', some important leaders like Mahtab organised secret meetings to discuss the issues involved. Besides, a training centre was established at Alasuan village, bordering Nilgiri, to direct the state's people.[158]

The stage for a showdown was set when the Prajamandal submitted a list of 31 demands. The most important of these demands reflected the extremely strong anti-feudal current. For example, it included the abolition of all kinds of *bethi*, lowering of rents to the level of Balasore's and forest rights. The demands also included the abolition of restrictions on *handia* (rice liquor) manufacture and the standardisation of rent assessments for the Bhumijs, Santhals and other tribals as well as caste Hindus. These reflect the interesting combination of Gandhian (symbolic common dinner) and non-Gandhian features (encouragement of *handia*) and how through these the Prajamandal united the tribals and non-tribals. These features created a broad social base for the Prajamandal,[159] and here the Communists of Nilgiri played a significant role. They operated secretly within the Congress and had set up sixteen cells in the state. Individuals like Banamali Das were associated with this trend and they played a prominent role in building up a strong Prajamandal. Das became the Secretary of the Prajamandal and this strengthened its organisation. It incorporated tribal methods (most probably Santhali) of mobilisation. Thus, a rope with a knot used to circulate and each time it changed hands, the news of the Prajamandal or its plan used to be relayed.[160]

The Prajamandal decided to impose a boycott on the Raja. This boycott was so complete that food provisions had to be procured from outside the state.[161] It also mobilised people for a demonstration to protest against the arrests and to violate Section 144 that had been imposed. What followed were regular demonstrations along strictly Gandhian lines of non-violence, although the state unleashed terror through merciless lathi-charges and beatings. People marched to the capital from various parts of the state to participate in these demonstrations and express their solidarity with the struggle.[162]

In order to crush the Prajamandal the state authorities decided to impose fines on prajamandal activists and villages which were identified as the backbone of the movement. Attempts to collect these fines created the basis for collective resistance. The state authorities decided to raise a fine of Rs.10,000 from the Machuapatana village. Prajamandal activists and villagers from different parts of the state, numbering around 10,000, remained at this place, surrounding the village, braving the rains and living on rice and *sag* (edible leaf). The gathering also included tribals.[163]

The Raja and the British Political Agent, Bazellgate came down to survey the situation. The Prajamandal activists asked the people to remain calm and they sang the *Ramdhun*.[164] An argument developed between Banamali Das and Bazellgate when the latter condemned the action of the gathering as treasonable. Das stunned Bazellgate by asking him in English why it should be condemned for after all the British people had also beheaded Charles I. Speaking with Bazellgate who symbolised terror and that too in English made Das a 'hero' overnight.[165] Popular perceptions identified him as a person who could match a white man in his own terms. This was a very important feature which consolidated people's faith in both Das and the Prajamandal and it was more so since the police did not open fire and the fines were withdrawn.

The Raja's next move was to drive a wedge between the tribals and the non-tribals. He set up a camp at Darkhuli, close to the Mayurbhanj border and asked the tribal chiefs to meet him. The Prajamandal decided to counter his manoeuvers and sent some activists, which included Banamali Das, to foil the Rajas's plan. A tribal leader of Hathikhulia village, Dalei Singh, wanted to meet the Raja and consulted Das who produced a blood-stained knife (which had been used earlier to dress meat), and asked him to kill him first and then go to meet the Raja. Dalei Singh broke down. The Raja had no callers, did not get even tea or dinner, and left the place the next morning. Soon afterwards an abortive plan was made to murder Das.[166]

By July 1938 the younger elements of the Prajamandal were contemplating a mass civil disobedience movement. A plan was being worked out to launch a no-rent movement from around October 1938 when rents had to be paid to the state.[167] Although the PCC tried to restrain this tendency, it was clear that there was every possibility that this could not be controlled. Things took a serious turn when Banamali Das was arrested. This was seen as the signal for action. Nearly 10,000 people offered *satyagraha* to protest against Das' arrest on the Hindu festival of Rathajatra. Given the nature of the cult of Jagannatha tribals were associated with and our evidence points to their participation at Nilgiri on the eventful day.[168]

What was new about the Rathajatra of 1938 was that it became a rallying ground for uniting both tribals and non-tribals. The oppressed rallied round the 'lord' to defy and fight their oppressors. Jagannatha—the symbol through which the oppressors had extended their hegemony—had been appropriated by the oppressed to fight their oppressors. This reflects some sort of an inversion of the logic of the cult.

As the movement gathered momentum there was an increase in the participation of tribals. We have evidence of Santhals joining as volunteer corps. Occasionally there are references to tribal humanism when tribals asked the police to arrest them and free the children whom the police had arrested.[169] Nevertheless, the repression continued. By mid-July around 116 people had been arrested. Some activists of the Prajamandal had been banned from entering the state and a few state officials had been dismissed for divulging the secrets of the *durbar* to the Prajamandal. Some Brahmins holding rent-free (*lakhiraj*) tenures were dispossessed for joining the movement.[170]

By the beginning of August 1938 the *durbar's* position appeared to soften a bit. On 4 August the Prajamandal was recognised but very soon the Raja retreated from this position. What followed was another spell of struggle culminating in a procession on 10 August. The police opened fire killing one person and injuring about 90 people. This was followed by another spell of repression on the next day.[171] However, immediately after this the Raja changed his mind and tried to reach a compromise with the Prajamandal, which suspended all processions on 12 August.

Negotiations for a settlement began from 13 August between the Raja, the Political Agent and Mahtab who represented the Prajamandal. The conflict between popular pressures and the Congress style of political adjustment surfaced. At a Prajamandal meeting that followed, Mahtab proposed acceptance of the conditional supply of services during *shikar* (hunting expeditions). This was resisted by the majority of the Prajamandal activists, including the Socialists and the Communists. In the voting Mahtab's proposal was rejected.[172]

Finally, by the end of August the Prajamandal emerged victorious when the Raja was forced to recognise it, abolish *bethi* and *rasad*, reduce the rent on the *bethia* jagirs by 25 per cent, abolish *salami* and grant concessions on the use of forests. He also agreed to abolish taxes on the sale of bamboo by Dombs and on brewing liquor for household consumption. The ban on *Krushak* was lifted. The Prajamandal emerged more powerful and organised than ever before.[173]

Resolutions passed by the Prajamandal reflected a broad and enlightened outlook. Identifying with the struggles of the states' people elsewhere, it sent out volunteers to assist the movement in Dhenkanal.[174] The Communist Party emerged as a strong and organised force in the state. As the Prajamandal leadership (especially most of the Congress office bearers) had shifted to Gadiamal, it was left to the Communists to organise popular pressures effectively. Although this aspect is not clearly recognised, the Nilgiri Prajamandal's popularity and organisational strength were appreciated by important Congress leaders like Mahtab.[175]

The growing strength of the Communists, who championed vital demands, caused anxiety among the Congress activists of the Prajamandal. Activities of Communists working through the Prajamandal were reported to the leaders of the PCC. Gouri Chandra Das, a Socialist activist, 'exposed' people like Banamali Das. When P.C. Joshi, the General Secretary of the Communist Party, toured Orissa in December 1938 Das had met him 'secretly' against the wishes of Malati Chaudhury and Nabakrushna Chaudhury. They reported this secret meeting to Mahtab.[176]

In 1939 Bazellgate's murder at Ranpur changed the balance of forces. The PCC retreated in this context and the colonial administration tried to crush the popular movements. The Raja of Nilgiri tried to go back on the various agreements around February 1939. Nevertheless, the strength of the Prajamandal seems to have prevented such a move and the *durbar* made a declaration on 21 February 1939 that the position remained unaltered.[177] However, by September 1939 the situation had changed with the state authorities attempting to reinforce the forest rules, take punitive actions against Prajamandal activists as well as tribal and Harijan supporters.[178]

Although 1939 marked a triumph for the PCC 'right' wing (and we have already sketched its implications as far as the peasant movement was concerned) the situation was different at Nilgiri. The PCC 'left' wing (especially the Communists) maintained its hold and worked within the Prajamandal. Once the *durbar* had accepted the major demands of the Prajamandal, the PCC activists' stress on recognition of the Prajamandal, rights over forests and pastures became redundant. They now shifted their focus to health, education, village reconstruction and responsible government and attacked the inefficiency and corruption of the administrative apparatus.[179]

In sharp contrast, starting in 1939 the Communists incorporated the following demands: (i) no forced levy by *sahukars* (moneylenders); (ii) a maximum of 25 per cent interest on loans; (iii) standardisation of a grain measure for the whole state since *sahukars* gave rice in small (Laxman) *gaunis* and received it in big (Ram) *gaunis*; (iv) fixation of a minimum wage at five seers of paddy per day.[180]

Consequently, the Communists shifted their focus to the question of internal exploitation. Moreover, since this included moneylender exploitation and the problems of agricultural labourers, these demands enabled the Communists to establish a strong base among the tribals. Besides, the Communists continued their campaign for the elimination of the 'dark-zones'.

It was the Nilgiri state peoples' struggle which was the spark for the popular movements in the various states of Orissa. The fact that the established order of the 'dark zones' could not only be questioned but also substantially altered through collective action was an important feature which undermined the hegemony of the princes. From around August 1938 the focus of the OSPC and the 'left' wing shifted towards Dhenkanal—undoubtedly the most oppressive Orissan state.

Coming more specifically to Dhenkanal, we find the people questioning the 'established order'. Issues like *bethi*, feudal levies and the absence of civil liberty provided the material needed to question things. A Prajamandal had been set up around June 1938 when the Enquiry Committee toured Angul to collect evidence from the Dhanakanal state people. Nearly 300 people from Parjang, Upardesh and Palasuni areas had gone to give evidence to the Committee, in spite of persuasion and threats by the state officials. It seems that initially Prajamandal meetings were held under the cover of *jagyans* and religious discourses.[181]

The first break came, interestingly enough, when the Prajamandal decided to oppose the monopoly system which led to the high price of popular commodities like *pana* (betel leaf). The decision for a *pana* boycott was taken on 2 July 1938. *Sankirtan* parties popularised the message of the Prajamandal throughout the state. Our evidence indicates that several mass meetings were held at Parjang and Palasuni Bisos to gather support for this boycott.[182]

Sarangadhar Das, Secretary OSPC, met and addressed the Dhenkanal state people on the borders of the state through the help of the Kisan Sangha workers. Besides, Communist Party activists like Bhagabati Charan Pannigrahi and Baidyanath Rath also met the people of the state. These meetings and discussions were aimed to awaken the people to the achievements of the peasant movement in British Orissa and the Nilgiri state peoples' struggle and to politicise them. The success of the PCC 'left' wing was due to the fact that as late as July 1938 there was no Congress organisation within the state.[183]

In the initial phase a young man—Baishnab Pattnaik—who was a painter in the Bengal-Nagpur Railway collected information from the villages of the state at night and despatched them for publication in the *Krushak.*[184]

The Nilgiri state peoples' struggle had made the *durbar* quite apprehensive. In an attempt to nip things in the bud, the Raja asked the people to represent to him directly—an obvious ploy devised to prevent the formation of a collective body. Around August 1938 the Raja decided to meet the people in order to discuss their grievances. This created a lot of confusion among the people since they did not know what to say.[185]

In early August 1938 the Raja met a gathering of about 15,000 people at Motagaon. His officials and favourites came on to the stage and asked the gathering to send 4 or 5 representatives to discuss things with the Raja. Since no one went the audience was told that unless they sent their representatives the Raja would go away. After this the Raja and the Rani came on to the stage. The Raja 'wept' and asked the people to state their grievances. Interestingly enough, this influenced some people. Purna Chandra Mahapatra got up and spoke with folded hands. He said that although their fathers had been great fighters, affluent and wise, the people of the 'present' were cowardly, poor and foolish. He appealed to the Raja to set things rights so that they could be like their ancestors.[186]

After this Maheswar Subaho Singh spoke about the grain shortage, forest grievances and the problem of unemployment. The Raja immediately ordered for the supply of grain, the suspension of forest officials who created problems for the people, and employment facilities.

When Baishnab Pattnaik's turn came he did not fold his hands and said that if the Raja was serious then he should not ask the people to state their grievances with the guns pointing at them. He focused on the question of civil rights. At this point the Raja 'wept' again and said how he was not aware of this aspect and that his officials had kept him in the dark. The audience thundered approvingly that they were 'forced' to speak and contradicted the Raja by mentioning how he was himself a party to everything. The Raja's scheme ended in a fiasco.[187]

After this the state people organised mass demonstrations against the misrule and demanded a responsible government. To counter it the state police surrounded Parjang and Palasuni, which were identified as rebellious areas, for two weeks in order to prevent other areas from being poisoned. It also set up an enquiry committee and asked for two representatives from each village.

In the meantime the Prajamandal finalised its demands. Along with the demand for civil liberty and representative government, it included the abolition of *bethi*, *magan*, forced contributions, the monopoly system (over certain commodities like *pana)* and a restructuring of the forest and tenancy laws.[188] Most of these were drawn up along the lines of the Kisan Sangha inspired peasant movement as well as the Nilgiri Prajamandal.

Between 10 and 20 August 1938 a massive campaign was organised and hundreds of meetings were held all over the state to discuss and pass a resolution supporting the demands. At the call of the Prajamandal around 10,000 to 12,000 people assembled at Jenapur in Cuttack district to press their demands and express their solidarity.[189]

As things seemed to go out of control, the Raja invited Subaho Singh and other Prajamandal leaders to meet him. People from various parts of the state joined him and at the head of some 40,000 people Subaho Singh reached the palace. Slogans like 'Down with Tyranny' and 'Grant Responsible Government' rent the air. Subaho Singh was not allowed to address the gathering and only the Raja spoke. He made vague promises and it became clear that the autocracy was not in a mood to submit to popular will.[190]

The next milestone was the massive Kisan Day rally of 1 September 1938 at Jenapur. A large contingent of people from Dhankanal attended it carrying the national flag and the red flag. Many of them had walked about a hundred miles to reach Jenapur. They donated Rs. 500 to the Kisan Sangha and had carried a considerable amount of rice and vegetables with them.[191] It is not clear whether it was only for their own consumption or whether this (along with the cash donations) was meant to be *vethi* (gifts) for the Kisan Sangha—instead of the state authorities. Although we are not sure, but if this had happened it indicates the way peasants and tribals viewed authority, which was central to their existence, and how the 'old' authority was being replaced by a new one in their perception.

September 2 was declared 'Dhenkanal Day' where the Prajamandal's demands were reiterated. From 6 September the peasants and tribals stopped paying the customary *suniya vethi* (new year's gift).[192] What needs to be pointed out at this juncture was the fusion that was taking place between the peasant movement in British Orissa and the popular movements in the princely states.

The *durbar* decided to meet the leaders but wanted the demonstration and the meetings to stop. The Prajamandal could not agree to this since it realised that the pressure should not be relaxed. Meetings and demonstrations continued and the state tried to strengthen itself by getting policemen from the neighbouring states. Things took a serious turn when the President of the Prajamandal, Manmohan Pattnaik, and the Secretary, Subaho Singh, were arrested, and the state unleashed terror when thousands of people followed their leaders to the jail gate.[193]

As the news spread to different areas people marched to the capital town. Women also joined in. In a state of panic the *durbar* decided to unleash its machinery of repression and besides lathicharges, in one day three firings were ordered. However, on 14 September around 50,000 people paraded the streets of the capital (this included people from the adjoining states of Athgarh, Hindol and Tigiria) and the state authorities responded by releasing the prisoners before they were actually rescued and provisionally recognising the Prajamandal.[194]

It was in this context that the PCC decided to intervene through Mahtab to reach a compromise. Mahtab advised the Political Agent, Bazellgate, and the *durbar* to settle things with the Prajamandal after considering its demands and to order an enquiry into the reasons for the clash between the state police and the people. The *durbar* made false allegations of attacks on state officials by the people. Interestingly, Mahtab thought that it was necessary to counter these through evidence. However, he did not have any perspective on the struggle which had assumed a high degree of militancy. The idea was to try for a compromise. This reflected the ambiguity of the PCC and a clear preference for toning down struggles of the states' people. It also reflected a tension between the PCC 'right' wing and the 'left' wing, Kisan Sangha and the Prajamandal. In fact, the Secretary of the OSPC criticised Mahtab's moves.[195]

Given a change in the balance of forces the Prajamandal organised several meetings in various parts of the state. Students joined in by calling for a strike. However, the *durbar* waited for a contingent of 200 British troops (King's Own Scottish Brigade) to arrive. The train carrying these troops escaped a sabotage attempt and reached the state on 20 September.[196] This illustrates a comprehension of the terror that was expected to follow as well as the way popular perceptions linked the *durbar* with colonialism. At a deeper level it reflected the way popular perceptions looked at 'modern' things like railroads which were associated with repression.

After this the *durbar* again unleashed terror. Popular memory still retains the shooting down of several Prajamandal activists and sympathisers. People were forcibly recruited for *bethi* and publicly lashed and told that this was their 'Civil Liberty' and 'Responsible Government'. The armed soldiers and the state police used to confront people by boasting that the Raja had secured a license to kill, for three years. Villages were encircled to strike terror and shootings, rapes, plunder and beatings became the order of the day. The Rajas of Dhenkanal and Talcher and the Political Agent of Orissa, Bazellgate, personally supervised these operations when they were conducted in areas which had emerged as the bastions of the Prajamandal (Parjang). Loyalty tickets were sold and there are references to attempts made to split the movements along lines of caste through the deployment of untouchables to beat and arrest people of high caste.[197] This was also an indication of some weaknesses within the Dhenkanal Prajamandal which, unlike the Nilgiri Prajamandal, had not consolidated itself among outcastes and tribals.

The PCC 'left' wing tried its best to publicise the terror of the *durbar*. In a moving piece Bhagabati Pannigrahi wrote how the people of Orissa who were used to deaths through floods, famines and starvation were learning to die through bullets.[198]

How did the Prajamandal cope with this organised terror? In fact, it was not adequately prepared to meet the repression. Its relative isolation from the overall bearings of the Congress and the anti-imperialist struggle as well as the lack of a clear perspective of the 'Mahatma' made the situation extremely difficult. Along with the Raja the Congress leaders criticised the state people for carrying *lathis* (sticks) and it was condemned since it symbolised violence. In response the state people stopped carrying *lathis.*[199] After all, the sanction from the 'Mahatma' and the Congress was extremely vital for their struggle. The PCC mediated through a minister to put pressure on some of the leaders of the Prajamandal, against whom warrants had been issued, to return to the state.[200] Thus while on the one hand the Congress ministry did not agree to arrest these people (against whom extradition warrants had been issued), on the other it wanted them to return to the state and surrender to its law.

However, we have evidence of some resistance. For one, state officials were boycotted and conches were blown as warning signals and to get people together. There were also stray cases of retaliation against state officials and the police. In any case this was an obviously impossible task for the unarmed peasants and tribals. The microscopic Communist Party cadre, of course, used arms to retaliate on a few occasions. Veterans of the Nilgiri Prajamandal used this method to foil mass rape campaigns.[201]

Under these circumstances around October 1938 the Prajamandal gave a call for *hizrat*. Nearly a lakh of people left the state and crossed over to the adjoining zamindaris of British Orissa. What needs to be emphasised is that for the state people this was a form of protest which, perhaps, had some connection with similar modes of protest in the pre-British past.[202] The *hizrat* refugees were received cordially by the people of British Orissa. We get touching references to men folk staying outside in the field along with their counterparts of Dhenkanal, leaving their huts for women, children and invalids.[203]

Those who stayed back, including women, helped in collecting funds and organising secret meetings. In this context we come across desperate attempts being made to keep the morale high. Shortly after the firing at Kandazsingha, Baishnab Pattnaik reached the village and wanted to organise a meeting at night. Most of the villagers had deserted the village and the local activist did not agree to a meeting. Pattnaik sang a song on how the Prajamandal would be victorious and walked around the village. Next morning the women folk talked of how their village goddess had come out at night and had prophesied the victory of the Prajamandal. This demonstrates how inspiration was drawn from the village goddess—quite important in the life of the village folk— at a point when the state people were helpless, given the nature of state repression and the desertion by the Congress.[204]

Similarly, at Bhuban, Prajamandal activists Srikant and Rabi Ghosh organised a meeting after the place had been looted and in a context when the upper crust showed signs of shifting its allegiance to the Raja. The two young activists sang songs to inspire and gather people for a meeting where

The princely state of Ranpur, however, became a centre of importance because of Bazellgate's murder in January 1939. Here again we find broadly similar conditions. The state was oppressive and the initial efforts to organise the Prajamandal was confined to Tangi, Siko, Sanpadar and Bolagad which were outside the state. Left-wing activists of Puri like Prananath Pattnaik and Gokul Mohan Rai Chudamani played an active role in this process. Inside the state Kandha-Nayagada (Tangi was 2 miles from it) became the secret headquarters of the Prajamandal.[229]

The Prajamandal was formed with Banamali Ram as its President, Raghunath Mohanty as the Secretary and Krupasindhu Misra as the Vice-President. Its activities were directed from Tangi and Krupasindhu Misra resided at this place. The development of popular movements had hardened both the colonial authorities and the Ranpur *durbar* and this meant serious hurdles from the outset. Around October 1938 the *durbar* tried to nip the formation of the Prajamandal in the bud and arrested some of its activists at Chandapur village who were on their way to Tangi. Banamali Ram mobilised about 1,000 people and marched towards the capital. At Chandapur the formation of the Prajamandal was declared. Its basic demand centered on the release of the arrested activists and the recognition of the Prajamandal. Even at this juncture some people of the state did not favour the formation of the Prajamandal.[230]

An organisation of the Prajamandal developed within a very short tie. It had representatives from various parts of the state. A mass meeting s held at Dasadola followed by the distribution of a leaflet in every age. It attracted the attention of the people to the struggles launched by people of Nilgiri, Dhenkanal and Talcher and the efforts for settling the plems by the rajas as a result of these struggles. It emphasised the need unity and struggle to counter the exploitative machinery at Ranpur. le emphasising the need for 'truth' and 'non-violence' it pointed out s for a future meeting at the state capital. It appealed to the peasants the agricultural labourers to get united.[231]

The *durbar* swooped down on the Prajamandal leadership. Banamali and Achyutanand were arrested and sent to jail. This set the stage for wdown. The Tangi office was closed down and Krupasindhu Misra d the Chandapur area extensively to mobilise the people for a march capital. People from different parts of the state decided to join the h. By the time Misra reached Kandha-Nayagarh about 5,000 people d to receive him. It was the harvesting season and peasants with s in their hands left their fields to join the march. The people of the xpressed their solidarity with the processionists by providing them

a loyalist was forced to apologise.[205]

The developments led to the emergence of a new consciousness among the people of the state.[206] They refused to remain as 'Dhenkanalias' anymore. They had grasped the meaning of collective strength and expressed their solidarity also with other states' people. For example, the Dhenkanal Prajamandal wanted to collect funds for the Nilgiri Prajamandal. It directed that everybody should contribute one pice for this, which was paid by everyone. The movement had a multi- caste basis, and outcastes as well as tribals united under the banner of the Prajamandal. In some of the bastions of the Prajamandal, like Palasuni, Harijans were members of its executive.[207]

By November 1938, the *durbar* announced some paltry concessions but continued to terrorise the people. It also decided to attach paddy fields in January 1939. In this situation the people decided not to return and things did not show any signs of improvement.[208]

The PCC politics continued to oscillate between 'non-interference' and a compromise. What was being emphasised from about November 1938 in most of the meetings was that the British government was at the root of the trouble and that the agitation in the states was a part of a general struggle against imperialism.[209] The internal anti-feudal contradiction was abstracted from its politics.

In December 1938 Nabakrushna Chaudhury resigned from the legislature as well as the post of Secretary of the PCC and led the first batch of *satyagrahis* into Dhenkanal on 3 December 1938. The 'Mahatma' did not approve of it and a section of the PCC put pressure on him not to undertake this mission. After this seven more batches of *satyagrahis* crossed into Dhenkanal.[210] However, even this attempt of the PCC 'left' wing was admonished by the 'Mahatma' as a 'mistaken zeal'. His alternative was to help the Dhenkanal people from outside by 'an examination of terrorism'.[211] As a result of this criticism of the role of outsiders in the state the focus shifted to training the state people outside and diverting their energies towards spinning *khadi*.[212] This was followed by a decision of the Congress Working Committee (21 December 1938) which was against this 'interference.[213] In a situation, when the All-India leadership 'failed to move'[214], the *satyagraha* was abandoned and the exodus continued.

This situation lasted till March 1939 when a *dewan* was appointed and the Raja's powers were withdrawn. Some minor concessions were given. It was only after this that the people started returning to the state.[215]

Talcher had collieries and was strategically important for the British. The presence of mines and the railway system meant that there were some workers, some of whom were from 'outside'.[216] It had close geographical proximity to the citadel of feudal oppression—Dhenkanal. The situation, as well as the time-frame of the Talcher people's movement, roughly coincided with that of Dhenkanal. The politics of opposition to the established order began around January 1938 with a students' strike. In an attempt to promote the sales of a cloth store owned by the Raja's brother, *khaki* dress was made compulsory for the students. When they protested against this, some of them were rusticated from the school.[217]

The Prajamandal was formed on 6 September 1938 in Kosala (Angul). The Prajamandal's demands included the right to form associations, hold meetings, the abolition of *bethi*, *magan* and *vethi*, modification of tenancy and forest laws and better working conditions in the collieries.[218] Consequently, its support base included the microscopic work force in the state. When the Prajamandal presented this list of demands to the Raja, he struck back by banning the Prajamandal since it was 'revolutionary' and ordering repressive measures to counter it.[219]

About 10,000 people of Talcher assembled at Kosala (Angul) on 16 September 1938 and resolved to struggle till their demands were accepted. A local Congressman (member of the legistature) addressed them and asked them to remain 'peaceful' and get recruited as Congress members.[220]

The Prajamandal decided to boycott the Raja and directed the people not to offer *bethi* or pay customary feudal dues and taxes and to violate the forest as well as other oppressive laws. Along with this they were asked not to recognise the British and the state authorities,[221] implying a non-recognition of the two levels of authority. This anti-imperialist and anti-feudal link-up perhaps resulted from two factors mentioned earlier: the physical presence of colonialism in the state and the arrival of the British army at Dhenkanal on 20 September.

A training camp for Prajamandal activists was set up at Panigola (Angul). However, even at this stage the faith of the people in the Raja had not been shaken. They looked forward to the Dussehra Day (4 October) when the *durbar* had traditionally announced concessions. Since no concessions were announced, the illusion about the Raja ended and the Prajamandal decided to launch a *satyagraha*. Volunteers from the training camp were sent over to Talcher and within two months about 1,400 of them had crossed into the state to campaign for the Prajamandal's demands and to implement its action-oriented *satyagraha*. The Prajamandal also set up small shops to sell commodities which were declared to be under the monopoly system.[222]

The durbar seems to have timed its repression after the British troops

had reached Dhenkanal on 20 September. Arrests, rapes, firin ment of crops and destruction of the houses of Prajamandal l activists were carried out to smother the movement. People we on their buttocks and their forearms were tattooed with the wo *haram*'. There are references to the increasing association bet and state-sponsored violence.[223]

By November 1938 the training camp to train volunteers w down. The 'Mahatma's', intervention altered the situation. He a thousand people left the state and resided outside, the British a would be forced to take remedial measures.[224] This was a sig exodus and the people of Talcher crossed over to Angul to counterparts from Dhenkanal. Rumours floated in the cam Talcher refugees that Nehru and the 'Mahatma', as well as th were coming to their camps to help them.[225] This demonstrates of 'saviours' of the Congress with a 'distant authority' in popular in a context of repression, helplessness and desertion by the C

By March 1939 the colonial government intervened to find for the Talcher refugees. Accordingly, the Assistant Politi Major Hannessey was deputed to negotiate a settlement. At th PCC became keen on a settlement negotiated through Ma emerged was the Mahtab-Hannessey Pact which shows how t anxious to tone down as well as compromise the anti-feudal di had developed out of the struggle. For example, this Pact ac recruitment for 'public purposes' on payment of wages. As Pabitra Mohan Pradhan (President of the Prajamandal) it w settlement. It was agreed that if the Raja accepted this refugees would go back.[226]

However, after about a month it was clear that the mood to accept even this agreement to which the colonial g a party. This created a deadlock but given the pressu government forced the Raja to accept some of the majo 1939) like the abolition of *bethi*, customary dues, religio right to kill animals destroying crops.[227] In another majo 'Mahatma' announced on 2 June 1939 that the civil disob should be suspended indefinitely, that demands should that the stress should be on negotiations.[228] With this, full circle and the Prajamandal called to the people t Thus the 'Mahatma's' intervention decided the co adopted and demonstrated how the struggle against the colonialism and feudalism—had been compromise

with food and shelter and by joining them. The *durbar* tried to prevent this procession from reaching the capital and tried to persuade Miśra to call it off with an assurance that the Prajamandal's demands would be accepted.[232]

When the procession reached Ranpur Garh it had swelled to 10,000 people. The state authorities were quite shaken. Not only were the prisoners released but the processionists were given lunch by the Raja. Around 4.30 p.m. when lunch was over the Prajamandal had already been recognised.[233]

The Prajamandal held a huge meeting and reiterated its demands: recognition of civil, democratic and social rights, the abolition of *bethi* and customary feudal levies. An analysis of these demands makes it clear that the Prajamandal's base included tribals as well as out-castes like Hadis and Dombs. At Sunakhela 8 to 10 prominent Prajamandal activists were tribals.[234]

The *durbar* made a determined effort subsequently to deal directly with the people and in a proclamation every *mauza* was asked to send two of their representatives to a meeting scheduled for 25 November 1938. The Prajamandal also campaigned for this and asked the people to send their representatives and to attend this meeting. Accordingly, a huge gathering waited on the fixed date but the *durbar* did not send anyone. The colonial administration had succeeded in disrupting the proposed meeting and through its intervention had convinced the Raja to cancel the meeting as it would mean a victory of the Prajamandal and enhance its credibility. The experience with the popular movements in the states had made the colonial administration harden its stand.[235]

In this context, on 29 December 1938 the Prajamandal organised a meeting at Sunakhela. At this meeting Banamali Ram criticised the *durbar* and reiterated the demands. It decided to send out processions and organise demonstrations in the capital till the demands were met. What followed was ruthless repression aimed to smother the popular movement, beginning in January 1939. The Prajamandal was declared unlawful; arrests, searches, lootings and the destruction of Prajamandal offices were to force its leadership to go underground.[236] Krupasindhu Misra was arrested and this angered the people who decided to march to the capital. Malua tribals and women too participated in this march. A rumour circulated that Misra and other activists would be removed from the state and that they would even be killed. To prevent the removal of the Prajamandal activists the people blocked all the roads to the capital with trees.[237]

On 5 January 1939 the Political Agent of Orissa, Bazellgate, went over to Ranpur Garh. On his way he asked some peasants to clear the road at village Lodhachua but since there was a directive from the Prajamandal to keep the roads blocked these people refused. They were badly beaten and injured for this and people from the neighbouring areas rushed to their help, put them on a bullock-cart and took them to Tangi for treatment. The Political Agent reached the capital and found a huge gathering.[238] The police report reveals the predominance of agricultural castes (appx. 14), the presence of Brahmins and Karanas (35) as well as some professional castes among the 104 people arrested. They also included a few tribals (3), an outcaste and a Muslim. This can be, perhaps, taken as a rough index of the social composition of the gathering which included people of different social strata.[239]

Soon after Bazellgate's arrival the bullock-cart also reached the Garh on its way to Tangi. A rumour circulated that Bazellgate had killed two people. As Bazellgate moved to the bullock-cart to examine the two bodies the people surrounded him. A person who struck terror in the 'dark zones' was in a state of panic, perhaps for the first time in his life. He fired from his service revolver killing one person on the spot. After this Bazellgate was disarmed and beaten to death.[240]

Bazellgate's death created a serious crisis. Throughout the phase of the popular movements in the states various methods had been adopted to provoke the people to violence by the *durbars*.[241] The PCC (including the Socialists and the Communists) as well as the OSPC had managed to keep these movements 'acceptable' to the Gandhian framework. The people had faced ruthless terror and death 'non-violently'. However, with the death of Bazellgate the 'violence/non-violence' debate raised its head again and in fact manifested itself as another Chauri Chaura. The PCC as well as the Congress leadership took this as the signal for retreat. While Mahtab called for a suspension of mass movements in the states, the Secretary of the OSPC, Sarangadhar Das, called for halting mass movements for direct action. Thus, the 'dead' Bazellgate could achieve what the 'living' one had not. Along with the Congress retreat the colonial administration sent 1200 soldiers from the army to Orissa in order to strengthen the coercive apparatus.[242] In this context, the Prajamandal could not think of any militant course of action.

The position of the Congress and its retreat after Bazellgate's death and the presence of troops created an atmosphere of terror which climaxed with the massacre of 32 unarmed tribals at Gangpur on 28 April 1939. Those who had rebelled were Mundas who had been converted to Christianity around the 1880's.[243] In the absence of a Prajamandal, Christianity became a source of strength for the Mundas to fight their oppressors. This reflects the changing nature of Christianity and its association with a struggle against oppression as well as its role as an instrument of solidarity. The way in which Christianity, which was a product of the west, came to become a rallying point to fight both internal and external exploitation suggests an obvious transformation or even a possible inversion of its fundamentals. After all, in the remote state of Gangpur a social historian would expect it to be an instrument of legitimisation of both colonialism and the structure of internal exploitation. That the Mundas sought to set things right in this world through Christianity is both representative of this changing nature of Christianity as well as the dynamism of popular militancy.

There was a campaign for a no-rent movement around January-February 1939 by Nathaniel Munda.[244] The immediate issue centred around the sudden increase in the rate of rent which had been raised by about 100 per cent to 150 per cent over the 1910 Settlement. The Regent Rani had announced some meagre concessions[245] (which were not satisfactory) perhaps to prevent any untoward events as in the other princely states.

Perhaps as 'good Christians' who had partly accepted the hegemony of the colonial administrative apparatus the people submitted a petition to the Rani, the *dewan* and the tahsildar at a meeting on 2 February 1939. This was attended by about 5,000 people from about 30 villages. This petition, besides wanting the rent structure to remain at the 1910 level, articulated the anti-feudal feelings which had been kindled by Christianity (of the 'native' preachers), the Orissa States Enquiry Committee and contacts with the anti-imperialist and anti-feudal movements in the province as well as the princely states. It included the abolition of *bethi*, customary levies, restriction on land transfers, forests and forest products, the right to use roads, irrigation and employment facilities and the freedom to buy and sell (since this was the only state which levied an income tax). Since the state kept quiet about this petition, the tribals appealed to the Viceroy—the 'good' Christian—which failed to produce any result.[246]

It was only after these developments that a no-rent movement developed in the state. Out of a population of 60,000 Mundas there were 17,000 Lutheran and the rest were Roman Catholics. What needs to be pointed out is that only the Lutheran Mundas rebelled. It is quite possible that they were translating into action the plebianised version of Christianity as preached by their 'native' preachers, in line with their own perceptions, since our evidence indicates that the Lutheran mission was initially indifferent to things. In sharp contrast, the Roman Catholic Church of the state considered the hike in rent to be reasonable. In fact, it felt that this would be 'beneficial' for the people in the long run as it would force the cultivators to work their lands better. Its hold over its following seems to have been quite strong since it seems to have accepted the position of the Catholic establishment.[247] .

By the end of March 1939 the no-rent movement was launched. Nearly 5,000 Lutheran Mundas refused to pay the second *kist* to the *durbar*. The rest of the Lutheran and the Catholic Mundas continued to petition against the Settlement. As the no-rent movement gathered momentum there was a shift in the position of the Lutheran establishment—from indifference to anxiety. However, its 'holy' intervention proved to be ineffective. Its following seems to have been influenced by two Munda pleaders of Ranchi and the 'native' preachers, and this reflects the complexities of tribal and urban linkages as well as the popular interpretation of Christianity by the 'native' preachers.[248]

In its anxiety the *durbar* approached the Lutheran Church Council (Ranchi) to send a deputation to Gangpur to show the rebellious Mundas that the path of the *durbar* was correct. The deputation reached Gangpur around the beginning of April 1939 but failed to achieve the desired results. The Secretary of the Church, in fact, advised the *Dewan* that only strong action would make the Mundas 'see reason'.[249]

The *durbar*, the colonial administration and the Church establishment viewed the situation seriously, for Ranpur had opened their eyes. On 25 April about 90 troops and 60 state policemen led by the Assistant Political Agent went over to village Sikmo, a mile and a half away from the village of the 'rebellious' Mundas. The state police were ordered to advance and arrest Nirmal Munda for assaulting a chaukidar. At the arrival of the police, the Mundas collected together and refused to surrender Nirmal.[250]

At this point the Assistant Political Agent addressed the gathering of about 800 people who were asked to keep away their *lathis*, bows and arrows and proceed to a nearby maidan for a meeting to discuss their grievances. The Mundas agreed to this proposal and reached the maidan. Here they were surrounded by the military and policemen and were asked to surrender Nirmal. The tribals refused to be cowed down by threats of firing and one man exposed his chest saying, 'Let us see how you will shoot us'. At this point a gunshot was heard and one of the villagers hit the Assistant Political Agent with a stick. After this a firing was ordered which left 32 dead and 19 injured.[251] The leaders were arrested and the movement smashed in a context of its relative isolation from other movements in the states and the Province, the atmosphere of repression (especially from about September 1939) and the retreat of the Congress.

In July 1939 the much publicised report of the *Orissa States Enquiry Committee* was published. It hardly offered anything new and clearly compromised with landlordism. It advocated that the treaties (*sanads*) with states should be cancelled and they should be treated as permanently settled estates 'without doing any violence to the rights of the Chiefs'. It suggested certain controls on their privy purse and the shifting of the states to the jurisdiction of the Orissa province. It wanted the preservation of the states and reinforced the 'Mahatma's', position that activities such as freedom to enter the states by outsiders and those connected with civil liberty and freedom of association were all right 'so long as . . . (these) are not directed towards the destruction of the states'.[252] This Report came out in a context in which the popular movements in the states had already declined.

III

Conclusion

In conclusion it can be said that this phase was marked by a combination of the anti-imperialist and anti-feudal currents in Orissa.[253] From a position of a non-entity in the princely states and the Jeypur zamindari, the PCC became organisationally established, expanding/consolidating its social base. Besides, one cannot miss the undermining of the hegemony of both colonialism and the feudal order. This is corroborated by the emergence of the peasants and tribals as a significant political force. This is also visible in the politics of the Kisan Sangha, the Prajamandal movement and the developments seen in the Jeypur zamindari. In fact, as already observed, the sweep of the peasant movement created a polarisation within the PCC and contributed significantly to the development of a Socialist trend and the birth of the Communist Party in Orissa. And, needless to say, by stirring the middle class intellectuals the peasant movement narrowed the gulf between them and the common people.

A new feature of this phase was the emergence of powerful movements in some of the princely states. Any generalisation locating this as a shift of the dominant peasant leaders towards the Congress[254] can be misleading in the light of our discussion, if one keeps Nilgiri in mind, and, as long as the focus is not only on the leadership. Besides undermining the authority of the rulers these movements had a distinct anti-imperialist edge, and demonstrated to the states' people how their rajas and the British were one when it came to facing the Prajamandal movement.

These struggles also undermined the hierarchies (caste, class and tribal/non-tribal) which had been sought to be carefully preserved in the princely states. The relationship between the PCC and the states' people shifted from that of 'non- intervention'[255] to taking a back seat when the movements began, and, then to try to enforce a settlement as soon as it was possible.[256] Our discussion illustrates that the states' people needed the Congress as much as the Congress needed them. This—coupled with the fact that the colonial power and the princes accepted the Congress as a representative of the states' people—gave the Congress the necessary legitimacy to negotiate.

And, all these features we have discussed so far led to the consolidation of the depth of the national movement in Orissa. Nevertheless, this co-existed with a virtual retreat of women from it. The space offered to women during the Civil Disobedience Movement seems to have been visibly altered in this phase. Women figured primarily as victims of terror/refugees from the princely states. Their participation in the leadership of the Kisan Sangha (Malati Chaudhury) or in the Legislature (Sarala Devi) was only a token one. Thus, they remained outside the mainstream of the mass movements which was no longer perceived as an acceptable sphere of women's participation. This loss of space for women was marked by a continuity in the succeeding phases, and reflects a shift backwards.

This phase also demonstrates the shifting position of the PCC. We have seen how its anti-zamindari position[257] changed once the elections were over. Besides matching with the all India position of the Congress, it was also related to the shifting position of the landlords—i.e. from that of antagonism *vis-a-vis* the Congress, to that of accepting its crucial role as a bulwark against the sweep of the peasant movement.

Seen in its totality, the PCC struck compromises and retreated in the face of movements. Its position *vis-a-vis* zamindari abolition and the struggle in the princely states illustrates this point most unambiguously. In this sense the PCC's logic seems to have been to associate itself with movements, or, as in the case of the princely states, enter the arena (after maintaining an ambiguous silence) when movements had already developed, strike compromises and then retreat.

However, it might well be asked, how could the PCC do all this and yet increase its popularity? This riddle cannot be solved only by locating the manoeuvres of the PCC, or its ability to regulate and demobilise the peasant movement. It is here that we have to turn to popular perceptions which identified the Congress as an instrument of struggle, and the way the Congress appealed to popular imagination by accommodating a wide variety of concepts and beliefs ranging from what was located as *swaraj* or the desire to gain respectability by being associated with the Congress, to the complexities associated with the Hinduisation of tribals. And, after the elections this process was also accompanied by the expectations from 'our ministry' which would solve various problems. And, given all this, one can perhaps explain how the PCC reaped the harvest of the movements in this phase, in spite of its compromises and retreats. Consequently, the consolidation of the depth of the national movement coexisted with the hegemonisation of the peasants and tribals by the Congress.

One can, however, end by adding that this process was marked by an unevenness. One can cite here the case of the Nilgiri Prajamandal. Here the Prajamandal included the Communists who were at the forefront of the struggle and whose intervention meant the combination of class struggle with anti-imperialism. This created an alternative to Congress politics, especially after the authority of the *durbar* had been undermined through a powerful movement. The consolidation of the social base of the Communists caused a serious concern to the Congress—something that we shall return to subsequently.

Notes

1. Gandhi visited Orissa in 1934. I was told that Bhaigabati Charan Pannigrahi could not reconcile himself to the Gandhian 'retreats' and 'compromises'. Interview: Kalindi Charan Pannigrahi (Cuttack, June 1981), the elder brother of Bhagabati.
2. Surendranath Dwivedy, *Quest for Socialism: Fifty Years of Struggle in India* (New Delhi, 1984), pp. 29-30.
3. *Ibid,* p. 59.
4. Home Political 18/10/1933 (National Archives, New Delhi), hereafter HP It may be added here that Mahtab was also involved in the Harijan uplift programme and as mentioned by him in *Sadhanara Pathe* (Oriya; Cuttack, 1972) p. 154, he kept a Harijan servant, after his father's death, in line with this programme.
5. Indulal Yajnik Paper, Subject file 14, p. 2 (hereafter, IYSF 14), Nehru Memorial Museum and Library, Private Papers Section (New Delhi). This was a report on the Utkal Kisan Sangha, drafted around mid-1939.
6. *Sarathi,* 19 March 1934.
7. IYSF 14, *op.cit.,* p. 2.
8. *Ibid,* p. 3.
9. S.N. Dwivedy, *op.cit.,* p. 52.
10. This narrowing down of the gulf was an extremely important facet. IYSF 14 p. 3 mentions the role of *Sarathi* for preparing the ideological background to work with the peasants.
11. *Ibid,* p. 5.
12. *Ibid,* p. 3.
13. Accession No. 33 (hereafter Acc. No.), Special Branch Police Reports, Orissa State Archives, Bhubaneshwar, p.2.
14. M.A. Rasul, *A History of the All India Kisan Sabha* (Calcutta, 1974), pp. 4-5.
15. Mahtab, *op.cit.,* p. 176, mentions that it was mostly the Socialists who worked seriously for the PCC.
16. Dwivedy, *op.cit.,* pp. 65-6.
17. Acc. No. 33, *op.cit.,* pp. 1-14.
18. Dwivedy, *op.cit.,* p.68.
19. Acc. No. 33, *op.cit.,* pp. 14-45.
20. *Ibid,* p. 22.
21. Dwivedy *op.cit.,* p. 69.
22. HP 18/10/1936 and P.N. Chopra (ed.), *Towards Freedom 1937-47* (New Delhi, 1985) from Hubback to Linlithgow, 1 February 1937, pp. 81-4.
23. IYSF 7. In fact, the PCC's agrarian manifesto was the most radical one; interview: Sarat Pattnaik (Cuttack, December 1980).
24. Acc. No. 33, *op.cit.,* p. 25. Although we do not know exact details of the United Party, the National Party was born in September 1936; HP 18/10/

1936.

25. Bipan Chandra, 'Jawaharlal Nehru and the Indian Capitalist Class, 1936' *Economic and Political Weekly*, Vol.X, August 1975, sees this period as the most radical phase of Nehru.
26. HP file No, 4/38.36 gives us an insight into Nehru's tour. Besides asking people to vote for the Congress, Nehru launched a frontal attack on both imperialism and feudalism.
27. *Ibid.* In fact, this seems to have surprised the colonial authorities.
28. IYSF 14, *op.cit.*, pp. 4-5; Acc No. 33, *op.cit.*, p. 35-36.
29. HP 18/11/1936.
30. S.N. Mozumdar, *Report on the General Elections in Orissa-1937* (Cuttack, 1937), pp. 14-16.
31. *Ibid.*
32. *Ibid.* p. 15.
33. HP 18/2/1937; this happened in the Jeypur zamindari.
34. Chopra (ed.), *op.cit.*, pp. 81-4.
35. Mozumdar, *op.cit.*, pp. 14-15, HP 18/1/1937; 18/2/1937; Chopra (ed.), *op.cit.*, pp. 81-4.
36. Mozumdar, *op.cit.*, p. 14. In fact, 32 of the defeated candidates forfeited their deposits; *ibid.* p.31.
37. All India Congress Committee, Private Papers Section, Nehru Memorial Museum and Library (New Delhi), pp. 21-2, part III, 1937, Mahtab to Kriplani, 15/2/1937; thus, even someone like Mahtab was looked upon suspiciously.
38. *Congress Socialist*, 20 March, 1937.
39. HP 18/1/1937; 18/2/1937; thus, the tribals of the Jeypur zamindari stopped paying the plough tax; Acc. No. 33, 34, shows a great deal of enthusiasm to get recruited as Congress members.
40. Chopra (ed.), *op.cit.*, Linlithgow to Hubback, p. 137-38; Linlithgow to Zetland, pp. 139-40, Linlithgow to Zetland, pp. 99-104; Hubback to Linlithgow, pp. 81-4; HP 18/3/1937.
41. Linlithgow papers, microfilm, NMML, Provincial Reports, Vol.II, Accession No. 1166 Hubback to Linlithgow, 16 May 1937; Hubback expressed this feeling, and it obviously had a basis.
42. HP 18/4/1937.
43. *Congress Socialist*, 14 May, 1937.
44. Acc. No. 34 *op.cit.*, pp.64, 67.
45. *Ibid*, p. 68.
46. HP 18/5/1937; Linlithgow papers, microfilm, *op.cit.*, Hubback to Linlithgow, 18 June 1937.
47. IYSF 14 *op.cit.*, p. 6; Acc. No. 34, p. 69; Linlithgow, microfilm, 16 May 1937 op.cit.; *Congress Socialist* 14 May, 1937; 5 June, 1937.
48. Mahtab, *op.cit.*, p. 166.
49. Acc. No. 34, *op.cit.*, pp. 54-64.

50. IYSF 14, p. 6.
51. *Congress Socialist*, 5 June, 1937.
52. For example, Acc.No.34, p. 54, mentions of how the Kisan Sangha convinced the Lok Sabha of Delang (Puri) to identify itself with the Sangha, instead of trying to redress grievances of peasants constitutionally as planned by the Sabha.
53. *Report on the Land Revenue Administration of the District of North Orissa for the Year 1936-37* (Cuttack, 1938), pp. 8, 11.
54. Acc.No.34, pp. 65-66; although details are unfortunately not articulated.
55. *Krushak*, 20 January, 1938; the violation of pledges secured by the peasants we have noted, is extremely significant.
56. Acc. No. 34, p. 65; this was a proposal of the Puri Kisan Sangha in May 1937.
57. HP 18/1/1938.
58. Acc. No. 34, p. 71.
59. This was released through the press around the beginning of July, 1938; Acc. No. 34, p. 73.
60. Acc. No. 34; p. 79; B.Das made this statement at a gathering of five thousand people in the Puri town in early August 1937.
61. Acc.No. 34, p. 74.
62. Acc. No.29, p.3; this trend can be observed from about August 1937.
63. *Congress Socialist*, 6 August 1937.
64. IYSF 14, p. 7; *Congress Socialist*, 17 September 1937; Acc. No. 29, pp. 5-6; HP 18/9/1937.
65. *Ibid.*
66. Acc. No. 29, *op.cit.*, pp. 5-6.
67. *Congress Socialist*, 17 September 1937; HP 18/9/1937.
68. *Congress Socialist*, 17 September 1937; Acc.No.29, p.8.
69. IYSF 14, p. 7; Acc. No.29, p. 8, 29; this is clearly visible between September and November 1937.
70. *Indian Annual Register, 1937*, pp.265-68; hereafter *IAR*.
71. K.M. Patra, *Orissa Legislature and Freedom Struggle 1912-47* (New Delhi, 1979), pp. 118-19.
72. Valmiki Choudhary (ed.), *Dr. Rajendra Prasad: Correspondence and Select Documents*, Vol.I (New Delhi, 1984), pp. 86-7.
73. Interestingly, we may add here that the Congress had supported a ministerial crisis over the appointment of Mr. Dain in the absence of the Governor in May 1937 (during the minority ministry period) and the central leadership also supported such a policy; Patra, *op.cit.*, p. 112.
74. *Congress Socialist*, 22 July 1938.
75. *IAR 1938*, p. 351.
76. Patra, *op.cit.*, p. 125.
77. *Orissa Legislative Assembly Proceedings vol. II, Part I, 1938* (Cuttack, 1938) p. 901; hereafter *OLAP*.

78. Acc. No. 29, p. 17.
79. *OLAP, Vol. II, Part.II*, pp. 938, 1230.
80. *Congress Socialist*, 26 November, 1937.
81. IYSF 14, *op.cit.*, 7; *IAR*, 1938 p. 351. The Orissa Tenancy Amendment Bill was enforced on 1 November 1938.
82. IYSF 14, *op.cit.*, p. 7.
83. Patra, *op.cit.*, pp. 131-34.
84. IYSF 14, *op.cit.*, p.11.
85. Chopra (ed.), *op.cit.*, pp. 1194-95, Nehru to Pant (25 November 1937) reflects on the general nature of this problem. As felt by Nehru: 'I am greatly distressed at the turn of events.... If I may put it in technical language, the Congress ministries are tending to become counter-revolutionary'.
86. HP 18/10/1937; Acc. 29 p. 30 (17 November 1937).
87. Acc.No. 29, *op.cit.*, p. 20 (5 october 1937).
88. HP 18/12/1937.
89. Rajendra Prasad Private Papers, microfilm, roll no. 5, NMML; (hereafter, R.P.) in response to Nityananda Kanungo (Minister of Revenue and Public Works, Orissa) to Prasad - 6 December 1937, Prasad suggested Nilakantha Das' name - 11/12/1937.
90. Linlithgow, microfilm, *op.cit.*, August-December 1938, from Raja of Khallikote to Prasad (7 August, 1938).
91. *Amrita Bazar Patrika*, 14 January 1938.
92. R.P. *op.cit.*, Biswanath Das to Prasad, 12 December, 1937. Thus, rents had been assessed as high as Rs. 12 to Rs. 18 per acre and Das was conscious of the fact that this was a wrong thing since, it 'was one of our election pledges that we give them (peasants) relief'.
93. H.P. 18/12/1937 - Biswanath Das' statement; Rajkrishna Bose at a meeting (Mahanga, 28 November 1937) also expressed a similar position, and focused on the 'middlemen'.
94. *Krushak*, 13 January, 1938.
95. Acc. No. 29, *op.cit.*, p. 34.
96. *Ibid, op.cit.*, p. 29 (17 November, 1937).
97. *Krushak*, 13, 20, 27 January 1938.
98. IYSF 14, *op.cit.*, p. 10, mentions how the Kisan Sangha was not allowed to develop in Jeypur and Ganjam; Acc. No. 29, p. 16 (7 October, 1937), R.K. Biswasroy visited different areas in the Jeypur estate and advised the people not to pay taxes till the crops were cut.
99. Acc. No. 29, *op.cit.*, p. 32 (27 November 1937); HP, 18/9/1937; *Krushak* January 13, 1938.
100. Acc. No. 29, *op.cit.*, pp. 17-18; HP 18/10/1937.
101. HP 18/12/1937.
102. IYSF 14, *op.cit.*, p., Acc 8 .No. 29, *op.cit.*, p. 13 (September 27, 1937), p. 25 (3 November, 1937); p. 35 (3 December 1937).

103. *Dr. Rajendra Prasad: Correspondence..., op.cit.*, Vol. II, pp. 233-39, from Godavaris Misra to Prasad (24 March 1938).
104. HP 18/12/1937; Acc.No. 29, *op.cit.*, p. 21 (27 October 1937) p.p 27-8 (10 November, 1937), IYSF 14, *op.cit.*, p. 8.
105. HP 18/11/1937 and 'Communist Conspiracy Against the Congress Socialist Party', 9 May 1938, 49-C (1938) at the P.C. Joshi Memorial Archives (New Delhi) point to a tension within the 'left' wing itself, especially centered around the 'slide back' of Nabakrushna Chaudhury who was viewed as a 'reactionary' by some.
106. Mahtab, *Sadhanara..., op.cit.*, p. 166.
107. *Dr. Rajendra Prasad: Correspondence..., op.cit.*, Vol. II, p. 5, Mahtab to Prasad, 24 January, 1938.
108. HP 18/2/1938.
109. HP 18/4/1938.
110. *Ibid.*; Acc. No. 30 (6 April, 1938).
111. *National Front*, 24 April, 1938. In fact, P.C. Joshi pointed to this serious omission.
112. HP 18/3/1938; Acc .No.38 -April, May 1938; *Krushak*, 20 January 1938, locates peasant militancy of Tirtol to have been precipitated as a result of a landlord beating a peasant at Govindpur (Tirtol); *Congress Socialist*, 18 March, 1938.
113. *Report on the Land Revenue..., op.cit.*, 1937-38 (Cuttack, 1939), pp.9-10.
114. *Krushak*, 19 February, 1938, pointed to this in its editorial.
115. For example, HP 18/7/1938, reported Biswanath Das addressing a large gathering at Jenapur (Cuttack district) on 14 July where he deprecated the use of slogans like 'Destruction to the Zamindari System' as well as the 'violence' of the Kisan Sangha, and advised peasants to pay their due to the landlords.
116. IYSF 14, *op.cit.*, p.11, mentioned: 'The Kisans of these parts now look upon the ministry for delivering them some boon. They are forgetting their task of fighting their enemy. The enemy has made room for their own Minister. The enemy no longer appears before them. They are now face to face with their own Ministry whom they must not fight but always ask for favours'. As can be seen, this hegemonisation implied a dampening of the anti-imperialist struggle as well.
117. This happened from about June 1938. We shall discuss details in the course of this chapter.
118. IYSF 14, *op.cit.*, p. 4; as pointed out: 'The approved list (of members appointed by the top leadership) would be pressed in the Kisan Committee, and carried. Insistence on having the Committee, democratically elected, would mean disruption'.
119. *Report on the Land Revenue....,op.cit.*, 1938-39 (Cuttack, 1940), p. 7.
120. *Report on..., Ibid*, 1937-38, pp. 9-10.
121. *Krushak*, 20 January, 1938.

122. HP 18/7/1938.
123. *IAR* 1942, p. 194.
124. *Ibid.*
125. HP 4/13/1938.
126. HP 18/10/1938.
127. HP 18/6/1938.
128. HP 4/13/1938; HP 18/11/1938.
129. B.Singh Deo, *The Goti System in Jeypur Agency* (Jeypur, 1938) p. 7. Unfortunately, I have not been able to locate his paper on *bethi.*
130. HP 18/11/1938; HP 4/13/1938; Interview: Damodar Samantarai (Jeypur, June 1981).
131. S. Sanganna, 'Revolts in Orissa - Martyr Laxman Naik: A Hero of the Freedom Movement'; in V. Raghvaiah (ed.), *Tribal Revolts* (Nellore, 1971), p. 249.
132. HP, 18/1/1939; 18/2/1939; 18/4/1939; Acc.No. 38, February, June, 1939.
133. Mahtab *et.al., Report of the Orissa State's Enquiry Committee* (Cuttack, 1939), p. 59, recommended that the princely states should be converted to permanently-settled estates without violating the rights of the chiefs, thereby indicating the new position.
134. IYSF 14, *op.cit.,* pp.4-5.
135. *IAR*, 1939, p. 405.
136. HP 18/4/1939; 18/5/1939; Acc.No.38, 10 February 1939, 22 May 1939.
137. HP 18/4/1939.
138. HP 18/6/1939.
139. *National Front*, 27 August, 1939; Acc.No. 38, 22 September 1939; HP 18/10/1939.
140. *Report on the Land Revenue...*, 1939 *op.cit.,* (Cuttack, 1940), pp. 7-8.
141. Acc. No. 38, 8 April, 1939.
142. HP 18/8/1939; 18/9/1939.
143. HP 18/10/1939.
144. *National Front*, 12 February, 1939.
145. *Ibid,* 25 December 1939. The Congress Ministry resigned on 4 November 1939.
146. HP 18/11/1939; 18/12/1939; Acc.No.38, 8 November 1939.
147. See H.K.Mahtab, *et.al* (eds.) *Report of the Orissa State's Enquiry Committee* (Cuttack, 1939), especially pp. 18-23; Nilgiri Prajamandal History Compilation Committee, *Nilgiri Praja Andolanara Itihas* (Oriya; Balasore, 1981), pp. 46-59; (Oriya; Cuttack 1986), pp. 99-103; and Krupa Sindhu Biswal, *Saheed Raghu-Dibakara* (Oriya; Cuttack, 1982), pp. 7-15; R.K. Ramdhyani, *Report on Land Tenures and the Revenue System of the Orissa and Chattisgarh States Vol.I-III* (Berhampur, ?), pp. 95-96.
148. All India Congress Committee (hereafter AICC) Papers, file G-27, 1934, Private Papers Section, NMML, New Delhi; Gandhi to Kelkar (President, AISPC) July 1934.

149. Dwivedy, *op.cit.*, p. 61.
150. Correspondence of Sarangadhar Das, NMML, file No. 127.
151. AICC file No. G-35, Part I, 1938; Statement of Sarangadhar Das (27.11.1938).
152. *Ibid.*
153. Ramchandra Ram, *op.cit.*, pp. 100-101, mentions how every educated person in the Ranpur state was an enemy of the Raja and how the Raja was a bit wary of such people.
154. Linlithgow, Private Papers (NMML) Acc. No. 1060, microfilm from Zetland to Linlithgow (8 November 1938); this will become clear once we go over to discuss the movements and the demands of the Prajamandal.
155. *Nilgiri Praja Andolana Ra Itihasa* (hereafter, *NPARI*), *op.cit.*, p. 69; appendix pp. 26-28.
156. *Ibid.*, p. 64; *Krushak*, 3.1.1938.
157. AISPC Nilgiri file no. 124 (NMML) 1938-40, 16 May, 1938.
158. *National Front*, 19 June, 1938; *Krushak* was banned from 23 May, 1938; HP 4/4/1938 (NAI); *NPARI*, *op.cit.*, p. 74.
159. *NPARI* appendix, pp. 52-55.
160. Interview: Banamali Das (Nilgiri, May 1982).
161. AISPC file no. 124, *op.cit.*, analysis of L.M. Sahu 6 September 1938.
162. *NPARI*, *op.cit.*, pp. 71-72.
163. Interview: Banamali Das; Sadasiba Pradhan, *Agrarian and Political Movements: States of Orissa: 1931 to 1949* (New Delhi, 1986) p. 99 mentions wrongly that the majority of these people were aborigines.
164. *NPARI*, *op.cit.*, p. 76.
165. Interview: Banamali Das.
166. *Ibid.*; *NPARI op.cit.*, 78.
167. AISPC correspondence of S.Das, file 127, *op.cit.*, Mahtab to Mehta 15 July, 1938.
168. Interview: B. Das; *Final Report on the Nilgiri Settlement (1917- 1922)* (Berhampur, 1922), p. 23, mentioned: 'Most of them (i.e. tribals) join in Hindu festivals...such as Rath Jatra and are allowed to pull the car of Jagannath'.
169. AISPC file 127, *op.cit.*, S.Das to P. Sitaramayya, 12 July 1938.
170. *Ibid.*; S. Das' statement (undated); 'Nilgiri Ra Aitiha' (in Oriya), *Gyanamruta* (? 1972), p. 57.
171. *Indian Annual Register*, July-December 1938, Vol. II, p. 297; Mahtab *et.al* (eds.) *History of the Freedom Movement in Orissa* (Cuttack, 1957), Vol. IV, p. 17.
172. Interview: B. Das.
173. *NPARI*, op. cit., pp. 87-88.
174. Interview: Das; AISPC file no. 124, resolution of a meeting (26 September, 1938) of the Prajamandal.
175. Mahtab, *Sadhanara Pathe*, *op.cit.*, p. 189.

176. Joshi visited Cuttack and Dhenkanal; HP 7/3/1939 (NAI); Interview: Das.
177. AISPC file no. 124, *op.cit.*, Nilgiri News 28 February 1939.
178. *National Front*, 3 September 1939.
179. AISPC file no. 124, *op.cit.*, 'Statement of the Working Committee', September 1940.
180. Interview: B.Das.
181. AICC, file no. G.35 part I, 1938; S. Das' Statement 27.11.1938; and B.N. Banerjee, *Dhenkanal Unrest - A Review* (Cuttak ?); Interview: Baishnab Pattnaik (Dhenkanal, June 1985); *National Front*, 25 September 1938.
182. S. Das' statement, *op.cit.*,; Interview: B. Pattnaik.
183. Interview: Pattnaik; Sarangadhar Das' Correspondence, AISPC 127, *op.cit.*, Das to Balwantrai Mehta (29 August, 1938), H.K. Mahtab to Mehta (7 July 1938).
184. Interview: B. Pattnaik; *National Front*, 29 January, 1939.
185. Interview: B. Pattnaik.
186. *Ibid.*
187. *Ibid.*
188. S. Das' statement (27 November, 1938), *op.cit.*
189. *Ibid.*
190. *National Front*, 25 September, 1938.
191. IYSF file 14, *op.cit.*, p. 105.
192. Sadasiba Pradhan, *op.cit.*
193. *National Front*, 25 September, 1938.
194. Statement of S. Das (27.11.1938), *op.cit.*, indicates three firings being ordered on 12 September—twice to prevent people from entering Dhenkanal town and once at a gathering at Alasua *hata*, where about 20,000 people were asked to withdraw. They refused and demanded the release of their leaders and firing was ordered. By the evening when Malati Chaudhury appealed to them to remain non-violent some people had felt that all these had happened because they had remained non-violent. By 27 November 1938, 15 people had died and 133 people were injured as a result of these firings; *National Front*, 25 September/20 October 1938; Pradhan *op.cit.*, pp. 106-07.
195. Mahtab, *Sadhanara Pathe*, *op.cit.*, pp. 188-89.
196. *National Front*, 2 October 1938; HP 18/9/1938. We may add here that the Congress Ministry was kept in the dark about this.
197. S. Das' statement (27 November, 1938), *op.cit.*, *National Front* 23 October, 1938; *Congress Socialist*, 16 October, 1938; S. Das correspondence, file no. 127, *op.cit.*, *Orissa States News Bulletin* (Nov. 10 and 18, 1938) Das report (14 December, 1938).
198. *Krushak*, 10 September, 1938.
199. S. Das' statement (27 November 1938), *op. cit.*
200. S. Das' Correspondence, *op.cit.*, 'Our Orissa Letter' (6 January 1939).
201. Banerjee, *op.cit.*, S. Das statement (27 November 1938), *op.cit.*, Interview:

Banamali Das.

202. See for example, Irfan Habib, *Agrarian System of Mughal India* (Bombay 1963), pp. 328-29, where he discusses the flights of the peasantry.
203. IYSF 14, *op.cit.*, pp. 9-10; this *hizrat* was also a feature in Gujarat and is discussed by David Hardiman. *Peasant Nationalists of Gujarat: Kheda District 1917-1934* (New Delhi, 1981).
204. Interview: Baishnab Pattnaik; *National Front*, 29 January, 1939.
205. *National Front*, Ibid.
206. Even Banerjee, *op.cit.*, recognises this, although he was very critical of the movement.
207. S. Das' statement (27 November 1938), *op.cit.*; *National Front*, 30 July, 1939.
208. S. Das' correspondence file no.127, *op.cit.*, report of 18 November, 1938.
209. Acc.No.38 (3 November, 1938), Special Branch (Police) Reports, Orissa State Archives (Bhubaneswar).
210. HP 18/12/1938; *National Front*, 11 December, 1938.
211. Gandhi to Mahtab (12 December, 1938), cited in H.K. Mahtab, *Gandhiji O Orissa* (Oriya; Cuttack 1971), p. 209.
212. S. Das' correspondence, *op.cit.*, Das to Rangildas (29 Dec. 1938); Gandhi to Mahtab (11 November, 1938) in Mahtab, *Gandhiji...*, *op.cit.*, p. 206 expected the refugees to spin *khadi*.
213. Pradhan, *op.cit.*, p. 112.
214. S.Das' correspondence, *op.cit.*, Das to Rangildas, *op.cit.*,
215. *Ibid.*; Das' report (undated); even these were looked upon to be the result of the struggles of the state people.
216. Foreign Political 386 I/1924 (National Archives, New Delhi); *Final Report on the Settlement of the Dhenkaṇal Feudatory State Orissa 1923-24* (Berhampur, 1966), p. 14; *Memoranda on the Indian States 1930* (Calcutta, 1931), p. 234.
217. Pradhan, *op.cit.*, p. 113.
218. AISPC Private Papers, NMML, file no. 164, 'History of the Political Movement in Talcher' written by Pabitramohan Pradhan; *National Front*, 4 June, 1939; Acc. No. 38, *op.cit.*
219. AISPC file no. 164. *op.cit.*
220. Pabitra Mohan Pradhan, *Mukti Pathe Sainika* (Oriya; Cuttack, 1979), p. 61. HP 18/9/1938; AISPC file no. 164 mentions that about another 15,000 people from Pal-Lahara state attended this meeting.
221. Pradhan, *Mukti Pathe...*, *op.cit.*, pp. 65-66.
222. *National Front*, 4 June 1939 Pradhan, *Mukti...*, pp. 66; AISPC file no. 164.
223. Pradhan, *Mukti...*, p. 66; *National Front*, 4 June 1939; AISPC file no. 164, *op.cit.*
224. *Talcher Prajamandalara Itihas* (Oriya; Calcutta, 1950), p. 24-25.
225. Linlithgow Private Papers (microfilm), NMML, Acc. no. 1134 August-December 1938, From Boag to Linlithgow (5 December, 1938); H.P. 18/

6/1939.

226. Pradhan, *Mukti* .., *op.cit.*, pp. 73-81.
227. Sadasiva Pradhan, *op.cit.*, p. 123.
228. *Amrita Bazar Patrika*, 3 June 1939.
229. Ramachandra Ram, *Sangrami* (Oriya; Cuttack, 1986); pp. 99-103; Krupasindhu Biswal, *Saheed Raghu-Dibakara* (Oriya; Cuttack, 1982) pp. 7-15.
230. Ram, *op.cit.*, pp. 104-05.
231. *Ibid*, p. 105.
232. Interview: Krupasindhu Misra (Ranpur, June 1984); Ram, *op.cit.*, p. 105.
233. Interview: Krupasindhu Misra.
234. Ibid; Ram, *op.cit.*, pp. 113-16.
235. Ram, *Ibid*, pp. 117-20; another meeting scheduled for 17 November 1938, also ended in a fiasco.
236. Interview: Krupasindhu Misra; the *durbar* looted around Rs.15,000 from the Kandha-Nayagada office of the Prajamandal; S. Pradhan, *op.cit.*, pp.124-25.
237. S.Pradhan, pp. 124-125; Mahtab, *Sadhanara..*, *op.cit.*, pp. 194-98.
238. *Ibid.p*
239. Ram, *op.cit.*, pp. 134-38.
240. Interview; K.Misra.
241. S.Das' statement (27 November, 1938), *op.cit.*, mentioned how the *durbar* of Dhenkanal incited people, through *khadi*-clad men, to violence.
242. *National Front*, 15 January, 1939; 29 January, 1939.
243. HP 18/3/1939; *National Front*, 18 June, 1939.
244. HP 18/2/1939; 18/3/1939.
246. AICC file no. G12/1937-39; *National Front*, 18 June 1939.
247. HP 18/3/1939.
248. *Ibid.*
249. *National Front*, 18 June 1939.
250. *Ibid.*
251. *Ibid.*
252. Mahtab et.al (eds.), *Report of the Orissa States: Enquiry Committee* (Cuttack, 1939), pp. 57-60.
253. K. Gopalankutty, 'The Task of Transforming the Congress in Malabar, 1934-40', in *Studies in History*, July-December, 1989, also identifies a similar movement developing in Malabar; p. 177. However, his method tends to dichotomise class struggle and the anti- imperialist struggle (see p. 193). This raises a serious theoretical problem. Is is possible to dichotomise anti-imperialism and class struggle, and concentrate on locating primary and secondary structures? Was not a struggle against a moneylender or a landlord also a struggle against the British?
254. This seems to be the general tone of Manor, 'Gandhian Politics and the Challenge to Princely Authority in Mysore' in D.A. Low (ed.), *The*

Congress and the Raj (London, 1977), and Richard Sisson, *The Congress Party in Rajasthan* (Berkeley, 1972).

255. On the face of it the Congress' position, however, had changed by the time of the Haripura Session (1938). As reported: 'The Congress stands for the same political, social and economic freedom in the states as in the rest of India and considers the states as an integral part of India.... Purna Swaraj... is for the whole of India inclusive of the States. *Leader* 10 February 1938.

256. Thus, Robin Jeffrey, 'A Sanctified Label - Congress in Travancore Politics, 1938-48' in Low (ed.), *op.cit.* refers to the state people's 'hope for strong support from outside' which does not seem to have materialized when it came to the Congress in Orissa.

257. In fact, Orissa offers a sharp contrast to other parts, since the PCC's position was quite radical and the zamindars were on the opposite side of the fence during the election. One can cite here Lance Brennan, 'From One Raj to Another: Congress Politics in Rohilkhand, 1930-50' in Low (ed.), *op.cit.*, to explain this point. Thus, Brennan locates the Congress election campaign to be based on a moderate agrarian reform programme and mentions that apart form Moradabad, zamindars were selected as Congress candidates from each district of Rohilkhand; pp. 478-79. Similarly, Bihar offers a sharp contrast since the abolition of the zamindari system did not surface in the Bihar PCC's election manifesto in spite of the strong sweep of the peasant movement; see, for example, Stephen Henningham, *Peasant Movements in Colonial India: North Bihar 1917-1942* (Canberra, 1982), chap. 6.

Chapter IV

The Quit India Movement: The Climax of Popular Protest

The chapter begins by focusing on 1940 and 1941—the efforts to form a Coalition Ministry (which was installed on 24 November 1941), the situation created by the outbreak of the Second World War, colonial policy and the strained communal situation in some areas of the Balasore district (viz. Bhadrak). It deals with the state of the peasant movement and the Prajamandals and explores the activities of the landlords and princes to reassert their position which had been undermined in the 1936-39 phase. It locates the organisational state of the Provincial Congress Committee and the evolution of *satyagraha* of a 'new type' (i.e. 'individual *satyagraha*') in response to popular pressures, especially against the War. Highlighting the intra-regional variations that this restricted mobilisation evoked, it emphasises the unifying effect of wartime pressures. At the same time certain features like communalism, the friction within the Provincial Congress, as well as its efforts to contain the growth of the Kisan Sangha and the Communists presents a contrasting picture of disunity. This co-existence of apparent contradictions needs to be emphasised, given the complexities and shifts of this phase.

This chapter also explores the immediate background of the Quit India Movement (January to August 1942), delineating the way popular perceptions related to its build-up. And, finally, it charts out the Quit India Movement in Orissa—from 8 August 1942, when Gandhi and the Congress passed the Quit India Resolution at Bombay — highlighting in the process the variations, the scope and extent of the movement as well as the social composition of the participants.

Perhaps it will not be far-fetched to identify the Quit India Movement as the most powerful mass movement in colonial India. Its importance lay not only in its reflecting the climax of the anti-British struggle but also in its vision for the future. It was characterised by a broad popular participation as well as by certain currents which questioned the internal contradictions within Indian society — a feature that is often ignored. The Quit India Movement needs to be located, along with other features, within the complexities of popular perceptions.

Conventional and stereotyped approaches tend to focus on the role of the Congress,[1] the 'economic' motivations[2] and the 'spontaneity'[3] and 'violence'[4] associated with the Movement. For the bourgeoisie in free-India the annual rituals of observing its anniversary (which climaxed in 1987 with the politics of soil mixing!) reflects an attempt to draw legitimacy from a struggle with which the entire Congress leadership had a tenuous link, especially in so far as the course of events or the form the Movement assumed was concerned.[5] And this is precisely where regional studies as well as the realm of popular perceptions become important.[6]

I

The Background

We can now begin our discussions on the Quit India Movement by constructing its background. As discussed earlier the Congress ministry in Orissa resigned in November 1939, having lost all hopes of changes in the imperialistic policies. The War had created a new situation which had important consequences for India as well. We have seen how the colonial government had tightened its grip and had come down heavily on the Kisan Sangha in Orissa. This trend continued in the 1940-41 phase as well[7] and climaxed with the Viceroy rejecting the Madras Estates Land (Orissa Amendment) Bill, 1937, in February 1941.[8] There were also attempts by imperialism to shift the pressures on to the peasants and tribals of Orissa through what came to be known as War subscriptions.[9]

The economic pressures on the people increased, as is evident from the observations of colonial administration, the political groups and Oriya newspapers. The problem was two-pronged. At one level the scarcity, which resulted from an ill-conceived plan to export rice out of Orissa, caused a rise in prices. Besides, the scarcity of rice as well as other essential commodities (like kerosene) led to hoardings for profits which reinforced both price rise and scarcity. Given the logic of monopoly restrictions on rice trade in the princely states, the problem was also acute there.[10]

However, the question of increased pressures should not be taken in simplistic or mechanical terms to explain the receptivity to the Quit India Movement in Orissa. What is important here is that the combination of repression and increased burdens had a unifying effect on the people of the Province. The War with all its remoteness and obscurity had a profound impact, for popular perceptions identified it as a thing forced on the people by the British—from the Governor to the *chaukidars*[11]—which added to their miseries.

Along with this, imperialist policy intervened to reinforce communal divisions. Thus, one sees a collaboration between the colonial administration and the Muslim League at Bhadrak[12] — a traditional zone of communal tension.

The discussion of pre-1942 should also take into account the position of the landlords and the state chiefs. One thing that comes out clearly is that the landlords of Orissa took steps to realign the balance in their favour. Their hegemony had been seriously undermined in the earlier phase (as we have seen). Encouraged by imperialism, they launched attacks on the Kisan Sangha. What is interesting is that, given the close identification of the Congress with the Kisan Sangha in Orissa, they also made the former a target of attack. Here we can cite the conference of the landlords of Orissa (February 1940) which was presided over by the zamindar of Kanika. Among other things, it swore to fight any trend which sought to sever India's connections with Britain. The position of the Congress *vis-a-vis* Independence was described as 'unreasonable' and 'uncompromising'. It reiterated its 'loyalty' and 'devotion' to 'His Majesty the King Emperor' and requested the people of Orissa to contribute in every possible way to the War.[13] And, the landed sections were keen to have a coalition ministry.

As for the princely states—especially Nilgiri, Dhenkanal and Talcher, where the popular movements had not been crushed—the *durbars* also attempted to re-establish their authority which had been seriously affected in 1938. There are references to the Nilgiri *durbar* trying to victimise *lakhrajdars* and prosecute people illegally;[14] the resumption of land grants by the Dhenkanal *durbar*;[15] and, the Talcher states' drive to reassert itself through oppression and arrests of Prajamandal activists.[16] It may also be noted here that the Eastern States Rulers Council passed a resolution (July 12 - 13, 1941) recommending that a spitfire aircraft be presented to defend India and that the money for this be raised from the states through subscriptions.[17]

Coming to the Provincial Congress Committee (hereafter PCC) one can, perhaps, say that it was in serious disarray and far from being an organisation capable of leading the Quit India Movement. The PCC's taste of power (1937-39) had made Gandhi an almost abstract entity.[18] However, once outside the corridors of power a shift had began to take place.

The tension within the PCC centered around the differences between the factions led by Nilakantha Das and Godavaris Misra and the 'ex-ministers party'.[19] Indiscipline within the PCC became virtually the order of the day. It ranged from violating the basic principle[20] of staying out of municipal elections, refusal of municipal commissioners to resign from their posts and their open association in several bodies where resolutions were passed supporting the War efforts,[21] to attempts by Nilakantha Das and Godavaris Misra to form a coalition ministry from July 1940. We get references to some members of the Legislative Assembly refusing to resign on being asked to do so by the Congress High Command, for their support of the efforts for the formation of a coalition ministry.[22] This dissidence was difficult to cope with and Gopabandhu Choudhury as well as Hari Har Das expressed their unwillingness to work in order to sort out differences within the PCC.[23]

As the *Samaj* lamented, 'moral ascendancy' and 'sacrifice' had been replaced by 'self-interest' and the 'pursuit of power'. Imperialism legitimised this dissidence within the PCC by installing a coalition ministry headed by the landlord of Parliakhemedi in November 1941. He led a group of ten members, most of whom had broken away from the Congress.[24]

The PCC as well as the AICC High Command had dragged its feet till December 1940. Whereas the PCC's campaign had stressed the need to stay prepared for a fight, and its leaders like Mahtab toured various parts of coastal Orissa,[25] the only concrete activity was to organise marches in rural areas. Here one can cite the march undertaken by Gopanbandhu Choudhury and some other Congressmen from Ganeshwarpur (Cuttack) to Bari (April 1940) where a Congress training camp had been set up. On the way meetings had been organised to explain the political situation to the peasants and to secure their support for the Congress.[26] A *khadi* march was organised from Soro to Jajpur (Cuttack district) in November 1940.[27] The evidence we have also suggests the activisation of the *satyagraha* training camps.[28] Besides, in April 1940, the PCC was reorganised and transformed into a *satyagraha* committee. It began enrolling *satyagrahis* and projecting the Gandhian alternatives of spinning *khadi* and the promotion of constructive work. It also issued three leaflets which focused on the non-cooperation with the War.[29]

However, the general atmosphere continued to be one of uncertainty and a lack of enthusiasm within the PCC, with some Congressmen wanting Gandhi to initiate a Mass Civil Disobedience Movement instead of a *satyagraha*. By October 1940 the PCC circulated its plans for a 'new type' of *satyagraha* which was initiated by Gandhi.[30] The approach marked an attempt to reconcile the existing popular pressures (especially against the War[31]) with the politics of demobilisation, and led to the evolution of the 'individual *satyagraha*'.

The 'individual *satyagraha*' was extremely selective about the participants. It was made adequately clear by the PCC (as well as Mahtab) that no Congressmen was to carry out any propaganda against the War or disobey the law except those *satyagrahis* who were selected by Gandhi.[32]

II

The State of the Peasant Movement (1940)

We can examine how the peasants and tribals of the province interacted with the various processes and begin by focusing on the three coastal districts of Cuttack, Puri and Balasore. What seems clear is the dampening of the peasant movement in comparison with the 1936-39 phase.[33]

The Kisan Sangha's first important task was the observance of 'Independence Day' celebration of 26 January 1940. The idea was to link this celebration with Kisan rallies and the student movement. This was accompanied by drastic efforts made by the PCC to increase its influence (especially in Balasore). The militant peasants of the coastal tract responded favourably to these moves and a number of peasant meetings were arranged which attracted between 300 to 1000 people. The central focus at these meetings was on anti-imperialism with references to the resignation of the Congress Ministry and the Viceroy's role in blocking the Madras Estates Land (Orissa Amendment) Bill, 1937.[34]

Around this time the All India Kisan Sabha had its 5th session at Palasa (Andhra Pradesh) between 23 and 27 March. Although held in an atmosphere of repression with the President-elect, this Palasa session attracted the Oriya press to a large extent. Orissa was represented by Sachidananda Routroy.[35] His evolution—as a person who was from a Congress family background and who demonstrated excellent literary sensibilities, to an activist in the left-wing student movement, the Prajamandal movement and the peasant movement—reflects the thinning down of the gulf between the intellectual and the peasant.

It was after the Palasa session that the Kisan Sangha began planning for a no-rent campaign as a possible alternative to the Congress' *satyagraha* and constructive programme. Its position attracted some members of the Servants of India Society (like Shyam Sundar Misra and Laxminarayan Sahoo)[36] and this, perhaps, demonstrates the feeling of some Congressmen for a more militant course of struggle which the Kisan Sangha advocated. The Kisan Sangha set up schools in some areas to politicise the peasantry.[37] However, these activities received a setback due to the floods of July 1940 which ravaged the districts of Cuttack and Balasore, and the arrest of some Communists who worked for the Kisan Sangha.[38] The Kisan Sangha observed the Kisan Day (September 1, 1940). The central focus was to criticise the British War policy, especially War recruitment and the fund collection drive.[39]

There was an absence of serious conflicts in the government estates. This perhaps matches with the overall decline of the anti-imperialist struggle and reflects on the role of intermediary agencies of control created by the colonial administration. However, the pressure of the peasant movement led to tension between the landlords and peasants of Kanika, Aul and Dompara. The district of Puri seems to have emerged as a centre of the peasant movement. There are references to smaller landlords (i.e. Mahiprakash Math, Sankarananda Math and Samadhi Math) trying to reassert their position which had been undermined in the 1936-39 phase. There was tension between the peasants of Erbang and the Mohunt of Neuldas Math. That the 1936-39 phase had drastically altered peasant consciousness was reflected in the friction between the 'mobile Vishnu'—the Raja of Puri—and his peasants, which was centered around the levy of mutation fees.[40]

The militancy of the Puri peasants is also visible if one compares the violations of the salt laws between 1938-39 and 1939-40.

Table I

Cases of abuse of salt laws[41]

	1938-39	1939-40
Cuttack	34	38
Balasore	164	114
Puri	670	1654

The above table shows that the violation of salt laws increased considerably in Puri district. Besides, we do get a reference to a case of 'assault' in Puri (1939-40), when 'contraband' salt seized by an excise officer was 'forcibly' taken away and 'made over' to the 'illicit traffickers'.[42] These are indicators which point to regular attempts at self-assertion with which the active role of the Kisan Sangha in Puri did have some connection.

Our evidence also suggests the existence of strong pressures against the War collections in Puri district. This prompted the Puri District Congress Committee (DCC) to issue a circular (September 1940) criticising, and giving details of forced War collections[43] in rural areas. Further, a leaflet entitled 'Ranabehari" was circulated at the Jaleshwar *hata* (Balasore district) in June 1940, which demonstrated anti-War sentiments in the Balasore countryside. It read:

> 'Bande Mataram!
> Warning to Kisans! Beware! Let not the villages pay War tax to the hypocritical Britishers. Let them devise means, to drive out white men from India. In every village Youth Volunteer Corps should be formed. Remove all fear from the country. Do not be at all afraid of people with red *pagrees*.'[44]

While discussing the coastal tract, mention must be made of the increase in small-scale crime, especially in the districts of Cuttack and Balasore. This took the form of 'thefts' of foodstuffs and utensils,[45] and perhaps reflects the conditions of the people in a context of increasing pressures. Besides, we also get references to communal tension in Cuttack, attempts to organise the Hindu Mahasabha in Puri and the increasing identification of the Muslim League as 'pro-imperialist' in Balasore (given its campaign to support the War effort.)[46] Although these communal tendencies were urban, it needs to be stressed that they reflected developments which were neither sudden nor based on purely local issues.

As for the five princely states, we find the *durbars* successfully reasserting themselves in Gangpur and Ranpur.[47] However, the pulls and pressures of the Prajamandals of Nilgiri, Dhenkanal and Talcher *vis-a- vis* the state authorities continued, although there was a marked decline in the Prajamandal movement if one compares it with 1938.

Let us take the case of Nilgiri. Evidence indicated the formation of a 'defence committee' to render financial assistance to the victims of the chief. It had meetings at the Nilgiri Garh where resolutions were passed against the victimisation of certain *lakhrajdars* by the *durbar*.[48] The attempts of the colonial administration to come down on the Communists in the coastal tract had its repercussions in Nilgiri as well. What is significant is the close collaboration offered by the *durbar*, as well as the Congressite section in this process of isolating the Communists, who worked actively and had contributed significantly to build the strong Prajamandal.

This position adopted by the Congressite section was dictated by two major issues. During the National Day celebration (1940) slogans like 'Na ek bhai, Na ek pai, Samrajyabad ka ladhai' ('Not a single brother, not a single paise for the Imperialist War'[49]) and 'Lalajee ke badla lena' ('Avenge the murder of Lala Lajpat Rai') were raised. Banamali Das made speeches exhorting 'the audience consisting mainly of innocent and illiterate people, mostly aborigines to raid police stations, to take possession of the jail, to make over dues payable to the state not to the state but to the Congress office, and to forcibly appropriate the granaries of the rich people according to their necessities, when called upon to do so.' This was described as antithetical and 'offending ...the four-fold constructive programme of Mahatmajee'.[50]

Secondly, when Das' house was raided by the police it seized literature published by the Communist Party of Great Britain, from Moscow as well as the Orissa papers of the Communist Party of India. The wrath of the colonial government, the *durbar* as well as Congress activists in the Prajamandal fell on Das. Besides being arrested, he was expelled from the Prajamandal.[51] The resolution which expelled Das was forwarded to the *durbar* and K.C. Mohanty met the Raja in this connection.[52] There is evidence of Mahtab's presence around this time at the state to settle the matter.[53]

The correspondence between Mohanty, Das and the State Peoples' Conference High Command[54] reflects how the forms of struggle organised by the Communists were sought to be smashed from above. K.B. Menon, Secretary of the All India State Peoples' Conference, went to the extent of admonishing Mohanty for the action. As he put it: 'I feel that you unnecessarily created a fuss about the matter. It was unwarranted ... action against a colleague on the basis of police reports and perhaps out of panic. ... It was exposing him to the Government's wrath ...you could have as well privately negotiated with him to quit'.[55] However, the High Command stuck to its 'Gandhian principle' and stood behind the decision of expelling Das, advising him to work outside the Prajamandal.[56]

This purge created some confusion in the Prajamandal. However, through this the PCC attempted to extend its control over the Nilgiri Prajamandal which was very powerful and highly organised, and, given the intervention of the Communists, had focused on class issues since

1939.

As for Dhenkanal, by early 1940 the refugees had returned to the state.[57] There is very little evidence of any militant action by the Prajamandal. The *durbar* continued to unleash terror through arrests, obstruction to the enrolment of Congress members and arrests of Prajamandal leaders like Subahu Singh and Baishnab Pattnaik. However, what seems to have happened is the development of co-ordination between the various states, with Nilgiri and Talcher taking the lead.[58]

In this phase Talchar became a storm centre of the state peoples' movement. We get innumerable references to the state Prajamandal having meetings (on occasions with other states). Various oppressive features in the state were criticised and memorials were addressed to the colonial authorities. The focus was on reorganising the '*parishad*', the right to kill wild animals destroying crops and the complete abolition of miscellaneous cesses.[59] It noted with concern the revengeful attitude of the *durbar* which took the form of dispossessing peasants, reinforcing forest laws and grazing restrictions, preventing the people from using the state roads and instituting certificate cases for recovery of rents from people who were in no position to pay. It appealed to the Political Department to rectify the administration of the state.[60] In addition, there was restlessness among the colliery workers and plans for a strike to improve working conditions.[61]

The Talcher Prajamandal took up the constructive programme of the Congress, especially the question of Harijan uplift and prohibition. It seems that Harijans gave up beef and liquor, and going by the evidence cited by Pabitramohan Pradhan President of the Prajamandal as many as seventy percent of Harijans gave up *tari*, and it ceased to be extracted.[62] Whereas the anti-untouchability campaign served to unite and strengthen the Prajamandal, changes in diet and the temperence movement reflects the emulation of upper caste norms by Harijans, as well as the hegemonisation by the Congress.[63]

As for the Jeypur zamindari, a series of Congress meetings were held. The focus was on the forcible War collections, and on occasions appeals were made to women to become politically active. Evidence indicates a massive campaign against the War collections including the distribution of a cyclostyled leaflet.[64] It was this campaign that proved to be the basis of the strong anti-imperialist current which swept the zamindari. We get references to 'Congress workers'— a category used rather liberally by the colonial administration — in Jeypore being arrested and prosecuted for trying to dissuade people from subscribing to the War funds (October and

November 1940). And it was perhaps this trend that made the PCC leadership apply brakes with the argument that the people had not got permission to begin anti-War propaganda.[65]

What is remarkable is the toning down of the anti-feudal struggle, which marked a continuity of the post-1937 election pattern. The stress on the anti-imperialist struggle served as a vital component through which the Congress hegemonised the peasants and the tribals of the Jeypur zamindari. How effective this hegemony was and the extent of strain it could take is something that we shall see later on.

Moreover, there was the growing popularity of tribal Congress activists in the zamindari like Laxman Naiko of Tentuligrumma (Malkangiri). He moved extensively in the forest tract of Malkangiri, usually covering 30 to 40 miles a day. Popular perceptions regarded him as the 'Gandhi of Malkangiri'. People followed him in crowds wherever he went.[66] However, one observes a shift to more acceptable forms of PCC politics, in line with what we have witnessed in the post-election (1937) phase. In spite of this, his activities did cause some concern to the colonial as well as the estate authorities.[67]

We can round off our discussion of the Jeypur zamindari by mentioning the sudden increase in 'petty' crimes like 'thefts' of food-stuff.[68] Besides, the trend of tribal supporters of the Congress giving up meat and liquor continued. This reflected the emulation of features of Hindu society and was, perhaps, associated with the complex process of the hegemonisation of the tribals by the Congress. But emulation could also be a kind of self-assertion although we have no evidence of conflicts with liquor distributors in this phase.

III

Between Mass Pressure and the Politics of Demobilisation (1941)

By the end of 1940 it was clear that there had been a decline in the primary membership of the Congress. The following table illustrates the connections between this trend and the decline of the anti-imperialist struggle and the peasant movement in Orissa.

Table II

Table showing the number of primary Congress members in Orissa.[69]

1938	1939	1940
1,98,325	1,23,900	45,837

Besides the sharp decline in the Congress membership in 1940 there were as many as 27,769 renewals. The total strength of the Congress in the urban area was 2,370 as against 43,467 in the rural areas, a phenomenon which reflects the stronger hold of the Congress in the countryside.[70] However, what needs to be emphasised is that this decline in membership did not denote a decline in its popular acceptance as an instrument of struggle.

Keeping this in mind we can now discuss the next phase which began with the inauguration of the 'individual *satyagraha*' on 1 December 1940.[71] In the coastal tract prominent leaders of the PCC like Mahtab, Biswanath Das, Nabakrushna Choudhury offered 'individual *satyagraha*'. In speeches delivered before their arrest these leaders focused on the need to remain peaceful, and reiterated Gandhi's appeal to promote unity with untouchables and Muslims, spin *khadi* and promote *swadeshi*. As for the War, they stressed the 'non-violent' approach to it, criticised the colonial government for dragging India into the War and appealed to the people not to pay the War subscriptions.[72] On some occasions *hatas* were selected to attract the attention of the rural folk.[73]

At this juncture let us try to say something about the type of people who were involved in anti-war activities and the 'individual *satyagraha*' movement. We shall concentrate on the first detailed report available to us for January 1941.

Table III

Persons prosecuted in January 1941 for anti-war activities[74]

District	*First half*	*Second half*
Cuttack	17	28
Puri	3	10
Balasore	2	9

Table IV
Approximate caste pattern of those arrested between 15-31 January 1941[75]

District	*Brahmins/ Karanas*	*Agricultural (i.e. Khandayats)*	*Cowherds*	*Artisans*	*Others (includes unidentified castes)*
Cuttack	12	10	1	-	5
Puri	4	4	-	1 (potter)	1
Balasore	3	-	1	1 (carpenter)	4

As can be seen, our evidence points to the participation of different castes. Along with the upper castes (Brahmins and Karanas) some agricultural castes (Khandayats), cowherds and artisans also figure in the list of those arrested. However, there was the absence of outcastes as well as tribals which was perhaps representative of the coastal belt as a whole.

In February 1941 all the District Çongress Committees and the Primary Congress Committees were suspended and Gouranga Charan Das, Satyabadi Nanda and Nilambar Das were appointed to conduct the 'individual *satyagraha*' in the districts of Cuttack, Puri and Balasore respectively.[76] The AICC wanted to keep this movement confined to its political framework. This was hoped to be achieved through the selection of *satyagrahis* by Gandhi and the instruction that villagers should not go to towns to offer *satyagraha*.[77] The PCC also sought to reinforce this thrust by tightening *satyagrahi* recruitment, as well as permitting only *satyagrahis* to make speeches.[78]

After February 1941 there developed a gradual lull in the 'individual *satyagraha*' movement.[79] While the colonial government adopted a 'leave them alone' attitude[80], we find some reluctance among the released *satyagrahis* to get re-arrested.[81] As a result, by May 1941 the 'individual *satyagraha*' movement started fizzling out in coastal Orissa, and had in fact died by the time it was formally suspended in December 1941.

As can be observed, The peasants and tribals of coastal Orissa were kept out of this movement. As for the Kisan Sangha there are references to a conference at Khurda (8 June 1941) which was presided over by Jamunalal Karzi, the peasant leader of Bihar. Domodar Misra, the Chairman of the reception committee, emphasised the dictatorial character of the Congress while Karzi pointed to the futility of the 'individual *satyagraha*' and recommended relief to the peasantry in the form of *taccavi* loans, rent remission and setting up of free food centres. The conference focused on the sufferings of the peasants at the hands of imperialists, the capitalists and the zamindars. It charaterised the War as an 'imperialist' War into which India had been dragged. The Kisan conference reiterated its position of cooperation with every anti-imperialist organisation in order to achieve freedom and criticised the Viceroy for turning down the Madras Estates Land Act (Orissa Amendment) Bill.[82]

The year 1941 saw the Kisan Sabha quite active in the coastal tract. Around thirty thousand rent suits were filed in the Cuttack district. These were attributed to the inspiration generated by the past struggles of the Kisan Sangha. The Madhupur estate (Cuttack) continued to attract the attention of the colonial administrators as a zone of peasant militancy. The Kisan Sangha was also active in Puri.

However, in this phase it was Balasore where the Kisan Sangha made deep inroads. There are reference to Kisan Sangha activists like Sachindananda Routroy moving extensively all over the district.[83] At Dhamnagar a Water Tax Association was established to oppose the government's policy of levying water,[84] which culminated in the establishment of a Kisan Sangha.[85] There are also references to the opposition to the 'individual *satyagraha*' form of politics in certain areas like Eram, Basudevpur and Bhadrak.[86] And, in the context of food scarcity in Balasore the 'individual *satyagraha*' assumed a form unforseen by the Congress, with local people offering *satyagraha* in front of the houses of paddy hoarders.[87]

The Kisan Sangha observed the Kisan Day (1 September 1941) with week-long meetings at different parts of the coastal tract.[88] In some parts people from the adjoining princely states joining in to celebrate the Kisan Day.[89]

These efforts of the Kisan Sangha, especially the Communists, were 'frowned upon by the official Congress Party'. In an attempt to maintain its position the PCC did try to set up a parallel Kisan organisation which did not succeed.[90] The PCC President issued a statement asking the Congress workers to stay out of the Kisan Sangha's activities as it preached class war, which would retard the political progress of the country.[91]

Finally, we must mention the continuation of certain trends we had observed in 1940 — 'petty' crime[92], and increase in the violations of salt laws (especially in Puri)[93], communal tension and the phenomenon of scarcity and price rise of essential commodities (which became accute with the declaration of War).[94] There was also a caste conflict between cowherds and Khandayats at Kendrapara (Cuttack) which resulted in a clash (November 1940).[95] The two districts of Cuttack and Balasore suffered extensive damages as a result of floods (August 1940).[96] And the War led to an exodus of hundreds of Oriyas from Calcutta and its suburbs, back to their villages. This led to a host of rumours[97] which had an electrifying effect on the countryside.

As for the princely states, the 'individual *satyagraha*' failed to evoke much response from Nilgiri. Kailash Chandra Mohanty was arrested at Ambodia *hata* (16 December 1940) after offering 'individual *satyagraha*' and delivering an anti-war speech.[98] However, unlike Nilgiri the pressures exerted on the state people of Dhenkanal was much more. The *durbar* went back on its promises and raised local cess and *bethi*. The Prajamandal organised several meetings to protest against the *durbar*.[99]

As for Talcher, Prajamandal activists like Pabitra Mohan Pradhan were arrested for offering 'individual *satyagraha*', (December 1940). The Prajamandal appointed new leaders in January 1941 to keep the organisation ready for the future. The pressures exerted by the colonial administration and the *durbar* forced many activists of the Prajamandal underground. The prajamandal criticised the maladministration of the *durbar* and the PCC's alternative programme of constructive work continued as in 1940.[100]

As for the Jeypur zamindari we have already noted the strong anti-War agitation, even before the PCC and the AICC launched the 'individual *satyagraha*'. Consequently, the peasants and tribals of the zamindari were extremely responsive to the 'individual *satyagraha*' movement.[101] Prominent tribal Congress supporters like Laxman Naiko offered 'individual *satyagraha*'.[102] The popular enthusiasm generated by the 'individual *satyagraha*' can be judged, however, if one analyses the facts which indicate the type of people who participated in it. One common feature was the predominance of tribals and outcastes. These people were mostly small cultivators (who 'looked after...their own cultivation') and a few were agricultural labourers (who 'worked in the fields'). Most of them gave up eating beef and drinking liquor, spun *khadi*, instructed people about cotton cultivation and recruited members for the Congress. They went to Jeypur town regularly in connection with *khadi* or meetings. They engaged themselves in village reconstruction (eg. clearing roads and ponds) and worked towards eradicating illiteracy. There are interesting references to some tribals working in Harijan *bastis* to uplift the latter, and one reference to an aspiring *satyagrahi*, who was a tribal, stopping an early marriage.[103]

There were some *satyagrahis* who were unemployed, some who described themselves as 'coolies' and others as 'beggars'. In one case released *satyagrahis* asked people to 'give up' brass ornaments (worn mostly by the hill folk and not in Hindu society) and eating pigs and fowls.[104] The *charkha* penetrated the remotest corners of the estate and *ashram* schools were also set up in various parts (e.g. Udoyogiri, Pandra Guda and Tentuligumma).[105] These features indicate the popularity as well as the expansion of the PCC and although we do not have any data for the district, the fact that in 1941-42 even a remote village like Tentuligumma boasted of 200 primary Congress members[106] proves this point. And, taken together, these features also reflect the deeper processes which led to the hegemonisation of the peasants and the tribals by the Congress. Besides the twin process of Hinduisation of the hill people and their emulation of features of Hindu society in order to seek identification with the Congress, there was also a social reformist current among the people of the estate.

Seeing things in this perspective one can understand how the Congress merged with popular aspirations and why the 'individual *satyagraha*' evoked militant responses in Jeypur, unlike in the coastal belt. This created a serious threat to the colonial administration[107] and, perhaps, influenced Padhiary's circular to the DCCs instructing them to restrict recruitment of individual *satyagrahis*.[108]

IV

The Shifts, Changes and the Preparation for 'Quit India' (January 1942 - July 1942)

The 'individual *satyagraha*' was suspended in December 1941.[109] In January 1942, the PCC leaders like Mahtab, Nabakrushna Choudhury and Malati Choudhuri initiated a programme of mass contact.[110] Their approach implied a criticism of the colonial government which had first repressed the people and then turned to them when faced with a crisis. They described the War as an 'imperialist war' which had no relevance for the peasants and workers. Reiterating the need to strengthen the Congress they advocated the promotion of Gandhi's constructive work. The coalition ministry of Orissa was also a common target of attack.[111]

In most of these meetings the PCC leaders hinted at a 'break-down' which was linked to the British leaving India owing to a civil disorder, or a political upheaval, or a possible Japanese invasion. The British were either asked to go or were referred to as 'already gone' since their condition was like that of a dying man, surviving on medicines. The 'enemies' who 'looted' the people were distinctly identified and they ranged from the Viceroy and the police to the zamindars, *sahukars* and *chaukidars*.[112]

It was also given out that with the departure of the British there would be a collapse of the police system which would not be in a position to help the propertied classes. Since the landlords would not be able to face the people in this altered situation they were thus urged to give up their old policy and live harmoniously with the common people.[113]

The PCC leaders also projected the alternatives on how to survive the 'breakdown'. Thus, the people were advised to store grain, grow cotton, spin and weave *khadi* and organise Congress volunteer corps to protect their villages. These, it was stressed, would transform the villages into invincible forts.[114]

The 'Mahatma's', initial position, although ambiguous, also operated within the framework of a 'breakdown' resulting out of a possible Japanese invasion. His idea (which must have been popularised by the PCC leaders) was that if the Japanese occupied a part of Orissa it had to be considered whether the people were prepared to 'non-cooperate' with them. In case they were not prepared to do so, the believers in non-violence were advised to desert the area.[115]

When Mira Ben toured Orissa as Gandhi's emissary in May 1942, she focused on the fact that even if the British 'withdrew' the Congress 'would stay' and look after the people.[116] She forecast an early Japanese invasion and emphasised that in such a situation the British would immediately destroy railroads and roads and then retreat.[117] She criticised restrictions on salt 'manufacturing' and advocated their removal in view of the scarcity of salt. She also visited Chaudwar where people had been evacuated so as to build an aerodrome and desired that the evacuees should be compensated.[118] Consequently Mira Ben's tour also reinforced the idea of a 'break-down'.

These apocalyptic notions were, of course, largely reinforced by the popular tradition itself. The concept of '*pralaya*' or 'the end of the world' (present in one form of the other in Hindu as well as tribal 'world views)[119] philosophised about the periodic destruction of the world for a better one. While it is impossible to gauge popular perceptions, these apocalyptic notions seemed to indicate the end of the British empire and its replacement by the one created by the 'Mahatma' and the Congress, which would be better (*swaraj*).

With the distinct possibilities of a Japanese invasion and the return of evacuees from Calcutta and Rangoon (captured by the Japanese in March 1942) this belief in a 'breakdown' got strengthened and a wide variety of rumours circulated in the coastal Orissa countryside.[120]

Moreover, almost every major step taken by the colonial administration seemed to strengthen the notion of an 'impending doom'. Thus, the arrival of a military contingent in January 1942 to counter the possible Japanese invasion, caused serious alarm. A rumour circulated that cattle and grain would be 'commandeered' and people considered shifting these possessions to safety. There were also rumours in some areas regarding the possible molestation of women in the areas in which this army would be posted and hence their evacuation from such zones was considered as well.[121] Although born out of the immediate context, such perceptions were shaped by the experiences and interactions of the peasants and tribals with the colonial army.

Lightning restrictions[122] from 15 January 1942 and low-flying aeroplanes[123] meant to defend the coastal tract also reinforced such 'apocalyptic' notions. We get a reference to a leaflet entitled 'We are your friends', dropped from a Royal Air Force plane, causing serious alarm among the peasants of Balasore.[124] In another instance an evacuee from Burma hoisted a Congress flag on his house, and explained that he had heard that this was the 'immunity' from Japanese air raids.[125] There were similar reports from the Jeypur estate, and the case of an aeroplane flying overhead without causing any damage was attributed to the flying of the Congress flag.[126] Besides indicating a fear of the unknown 'bomb' which symbolised destruction and 'doom', such actions also demonstrated popular belief in the invincibility of the Congress.

The shifting of the secretariat from Cuttack to Sambalpur necessitated by the fear of a Japanese invasion[127] was another such policy. This news spread like lightning. It not only implied a 'breakdown' of colonial authority, but was also looked upon as a signal for rebellion.[128]

In an attempt to delay the movement of Japanese troops, in case of a possible invasion, the colonial administration seized boats, bicycles and buses within twenty miles of the coast. Orders were also issued banning people from stocking paddy in this 'war zone'.[129] The effect of this can be judged from a rumour in coastal Orissa that the government had arranged for wagon-loads of sickles and scythes for destroying the harvests in the event of an invasion.[130] The construction of a 'war zone' together with the effort to evacuate people from some places in order to strengthen the system of air defence seem to have generated a rumour that villages three miles on either side of the Grand Trunk road would be evacuated, which caused serious alarm.[131] These policies were perceived as those of an alien government, thereby indicating a serious undermining of colonial hegemony.

Popular conceptions of a 'breakdown' were also strengthened by violent explosions off the coasts at Jagatsingpur (Cuttack district) in April 1942 during a naval raid directed against British ships by the Japanese. Besides leading the people to believe that the Japanese had already landed on the Orissa coast, it was also looked upon as a supernatural phenomenon.[132] The impact thus produced can be judged from the fact that the population of Cuttack town got reduced by twenty thousand, with the populace fleeing mostly to the adjoining rural areas[133], carrying with them their version of the incident. One can also mention here the appearance of a stray barrage-baloon (with about two thousand feet of wire trailing from it) at a village in the Puri district. A peasant who saw the balloon settling down near his house in the moonlight was reported to have devoted the whole night to prayer.[134]

It was in such a context that the 'Mahatma's' position veered towards unprecedented militancy. By May 1942 he declared: 'Leave India to God. If that is too much, then leave her to anarchy. This ordered disciplined anarchy should go, and if there is complete lawlessness I would risk it'.[135] Explaining that his attitude had undergone a change he declared that he could not afford to wait any more.[136] However, as late as July 1942 nothing concrete had been envisaged by him or the AICC excepting that the British had to leave India.[137] Mahtab who returned after meeting the 'Mahatma' at Wardha in July 1942 expressed this ambiguity and perhaps reinforced it by his mystification of things.[138]

At the crucial Bombay session of the AICC which passed the 'Quit India' Resolution on 8 August 1942 Orissa was represented by Mahtab, Malati Choudhuri, Radhakrishna Biswasroi and Surendranath Dwivedy.[139] This Resolution reiterated in most unambiguous terms that the British had to go. It focused on the non-violent path and envisaged the possibility of the AICC not being able to instruct the people. In such a situation every participant was expected to function within the framework of the general instructions. The Resolution visualised a free India in which power would belong to the people as a whole.[140] Consequently, the Resolution was rather vague about the details of the on-coming struggle. Gandhi in his militant 'Do or Die' speech at the 8 August meeting called upon every Indian to 'consider himself to be a free man' who should be ready for the actual attainment of freedom or perish in the attempt.[141]

Within a week of the arrest of the Congress leaders on 9 August 1942, we get references to hand-written leaflets circulating (secretly) in Orissa.[142] It acquired legitimacy from the 'Mahatma' and the leaflet carried his instructions regarding the 'last struggle of the Congress'. Besides advocating that every person was expected to consider that he was a citizen of free India, destruction of the present government and the setting-up of an alternative panchayat-based government, it mentioned features outside the framework of the AICC's 'Quit India' Resolution or the 'Mahatma's, pronouncements. For example, the people were asked to disobey rajas and zamindars. They were expected to demand zamindari lands and excess of paddy from the zamindars. In case of refusal, they were asked to seize the lands and paddy forcibly. This leaflet also asked people to resort to illegal acts such as non-payment of rent, cutting forests and manufacturing salt.[143]

Finally, as late as in August the colonial government was unaware about the extent of popular anger in the province.[144] It tried to align itself with some anti-Congress[145] organisations and planned a propaganda campaign against the 'Congress Resolution'.[146] As for the coalition ministry, it was too cut-off from the masses. Besides advocating the need to support the War and failing hopelessly to control prices and food shortages, it recommended strict measures to face the Quit India Movement.[147] In fact, its lack of credibility, also contributed towards strengthening the notions of a 'breakdown'.

V

Charting the Quit India Movement in Orissa (August - December 1942)

We can now discuss details of the Quit India Movement in Orissa, and begin by directing ourselves to coastal Orissa. The beginnings of the Quit India Movement can be located in Cuttack town. There were no demonstrations during the arrest of about fifty prominent Congressmen of the Province or the seizure of the Congress offices between August 9 to13. However, immediately after this we find *hartals* and strikes in Cuttack town. This remained confined to educational institutions like Ravenshaw College. The students of the college went on a strike, began to hold regular meetings which were addressed by activists of the Students Federation (the Communist Party's student wing) and finally some records and furniture of the college were burnt. Most of the Students Federation leaders were arrested. There was also the involvement of some school students of Victoria School, Mission School and Academy School. In the absence of any other major happenings, this trend dominated till about 15 August

1942.[148]

Around this time the Quit India Movement began spreading into the rural areas of Cuttack district. Features like taking possession of Congress *ashrams*, like the one at Bari, were associated with this shift, and reflect the symbolic importance attached to them.[149] Rural schools and *hatas* also played an important role through which the Quit India Movement seems to have percolated into the countryside.[150] Between 15 and 30 of August we witness innumerable instances of cutting of telegraph and telephone wires, 'attacks' on post offices, which also included burning , in various parts of the district and a case of a mail runner being robbed. There were instances of burning of the uniforms of policemen, *chaukidars* and *daffadars* and on occasions they were left naked. There were 'attacks' on rest houses of the Forest and the Irrigation Departments and the burning down of certain Canal Revenue offices. In Jajpur the embankment of a distributory canal was cut at Andola and the water diverted. Records of an opium shop were destroyed and a liquor shop 'looted'. Symbols of colonialism—road mile-posts, signboards—were thrown away.[151]

This phase also saw attempts to tamper with the railway lines. On 20 August a 'military special' was derailed between Mandaso and Baruva. Railway lines were also damaged at Sonepata on 25 August, and the Madras Mail encountered an obstruction on the midnight of 30 August near the Jenapur station.[152]

The selectivity of the targets support the dominance of an anti-imperialist current. However, we also get references to the development of an anti-feudal struggle as well. Various meetings were held at the Sukinda and the Madhupur estate where plans for a 'no-rent' movement were discussed. There were also 'attacks' launched against the *kutcheries* of some estates. During the last week of August six *kutcheries* of zamindars were burnt in the Jajpur sub-division, and a similar action was taken against the *kutchery* of the Sukinda estate. We also get references to the 'looting' of granaries.[153] These features indicate a struggle against the landed section—howsoever marginal—something that is glossed over by nationalist historiography.

Another notable feature in this phase was to 'rescue' people arrested by the police. This reflected not only a defiance of authority but also the level of solidarity created by the Quit India Movement. Here we can cite the example of an arrested person being 'rescued' by around two hundred people from the clutches of a constable and some *chaukidars* at Tirtol.[154]

'Crowd' behaviour in this phase can be an extremely fascinating aspect of study. About 10,000 people entered Jajpur town in about eight batches on 27 August. Shouting slogans, they also invited the people to join them. Two liquor shops were 'looted' during the march towards the police station and the office of sub-divisional officer. They halted about eighty yards from the armed guards who stood at the office complex. Three 'leaders' were permitted to approach the officers. In the course of their meeting these men said that they had come to prevail upon the local officers to resign from their posts. The 'crowd' was getting excited and the police were contemplating dispersing them through firing. Suddenly a low-flying aeroplane dropped dynamite on the 'crowd', scattering the people. Although some people remained, the 'crowd' dispersed, and continued its march quietly. It set fire to the Rambagh post office which was about four miles away.[155]

September saw the continuance of all the features we have already seen. The 'attacks' on the symbols of colonial authority and colonialism continued on a wider scale.[156] Alongside, we get references to the 're-capturing' of Congress *ashrams* seized by the colonial administration which demonstrate attempts at self-assertion. However, there was a shift insofar as the 'attacks' on zamindari *kutcheries* were concerned; this trend died down, although we get references to meetings where such actions were planned. The target seems to have shifted to the court rooms of the colonial administration.[157]

Although these activities eclipsed happenings in urban areas, a merging of hopes and aspirations between the rural and urban areas can be perceived. Students at Cuttack appealed to the people to burn *thanas* and government buildings and cut telegraph lines[158] —actions which were enthusiastically being implemented in the countryside.

Ersama had emerged as a centre of militancy. On the morning of 6 September a 'crowd' of about 700 persons 'armed' with various kinds of 'weapons' from thirteen villages reached the police station. The sub-inspector and his assistant 'requested' the 'crowd' to refrain from violence. The people 'seized' the sub-inspector and kept him in 'confinement' and the other policemen were forced to remain inactive 'on pain of being put to death'. After this the 'crowd' destroyed the doors, windows and the furniture at the police station and set them on fire along with the records. They shouted that the British government 'should go away from India' and that the policemen should resign from their posts and burn their uniforms. Slogans like 'Mahatma Gandhi Ki Jai' and 'Swadhin Bharat Ki Jai' were also raised. After this the 'crowd' proceeded to the local post office which was set on fire. Next, the *ganja* and the opium shop was 'looted'.[159]

After the initial shock the colonial administration made arrangements to face the challenge posed by the Quit India Movement. Besides *lathi* charges and arrests, 'collective fines' were imposed.[160] One Gokul Chandra Mohanty, most probably a landlord of village Ahiyas in the Jajpur sub-division, who had become a target of some 'Congressmen' for sheltering the police, collected about hundred Muslims who dispersed the 'raiders' with their *lathis*.[161] This indicates the role of the landed sections *vis-a-vis* the Quit India Movement as well as the working of communal politics.

By October, the Quit India Movement seems to have lost its explosive form in the Cuttack district. A bulletin issued by Surendranath Dwivedy on 2 October Gandhi Jayanti tried to infuse militancy and enthusiasm. It called out: 'The funeral pyre of this weak Government is burning in flames throughout the country. On the ashes of the Government on the carcasses of this beastly administration and the grave of this sinful kingdom will be erected the Government of our labourers and cultivators and administration of justice and righteousness'. It directed its anger at the coalition ministry and called it an agent of the British. However, its call for a '*hartal*' was not successful.[162] As for the countryside instances like wire cutting, 'attacks' against government buildings and schools, regular meetings and processions were witnessed.[163]

By November 1942 the Quit India Movement had almost died down in the district. There were a few cases of wire-cutting and an instance of a vaccinator being attacked at Kissenagar (Binjharpur) by some 'Congressmen'. His registers were snatched away and burnt. Besides, some people entered the tehsildar's office at Napang, destroyed his papers and 'took away' cash amounting to Rs. 700. At Salepur some people entered the office of the sub-registrar and asked him to resign. Although 'Congress workers' toured the countryside campaigning for a 'no-rent' movement but our evidence does not suggest the development of any such movement.[164]

The only major activity that we come across in December 1942 is in the Sukinda estate. Some Panas (outcastes) initiated a movement to cut off paddy of 'loyal' tenants. This was inspired by the arrest of a Pana leader in August 1942. Flag marches and warnings by the police seem to have dampened the movement.[165]

The following tables[166] which carry details of some prisoners give us an idea of the type of people who participated in the Quit India Movement in the Cuttack district.

Table V

Name	*Place*	*Land held*	*Whether Employed*	*Nature of employemnt*	*Income*
Srinath Mohanty	Tirtol	8 acres	No	-	-
Rusinath Sahoo	-do-	1 acre	Yes	Calcutta	Rs. 10/- a month
Govinda Kasta	-do-	None	Yes	Daily labour	Rs. 4/- a day
Sridhar Das	-do-	-do-	No (beggar)	-	-
Daitari Misra	-do-	4 acres	No	-	-
Pranakrishna Nath	-do-	None	Yes	Calcutta	Rs. 10/- a month
Dibakar Pradhan	-do-	4 acres	No	-	-
Puri Kasta	-do-	None	No	-	-
Mayadhar Mohanty	-do-	10 acres	No	-	-
Anam Charan Das	Binjharpur	?	Yes	Calcutta (cook)	Rs. 10 a month
Rasananda Sukla	-do-	?	(Lived on father's income)		
Indramani Tripathy	-do-	?	(Lived on his land and cultivated the land of others)		
Balakrishna Sukla	-do-	?	(Lived on produce of his own land)		
Benudhar Samal	-do-	(Landed Property)	No	-	-
Muralidhar Roy	-do-	?	(Lived on produce from own land)		
Dambarudhar Rai	-do-	None	Sold rice of his elder brother's wife and earned money		
Vipin Bihari Mohanty	-do-	?	Yes	Mem. district board ?	
Sachidananda Jena	Mahanga	?	Yes	-do-	Rs. 15/- a month
Brundaban Sarangi	-do-	?	(Used to earn Rs. 15/- a month from the Congress office)		
Bibhuti Bhushan Acharya	Govindapur	1.5 acres (Rs. 13/- to Rs. 15/- a year)	Yes	Teacher	Rs. 5/- a month
Sudarshan Naik	Dharamsala	Sons cultivated land	-	-	-
Bhagat Samal	?	?(Lived on land)	No	-	-

TABLE VI

Approximate caste pattern of the prisoners (total - 22)

Brahmins/ Karanas	*Agricultural castes (i.e. Chasas and Khandayats)*	*Oilmen*	*Unidentified persons*
11	4	1	6

TABLE VII

Class/Profession of the prisoners (total -22)

Peasants Amount of Land held		*Landless people*			
		Locally employed	*Employed at Calcutta*	*Beggars*	*Details of land-holding not known*
1-4 acres	8-10 acres				
4	2	1	3	1	11

What can be seen is the presence of different castes, including agriculturists and an oilman. Our evidence indicates the prominent role of some landless rural folk who came back to the countryside from Calcutta —a trend noted while discussing the background to the present chapter. The active role of these landless people is particularly striking and reflects their heightened consciousness which resulted from their exposure to various complexities at their working place as well as at their villages. There was also participation of 'poor' peasants.

In the Balasore district, the colonial administration launched an offensive by arresting prominent Congressmen and seizing the Congress offices at Balasore, Soro, Bhadrak, Agarpara and Dhamnagar.[167] Till about 15 August nothing much seems to have happened. There is a reference to a meeting at Chandbali where Muralidhar Jena insisted on the payment of compensation to people whose boats and lands had been taken over. He seems to have campaigned in a similar fashion in some interior parts as well.[168]

The educational institutions were the first major centres of activity. Students in a large number of schools went on strikes, picketed schools and took out processions.[169] Some furniture of the Mission English School was also burnt. The students of this school distributed a leaflet on 16 August which, among other things, asked the people to 'plunder' salt depots, thoroughly boycott government officials and induce them to resign, to observe '*hartals*' in schools and colleges, to paralyse the communication system, cut telegraph wires, 'loot' post boxes, store food in villages, form *swaraj* panchayats, to stop payment of rents and taxes and violate forest and other laws through mass civil disobedience.[170] Whereas the '*hartal*' was observed between 14 and 18 August and developed into picketing of excise shops by students,[171] the appeals to the countryside demonstrate the thinning down of the barrier between town and country.

The first major break came on 17 August at Bhandaripokhari, which indicated the permeation of the Quit India Movement into the countryside and its new form. A meeting had been planned at Kahanrapokhari on 17 August. Around 500 processionists from Bhandaripokhari and a number of adjoining villages got together at Kahanrapokhari. They marched to Bhandaripokhari and then returned to Kahanrapokhari for the meeting. On the way it rained and the police party that accompanied them took shelter in the *thana*. A police sub-inspector who came to survey the situation was asked to say 'Mahatma Gandhi Ki Jai'. On refusing, he was stripped and his cycle taken away. He was 'struck' on the head, but because he was an old man he was given a *gamcha* and allowed to go. After this the 'crowd' pursued other police officials who hid in some neighbouring houses.[172]

On attaining success the 'crowd' set about burning almost everything that came on their way to the police station, as well as at the officers' quarters. An unsuccessful attempt was made to burn the money in the post office strong-box at the police station. The opium chest was forced open. While the opium was left, about Rs. 80 were taken away. All the confidential papers and the rest of the cash was left intact. The post office situated in the same compound was also burnt. Fearing that these actions would invite repression the 'crowd' dismantled the bridge to prevent the movement of troops and cut the telegraph wires to prevent this news from spreading.[173]

In September the Quit India Movement gathered considerable momentum and militancy at Balasore. Villagers joined in groups and planned to resist colonial authority. There are instances of widespread adoption of popular methods like blowing conches and drumbeats to signal the advent of the police. These attracted the villagers to assemble in large numbers to face the police force. In many areas paralell panchayats sprang up to settle disputes. Besides, appeals were made to police officers to disobey their superiors. An effigy of the British government was slapped and its ears boxed before it was burnt at Jaleswar.[174] This trend also implied the rescuing of properties of Quit India Movement activists attached by the police.[175] In September Dhamnagar emerged as a strong centre of the Quit India Movement.[176] The people 'extorted' paddy from *mahajans* and also burnt uniforms of *chaukidars*—which show the coexistence of two strands of the struggle.[177] Dhamnagar was identified as a 'disturbed area' and the police staged a 'flag march' on 2 September. A 'crowd' of about 200 approached the police and asked them to leave the place and resign from their posts. As the police began to fix bayonets, the 'crowd' dispersed.

In an effort to arrest Muralidhar Panda, who was a leader of the Dhamnagar area, the police force reached Katasahi on 22 September where they faced a 'crowd' of three thousand people. On seeing the police force approaching the 'crowd' blew conches and signalled through drum-beats to the neighbouring villages. Very soon their numbers swelled to about 5,000. Muralidhar Panda asked the police sub-inspector the reason for his visit and asked the police party to leave immediately. When the policemen refused Panda informed the 'crowd' that the police were there only for 'show'. They had no ammunitions and were never known to shoot.[178]

In the events that followed the sub-inspector's hat was 'damaged' by a *lathi* 'blow', he was pushed, his shirt torn and as a result he fell down. An abortive attempt was made to snatch a rifle from a constable. What followed was a firing without any formal order. About 10 people fell down and the 'crowd' retreated by about five hundred yards. People murmured that their brothers had been killed and the policemen should never be allowed to escape. After this the police force withdrew. The next morning Panda accompanying the dead and the injured went over to Bhadrak and surrendered to the police.[179]

Equally militant and enthusiastic were the people of Khairadhi. In an attempt to restore 'order' a police party went over to Khairadhi on 22 September and arrested Baidyanath Raut, a prominent activist of the Quit India Movement in this area. At night the police party camped at the house of the union president. A 'crowd' of about 500 people 'armed' with *lathis*, axes, bows and arrows 'attacked' the police camp and 'rescued' the prisoner. The sub-inspector was bound with a rope and the other policemen were 'assaulted' and their uniforms and records burnt. The union president was also made a target of 'assault' and his shop was 'looted'.[180]

After this a strong police force was despatched. At Tudagadia *hata* some people 'insulted' the sub-inspector and took off his hat. When the policemen reached Khairadhi they were received by a 'crowd' of about 300 to 400 people who were 'armed' with *lathis*, and who blew conches drawing a large number of people from the adjoining area. The sub-inspector was asked why he had come, and was warned that the police would have to arrest everyone or shoot before they could arrest Raut. The police opened fire but no one was hurt. After this the policemen withdrew.[181]

The police made another attempt the next day. They were greeted with conch blasts. At Panisiali some searches were made. After this the police force went to Khairadhi. When they had gone into a house for a search someone set it on fire and cried out to 'attack' the police party. The police opened fire killing two people. After this the police force retreated from the scene with the dead bodies.[182]

At about 3 p.m. a 'crowd' of about 100 people surrounded the police at Tudigadia in order to 'rescue' the dead bodies and the arrested people. They were 'armed' with *katuris*, *lathis*, bows and arrows. The police opened fire killing three Santhals of Nilgiri and also caught hold of 19 people.[183]

These was a marked enthusiasm in Basudevpur.[184] The Quit India Resolution was received very enthusiastically and the movement began with the boycott of educational institutions and a 'no-rent'/tax movement. The picketings in front of the government offices, meetings and procession served to raise the consciousness of the people. As the news from various parts of the country poured in, four Karmee Sammelans were held at Iram, Suan, Baranda and Guda. We get a reference to a meeting at Iram where a message was brought from the Congress *ashram* at Bari by Shyamasundar Pani. Important activists of Iram endorsed the Quit India Resolution at this meeting.[185]

Iram got regular news and directions from the underground Congress Socialist Party leaders like Surendranath Dwivedy and Gourmohan Das. In the Basudevpur area Iram became the focal point of the Quit India Movement. A '*banara sena*' led by Anirudh Mohanty and a 'guerilla *sena*' led by Ramanaryan Das were set up. Along with this, big meetings were organised at Iram on 27 August; 7, 17, 22, September, Sankaru on 9 September, Guda on 13 September, Bedhada on 11 September, Brahmana Gaon on 13 September and Basudevpur on 18 September. The triangular tract between the rivers Kansabausa and Gamei was declared to be a 'liberated' zone on 17 September. Interestingly, this was referred to as the

'Swadhin Banchanidhi Chakla' after the famous nationalist poet/singer Banchanidhi Mohanty. This was an inaccessible tract during the monsoons, and it was here that a parallel government with its administrative parishad, court, jail and secretariat was set up.[186]

In the 'liberated' zone all the government institutions were rejected. Licensed vendors of the government selling intoxicants were sentenced to seven years imprisonment. Boatmen were asked not to ferry policemen across the rivers. One Basu Tarai of Basudevpur campaigned against the order of restrictions imposed on using boats. The '*Santi Sena*' conducted marches in the area which heightened the consciousness of the people and led to the enrolment of recruits for the volunteer corps.[187] It came to be believed that the British government 'had been destroyed' and that under a *swaraj* government 'no taxes would be paid' and the 'paddy' of the rich would be available to the poor.[188]

Very soon, people stopped paying the *chaukidari* tax. A 'raid' on the coastal watching station at Kulkati was conducted on 20 September in which the staff present were 'assaulted' and driven out.[189] Instructions were also issued at meetings to burn the uniforms of *chaukidars* and *daffadars*.[190] A strict watch was kept over Radhakanta Padhi, the zamindar of Iram, who tried to mediate between the government and the peasants.[191] Consequently, in about 25 villages in the 'Swadhin Banchanidhi Chakla' the authority of the colonial government was reduced to an abstraction for three weeks.[192]

The colonial administration began to plan the restoration of its authority in the 'liberated' zone. A police party was sent out and, by terrorising the boatmen, it managed to cross the river. However, once in the 'liberated' zone it faced non-cooperation by the people and as a result, was forced to camp at the residence of the zamindar, Radhakanta Padhi. Its first major action was symbolic—the *satyagraha ashram* at Sudeipada was locked up. Important leaders like Banchanidhi Agasti and Arjun Biswal were arrested on 19 September. This was opposed through '*hartals*' at the *hatas*, especially at Basudevpur, Bedhada, Iram, Padmapur and Brahmana Gaon. A protest meeting was organised at Iram on 22 September to condemn these arrests.[193]

Around this time the peasants were exposed to seven acute spells of floods which destroyed the crops and created serious shortages. While carrying on the struggle against imperialism there are instances of people's committees forcing *mahajans* to release grain from their hoarded granaries to the affected people. The anger against Radhakanta Padhi also led them to seize his grain stock on 28 September.[194]

The police decided to act. As they advanced towards Iram conch warnings were relayed from village to village. People marched to Melanapada (Iram) from different adjoining villages like Suan, Sudarshanpur, Artu, Padhua, Bachchada and Sankarpur[195]. Slogans like 'Bharat Mata Ki Jai', 'Mahatma Gandhi Ki Jai', 'Angrezi Raj Ra Dhwansa Hou',[196] which expressed popular aspirations, were raised. Around 500 women turned up for the meeting. The people were determined to resist the 'illegal' entry of the police force into their 'liberated' zone.[197]

At the meeting at Melanapada, Kamala Prasad Kar addressed the people and explained that by having the meeting they had violated colonial authority, since Sec. 144 had been clamped. He warned that they might have to face *lathis* and bullets and advised the people to remain non-violent. At this time some *chaukidars* passed that way, carrying the baggage of the policemen which were seized but returned.[198]

After this the police landed at the place and fired at the 'crowd', killing 26 and injuring 46 others.[199] Following this, around 200 women came out and stood before the police and 'declared *swaraj*'. They went back to their villages and distributed hoarded grain to the needy. Close upon this the colonial administration unleashed repression on the villages which led many people to desert the area. When some people went to protest in front of the court at Bhadrak they were arrested as 'Communists'.[200]

At this stage, let us mention something about the type of people who participated in the Quit India Movement at Iram. The list includes those who were killed or injured as a result of the firing. The following table illustrates this.:

TABLE VIII

Approximate caste pattern of the people killed or injured in the police firing at Iram (total - 72).[201]

Brahmins and Karanas	Agricultural (i.e. Khandayats)	Cowherds	Oilmen	Washermen	Outcastes	Tribals	Unidentified
21	17	11	6	2	4	3	8

The above table shows the presence of people from different castes, which was perhaps true of the Quit India Movement in Iram as well. What needs to be emphasised is the participation of outcastes and tribals along with high castes like Brahmins and Karanas. There was active participation of landless agricultural labourers[202] as well, which not only demonstrates the broad social composition of the Quit India Movement but also a rise in the level of consciousness, making it possible for these people to relate to the anti-imperialist struggle. However, class struggle got muted simultaneously.

By October the Quit India Movement had become considerably subdued in Balasore. The imposition of collective fines,[203] attachment of property and repression were used to restore colonial authority. Nevertheless, there are references to people being asked to non-cooperate with the government, not to pay the *chaukidari* tax and other government revenues in the district. In the Gurpal area an organisation called National Government was established, which advised the people to implement these instructions, and to force the rural police to resign.[204] However, the arrest of Surendranath Dwivedy in October, 1942[205] signalled the end of the underground bulletins which had spread the message of revolt like wild fire.

In October Balasore was hit by a severe cyclone. This left a large number of people homeless and paralysed the communications system. A 'crowd' of 2,000 people affected by the cyclone 'attacked' the Laxmi Nath rice mill at Basta with a desire to 'loot' it.[206]

But after October the Quit India Movement almost ended in the Balasore district. There were some meetings and plans to damage government buildings, which could not be implemented. The Quit India Movement survived, if at all only in symbolic acts like the 'taking over' of the Kumbharia Congress office in Bhandaripokhari by a lady Congress worker.[207]

At Puri a similar pattern was witnessed. With the arrests and seizures of Congressmen and Congress offices, nothing happened till about 15 August excepting for some protest meetings. After this we get references to strikes in educational institutions, viz. the Sanskrit College and Puri Zilla School at Puri, the high schools at Nimapara, Olsing and Banpur. The Quit India Movement spread into the countryside through these schools, although nothing much seems to have happened till about the end of August.[208]

In September, the Quit India Movement spread into the countryside. It began with the cutting of telephone wires at the Bhubneswar railway station and at Delang.[209] The first major indication of this shift is evident from a meeting at Nimapara on 16 September. People from villages like Hanspada, Bhatbanda, Chanarpada, Miniganj, Adhia, Dihasahi and Villigram as well as some Bauris (outcastes) from Dihabari assembled at the Barabati field.[210]

The tension and conflicts against both the internal and the external exploiters surfaced at this meeting. An unknown person asked the audience not to pay rent to the zamindars as well as the government. A 'crowd' of about 500 people then proceeded to the police station in order to persuade the policemen to resign. On their way to the police station they met a police inspector who was 'requested' to give up his job.[211]

As the 'crowd' reached the police station it was asked not to enter the compound. This led to their pelting the police station, and the police resorted to firing which resulted in the death of one person and the injuries to some others. The 'crowd' retreated but very soon abortive attempts were made to burn a Public Works Department bungalow and a post office. On 19 September, the villages of Hanspada and Chanarpada were raided by the police to smother the rising. Three important leaders were arrested and a collective fine of Rs. 1500 was imposed on the villagers.[212]

In September strikes in some educational institutions, viz. Puri Zilla School and Sanskrit College continued. Besides, about 400 weavers from the adjoining state of Nayagarh assembled at Bolgarh (Puri) on 28 September to demonstrate before the sub-divisional officer demanding the release of the Dighri Khadi Centre which had been seized. When told by representatives of the colonial administration that this matter was being considered by the government, they dispersed.[213]

Thus by October 1942 the Quit India Movement seems to have died down in the Puri district. Still some people continued courting arrest and some 'objectionable' speeches were being made by prisoners while they were being taken from the jail to the court.[214]

As for the princely states, at Nilgiri the Quit India Movement began on 15 August with a boycott of officials and the burning of their uniforms aimed to protest against the arrest of some prominent Congressmen. Some meetings were also arranged to violate prohibitory orders. Very soon these assumed a mass character and virtually every village joined in. It was a regular feature to have 12,000 to 14,000 people march up to the Nilgiri town from different parts of the state singing songs and beating drums and having meetings. Some activists of the Prajamandal like Banamali Das went underground as jail-going was not considered to be enough.[215] A noticeable feature of this phase was the large-scale violation of forest laws.[216] Appeals were also made to state officials to join the Quit India Movement. This was sometimes accompanied by the burning of uniforms of state officials, which became a popular form of protest. In this contest the Prajamandal had a meeting on 22 August where it was decided that the leading activists would go underground. The police arrived at this meeting and arrested the leading Congressmen present, including Kailash Chandra Mohanty.[217]

People got news of this and followed their leaders to the jail gate at Nilgiri town. An activist of the Prajamandal, Shyam Prasad Chaudhuri, mentioned that a day would come when the state people would remove every brick from the jail. This alarmed the *durbar* which requisitioned war planes and two hundred men from the Eastern Joint Union. This altered the situation considerably. There are references to aerial attacks on 'crowds' at Ayodhya who were marching in a procession, and on people in boats when they were crossing the Son river for a meeting. Besides, there were aerial attacks and military repression on processions at Chandipur, Gopinathpur and Kathapada. At Berhampur around 80 people gheraoed the police party. At the intervention of the Political Agent the 'crowd' withdrew. Once the policemen were set free the Political Agent ordered a firing, killing three person. The 'crowd' retreated and re-assembled to find that the police force had gone away. At Ishwarpur an attempt was made to burn the police station. However, the plan failed for want of favourable weather. There seems to be some relationship between *hatas* and this form of 'crowd' behaviour.[218]

The Raja of Nilgiri tried to prevent meetings associated with the 'unity week' in November 1942 through arrests. This 'unity week' was supported by the Prajamandal activists like Banamali Das who had gone underground. Around this time the major demands of the Prajamandal included the release of political prisoners, cancellation of warrants and collective fines and the restoration of rights to organise meetings. A signature campaign was launched in some parts of the state like Panchakhada and Athakhunt, demanding exemptions from taxes and fines which had been imposed. The peasants who had links with the Kisan Sangha were not given loans by the moneylenders. However, they held out depending on the forests for their food.[219]

In this phase the people were exposed to ruthless repression. The machinery of repression was personally supervised by the Political Agent. From every village two to three people were arrested. Some people were forced to leave the state; collective fines were imposed at the rate of Re. 1/- per person or Rs. 78/- to Rs. 154/- per village and lootings, firings, rapes and beatings became the order of the day. The Prajamandal retaliated through a total boycott of state officials.[220]

The repressive policy was also directed against the Communist Party at Nilgiri, with arrests and imprisonment of its cadre, for periods ranging from 15 days to 3 to 4 months, and on occasions some activists were kept under house arrest or forced to leave the state. A meeting, where the Communists were explaining their policy of support to the War, was attacked.[221]

It is not possible to have a clear picture of the participants in the Quit India Movement. However, the facts related to 80 people arrested on 'serious' charges perhaps throws some light on the social composition of the participants. About 50 per cent of these belonged to dominant castes i.e. Brahmins and Karanas; there were 12 people from agriculturist castes; 13 cowherds, 3 outcastes and 1 Santhal. Thus, Nilgiri saw the participation of people from different castes. Outcastes and tribals also joined in the Quit India Movement.[222]

A very significant development of the Quit India Movement in the state was that the Raja was forced to stay outside the state till 1946. This had important consequences insofar as popular perceptions regarded this as a symbol of victory of the Prajamandal struggle.[223]

As for Dhankanal, the *durbar*, in its drive to smother the Prajamandal movement, had arrested some of its leading activists. After the news of the Quit India Movement reached the state, Baishnab Pattnaik escaped from house arrest and moved in the Palasuni and Parjang area mobilising people for the Quit India Movement. Nearly 300 people got together in the forest and planned to raid the armoury at Madhi with muzzle-loaded guns. On 26 August about nineteen people including some daily wage labourers 'liberated' the armoury at Madhi with crowbars and swords. Their job was quite easy since the armoury was left relatively unguarded as the chief's son's birthday was being observed and the guards had gone over to the capital. Two policemen and a few *chaukidars* were locked up in the *hazaat*. Shouting slogans like 'Prajamandal Ki Jai' and 'Mahatma Gandhi Ki Jai', the symbols of the British and the Raja, e.g. barracks, were burnt.[224]

After this a meeting was held in which about 15,000 to 20,000 people participated. Here the decision to set up a popular government was articulated. Accordingly local committees and 'death squads' were set up.[225]

Subsequently, the Raja's granary at Malapara was 'looted' and the grain distributed to the people. Papers of *sahukars* were burnt, along with a local school and the police station at Chapur on 2 September.[226] The *durbar* got news of these developments. With the assistance of three platoons of the colonial army and aerial support the *durbar* met the rebels. Two activists—Benu and Bira—were killed and Baishnab Pattnaik got seriously injured and had to flee the state. Here, too, the state smothered the Quit India Movement through repression.[227]

The Quit India Movement evoked sharp responses from the state of Talcher. With their experience of the 1938 *hizrat* the people felt attracted to a movement which called for a direct confrontation with the British and which asked them to be their own leader. In the beginning the state people attempted to establish some coordination with the people of adjoining states like Dhenkanal. The *durbar* decided to deal with the Prajamandal with an iron hand. This led to the arrest of the entire Prajamandal leadership and some activists were forced to go underground. However, it seems that the Prajamandal leadership could send out directions to the people from jail. This situation was altered when around the end of August 1942 Pabitra Mohan Pradhan, President of the Prajamandal escaped from the state jail. It came to be widely believed that Pradhan had been murdered by the state authorities.[228]

The past experiences of struggle, a rise in consciousness, the desire to fight British imperialism and the oppressive *durbar* rallied the people to militancy.[229] Popular perceptions wanted an end of the Raja, viewed the 'passing of the *lathi*' by the 'Mahatma' approvingly and aspired to establish a '*praja raija*' (*swaraj*).[230] In fact, when the Prajamandal leadership conceptualised the establishment of a '*chasi-mulia*' raj in response to the Quit India Resolution or the resorting to a militant struggle through guerilla warfare, in coordination with adjoining states, it mirrored the popular perceptions and the heightened consciousness of the state people.[231]

In this context Pradhan's 'death news' spread like wild fire in the state. On 1 September, at a meeting at Paniola (Angul), the Prajamandal considered breaking the jail.[232] At a meeting on 3 September at Kumunda it was decided to abide by the Quit India Resolution, destroy the state authority and the ruling dynasty and set up a '*chasi-mulia*' raj. It was also decided to capture the capital and the palace on 6 September at 1 a.m.[233]

People all over the state refused to submit to the authority of the *durbar*. Schools, courts and offices were closed down. The refrain to destroy the ruler's family and the state authority was on everybody's lips, along with Gandhi's instructions of driving out the British and setting up panchayats at the village level. The officials of the state were won over, either voluntarily or through demonstrations of popular anger, which were directed against the uniforms and papers of state officials. On occasions we are told how they were made to swear (on symbols of Hinduism) that they had given up links with the *durbar* and that they accepted the Prajamandal *sircar*. Some arms were also seized from state officials.[234]

As the movement developed we get references to the destruction of telephone and telegraph lines in order to prevent the movement of colonial troops. The Cuttack-Talcher railway line was destroyed for several miles. However, it seems that the communication network controlled by the '*chasi-mazdur*' raj was left undamaged. With the '*chasi-mazdur*' raj taking over the police station and the sub-divisional offices, a parallel system of the people was established.[235]

The Prajamandal's programme reflected a popular peasant utopia. It aimed to provide food, shelter and clothing to all, reduce rents, help the unemployed with jobs and land and improve the system of education, health and water supply. Given the presence of mines and factories in the state, it planned to increase wages and take over these from foreign companies.[236]

On 3 September the Raja approached the colonial government for help. He requisitioned the services of the Royal Air Force and the Royal Military Infantry from 4 September 1942. From this day aeroplanes circled over the state and in some areas dropped leaflets asking people to give up their path of confrontation. In some places smoke-bombs and tear-gas shells were dropped to scare the people. It was in this context that the Prajamandal had its crucial meeting in its hill-base, attended by some activists of the adjoining states as well. It reiterated its plans to drive out the British, destroy the state authority and establish a '*chasi-mazdur*' raj. The idea was to open the attack on the Talcher *durbar*, and subsequently send the peasant army to the adjoining states on a similar mission. Some leaders like Prabitra Mohan Pradhan were opposed to the militant course but popular militancy seems to have prevailed and even Pradhan was forced to approve of this action plan.[237]

The popular enthusiasm this struggle generated can be judged from the fact that every family sent all its able-bodied male members (excepting one son) to join the militia. By 6 September the '*chasi-mazdur*' raj had been established all over the state,excepting the four square miles of Talcher town. The focus now was on the bastion of oppression —the Talcher town, which housed the palace and symbolised power and authority. People from various parts of the state began their march towards the Talcher town, carrying at least a *lathi*, rice, *sag* and *mudhi*. In many cases villagers gave them rice as they passed through their villages. There was no serious arming and people carried *lathis*, axes and sickles with them. Some dynamite and some gunpowder (seized from the stores of the collieries) and a few guns were also carried by some people. Slogans like '*Bharat Chada*' (Quit India), '*Kara ba Mara*' ('Do or Die') '*Karibu*

Maribu' ('Will do and Die'), '*Bharata ru Tadiba*' (Will drive out from India) *Talcher ru Tadiba*' (Will drive out from Talcher'), '*Raja ku Mariba*' ('Will kill the Raja') '*Chasi Mulia Sircar Gadhiba*' ('Will build Chasi-Mulia Sircar'), drumbeats and conch blasts rent the air.[238]

The people reached the outskirts of the Talcher town and camped in and around a mango grove in a semi-circle encircling the town on 7 September. They tried to negotiate with the ruler for transferring power to the newly constituted '*chasi-mulia*' raj. Failing, they attempted to break through the enemy lines. This triggered off a conflict in which they were machine-gunned from the air and under cover of smokescreen the military contingent opened fire on them. About 4 people died on the spot, around 100 were injured and nearly 300 arrested.[239]

This aerial attack along with ruthless firing continued the next day as well. The state authorities and the colonial administration 'restored order' through firings, lootings, plunder, rapes and flag marches through every village. The aeroplane assisted them in this operation. Collective fines to the tune of Rs. 45,000/- were imposed, though the money collected was as much as ten times more as no receipts were given. Besides, individual fines were also levied, many Prajamandal activists were to leave the state and properties of a large number of them were confiscated.[240]

The train derailment on 7 September, and the widespread destruction of bridges and telephone wires on 11 September[241] were the actions planned by the Prajamandal to neutralise repression by disrupting the communication system. However, these hardly served any purpose. The militia was forced to retreat and it resorted to guerilla tactics. Under increasing pressure these methods were to serve only marginally to neutralise repression. With the all-India movement almost over by December 1942 and the pressure of the *durbar* mounting, this form of struggle dragged on till May 1943 when the guerilla contingents were finally liquidated.[242]

Referring to Koraput we find that Biswasroi had been sent after a meeting of the DCC (Jeypur, 31 July) to Bombay to attend the AICC session. The Congress organisation was declared illegal on 9 August and on 11 August the colonial administration attached the DCC office at Jeypur. It seems that Dwivedy's instructions which he had sent in the 'Mahatma's' name also reached Jeypore. On 13 August two boys carrying cyclostyed copies of the 'Mahatma's call' roamed with Congress flags, reading out the 'call'. The initial thrust was to try to organise '*hartals*' by closing shops and to campaign for a no-tax movement. And, with the background as discussed earlier, this no-tax campaign seems to have percolated into the interior with remarkable speed. What fired popular imagination was the belief that the British were no longer ruling the country and that *swaraj* had been achieved. This conceptualisation of a breakdown of colonial authority has to be borne in mind while discussing the Quit India Movement in Koraput.[243]

There are references to tribals being told by 'Congressmen' that since the British government no longer existed taxes need not be paid and that the land belonged to the people. From about 15 August the Quit India Movement assumed a militant form. Attempts were made to close shops and court arrest (i.e. at Kundali 'shandy') and arrange huge gatherings (for example, at Dimla). There were 'interferences' with the functioning of the shops and in some cases 'lootings' and 'burnings' of stocks took place (for example at Pukkili 'shandy'). On 15 August a large 'crowd' of 'Congress sympathisers' attacked an arrack shop, the excise liquor depot and a cattle pound at Nandapur which resulted in considerable damage. An attempt was also made to 'invade' the Nandapur police station. The arrested people said that they were convinced about the end of the British regime and were happy to be jailed. On 16 August a 'crowd' of 1,000 people who 'attacked' the taluk office had to be dispersed through a *lathi* charge. On the same day a 'crowd' of 1,000 people assembled at the Jeypur police station, and had to be driven out by force. Later on a large 'crowd' which included tribals blocked the entrance of the police station and prepared to settle down for the night at the place.[244]

From this time we get references to hectic activity in the *hatas* which had assumed considerable importance as transmission points through which the Quit India Movement spread. It spread to Semiliguda soon.[245] Symbols of colonialism, like the Jeypore-Nowrangpur telegraph line, were badly damaged. By 18 August the Quit India Movement had reached Gunpur (which was at the eastern-most part of the zamindari). Here excise shops, courts and other government institutions were picketed. On 18 August a large 'crowd' surrounded and 'demanded the surrender' of the Dasmathapur police station since, according to them, the British had withdrawn and the Indians had attained *swaraj*. They dispersed after the arrest of eight leaders. A similar incident took place at Laxmipur police station where the 'crowd' managed to burn some records before dispersing. A selective 'attack' was made on Messrs. H. Dear and Company who were contractors who supplied railway sleepers. On several occasions sleepers made by them were destroyed and their labourers were threatened with dire consequences if they worked. The Quit India Movement also evoked considerable enthusiasm in the Guneipada and the Padwa area.[246]

Malkangiri and Nowrangpur were the most important centres of the Quit India Movement in the estate. We will now focus on Malkangiri and see the responses to the Quit India Movement in this area. On 16 August 1942 some 'Congressmen' threatened to 'loot' the opium shop at Badhigar unless Sadasiva Choudhury, the vendor, surrendered his stock immediately. The 'crowd', composed of tribals and non-tribals (i.e. agricultural castes) from the Mathili and Padwa area 'armed' with *lathis* and Congress flags, entered Sadasiva Choudhuri's compound. In a fit of panic The latter surrendered ten tolas of opium, his scales and weights. The leaders 'distributed ... the opium amongst their following. The purpose of this demonstration was to protest against government obtaining revenue from this popular means of relaxation'.[247]

After their success the behaviour of the 'crowd' took the form of demonstrations of their displeasure with the *mustajar*, Kesab Patro, 'whose ryots most of them were'. Patro had 'for long been unpopular for his alleged *zabardust* (strong-arm tactics) ways with many from whom *cist* (revenue) ... (was) due through him to the estate'. He had left his place to attend to his property matters at Govindapally, a neighbouring place. The 'crowd' felt disappointed on discovering this. It proceeded to Khogan, about three miles away. The 'crowd' then proceeded in a very enthusiastic way to the *hata* at Badhigar, 'trampling down the wares and produce for sale and knocking over people in their mad rush'. The official version labels this as an act of rioting. However, this reflected the climax of a chain of activities. Though this is not substantiated, it may be suggested that it was very likely that the 'crowd' had originated from this very *hata*. After accomplishing its mission successfully it perhaps went back to the source of its origin to share its triumph with others and then got merged with the people at the *hata*.[248]

On 23 August another interesting event was reported from Nuagaon, in the Mathili police station area. A 'Congress crowd' of about 200 threatened to burn the house of Gangadhar Guru (who owned a 'food store') of Nuagaon, unless he provided them with food. According to Guru's complaint, after satisfying their hunger, 'the intruders took also ... (his) valuables (i.e. clothes and Rs. 200/- in cash) lying invitingly there'. However, according to the police investigation report Guru's allegations regarding the theft were false.[249]

The Quit India Movement not only subsumed tribal/non-tribal dichotomy but also a division along lines of caste. A person of Malipara (Nuagaon) who was a Mali by caste was sent a chit which ordered him to keep food ready for two hundred 'Congressmen'. This person was affluent as compared to his 'co-villagers'. The self-invited guests numbering about one hundred attended the feast.The 'crowd' which was composed of both tribals and non-tribals (this included five Malis out of the ten leaders) invited their host to join them. Since the latter declined their offer on grounds of caste they 'threatened ... to break the caste barrier',[250] presumably by forcing him to eat with them.

There seems to be a difference at the popular level when one compares the 'crowd' distributing opium at Badhigar and the 'attacks' on the liquor shop led by Laxman Naiko at Kongrabeda, where liquor was destroyed, not distributed. After this Laxman led his 'band of rowdies' to Kuntipalli and 'attacked' the liquor shop at around noon on 17 August. The 'crowd' composed of tribals and non-tribals (like Gaudas) reached the place shouting slogans, 'brandishing' *lathis* and Congress flags. The pots containing the fermented *mohwa* and the distillation apparatus was destroyed. Although the owner estimated the damage to be around Rs. 500 'it was found later not to be more than Rs. 100'.[251] Laxman's 'attacks' reveal the absence of a total Congress hegemony, more so because of the specificity of the tribal areas where there was a close link between moneylenders and liquor dealers and where liquor ruined many families.

Laxman led another successful destruction of the Sindhabeda liquor shop on 18 August. After this he deputed Padlam Naiko (of Kaligada) and a 'party of soldiers' to 'raid' the opium shop at Salimi, 8 miles west of Sindhabeda. The contingent reached the opium shop owned by S. Chandrashekhar Pattnaik (who had his shop on the varandah of his house) around 3 p.m. The 'crowd' directed its wrath at 38 *tolas* of opium which was destroyed. Bhima Naiko tore up the account book of Pattnaik and he was then thrown out by the scruff of the neck. By this time Laxman's fame had spread all over Malkangiri and it came to be believed that he was the future king of Malkangiri.

This messianic trait, which formed an integral component of the revolt, was also associated with Lal Raja (whose real name was Moti Singh), the *naiko* of Tonguguda (in Malkangiri). He had been recruited as a four-*anna* member of the Congress in 1940. Being a village *naiko* 'he could naturally wield his influence' in the Tonguguda area. Laxman and Balram Pujari met him at the Damapalli 'shandy' (*hata*) on 19 August, and he was sent to 'attack' the 'out-still' liquor shop of Pushpalli. The 'crowd' composed of tribals, non-tribals and some outcastes 'raided' the shop at 4 p.m. on 19 August. The *sahukar*, Dayanidhi, was directed to close his shop for good as the British raj had ended and *swaraj* had been established and no taxes or revenue would be paid. A number of articles (distillation apparatus, buckets, etc.) were destroyed and the total loss amounted to Rs. 60. Since Dayanidhi 'interfered' during the 'raid' he was thrown out by the scruff of the neck by Lal Raja. The cash box containing Re. 1 just disappeared, but later on Dayanidhi 'recovered one anna six paise out of it'.[252]

The climax was a huge meeting organised at Mathili on 21 August. Since about 17 August the police had apprehended that this would take the form of a 'raid' on the Mathili police station.[253] What needs to be emphasised is that Maithili was the epicentre of a widespread campaign which had stirred up Malkangiri and the western portion of the neighbouring Jeypur *taluk* (especially Ambaguda and Udoyogiri). What seems to have made the estate authorities and the police panic was the fear that these activities would rouse the Bondas whom they dreaded since they had remained comparatively isolated and were looked upon as a fierce and war-like tribe.[254]

On 21 August the opium shop and the Revenue Inspector's office at Mathili were 'raided'.[255] Following this a 'crowd' of about 1,000 people reached the Mathili police station at about 9.30 a.m., singing the '*Ramdhun*' and carrying Congress flags. It raised slogans like '*Mahatma Gandhi Ki Jai*'. These people were stopped about two hundred yards east of the police station. After an argument with the police the 'crowd' withdrew to the nearby *hata* in a procession. Here Laxman made a speech informing the audience that the British government was gone and that Gandhi was their king. After this the 'crowd' (the number of which had swelled) marched enthusiastically towards the police station around 2 p.m. Here Laxman again made a speech through which he expressed the collective aspiration of the 'crowd'. As he put it, Gandhi Raj had replaced British Raj and the 'shandy' and forest dues no longer had to be paid.[256] Although portrayed in official reports as a violent mob, the 'crowd' remained peaceful. Its basic aim was to disobey orders, have a meeting and hoist the Congress flag in the police station as a symbol of defiance and to court arrest.[257]

In the tussle that followed the police got the pretext for a *lathi* charge and the subsequent firing. Laxman got injured during the *lathi* charge and fell down unconscious. It was the police firing that killed Ramayya, a forest guard and 9 to 11 demonstrators. The 'crowd' was termed as a 'violent mob' which wanted to burn the police station, kill the officers and loot the Malkangiri treasury. After this the authorities unleashed a reign of terror to smother the Quit India Movement.[258]

As for Nowrangpur, this area was to see the active role of some 'local leaders' who moved extensively in the villages of Nowrangpur, Mydalpur,

Tentulikhunti and Dabugam *thana* limits. They appealed to people to join meetings and focused on the no-rent campaign. The people were asked not to pay rent as long as their own government was not established, and to demand *swaraj*. They were advised to 'destroy' police buildings, 'attack' police/government officials, 'destroy' bridges and disrupt communication. After the Congress was banned in the district (9 August) there are references to meetings, 'attacks' on police buildings and bridges and policemen being 'threatened'. In some areas forests were cut.[259]

Madhav Pradhani planned to mobilise 'armed' men from Nowrangpur to Dabugam where a large 'crowd' from Umerkote was to join them. The idea of demolishing bridges, destroying police stations, cutting 'reversed' forests and declaring *swaraj* in this area was visualised. There are references to 'forcible recruitment' at Gumapadar for the Quit India Movement. As the 'crowd' advanced to Dabugam a pamphlet was distributed which asked the people to be prepared to die fearlessly; the importance of a no-rent campaign was also reiterated. The people were asked to think that they were independent and paralyse the government machinery.[260]

A large number of people joined in, 'armed' with bows, arrows, *lathis*, spades, *tangis* and rations for a few days. Plans of 'destruction' were implemented on the way. Trees were cut from a 'reserved' forest and a wooden bridge on the Ampani ghat near the Koraput-Kalahandi border was destroyed. A campaign was launched to attract people to Gumapadar. One Ananda Behera talked to people at the Maliguda *hata* and asked them to go over to Gumapadar. He also informed them about how the people were destroying symbols of British rule and violating forest laws.[261]

By the time the marchers reached Gumapadar a rumour circulated that the police stations at Papadahandi, Mydalpur and Kadinga would be 'attacked'. At Gumapadar Madhav Pradhani addressed a large gathering. After this the marchers moved towards Papadahandi. On 24 August a gathering of 5,000 people was fired upon by the police at Papadahandi, resulting in 19 deaths and 100 injured. Besides, 92 people were arrested. With this Quit India Movement gradually died down in the Nowrangpur area.[262]

It is not possible to say anything much about the social composition of the 'crowds' or the people who participated in the Quit India Movement in Malkangiri and the Nowrangpur area. However, some broad conclusions can be drawn on the bases of the following tables.

TABLE IX

Incidents prior to the meeting at Mathili (Malkangiri)[263]

Incident	*Date*	*Place*	*Total No. persons accused*	*Tribals & out-castes*	*Non-tribals*
1.	16.8.1942	Badhigar	8	4	4
2.	17.8. 1942	Kuntipally	27	23	4
3.	18.8.1942	Salimi	26	21	5
4.	19.8.1942	Pushpalli	29	27	2
5.	23.8.1942	Nuagaon	—Details are not known—		
6.	?	Malipara	10	5	5

TABLE X

Persons arrested in connection with the Mathili police station episode (total 54)[264]

Tribal group/caste					
Bhumiyas	*Kutias (Khonds)*	*Gaudas*	*Paikas/Ranas*	*Out-castes*	*Others*
36	*5*	*3*	*2*	*3*	*5*

Occupation			
Naikos	*Cultivators (including Naikos)*	*Agricultural and non-agricultural labourers*	*Teacher*
13	45	8	1

TABLE XI

Persons arrested at Papadahandi (total 92)[265]

Tribals	*Cowherds, Ranas and Telis*	*Outcastes*	*Karanas*	*Unidentified*
58	15	7	4	8

The predominence of tribals is obvious, which was true of the Quit India Movement as a whole in the district of Koraput. At Malkangiri this included Bhumiyas and Khonds and at Nowrangpur this saw the inclusion of Parajas, Gonds, Bhatras, Amanatyas and Savaras. We also find the participation of outcastes (mostly Dombs; two at Malkangiri and three at Papadahandi). Of course, besides the tribals and the outcastes we find non-tribals as well. Thus we find inter-tribal as well as tribal/non-tribal unity in the course of the Quit India Movement in the district. The hill-men/plains-men dichotomy does not seem to have any relevance since most of the DCC leaders like Biswasroi, Sahu, Tripathy and Damodar Samantarai were technically men from the plains. Further, the Quit India Movement united various castes and also some *mustajars* with tenants, agricultural labourers and non-agricultural labourers (as is clear from Malkangiri). The latter phenomenon was possible because of the nature of stratification and the position of *mustajars* .

The Quit India Movement caused great alarm within the colonial administration as well as the estate authorities. Troops were requisitioned from the adjoining state of Bastar[266] and 'flag marches' were conducted in Congress 'strongholds'.[267] Arrests, *lathi* charges, canings and rapes were resorted to in various parts of the estate to smother the Movement.[268]

By September the Quit India Movement had lost its momentum in the estate. There are references to some activity in schools, like the Jeypur High School.[269] By October the Quit India Movement had almost died down, except for Gunpur where militancy among the Savaras was witnessed.[270] This situation continued for sometime and on 1 December large 'bands' of Savaras under the leadership of one Saura Pattnaik cut down unripe paddy. Saura Pattnaik was arrested.[271] His name, as well as his surname, perhaps indicates the complex process through which the tribals got linked to Indian nationalism in the Jeypur estate. After this we see the end of the Quit India Movement in the estate.

The Quit India Movement also saw the legalisation of the Communist Party in Orissa for the first time since its inception in 1938. Although most of its activists were either imprisoned or were underground[272] and the Communists remained isolated from the political mainstream, legalised existence provided fresh opportunities. In the first week of November 1942 the Communists began functioning actively in course of the National Week in the three districts of Cuttack, Puri and Balasore. The Communist Party's organ *Muktijuddhya* could convey reports about its activities.[273] Nevertheless, the mistake of opposing the Quit India Movement isolated the Communists from the mainstream of national politics.

The Kisan Sangha's effort was directed to the political education of the peasants, a consistent critique of the Minority Ministry and the government, as well as their wrong food policies. The need for unity and struggle was stressed. A large number of meetings were organised to campaign against 'sabotage'—which was implicitly against the Quit India Movement itself and which was a serious mistake—and to organise peoples' organisations to defend the country against possible attacks by Japanese fascists. The problem of food shortages attracted the Kisan Sangha and it set up food committees to distribute food and essential commodities and tried to fix maxium interest rates. It also suggested restructuring the taxation system to provide relief to the peasantry. It appealed to the peasants not to sell their foodgrains to *sahukars*, zamindars and the government but to organise peasants' cooperatives for this purpose.[274]

These activities of the Kisan Sangha coexisted with campaigns for the release of political prisoners and the demand to stop the export of rice from the province. Given its live contact with the countryside it speculated over the possibility of a famine by the end of 1942.[275] In a context of isolation of the Communists, these features made the Kisan Sangha stand out as an organisation which worked for the peasant masses. As the storm of the Quit India Movement passed away, we get references to the Kisan Sangha attracting the attention of the peasant and even some Congressmen.[276]

We can round off our discussion of the Quit India Movement by citing how it stirred the Oriya intellectual. Here one can refer to Kalindi Charan's 'Agami' ('Future': 1942) which conceptualises a brighter future and demonstrates how the popular struggles associated with the Quit India Movement had left a deep impression on him and had, in fact, led to his radicalisation:

> Through a poem...
> I construct a society of abundance.
> Where everybody has at least a room to live in
> And gets some food to eat.
> Where every boy and girl is qualified,
> And there is no shortage of clothes.
> Where no hurdles prevent people from reading and writing
> And where nobody has the right to remain unemployed
> Since the government provides jobs for all;
> Where everyone has a right to speak...
> I sit to write a poem of that society.[277]

The conceptualisation of independence and freedom associated with the Quit India Movement made Sachidananda call out in his 'Uthare Swadhina Jati' ('Rise Oh! Independent People'; 1942):

> If you do not look after your country
> Will the foreigners do it for you?
> You don't keep your house in order
> And you fight among yourselves
> What pleasure lies in this sloth?
> Fly the flag of indpendence
> Under freedom's sky.
> Don't forget your country is your own
> Don't become another Mir Jafar.[278]

The sweep of the Quit India Movement stirred sensitive people in the colonial bureaucracy like Gopinath Mohanty. There is definitely a connection between his *Paraja* (1943)—which centres around the Paraja tribals of the Koraput district (where he was posted around this time)—and the sweep of the Quit India Movement in this area.[279] Through it the author in fact projects a critique of the 'zamindar-*sahukar*-sarkar' nexus and its exploitation of the poor tribals. Not only does the author capture the life and the problems of the tribals in a context of decline and change but he also projects how they tried to set things right by axing the *sahukar* to death at the end. Although the novel is silent about the Quit India Movement Mohanty's construction of the Parajas perhaps explains the delicate links between him and the volatile nature of the Quit India Movement in Koraput.[280]

VI

Conclusion

The Quit India Movement perhaps marked the peak of popular protest. It united town and country, the coastal belt and the western interior and the tribals and non-tribals. This accounts for the widespread nature of the Quit India Movement in Orissa.

That the Quit India Movement incorporated a strong anti-imperalist current is fairly obvious. The identification of all those who were associated with the colonial power—from the Governor to the petty village offical—as the 'enemy', responsible for various problems, largely contributed to this. This perception was also precipitated by the existence of a Ministry which was thrust on the people and had no links with the peasants and tribals, except as a bulwark to defend all that they had struggled against in the preceeding phase. Nevertheless, any attempt to locate the Quit India Movement within the framework of anti-imperialism alone is contradicted by the selectivity and nature of 'crowd' behaviour, the clashes with the immediate oppressors (whether liquor merchants/ moneylenders, landlords or the princes). Moreover, decoding the act of wire-cutting in the perspective we have outlined in the first chapter enlarges the scope of what may appear to be a purely anti-imperialist action. These features disprove any narrow definition of nationalism in this phase.

Nevertheless, in spite of these features the fact remains that the Quit India Movement does exhibit the deep inroads made by anti-imperialism. This can be partly explained by the setting as well as the build-up of the Quit India Movement. It was also a reflection of the nature of Congress politics and the local leadership during the Quit India Movement. For example, in the Jeypur estate there was an absence of any struggle centred on *goti* or *bethi*, although these had been taken up in the 1936-1939 phase. There was, similarly, an absence of any struggle against the zamindari establishment. This was possibly due to the extention of the Congress influence as well as the nature of stratification in which *mustagirs*, who were leading activists like Laxman Naiko, played an important role.

Moreover, one can also discern links between this phenomenon and the position of the Communist Party and the Kisan Sangha. Going against the Quit India Movement not only implied an aloofness from anti-imperialism, but also toning down the anti-feudal struggle—the twin currents with which the Kisan Sangha and the Communists were intimately involved. Given this, one can understand why in the coastal tract, where the Kisan Sangha and the Communists had secured a base among the peasants and the rural poor, the struggle against the immediate exploiters did not last beyond the initial phase of the Quit India Movement. It also explains the toning down of class struggle by the Nilgiri Communists. Consequently, this reveals the dilemma of class struggle being muted in a phase which reflected a virtual peak of the anti-imperialist struggle. In this sense, the position taken by the Kisan Sangha and the Communists during the Quit India Movement proved to be a costly mistake. Moreover, it also lacked the depth witnessed in the 1936-39 phase.

The Quit India Movement consolidated the link between the

Prajamandal movement and mainstream nationalism, in spite of the relative unevenness of this process. It witnessed the close identification of colonialism with the princes, and a common desire of both to reassert their power/authority which had been undermined in the preceding phase. Features such as the desire to set up 'liberated' zones, guerrilla warfare[281] and the large-scale violence —unleashed on the states' people—illustrate both the level of involvement and the depth of the Quit India Movement in the princely states.

This takes us to the role of Congress and Gandhi. Their position underwent major shifts between 1940 and August 1942. And both were extremely crucial in legitimising the Quit India Movement in Orissa.[282] In fact it would be difficult to envisage the Quit India Movement without the sanction of both. This partly explains the 'presence' of both in popular perceptions in spite of their actual organisational absence from the events of the Quit India Movement (given the arrests of most of the prominent leaders).

However, given the nature of the developments it will be unhistorical to stop here without making significant qualifications. And, while doing so, one cannot but see the shaping of the Quit India Movement itself as a response to popular pressures. The shifting position of the Congress in the 1940-42 phase—through the 'individual' *satyagraha* to the Quit India Resolution, the slogans of Gandhi—support such a position.

Consequently, both Gandhi and the Congress shaped the popular level while also being shaped by it. Gandhi and the Congress emerged as 'saviours from above' for the popular masses. This process was based on the messianic appeal, especially of Gandhi and some local Congress activists (like Laxman Naiko) and can be traced to the process of Hinduisation. Complex apocalyptic notions associated with the Quit India Movement (in some form or the other) coexisted with the popular translations of *swaraj*—which went beyond selective targets associated directly with colonialism and internal exploiters, to 'stealing' and distributing opium, common feasting (perhaps in anticipation of a new age) or confrontations with the coercive apparatus of the colonial order and the princes and attempts to build up liberated zones in and outside the princely states.[283] In this sense a social historian cannot miss the extension of the logic of popular translations of *swaraj*—from non-payment of revenue, asserting rights over forests, 'grabbing' the land of the rural rich or actions against *chaukidars*—witnessed during the Non-Cooperation Movement and the Civil Disobedience Movement. It also reflects the quest for a more concrete alternative order resulting from the interaction of popular imagination with the national movement.

We conclude by mentioning how the processes we have sought to highlight combined with the repression and arrests of Congressmen left the field clear for the Congress to reap the political harvest of the Quit India Movement, and, through it, hegemonise the peasants and tribals.

Notes

1. This began with *Congress Responsibility for the Distribances: 1942-43* (New Delhi, 1943), which demonstrates how the people were 'misled' by the Congress. Bourgeois-nationalist writings, for example, H.K. Mahtab, *et.al. History of Freedom Movement in Orissa, Vols. IV* and *V* (Cuttack 1959) do focus on the common people, but operate with framework of locating the role of the Congress.
2. Mahtab *et.al., op.cit.*
3. As the District Magistrate, Cuttack, L.P. Singh, wrote to the Chief Secretary, Government of Orissa (September 18, 1942): 'It would be incorrect to say that the various incidents that have occurred...are due to spontaneous resentment of the lower orders at the arrest of Mr. Gandhi, and the other leaders'; Acc. No.53, Who's Who Compilation Committee, Orissa State Archives (hereafter, WWCC); such a position matches with contemporary works like F. Hutchins, *Spontaneous Revolution* (Delhi, 1971).
4. This is often romanticised.
5. Failing to see things in proper perspective has, of course, created another problem. Here one can cite the example of Stephen Hennigham, *Peasant Movements in Colonial India: North Bihar 1917:1942* (Canberra, 1982), especially chapter 7 and his article, 'Quit India in Bihar and Eastern United Provinces: The Dual Revolt' in Ranajit Guha (ed.), *Subaltern Studies II* (New Delhi, 1983) where an attempt is made to split Indian nationalism into two levels: that of the 'elite' and that of the subaltern.
6. Among the very few works that exist one can mention Mahtab *et.al. op.cit,* Henningham *op.cit.*, Max Harcourt, 'Kisan Populism and Revolution in Rural India in Low (ed.), *Congress and the Raj* (London, 1978) and Gyanendra Pandey (ed.), *The Indian Nation in 1942* (Calcutta, 1988).
7. For example we get references to the Defence of India Rules being used to arrest Kisan Sangha activists like Phani Pal (active in the Madhupur estate) as well as Communists who were associated with the peasant movement in Februrary and July 1940, respectively; Home Political (hereafter HP) 18.2.1940 and 18.7.1940.
8. *Indian Annual Register,* Vol. I, 1941, February 5 (hereafter *IAR*).
9. For example, this stood at Rs. 1,86,500 in November 1940 and Rs. 6,63,600 in November 1941; HP 18/11/1940; 18/11/1941. A fighter plane was brought for Orissa at 5,000 pounds sterling;/H.P. 18/11/1940.
10. The Home Political Fortnighly Reports for 1940 and 1941 present this picture by repeatedly pointing to price rise, hoarding and scarcity.
11. This was, in fact, articulated specifically by Mahtab in a speech at Remuna, Balasore (1 December 1940) and reflected deeper levels of popular perceptions; Acc. No. 60, WWCC. Around October 1940 we get evidence of plans to recruit people for the army from Orissa (especially Koraput) and

its princely states. Although we do not get references to large scale recruitment this suggests that, perhaps, such attempts were actually made in some parts which contributed to unite the people; HP 18.10.1940.

12. HP 18/2/1941; 18/5/1941. However, given the fact that the Muslim population was confined to some areas like Balasore and Cuttack and was around two per cent of the total population of Orissa the level of communalisation was not significant.
13. Acc. No. 30, WWCC; HP, 18.3.1940.
14. HP 18/3/1940; 18/1/1941.
15. Acc.No. 30 WWCC (December 1941).
16. HP 18/2/1940; 18/1/1941; All India State People's Conference (hereafter AISPC) file no. 164 Nehru Memorial Museum and Library (New Delhi), from Sudhakar Rath to Secretary, State People's Conference (16.12.1940).
17. *IAR*, p. 333.
18. We can cite here Mahtab's letter to Gandhi (7.2.1939) where he wrote: 'How I wish you could direct us as you did in 1921 and 1930. Of course, we are now twenty years older; our sincere purposes have been substituted by sinister desires'. Mahtab, Private Papers, Nehru Memorial Museum and Library , New Delhi (hereafter NMML).
19. HP 18/2/1940.
20. HP 18/4/1940; the Ganjam District Congress Committee violated the PCC's directive.
21. HP 18/7/1941.
22. AICC, Private Papers (NMML) File No. P-20/940, Rajendra Prasad to Nityananda Kanungo (22.9.1941) where he mentioned that Sarala Devi declined to resign, as directed by Acharya Kriplani.
23. HP 18/4/1940; this was the role assigned to a tribunal set up by the AICC.
24. HP 18/7/1941; interestingly, this dissidence sought legitimacy from Lord Jagannatha and we get a refrence to Nilakantha Das and Jadumani Mangaraj organising a meeting (July 1941) at Singha Dwara (in front of the temple), where Gandhi's way of *satyagraha* was criticised and support to the British was advocated: Mansergh *et.al* (eds.), *The Transfer of Power 1942-44, Vol. IV; The Bengal Famine and the New Viceroyalty* (London 1971), Document 564.
25. HP 18/1/1940; Acc. No. 56, WWCC (January 1940); Acc No. 59, WWCC (April-May, 1940) - Balasore; Acc. No. 30, WWCC, Mahtab to all DCC's November 1940, instructing them to follow their individual or collective policy in case the Congress was declared illegal.
26. Acc. No. 30, WWCC (22.4.1940); Ganeshwar was the venue for the annual session of the Gandhi Seva Sangh. This march echoes Gandhi's march to Dandi; we do not have the exact dates.
27. Acc. No. 59 (November 1940); this march was led by Nilamber Das, and the processionists marched about 5 miles a day, demonstrating *khadi*-spinning to the villagers on route.

28. Acc. No. 30; by June 1940 we get references to five such *satyagrahi* training centres in Orissa.
29. *Ibid.* (April and May; September, 1940); *IAR* 1940, p. 245; the PCC was reorganised into four departments —Mahtab was in charge of propaganda; Biswasroi was given charge of the Harijan department; M.M. Athar was given the responsibility of the Ministry department; and the *charkha* department was placed under a sub-committee.
30. Acc. No. 30 (26.10.1940).
31. In fact, as we shall soon see, an anti-war agitation developed in Orissa even before the PCC took the plunge for the 'individual *satyagraha*'.
32. Acc. No. 30 (26.10.1940); HP 18/10/1940; it needs to be added here that as late as October 1940, *Samaj*, the organ of the PCC, carried advertisements of War Savings and appeals for the War Fund; 18/11/1940.
33. We may add here that although the Socialists and Communists were inclined in favour of open disobedience, they accepted the position of the Congress in order to maintain the anti-imperialist front.
34. HP 18/1/1940; the week long Kisan rallies were addressed by leading Congressmen like Biswanath Das.
35. M.A. Rasul, *A History of the All India Kisan Sabha* (Calcutta, 1974), Chap. 5; Sachidananda Routroy, *Granthabali Part II* (Oriya; Cuttack, 1979), p. 10; HP 18/3/1940.
36. HP 18.3.1940; Acc. No. 30, WWCC (April 1940).
37. Acc. No. 30 WWCC (15.6.1940); thus a Kisan school was opened at Jankia (Puri district) on 7 June, 1940.
38. HP 18/7/1940; 18/8/40, the floods caused extensive damages to crops, and a large number of houses were destroyed in the districts of Cuttack and Balasore. The Communists were arrested in the second half of July, 1940.
39. HP 18/9/1940.
40. *Report on the Land Revenue Administration of the Districts of North Orissa for the Year 1938-39* (Cuttack, 1941), pp. 5-9.
41. *Report on the Administration of the Salt Department in the Province of Orissa 1938-39; 1939-40* (Cuttack, 1940), pp. 2, 3.
42. *Ibid.*, p. 3.
43. HP 18/9/1940.
44. Acc. No. 59, WWCC (13.6.1940); this was being circulated by Nata Satpathy (in Oriya) who was arrested. The reference to 'red *pagrees*' most probably indicates the police.
45. E.A.O. Perkin, *Report on the Administration of the Police in the Province of Orissa for the Year 1940* (Cuttack 1941), p. 14.
46. HP 18/1/1940; 18/2/1940; Acc. No. 59, WWCC (March 1940).
47. This trend continued in the Quit India Movement as well.
48. HP 18/3/1940.
49. Rasul, *op.cit.*, p. 73 informs us how this slogan had gained currency among the people and undermined the War efforts of the colonial rulers.

50. AISPC file no. 124, K.C. Mohanty to Secretary. AISPC (15.6.1940); Banamali Das gave a statement to the *Samaj*; interview: Banamali Das (Nilgiri, May, 1982).
51. AISPC file no. 124, B. Das to Secy. AISPC (undated) interview: B. Das was arrested on April 23, 1940 and released the next day.
52. AISPC file no. 124 Mohanty to Secy. AISPC (15.6.1940). It is surprising that Mohanty justified his action on the basis of the argument that unless it was done the *durbar* would ban the Prajamandal. After all, by this time the *durbar*'s authority had been virtually smashed by the Nilgiri Prajamandal.
53. Acc. No. 60, WWCC (13.5.1940).
54. AISPC file no. 124; B. Das to Nehru (30.4.1940) and the Secy. AISPC (undated); Mohanty to Secy. AISPC (15.6.1940); and, K.B. Menon (Secy, AISPC) to B. Das (4.7.1940).
55. *Ibid.*, Menon to Mohanty (4.7.1940).
56. *Ibid.*, Menon to B. Das (4.7. 1940).
57. Perkin, *op.cit.*, p. 9; even the Talcher refugees had returned, as reported, *ibid.*
58. AISPC file no. 164; P.M. Pradhan's (President, Talcher Prajamandal) statement on 'Activities in the Different States' (4.9.1940). At a meeting (Kosala in Augul) presided by Pradhan on 20 August 1940, people (numbering around 5,000) from Talcher, Dhenkanal, Pallalahara, Athamalik, Bamra, Hindol and Rairakhol were present. Among other things this meething resolved to investigate the reasons why the Prajamandal movement did not develop in some states with a view to launch movements there; *ibid.*
59. *Ibid.*; HP 18/2/1940; 18/3/1940; 18/4/1940; 18/9/1940; 18/10/1940 Acc. No. 30 WWCC (January 1940).
60. AISPC file no. 164; Resolution of a Prajamandal meeting (20.8.1940).
61. HP 18/3/1940.
62. AISPC file No. 164; P.M. Pradhan to Secy. AISPC (4.9.1940); it is quite difficult to accept that 70% of Harijans gave up *tari* —a liquor made by fermenting the juice of the palm tree.
63. It may be noted here that whereas the anti-untouchability campaign was similar to the one witnessed at the Nilgiri state, the temperance campaign was in sharp contrast to the demand of the Nilgiri Prajamandal to allow the distillation of liquor. This point needs to be emphasised since both areas had a tribal population.
64. HP 18/9/1940; Acc No. 30, WWCC (3.10.1940); these meetings were addressed by important Congress leaders of the zamindari like Radhamohan Sahu and areas like Nowrangpur, Jeypur and Gunpur were quite receptive to this campaign. We get an idea of the intensity of the problem from a reference to the Governor of Orissa collecting Rs. 15,000/- and Rs. 9,000- from Jeypur and Nowrangpur respectively, and the fact that Koraput district led in the matter of War collections in Orissa; HP 18/11/1940.

65. *Ibid.*; HP, 18/10/1940.
66. Interview: Krushna Chandra Bisoi (Jeypur, June 1981). When Laxman Naiko used to go out on such campaigns he used to tell his wife Manguli that he was going to get 'raija' (*swaraj*); interview: Kausalya, Laxman's daughter (Mathili, June 1981).
67. Dasarathi Nanda, *Saheed Laxman Naik* (Oriya: Berhampur, 1977), pp. 72, 76; S. Sanganna, 'Revolts in Orissa— Martyr Laxman Naik: A Hero of the Freedom Movement, in V. Rangavaiah (ed.) *Tribal Revolts*, (Nellore, 1971), p. 250.
68. Perkin, *op.cit.*, p. 14.
69. HP 18/12/1940; AICC Private Papers, G-1/1941.
70. AICC Private Papers, File No. G-1/1941.
71. As discussed earlier, through this the PCC tried to blend the existing mass pressure with the politics of demobilisation.
72. Acc. No.30, WWCC (26.10.1940); Acc. No. 60, WWCC (December 1940). Mahtab at Remuna (1.12.1940); Acc. No. 52, WWCC (January 1941) Nabakrushna Choudhury, Pranakrushna Padhiary, Gouranga Charan Das and Malati Choudhury at Salepur (6.1.1941).
73. Acc. No. 51, 60, WWCC; for example, Krupasindhu Bhukta—Baniabehal *hata*, Angul (1.12.1940); Surenderanath Das—Deula *hata*, Balasore (5.12.1940); Kailash Chandra Mohanty —Ambodia *hata*, Balasore (16.12.1940).
74. HP 18/1/1941.
75. *Ibid.*
76. Acc. No. 30. WWCC (19.2.1941).
77. *Ibid.* (26.10.1940); 19.3.1941).
78. HP 18/4/1941; Acc. No. 59 (8.3.1941).
79. HP 18/3/1941.
80. Acc. No. 51, WWCC; Chief Secy. Orissa to District Magistrates (11.2.1941): 'The time has come when persons offering *satyagraha* should not be arrested automatically but should be ignored where the circumstances...warrant such a course'. Acc. No. 59, WWCC (15.6.1941) gives an example of people offering 'individual *satyagraha*' in Balasore where no arrests were made.
81. HP 18/11/1941.
82. HP 18/6/1941.
83. Acc. No. 60, WWCC (18.1.1941); Acc. No. 59, WWCC (31.5.1941).
84. Acc. No. 59 WWCC (10.3.1941).
85. *Ibid.* (31.7.1941).
86. *Ibid.* (15.7.1941).
87. *All India Kisan Supplement*, October 18/19, 1941, Indulal Yajnik Private Papers (NMML), subject file no. 20.
88. HP 18/9/1941; the attendance, as reported, was between 60 to 300 in about 16 meetings in the Kissan Week.

89. Acc. No. 59, WWCC (15.9.1941); the reference is to Remuna (Balasore) where the Kisan Day celebration is reported to have been attended by people of Nilgiri.
90. E.A.O. Perkin, *op.cit, 1941* (Cuttack, 1942), p. 8.
91. I. Yajnik serial file no. 20, *op.cit*, 15.8.1941. We should add here that similar attempts were made to keep the Congressmen away from the Kisan Sangha at Balasore, when, in a meeting of the DCC (15.8.1941) the people present were asked to stand by the Congress and 'not to cause diversion by joining the Kisan Movement'; Acc. No. 59, WWCC (15.8.1941). We are also told how Nabakrushna Choudhury intervened to bring about a compromise as a result of which it was decided that no disciplinary action would be taken against Congressmen if they worked for the Kisan Sangha as long as they did nothing contrary to the general policy of the Congress; Acc. No. 30, WWCC (6.10.1941).
92. Perkin, *op.cit*; *1941*, p. 12.
93. *Rep. ... Administration of the Salt Dep.... 1940-41*(Cuttack, 1942), p. 2.
94. HP 18/2/1941; 18/5/1941; 18/12/1941.
95. HP 18/8/1941.
96. *All India Kisan Supplement*, 15.8.1941, Yajnik s.f. no. 20, *op.cit*.
97. HP 18.12.1941.
98. Acc. No. 60, WWCC (16.12.1940).
99. AISPC file no. 128; from Narotam Das to Secy. AISPC (29.1.1941); Resolutions of various meetings (held between 15-30 March, 1941) as described by Narottam Das (17.4.1941).
100. AISPC file No. 164, Sudhakar Rath to Secy. AISPC (5.3.1941 and 23.9.1941).
101. HP 18/1/1941 to 18/3/1941 shows that the zamindari either led or came second to the Cuttack district as far as the number of people arrested for participating in the anti-War agitation was concerned. HP 18/1/1941 (second half) reflects on the type of people who participated; thus, out of 26 persons arrested there were approximately 10 tribals and 4 outcastes and it is not possible to identify the remaining 12 people. Acc. No. 30, WWCC (19. 2.1941) informs us that Damodar Samantarai was appointed to conduct the '*satyagraha*' movement in Jeypur.
102. S. Sanganna, *op.cit.*, p. 250, Confidential Police File on Laxman Naiko at Mathili police station (hereafter CPFLN); Laxman offered 'individual *satyagraha*' twice: in the Ramgiri out post area and in the Mathili area.
103. AICC Private Papers (NMML), File No. P20/1940; Padhiary's list to the General Secretary, AICC (8.9.1941) of intending satyagrahis.
104. HP 18/10/1941.
105. CPFLN.
106. *Ibid.*
107. HP 18/8/1941; as felt, it was not possible to ignore that *satyagrahis* in the estate as in other parts of Orissa and that 'anti-War propaganda could have

most dangerous results' in the estate.

108. HP 18/4/1941.
109. Acc. No. 30 WWCC (29.12.1941).
110. HP 18.1.1942.
111. Acc. No. 52, WWCC; this was the overall approach of the PCC in January 1942.
112. *Ibid.*
113. *Ibid.*
114. *Ibid.*
115. Mehtab, *Sadhanara Pathe* (Oriya; Cuttack, 1972), p. 224.
116. Linlithgow Collection (microfilm collection, NMML), No. 84; Lewis to Linlithgow (25.5.42).
117. Mahtab, *op.cit.*, p. 228.
118. HP 18/5/1942; we should add here that the reference to salt 'manufacture' was bound to reinforce the rebellious tendencies we have observed in some parts of the coastal tract, like Puri.
119. K.D. Das and L.K. Mahapatra, *Folklore of Orissa* (New Delhi, 1979), pp. 56, 57; in fact, speak of such a perception developing in the context of the Quit India Movement. They also refer to this concept of a cyclical deluge existing among the tribals and cite folktales of the Bondas and Didayis to illustrate their point. Such notions were also strengthened by a severe cyclone which hit Balasore (October 1942) and Puri (November 42); HP 18/10/1942; 18/11/1942.
120. HP 18/1/1942; 18/2/1942. The Government agencies and the Oriya press expressed the distinct possibility of a Japanese invasion in January 1942.
121. HP 18/1/1942; Acc. No. 53, WWCC (September 1942); we get a reference to resist the construction of a wireless system at Jagatsingpur as the villagers thought that a military station would be built.
122. *Ibid.* These restrictions were observed at Cuttack, Puri, Balasore, Bhadrak, Chatrapur and Gopalpur from January 15, 1942, *Ibid.* Mahtab, *op.cit.*, p. 221 tells us how people were not even allowed to light kerosene lamps in villages.
123. HP 18/3/1942.
124. HP 10/4/1942.
125. HP 18/3/1942.
126. Acc. No. 98, WWCC.
127. HP 18/3/1942.
128. Surendranath Dwivedy, *August Biplaba* (Oriya; Cuttack, 1972), p. 22.
129. HP 18/4/1942; Mahtab, *op.cit.* p. 223.
130. HP 18/10/1942.
131. HP 18/4/1942.
132. *Ibid.* Dwivedy, *op.cit.*, p. 21, tells us how it was viewed as a 'supernatural' phenomenon.
133. Linlithgow collection (NMML), Lewis to Linlithgow (28.4.42).

134. HP 18/5/1942.
135. *Harijan*, 24.5.42.
136. *Harijan*, 7.6.42.
137. See, for example, R. Tottenham, *Congress Responsibilities for the Disturbances 1942-43* (New Delhi, 1943), pp. 51-52 for the text of the resolution adopted by the Congress Working Committee at Wardha (14.7.1942). The only striking element is its radicalism *vis-a-vis* the propertied Indians. As stated: 'For the first time in India's history, the realisation will come home that the princes, jagirdars, zamindars and propertied and monied classes derive their wealth and property from the workers in the fields and factories and elsewhere, to whom essentially power and authority must belong. *Ibid.*, p. 51.
138. HP 18/7/1942 states Mahtab's position after his return from Wardha; he is reported to have stated that after the breakdown of the Cripps Mission 'the Congresss fell into a spiritual conflicts....Now thanks to the Mahatma India has seen the way out of this conflict. The results are in the hands of God'. In his *Sadhanara...*, *op.cit.*, p. 209, Mahtab mentions how a light emanated from his eyes in this phase.
139. Dwivedy, *op.cit.*, p. 16; Surendranath Dwivedy, *Quest for Socialism* (New Delhi, 1984), p. 116; CPFLN, *op.cit.* Dwivedy, *op.cit.*, p. 77, refers to how Mahtab almost rebuked Malati Choudhury and him at Bombay when they asked him if there were any instructions for an underground movement in Orissa. He, however, adds that this was due to the fact that nobody could imagine the form the Quit India Movement would take.
140. Tottenham, pp. 52-55.
141. *Ibid.*, p. 62.
142. Dwivedy, *August...*, *op.cit.*, p. 42, mentions how he sent Gandhi's call to Cuttack, and says that this reached Koraput DCC. Most probably, the reference we have cited here is the same which circulated even in coastal Orissa; Acc. No. 30, WWCC (15.8.1942).
143. *Ibid.*; it also asked the people to form an 'army of peace' (*'santi sena'*), win over the police and boycott people who used force against Congress law breakers or bought property of Congressmen auctioned by the government. As can be seen the approach to the landlords was distinctly more radical than even the Wardha Resolution which we have discussed earlier, or even the demands of the Kisan Sangha in August '42 which called for the formation of a National Government, arming the peasants, reduction of land revenue and remission of outstanding revenue and free cultivation of untilled land; Acc No. 30/ WWCC (7.8.1942).
144. HP 3/16/1942; As Bowstead reported around 18 August 1942: 'Congress would not find it easy to stir the Oriyas of these (coastal) districts'. Although he felt that the 'hill people' were capable of 'giving us a great deal of trouble' they would not as 'Congress influence is low among them'.
145. Acc. No. 55, WWCC; unsigned letter to District Magistrate, Cuttack

(25.7.1942); this included representatives of Muslim League and some landlords.

146. Acc. No. 45, WWCC; this included a plan to have posters to counter the Quit India Movement.

147. HP 103/42; in a speech delivered by Godavaris Misra (undated) at a meeting organised by the Cuttack District War Committee; he is reported to have focused on the necessity to help the British government in the War so that '40 million will be saved'. Most of the evidence support the utter failure of the Coalition Ministry to check price rise and scarcity. Linlithgow Collection (NMML), Lewis to Linlithgow (13.8.1942) mentioned how Godavaris Misra advised stricter measures to deal with the Quit India Movement.

148. Acc. No. 98, WWCC, 'Incidents of the August Revolution 1942 (August-December)'; Dwivedy, *August...*, *op.cit*, p. 70; Ramchandra Ram, *Sangrami* (Oriya; Cuttack, 1986), p. 54. Needless to say the Students Federation of Orissa did not follow the 'People's War' line.

149. Acc. No. 30, WWCC (16.8.1942); the 'crowd' set fire to the Public Works Department building nearby where the property seized from the Bari *ashram* had been kept.

150. Acc. No. 98 WWCC; here one can refer to schools in rural areas such as the Salepur High School and the Kosala Mela (Angul).

151. HP 3/16/1942; 3/30/1942, part I & II; Acc. No. 30 WWCC (15-30 August); Acc. No. 97, Acc. No. 98, WWCC ('Narrative account of Congress disturbances in the different districts of the Province of Orissa from August to December 1942'); Acc. No. 53;55 WWCC. It is worth speculating whether wire-cutting also had an anti-feudal dimension, given the fact that landlords in coastal Orissa levied a *tar* tax in the nineteenth century—something we have discussed in the first chapter.

152. HP 3/30/1942, Part I and II; HP 3/16/1942; Acc. No. 98 WWCC.

153. Acc. Nos. 30;55;98 WWCC: we should perhaps add here that the position in the government estates was relatively better, where the intermediary linkages of power and control seem to have been rather effective; Acc. No 98, WWCC.

154. Acc. No. 98 WWCC.

155. Acc. Nos. 30(3.9.1942); 53(S.D.O. Jajpur to Collector, Cuttack, 28.8.1942); 55 (S.D.O. to District Magistrate, Cuttack, 28.8.1942) WWCC.

156. Acc. No. 30, WWCC (3.9.1942 and 10.9.1942), these included burning of the Canal Revenue Office at Nuapara (Jagatsingpur), 31 August, the Jagatsingpur dak bungalow, 3 September; Ersama police station, barracks and the official records, 6 September; the Revenue office and Rest Shed at Tirtol, 7 September. Besides, in many places in Tirtol area telegraph wires were also cut. Some telegraph wires were cut along the railway track between Jenapur and Jajpur. The social base of the Quit India Movement broadened with the fishermen of Kujang and some 'criminal' tribes (!) of

Binjharpur joining in.

157. *Ibid.*; also 17.9.1942; there was an attempt to take over the Angul Congress *ashram* on 13 September. For example, this shift can be seen in the attempt to destroy papers at the Peshkar's table in the courtroom of the Kendrapada S.D.O.; Acc. No. 98, WWCC.
158. Acc. No. 30 WWCC (10.9.1942).
159. HP 3/31/1943.
160. Gobind Sahai, *42 Rebellion* (Delhi, 1947), p. 352, puts this at Rs. 8,000 for the Cuttack district. We should add here that 'collective' fines were imposed in strongholds of the Quit India Movement like Bari and 5 adjoining villagers; Acc. No. 53, WWCC (From D.M. to Chief Secy., 3.9.1942).
161. *Ibid.* (D.M. to Chief Secy., 14.9.1942). What also needs to be emphasised is that a pro-British Hindu was leading a group of Muslims.
162. Cited in Mahtab, *et.al* (eds), Vol. IV, *op.cit.*, p. 25 (appendix). Only two schools remained closed for the *hartal*.
163. HP 18/10/1942; we get references to students of Salepur school leading the 'attack'/burning down of the Canal Revenue Tehsil Office on 4 October; Acc. No. 98 WWCC.
164. HP 18/11/1942; there was also a report of the burning down of a Canal office and the picketing of an excise shop; Acc. No. 98, WWCC.
165. HP 18/12/1942; besides, the Balichandrapur Canal Revenue Office was burnt down on 2 December. The report mentioned that although Congressmen were suspected, later on it was proved to be unfounded.
166. These tables are based on Acc. No. 49, from S.P. Cuttack to D.M. Cuttack (12.4.1944).
167. Acc. No. 98, WWCC.
168. Acc. No. 59, WWCC (13.8.1942).
169. *Ibid.*; Acc. No. 98, WWCC.
170. Acc. No. 59, WWCC (25.8.1942).
171. Acc. No. 30, WWCC (22.8; 24.8.1942); most of the shops were closed at Durgabedi, Garuda, Remuna and Balasore; excise shops were picketed at Balasore town on 23 August.
172. Acc. No. 98, WWCC. The policemen became common targets during this phase. Prafulla Das, *Bharatara Sasastra Mukti Sangram* (Oriya; Cuttack, 1980) tells us how two policemen were made to stand with Gandhi caps, sing 'Bande Mataram' and say 'Gandhi Ki Jai' at the Chandbali police station compoud and then allowed to go; p. 721.
173. *Ibid.*; it seems that one constable was about to be thrown into the fire, but this was 'prevented' by the villagers. When the police began enquiring into the episode many of the villagers deserted the villages and very few people were actually named; Acc. No. 59, WWCC.
174. Acc. No. 30, WWCC (15.9.1942; 22.9.1942).
175. HP 3/16/1942; thus two bullocks attached by the police were 'rescued' by

a 'crowd' at Remuna on 29 September.

176. In fact, the Bhadrak area was quite militant and although we are not told of the exact place, we get reference to 350 maunds of paddy being extorted from a landholder and distributed among the people on the basis of a list prepared by 'Congress agtitators' on 18 September; Acc. No. 30, WWCC (27.9.1942).
177. Here we are obviously talking of the anti-imperialist struggle coexisting with a struggle against internal contradictions.
178. Acc. No. 98, WWCC; Acc. No. 62, WWCC (from Collector to Chief Secy., 21.9.1942).
179. *Ibid.*
180. *Ibid.*; Acc. No. 30, WWCC (27.9.1942).
181. *Ibid.*; it seems that the constables did not take proper aim.
182. Acc. No. 62, WWCC.
183. *Ibid.*
184. The following part is based primarily on Sudhakar Acharjya, *Swadhinata Sangram Bhumi Iram* (Oriya; Cuttack, 1977), and also *Report of the Joint Enquiry by the Revenue Commissioner Orissa and I.G. of Police Orissa into the Eram Firing on 28th September 42* (Cuttack, 1942), hereafter *REF*.
185. Das, *op.cit.*, pp. 22-23. The activists included Laxmi Narayan Padhi, Sapan Pradhan, Nishakar Dalei, Banchanidhi Agasti, Bhagirathi Pati and Arjun Biswal.
186. *Ibid.*, pp. 24-25.
187. *Ibid.*, pp. 25-27; HP 18/11/1943; the marches were conducted between Barandua to Iram via Basudevpur - 12 miles (16 September); from Iram via Padhua, Bchchada, Sankharu to Artu - 15 miles (17 September), Iram via agricultural fields to Basudevpur - 6 miles (18 September); p. 28, *Ibid.* As can be expected, these brought in the peasants of the area.
188. *REF,* p. 1.
189. Acc No. 59, WWCC (28.9.1942).
190. *REF,* p. 1 and Das , *op.cit.* p. 34, tell us how this was also implemented in some areas.
191. Das, *op.cit.*, pp. 26.
192. Acc. No. 98, WWCC.
193. Das, *op.cit.*, pp. 26-30.
194. *Ibid.*, p. 31.
195. *Ibid.*, p. 39.
196. *Ibid.*, *REF,* p. 2.
197. Das, *op.cit.*, p. 31.
198. *Ibid.*, p. 40.
199. Acc. No. 62 WWCC.
200. Sahai, *op.cit.*, p. 346.
201. Acc. No. 62, WWCC.
202. *REF*. p. 5; they are referred to as people belonging to the 'landless class',

ibid.

203. Sahai, *op.cit.*, p. 350, puts this at Rs. 6,000.
204. Acc. No. 30, WWCC (8.10.1942).
205. Dwivedy, *August...*, *op.cit.*, p. 129, mentions a bulletin he had prepared before 'dussera' which was seized at the time of his arrest and hence had not been circulated. It was entitled 'Devi Aradhana' and read: 'The Devi wants Mandara (a red flower) of blood —her most favourite Archana (i.e. offering). Can't you satisfy the Devi? There is no time; the time to do Aradhana (i.e. worship) to the Devi is fast approaching. And, our struggle seems to reach its last and final stage...'. This perhaps illustrates the association of Hindu religion with the Quit India Movement and how even otherwise secular people like Dwivedy were also swayed by it.
206. HP 18/10/1942; Acc. No. 98, WWCC; Acc. No. 9 , WWCC (29.10.1942).
207. Acc. No. 98 WWCC; HP, 18.11.1942.
208. Acc. No. 98 WWCC.
209. HP 3/30/1942; 3.16.1942; Acc. No. 30, WWCC (27.9.1942).
210. Acc. No. 98 WWCC; HP, 3/31/1943.
211. *Ibid.*
212. *Ibid.*
213. Acc. No. 98, WWCC; it may be added here that although the Nayagarh state remained by and large unaffected by Quit India Movement, the concern of these people to come all the way and demand the opening of the *Khadi* store shows the symbolic importance attached to it and the popular enthusiasm created by the Quit India Movement.
214. *Ibid.*
215. Nilgiri Praja Andolana Compilation Committee, *Nilgiri Prajandolanara Itihas* (Oriya; Balasore; 1982), pp. 102-05 (hereafter *NPARI*).
216. Interview: Banamali Das.
217. *NPARI* pp. 106; 115-116.
218. *Ibid.*, pp. 105; Mahtab, *et.al* (eds.) Vol. IV, *op.cit.*, p. 86 (Appendix 1). See, for example, Georges Lefebvre, 'Revolutionary Crowds' in Jeffrey Kaplow (ed.) *New Perspectives on the French Revolution* (New York, 1965), pp. 173-190; George Rude, *Paris and London in the Eighteenth Century: Studies in Popular Protest* (London, 1974). E.P. Thompson, 'The Moral Economy of the English Crowd in the Eighteenth Century', *Past and Present*, no. 50, February 1971; and David Arnold, 'Looting, Grain Riots and Government Policy in South India, 1918' *Past and Present*, no. 84, August 1979, where attempts have been made to study pre-industrial 'crowd' behaviour in relation to the market-place.
219. Interview: Banamali Das; *Muktijuddhya*, 13/10/1942; 30/10/1942; 12/12/1942.
220. *NPARI*, pp. 106-120; thus, the boycott of state officials was so systematic that no one could get people to attend to their crops, and some had to get even firewood from Balasore.

221. *Ibid.*, pp. 113, 122.
222. 'Nilgiri Ra Itihas' in *Gyanmruta* (Oriya; ? 1972), p. 59.
223. Mahtab *et.al* (eds.) Vol IV *op.cit.*, p. 145. Basudev Panda 'The Prajamandal Movement of Nilgiri', *The Eastern Times* (Cuttack, 23 May, 1981) tells us how a body called the '*prajamangal*' was created by the *durbar* to counter the Prajamandal.
224. Interview: Baishnab Pattnaik (Dhenkanal, June 1985); HP 3/16/1942.
225. Interview: Pattnaik.
226. *Ibid.*; HP 3/16/1942.
227. Interview: Pattnaik.
228. Pabitra Mohan Pradhan, *Mukti Pathe Sainika* (Oriya; Cuttack, 1979), pp. 93-97, 123; AISPC file no. 164, p. 1.
229. AISPC file no. 164, p. 1.
230. Pradhan, *op.cit.*, p. 120; these were the questions and positions voiced by some boatmen to Pradhan in disguise after he escaped from jail.
231. *Ibid.*, pp. 126, 128.
232. Sadasib Pradhan, *Agrarian and Political Movements* (New Delhi, 1986) p. 145.
233. P. Pradhan, *op.cit.*, p. 125.
234. *Ibid.*, p. 135; AISPC file no. 164, p. 2.
235. AISPC file no. 164, p. 2; HP 3/30/1942 Part I & II; P. Pradhan, *op.cit.*, pp. 133-136.
236. P. Pradhan, *op.cit.*, p. 136.
237. AISPC file no. 164, p. 4; P. Pradhan, pp. 127-130.
238. *Ibid.*, pp. 133-134; AISPC file no. 164, p. 4.
239. *Ibid.*, pp. 5-6.
240. *Ibid.*, p. 7-10, P. Pradhan, *op.cit.*, p. 157-58.
241. HP 3/16/1942.p
242. P.Pradhan, *op.cit.*, pp. 142, 153, 157.
243. Acc.No.30 WWCC (14/8/1942, 21/8/1942, 31/8/1942). *Samaj*, organ of the PCC, was banned in the district; Mahtab, *et.al.* (eds.), Vol.V, p. 59. The 'Mahatma's call' that was popularised was actually the one sent by Surendranath Dwivedy from Bombay; Dwivedy, *August...*, *op.cit.*, p. 42.
244. Acc.No.30 WWCC (21/8/1942); Mahtab, *et.al* (eds.) Vol. V, p. 86-87. HP, 3/16/1942.
245. *Ibid.*, p. 87; Acc. No.WWCC (21/8/1942).
246. Acc No.30 WWCC (21/8/1942); Mahtab, *et.al.* (eds.), Vol IV, *op.cit.*, p. 89.
247. CPFLN. It should be noted here that it is common practice for people in any tribal area of Orissa to move around with *lathis*, bows and arrows; however, colonial administrators as well as bourgeois-nationalist historians like Mahtab look upon this as evidence of their being armed, which is counter to the whole logic of tribal existence.

248. CPFLN; Patros and Bisois are mostly non-tribals.
249. CPFLN.
250. CPFLN; in fact, the Nuagaon and Malipara events reflect the type of people who formed the 'crowds' and the obvious fact that they were neither rowdies nor criminals.
251. CPFLN.
252. *Ibid.*
253. SC No. 18/1942 'Judgement in Late Laxman Naik's Case'; I am thankful to the Collector, Koraput for allowing me to use this document.
254. Nityananda Das, 'Martyr Laxman Naik: A Hero of the Freedom Movement', *Adivasi*, Vol. IX, no. 1, April 1967, p. 27.
255. Mahtab, *et. al* (eds.), Vol. V, *op. cit.*, p. 88.
256. SC No. 18/1942; 'Patna High Court Decision', cited in Mahtab *et.al* (eds.), Vol. IV, *op.cit.*, pp.44-48 (appendix).
257. Nityananda Das, *op. cit.*, p. 25; Sanganna, *op. cit.*, p. 252 mentions about the attempt to hoist the flag; Laxman in a letter signed by him mentioned how these people were eager to court arrest; cited by Balabhadra Pujari, *Saheed Bira Laxman Naik* (Oriya; Bhubneshwar ?), p. 20. Interview: Gopinath Pujari (Jeypur, 1981) matched with this evidence.
258. Radhakrishan Biswasroi, *Orissa Rajniti Ebon Eka Nua Pradeshara Parikalpana* (Oriya; Jeypur, 1973), p. 26, for details of repression. We may add here that the Malkangiri treasury was nearly 45 kilometres away.
259. HP KW10 to 3/80/1942. The 'local leaders' included Madhav Pradhani, Sukru Jani, Bukra Muduli, Chaitan Dalei, Kanai Bhatra, Rukune Paraje, Sadan Paik and Ananda Behera.
260. *Ibid.*
261. *Ibid.*; Mahtab, *et.al.* (eds.), Vol. IV, *op. cit.*, p. 89.
262. HP KW10 to 3/80/1942.
263. CPFLN.
264. Dasarathi Nanda, *Saheed Laxman Naik* (Oriya; Berhampur, 1977), pp. 118-120.
265. HP KW10 to 3/80/1942.
266. HP, 3/16/1942.
267. Mahtab, *et.al* (eds.), Vol. IV, *op. cit.*, p. 90; also Biswasroi, *op. cit.*, p. 26; Acc. No.30, WWCC (3/9/1942).
268. Sahai, *op.cit.*, p. 347, mentions that fines to the tune of Rs.11,200 were imposed on the people of the district, property worth Rs. 9000 was confiscated, 12 women were raped, there were 24 *lathi*charges, 3 people were suspended by their legs from trees and beaten and there were indiscriminate canings throughout the district.
269. Mahtab, *et.al,* Vol V, *op. cit.*, p. 88.
270. *Ibid.*; there was tension in the Kujindri village of Gunpur taluk (8/10/1942) as a result of which 16 Savara men and women were arrested.

271. HP 18/12/1942.
272. *People's War* 6; 20th September 1942 informed how within a week from 9th August 1942 all leading Kisan activists, student and labour workers were arrested; some activists who had been released after two years were arrested within a fortnight of their release; *People's War*, 11th October 1942, mentioned that by this time the entire Kisan leadership has been arrested.
273. *Muktijuddhya*, 13th November 1942; it needs to be pointed out that the *Muktijuddhya* started coming out most probably from October 1942.
274. *Muktijuddhya*, 30th October 1942.
275. *Muktijudhya*, 11th December 1942. The wrong policy of exporting rice out of Orissa was also criticised by different political groups, including Congressmen.
276. *Muktijuddhya*, 20th November 1942, reported how three Congressmen of Dhamnagar supported the unity campaign.
277. See Kalindi Charan Pannigrahi, *Granthabati Part I* (Oriya; Cuttack, 1971), pp. 354-57, for the poem.
278. *Muktijuddhya*, 6th November 1942.
279. See Gopinath Mohanty's *Paraja* (Oriya, Cuttack, 1978) or the English translation of the same (Delhi, 1987).
280. This point has been made in Biswamoy Pati, 'Complex Fabric of Tribal Life', *Economic and Political Weekly*, 12 December 1987.
281. We witness guerilla warfare also at Tamluk (Bengal), Bihar and Satara (Maharashtra). For details, see S.C. Samanta, *et.al, August Revolution and Two Years' National Government in Midnapore* (Calcutta, 1946), Stephen Henningham, *op. cit.*, and Gail Omvedt, 'The Satara Prati Sarkar' in Gyanendra Pandey (ed.), *op. cit.*
282. Henningham in Guha (ed.) *op.cit.* makes a bold attempt to speak of the 'duality' of the Quit India Movement which consisted of an elite nationalist uprising combined with a subaltern revolt (p. 164). However, the author's facts—which show the growing influence of the Congress in the pre-1942 phase and the appeal of Gandhi's slogans in the area studied by him—not only refute his method of splitting Indian nationalism but also shows how the Congress and Gandhi legitimised the Quit India Movement. See, for example, Biswamoy Pati's review of Henningham's article in Sangeeta Singh *et.al* 'Subaltern Studies II: A Review Article' in *Social Scientist*, October 1984.
283. It is worth speculating why the struggle against the immediate oppressors took this sort of a form in Orissa, in sharp contrast to, say Bihar or the United Provinces. This was, perhaps, because the sweep of the peasant movement was a more recent phenomenon in Orissa (from around 1938 or so) and the exploiting classes had not been able to restructure themselves and their hegemonic influence unlike in Bihar and the United Provinces with their nearly two decades of peasant militancy.

Chapter V

From Raj to Swaraj: The Complexities of Transition, 1943-1950

The Quit India Movement survived in popular memory and the 1943-44 context saw a terrible famine in coastal Orissa, especially in Balasore. This created a serious situation for the peasants and tribals of coastal Orissa. It was a context which sharpened class, caste and communal identities. At the same time it was essentially the food situation which provided fresh opportunities to the Kisan Sangha to re-establish its links with the peasants of coastal Orissa, which had been snapped in the earlier phase. And this created apprehensions for the Congress which sought to counter the influence of both the Kisan Sangha and the Communists.

This chapter focuses on the post-War situation, with the Labour government in England declaring that the elections to the provincial legislatures in India would be held in early 1946. The Congress, which was in shambles in Orissa, entered the electoral scene drawing its legitimacy from the Quit India Movement. Its position marked a distinct shift from the 1937 elections, especially when it came to accommodating the landlords as candidates. In fact, the landlords and some local officials were equally eager to join the Congress. However, the electoral campaign at Jeypur focused on the internal contradiction, revealing the unevenness of this process.

The elections swept the Congress back to power in Orissa. Once saddled in power the Congress sought to strengthen its links with the landlords and the 'rich' peasants and retreated from its position regarding zamindari abolition. These years also saw the consolidation of the Congress and its plans for the future coexisting with organisational problems and indiscipline. It saw strained caste, class and communal relations in parts of coastal Orissa. The advent of freedom also witnessed a rise in 'crime' which cannot be viewed simplistically.

The chapter also focuses on a spell of peasant movements in response to the unresolved nature of the contradictions. In the coastal tract this led to a powerful share-croppers' movement. In the princely states it paved the way for the merger of the princely states with the Orissa province. And, in the Jeypur zamindari it was marked by a strong anti-feudal current.

I

The 'Survival of Quit India in Popular Memory, Famine and Popular Pressures

By the beginning of 1943 very few traces of the Quit India Movement were left in Orissa. Laxman Naiko (who was the only political prisoner to be awarded a death sentence) was secretly hanged in the Berhampur jail on 29 March 1943. Before his execution he had declared that he would have been much happier if he had seen *swaraj* before his death.[1] The colonial bureaucracy simplified the logic of peasant and tribal militancy of the Koraput district by talking about how they were 'mislead' by the Congress. And, even if we accept the point that some of the political prisoners in the Koraput jail felt that they 'require(d) and expect(ed) punishment'[2], it needs to be emphasised that this only symbolised their pathetic acceptance of circumstances. Yet we also get evidence of anger and frustration at the failure of the Quit India Movement which took the form of individual actions like the burning of an opium centre at Ghateswar (in Bhadrak). Although no political significance seems to have been attached to this act, it is difficult to accept that it merely expressed the anger of an 'opium addict' who could not 'get enough opium'.[3]

Popular memory retained the Quit India Movement as something signifying doom and repression. A booklet of poems composed by a popular poet prophesised the end of the world on 1 August 1943 and began with the lines:

> On the 1st of August,
> Sunday morning,
> Kalijuga will meet its doom.[4]

A series of rumours circulated in coastal Orissa (July 1943), which were based on astrological reasoning and which predicted that the last two days of July and the first day of August 1943 would be 'really dangerous'. This was accompanied by another rumour in July 1943 that 'Lord' Jagannatha would soon be leaving Puri. These rumours had an extraordinary effect and on the evening of 1 August 1943 the entire population of Cuttack town was out on the streets making offerings at temples to tide over the 'bad' days.[5] Similarly, the forecast, based on the Oriya calender, of bad harvests should be viewed in the context of apocalyptic notions which survived in the post-Quit India Movement phase.[6] Of course, we shall never know for certain whether the pains and sufferings associated with the Quit India Movement were located as necessary towards a 'new order' which would be better and brighter— i.e. *swaraj*. Nevertheless, given the structure of popular perceptions this element of rationalisation of failure should be borne in mind by any social historian attempting to construct how the Quit India Movement survived in popular memory.

The anger and disillusionment came to be, of course, expressed in clearer terms by the intellectual. Kalindi Charan burst out in his 'Kie Sala Saitan' ('Who is the Devil': 1944).

We are born as human beings
But lack any self-respect
They can take liberties with our women folk
And for them we are scoundrels!
Through rain and heat we toil for them
Providing them with shelter
We invite darkness into our homes
While lighting their world!
We lay the table for their children
While our young ones die of starvation
They are their 'Majesties', their 'Excellencies' and their 'Highnesses'
And, of course, we are only mean folk.[7]

If anything, this points to how the Quit India Movement had shaken intellectuals like Kalindi Charan, making him focus sharply on the class dimension in contrast to the 1930's when his literary sensibilities epitomised the impact produced by Gandhian politics.

The Provincial Congress Committee (hereafter PCC) made efforts to reach the people through minor demonstrations, organised to observe the anniversary of the Quit India Movement in August 1943. Besides, it also raised the issues of 'collective' fines and helping the victims and prisoners of the Quit India Movement. Some secret pamphlets were circulated, which called for reviving the Quit India Movement but which failed to evoke any response.[8]

The Quit India Movement had further undermined the credibility of the Coalition Ministry. It continued to be looked upon as an agent of British imperialism and its authoritarian character was criticised even by some landed elements.[9] It played a significant role in precipitating a famine by supporting the wrong policy of exporting rice out of the Province, even as the famine deepened.[10] In March 1943 the Government of Orissa agreed to send 25,000 maunds of rice, upto a total of 15,000 tons, to Bengal. Besides, our evidence for Koraput and some princely states reveals how rice was exported out of Orissa to Madras and famine-hit Bengal in 1943, when coastal Orissa itself suffered from a severe famine.[11]

The crisis deepened when the Central Government decided to introduce the free-trade policy in the eastern region.[12] This meant that the Provincial Government was no longer in a position to regulate either the movement of foodgrain or prices. Thus, as the dust of the Quit India Movement settled the famine occupied the attention of different political sections who criticised the wrong policies in the 1943-44 phase. The central and common point was to demand an end to the export of rice from Orissa.[13]

The famine situation worsened in 1943, creating an acute crisis for the peasants and tribals of the coastal tract. There are references to people dying like flies and mosquitoes[14], 'silently' as though 'resigned to fate'[15], in areas of the Balasore district, which was the worst affected.[16] People ate leaves and struggled over *shradh* rice with dogs and deprived outcastes of any food they might have been carrying[17] and families broke up due to sale of children or desertion by male members.[18] In the northern part of Balasore peasants sold land at very cheap rates. There was an increase in the transfer of land during the famine years, as is evident from the following table:[19]

TABLE I

Year	*Transfer of land in Orissa* (in acres)
1941	110,868
1942	104,465
1943	141,697
1944	125,278

Added to this was the problem of large-scale hoarding and black-marketing by merchants and landed elements.[20]

The famine widened the gap between the rich and poor in the coastal tract. The wealthier classes were totally indifferent to the condition of the rural poor. These affluent sections preferred to sell rice outside Orissa as they got high prices.[21] This polarisation had several manifestations. For example, from Banpur (Puri) we get a reference to Sania Tarai who was killed as a result of an assault by a wealthy merchant on 9 April 1943. Tarai had not repaid a loan.[22] Popular anger against *mahajans*, who sold essential commodities at very high prices was noticed, and on occasions this also led to clashes as in Salepur (Cuttack) around March 1943.[23]

The famine also strained caste and communal relations in coastal Orissa as is evident from the tension between Khandayats and Gopalas in Kendrapada in the 1943-1944 phase.[24] Although centred around caste, the conflict was between the dominant Khandayats who were the landowning caste and the Gopalas who were pastoralists. The relations between Hindus and Muslims were also strained in Balasore in this phase. The Muslims belonging to north Balasore, which had been ravaged by the famine, were mostly wage-earners. The fall in wages and employment opportunities provided the basis for a tension between them and the landlords who were mostly Hindus.[25] The colonial administration 'rallied round the cow' to reinforce already existing differences.[26]

Another manifestation of the famine was an increase in 'petty thefts', burglaries and food 'riots' in the Balasore district. There was also an increase in crime, with dacoities becoming a daily phenomenon. Another feature was the overcrowding of jails in Balasore because of the large number of such offences. We cannot rule out links between 'petty crime' and jail-going which 'solved' the problem of hunger temporarily. The sudden increase in crime, as the following table reveals, had a distinct connection with the famine:

TABLE II

Increase in crime in Orissa in 1943 as compared with 1933-37 Averages[27]

Murder	*Dacoity*	*Robbery*	*Burglary*
+58%	*+2,510%**	*+162%*	*+150%***

*(Highest in India, Bombay followed with 865%)

**(Second highest in India—next to Bombay where it was +166%)

The famine continued up to 1944. Faced with severe criticism the Government woke up to organise free kitchens to provide relief, which offered no solution to the existing crisis. Moreover, the policy of procurement was a distinct burden on the peasants. The colonial administration constantly claimed 'normalcy' in the 1943-44 phase, and by the end of 1944 the free kitchens were finally closed down.[28]

While discussing the broad trends in the 1943-44 phase we should also refer to the fall of the Coalition Ministry in June, 1944. This development was based on the differences between the Premier, the Maharaja of Parliakhemedi and Godavaris Mishra over the food situation. The Premier's underestimation of the distress in Orissa and his idea of exporting rice was at the root of this.[29]

This was the overall context in which the Kisan Sangha functioned in Orissa. Its relative isolation from the masses as a result of its going against the Quit India Movement had affected its membership, as is evident from the following table:

TABLE III

Orissa Kisan Sangha Membership[30]

Year	*No. of members*
1938-39	20,000 for Orissa 30,000 for the Princely states
1943	4,224 for the whole of Orissa

Nevertheless, it was in the 1943-44 phase that the Kisan Sangha began to break out of its isolation.

In this phase the Kisan Sangha combined the demand for providing relief with the release of political prisoners. It formulated an excellent critique of the famine and stressed the need for a National Government as well as the unity of the Congress and Muslim League. It sought to link itself with popular patriotism as is evident from the rural meetings of the Communist Party. What needs to be emphasised is that the food campaign of the Kisan Sangha was joined by organisations like the Gandhi Seva Dal and the Servants of India.[31]

On the food front food committees were formed in the coastal belt. On occasions 'food marches' were organised to focus on the food crisis.

In April 1943 we get references to 'mass hunger' marches in Balasore[32] and Khurda.[33] This reached a climax on 28 June 1943 when 2000 marchers (which included 200 children and 500 women) reached the Orissa Legislative Assembly carrying empty bags and baskets on their heads raising slogans against hoarders and blackmarketeers and demanding the release of political prisoners, as well as Congress and League unity in order to fight the food problem.[34]

The Kisan Sangha's rural propaganda combined an opposition to the colonial administration as well as to the merchants. Not only did the Kisan Sangha put pressure on the colonial administration to stop the export of foodgrain and prevent its procurement, but also on the merchants to release their hoarded stocks for local use. Simultaneously, it intensified its rural propaganda that the Government should procure rice from the merchants and sell them to the poor. It deputed its volunteers to control the supply and distribution of foodgrain. Villagers were mobilised to offer *satyagraha* before carts carrying foodgrains. The Kisan Sangha demanded fallow lands for the poor (along with agricultural implements) so that they could engage themselves in cultivation.[35] It also intervened to demand compensation for land taken over from the peasants by the colonial administration.[36]

The Kisan Sangha campaigned for the 'grow more food' programme, the formation of peasant cooperatives and Palliamangal Samitis to settle petty disputes among the peasants. These had a distinct anti-zamindar and anti-*sahukar* thrust. A number of schools were also opened in the rural areas where its politics was explained.[37] Of course, as in the previous phase, there are references to the organisation of Santisenas and Muktisenas with the addition of Balasenas, in the rural areas, and a frontal opposition to War subscriptions.[38]

On the Kisan Day, 1 September 1943, the Kisan Sangha reiterated its stand.[39] In the 1943-44 phase its interventions, especially on the famine front, led to its growing influence in the coastal belt, particularly in the Puri district.[40] Thus, by the end of 1943 its membership had risen to 15,000.[41] Its humanitarian concerns were, in fact, shared by some Congressmen, who on occasions, joined it.[42] This feature, as well as the Kisan Sangha's unity efforts gave rise to 'concern' among the colonial administrators.[43] Besides raids on the Communist Party's offices and the arrest of leading Kisan Sangha activists and disallowing of public meetings called by the kisan Sangha, it was prevented from opening its own relief centres or transporting relief.[44]

The All India Kisan Sabha session at Vijaywada (14-15 March, 1944) evoked considerable enthusiasm, with 23 delegates representing Orissa. At this session Sahajanand Saraswati was elected President of the All India Kisan Sabha. As many as 30,000 people, including 5,000 women, attended this session and listened to the Kisan Sabha's stand which included the focus on the famine, the question of relief, the release of political prisoners and the problem of landlessness.[45]

Inspired by the Vijayawada session, the Orissa Kisan Sabha organised several meetings. In some of these people from adjoining areas participated in order to discuss various local as well as general issues. A meeting of the Kisan Sangha at Paradeep (Cuttack) on 19 April 1944 illusliates this. Peasants from Jajpur, Dhamnagar and Balasore attended it in large numbers. The meeting was presided over by Prabodh Mohanty. Problems of the peasants in various areas were discussed—shortage of water for cultivation at Jajpur and Dhamnagar; the problems created by the Jajpur landlords for the 'grow more rice' programme; destruction of crops due to floods and famine at Bari; the problem of landlessness and how the *mahajans* hoarded huge quantities of rice.[46] Another feature of the Kisan Sangha's politics was to plan camps on the borders of the princely states to consolidate the Kisan Sangha and Prajamandal movement.[47]

As the political prisoners were being released in 1944 and the PCC began to stand up again, it viewed the rapid success of the Kisan Sangha with suspicion. Consequently, the PCC took concrete steps to isolate the Kisan Sangha by clearly formulating its guidelines regarding qualifications for being a member. These included, among other things, the non-membership of any 'leftist' organisation.[48] This attempt to 'purify' itself also led the PCC to exclude Communists from activities like constructive programmes.[49] The PCC also sought to counter the influence of the Kisan Sangha, especially in areas like Puri district where the latter had made deep inroads. Thus, around the end of 1944 there were proposals to form an anti-Communist front under the leadership of Jagannatha Mishra.[50]

As for the princely states, meetings were banned in some of them to counter the Prajamandal movement. When in 1944 the Orissa government began releasing political prisoners the *durbars* re-arrested them.[51] We do not find much of activity in the princely states, excepting Nilgiri, and repression at Dhenkanal.[52] In 1944 the Dhenkanal administration was taken over by the British. At Talcher there was an incident of firing in May 1943, which resulted in the death of two Prajamandal activists. This was part of the final offensive against the guerilla movement and ended with the movement being crushed.[53]

At Nilgiri prominent Prajamandal activities like Banamali Das, who had gone underground during the Quit India Movement, were arrested in early 1943. This attempt by the *durbar* to throttle the Prajamandal continued in the 1943-44 phase. However, the Prajamandal and the Kisan Sangha continued to make even deeper inroads. The Communists organised about 200 cadres who received political education and training in self-defence. By combining the demands for food committees with political demands (i.e. the establishment of a national government and the release of political prisoners) the Communists strengthened the Prajamandal as well as the Kisan Sangha in the state. In a context when the Congressites had been reduced to inactivity, the Communists consolidated their position, getting their activities co-ordinated with the prominent Congress leader Kailash Chandra Mohanty. The PCC's anti-Communist position did not cut much ice in Nilgiri in the phase and the Communists continued to remain active.[54]

As for the Jeypur estate the colonial administration expressed its anxiety when political prisoners were being released in 1943-44. There is a reference to a political prisoner taking revenge on a person who had given evidence against him during the Quit India Movement. However, there is no evidence of any serious anti-colonial or anti-zamindari tension, except for a suspicion of the procurement policy.[55] We can conclude our discussion of the Jeypur estate by mentioning how a police party which visited Tentuligumma in December 1943 found that Laxman's relatives and 'co-villagers' firmly believed that he was still alive in Sambalpur jail[56]—perhaps a reflection of the unfulfilled dreams of those who had risen during the Quit India Movement.

II

Orissa's New Ruling Class: Between Visions, Popular Expectations and Realities

In 1945, the end of the Second World War coupled with the victory of the Labour Party in the General Elections in Britain offered fresh possibilities for ending the political deadlock in India. By this time all the political prisoners in Orissa had been released. Soon after assuming office the Labour Government declared that the elections to the various legislatures would be held in early 1946. In line with this policy the Governor of Orissa dissolved the Legislative Assembly by a notification in September 1945.[57]

At this time the PCC in Orissa was in shambles. The order banning the Congress was still in force. It was only in August 1945 that the provincial government withdrew the ban order. It gradually became clear that elections would be held. The morale of the PCC was very much boosted by the victory of its candidates in the District Board elections held soon after the lifting of the ban.[58]

As the PCC machinery harnessed itself to fight the elections Mahtab attemped to keep the big landlords 'at least ... neutral' and promised the Congress High Command that he would prevent any 'organised party' from contesting the 1946 elections.[59] His success on both counts, of course, was not really a result of his individual ability, but a fallout of the post-1937 election attitudes of the landed sections, already discussed in an earlier chapter.[60] Thus at freedom's doorstep one observes a strengthening of this alliance.

In this context Biswanath Das stated that the landlords were anxious to join the Congress. Moreover, the son of the Kanika zamindar was selected a candidate of the Congress for the Central Legislative Assembly.[61] Some like Motilal Pandit, a landlord, became Congressmen before the 1946 elections and drew their legitimacy from the new power structure to exploit the peasants.[62]

However, it will be wrong to regard this trend as a one-sided affair. In fact, the Congress organisation was as eager as the landlords to have the landlords on its side. Here one can cite the selection of Ranjit Singh, son of the Raja of Borasambar, as a Congress candidate. Ranjit had served in the Royal Air Force during the Second World War and his selection violated at least one of the three basic norms that had been formulated by the Congress High Command to select candidates for the 1946 election.[63] Faced with widespread criticism Patel wrote to Mahtab that his selection 'would be a feather in your cap' since given his 'army discipline' he would prove better than many Congressmen in the Assembly 'who in spite of their sacrifices ... did not accept discipline'. Simultaneously Ranjit was advised to keep his 'ears and eyes open' but his 'mouth shut', to 'forget' that he 'was a landlord' and a 'superior person' and to 'try to be one of the people of Orissa'.[64]

Mahtab secured fifty thousand rupees from a businessman (who had amassed a lot of wealth during the Wartime scarcities) for the Congress fund by giving him hopes of an election ticket.[65] We also get a reference to a possible decision to accept candidates who paid twenty-five thousand rupees to the Congress fund.[66] In this context the *Samaj* warned the Congress not to accept some people who were hoping to get election tickets by paying huge donations.[67]

This support of the propertied sections became increasingly visible as the election campaign picked up. Far from remaining 'neutral', as Mahtab expected them to be, the landlords of the three coastal districts declared their support for the Congress candidates.[68] Some *chaukidari* Presidents, who exercised considerable authority in the rural areas, and, who hitherto had firmly supported the government, not only supported the PCC candidates but also raised funds for the Congress.[69]

By October 1945 the political atmosphere in the Province was charged with the PCC's election campaign. Its central theme, and indeed its very source of legitimacy was the role of the Congress during the Quit India Movement. Innumerable meetings were held in the three coastal districts as well the Koraput district where the PCC leaders harped on this theme on going back to the people, after a gap of nearly three and a half years. Whereas some like Mahtab claimed that the Congress alone represented India,[70] some others like Nabakrushna Choudhary called out to the people to get organised in order to carry out another 'revolution' like the Quit India Movement.[71] In fact, a general reference point was the need for another rebellion and the danger of repression in the future, especially given the fencing of and supply of arms to the police stations.[72] It sought to communicate to the peasants that, if elected, the Congress would stop oppression and punish erring government officials.[73] Although the PCC leaders frontally condemned the colonial government, a lot of flak was also directed against the Communists.[74]

What is really striking is the extremely militant posture of the PCC in the Koraput district. Prominent PCC leaders like Mahtab criticised the estate administration.[75] A number of *hata* meetings were organised to discuss the atrocities of the estate officials and condemn them. In this tract the PCC's election campaign also included non-payment of rent and forest cess to the estate and a drive against the small savings campaign of the colonial administration. On occasions 'election speakers' prophesised the inevitable disappearance of the zamindari along with the withdrawal of the British.[76] This focus on the internal contradiction, totally absent from the election campaign of the coastal region, marks out the Koraput district, where popular enthusiasm was considerably roused during the election campaign.[77]

How does one explain this militancy? The most obvious explanation, of course, is that in the absence of the Kisan Sangha the PCC could only gain by firing people's imagination with anti-imperialist and anti-feudal slogans, without losing anything. However, it is also possible that this militancy was a result of the popular acceptance of the Congress and its appeal as an instrument of struggle which reached heights far above the level which the Congress organisation of Koraput could control.[78]

The PCC's victory in the 1946 elections in Orissa was not surprising, and unlike at the 1937 elections the colonial bureaucracy did not expect anything else to happen. In 37 constituencies out of the total 60 the PCC's candidates were declared elected unopposed and the overall position reflected a clean sweep with the PCC winning as many as 47 seats, the Muslim League 4, Independents 4, and the Communists 1.[79] It is worth pointing out at this juncture that the organisational strength of the PCC had declined considerably, as the following table illustrates:

TABLE IV

Utkal PCC: Table showing number of primary members[80]

Years	1929	1935-36	1937	1938	1945-46
Members	6,945	6,829	5,760	1,98,325	1,03,216

As can be seen, the 1945-46 membership figures failed to be anywhere near those of 1938. This empirical detail is a simple index of how even the Quit India Movement had apparently not been able to stir up the PCC membership to the 1938 level. This was due to the repression and the fact that the PCC was legalised only in 1945. It was also because this phase lacked the sweep of the twin currents of anti-imperialism and anti-feudalism of 1936-39. Notwithstanding this, the mass appeal and popularity of the PCC had, if anything, only increased, and it continued to rouse popular enthusiasm and aspirations of the people of Orissa.

The formation of the ministry saddled the Congress with fresh responsibilities. One of its first tasks was to release all the remaining political prisoners and implement the promise to institute enquiries into the excesses during the Quit India Movement. At the same time Premier Mahtab was against the setting up of a general enquiry into the conduct of government servants as this would lower their morale. In fact he strove to allay fears by a public statement that for acts done in obedience to orders of a higher authority no blame would be given to any officers if they had not gone beyond the reasonable scope of such orders.[81] The new ministry also abolished the tax on salt manufacture.[82]

At the doorstep of freedom Mahtab asked for the retention of the Governor's advisers and for more senior Indian Civil Service officers.[83]

His vision of the future was conditioned by a need to unite the princely states with the Orissa province (since otherwise nothing could be done to improve things) and to improve the conditions of the tribals (as only during the earlier Congress government had anything been done to improve their lot). He recognised the fact that Orissa was an extremely poor province where people lived in semi-starvation conditions. He felt that the solution to all problems lay in the establishment of representative government at the centre, which implied a more favourable centre-state relationship.[84]

The Congress ministry also planned to improve the supply of essential commodities for which some schemes were planned. Besides, two laws were adopted to accord equality to untouchables in services and institutions maintained by the government and allowing them to enter temples. The agrarian reforms began by seeking to identify the problems. The PCC which had fired popular aspirations in the late 1930's now talked of how 'the actual abolition of zamindari present(ed) practical difficulties' and began speculating whether or not to compensate the landlords. To look into the question of agrarian reforms a committee was set up.[85]

Of course, the need for 'developmental projects' made the ministry contemplate means to acquire land for private companies. As the development of Orissa was being planned one of the first efforts was to implement the plans to build dams at Machkund, Duduma and Hirakud. This met with a lot of opposition on account of a variety of reasons. After all, there was a genuine fear of lack of adequate and proper compensation. Added to this was the notions of a society unprepared for the changes which were being planned. This can be illustrated by referring to how the appearance of certain 'ill omens' raised doubts in the minds of people about shifting to the alternative site offered by the government, or a belief current in Sambalpur at the time that power generation would syphon out all the important properties from the water, making it useless for agriculture. Added to this was the attempt of the western Orissan chiefs (especially Patana) to launch an agitation against the Hirakund dam project in order to demand secession of western Orissa from the Province. What is worth noting is the virtual identification of leading Congressmen like Bodhuram Dube and Laxminarayan Mishra with this separatist movement,[86] causing a lot of embarrassment to the Congress and its plan for regional development.

This takes us to the question of Congress indiscipline, which assumed serious proportions. Besides the close identification of leading Congressmen with the separatist movement, there are references to funds collected by unscrupulous persons in the 'name of the Congress'. In fact Congress indiscipline became more pronounced after Independence, forcing Mahtab to take steps in 1949 to tighten discipline within the Congress in order to have a strong and efficient administration.[87]

Then, there was the desire of the new ruling class to build a capital for the new centre of political power. This led to the consultations with the planners of the Tatas, and ended with the plan to build Bhubaneshwar as the new capital.[88] While laying the foundation of the new capital, Nehru had expressed the hope that Bhubaneshwar would not be 'a city of buildings for officers and rich men without relation to common masses. It will accord with our idea of reducing differences between rich and poor'.[89] However, this ideal has remained unrealised.

And, the same Congress which had only a few months before (during the 1946 election campaign) criticised the arming/fencing of the police stations, increased the budgetary allocation for, and also increased, the police force. This was rationalised as a feature associated with the very process of 'development' itself. The Congress in Orissa interestingly seemed to depart from the 'Mahatma' when it came to planning for 'development'. 'To bring Gandhi into the day-to-day business' like increasing the police force began to be frowned upon as this would obstruct 'big development all round'.[90]

Steps had to be also taken to check corruption of government servants and traders. In 1946-47, 500 cases were detected and a majority of the guilty were convicted. The trend of bureaucratic corruption worsened with Independence, government officials being sometimes caught red-handed taking bribes.[91]

Another feature was the sudden patriotism of some of the most oppressive officials. One can cite here the case of a magistrate, Mosaheb Khan (whose name was synonymous with terror during the Quit India Movement) who offered to rebuild the Congress *ashram* at Bari, which had been destroyed under his own orders during the Quit India Movement.[92]

At the doorstep to freedom the links between the Congress and the landlords were sought to be further strengthened. After the formation of the ministry the abolition of the zamindari system began to be shelved and seen as a step to be taken only after Independence was achieved. It was no more considered 'a simple matter ... as if the Ministers have to go ... to the Secretariat, ask for a slip of paper and just write on it that the zamindari system is abolished'. There was a clear attempt to side track the issue that had been so 'central' to the PCC's politics since 1936. By March 1947 it was made adequately clear that the government was in no hurry to abolish the zamindari system as 'with all its ills' it had been in existence for several centuries.[93] We also get references to Congressmen intervening as arbitrators to settle disputes between landlords and peasants.[94]

The landlords evidently realised that the Congress was the lesser evil and were happy to have a Congress ministry in power.[95] What is worth emphasising is a new aggressive character of the landed elements which, sometimes, took the form of organising the militia to counter the peasant movement in areas like Puri.[96]

In this phase we also witness an attempt by the Congress to strengthen its links with the 'rich' peasants. For example, the idea of increasing the procurement prices of grain and demanding a reclassification of different varieties of rice for the purpose of promoting a large number of varieties in the 'superfine' category was aimed not only to benefit the landlords but also the 'rich' peasants who came next in the rural social hierarchy. In the 1947-48 phase landlords and 'rich' peasants having surplus grain stocks also profited from the high prices of foodgrains.[97] Within months following Independence the system of control imposed on foodgrains was removed[98] to benefit these sections. Similarly, the conceptualisation of a ceiling on the agricultural income tax for those whose income was more that Rs. 5000 annually[99] was aimed at strengthening the links with the small landlords as well as the 'rich' peasants.

In this context the 'pink' allies of the Congress were no longer necessary. On the threshold of freedom the PCC had emerged as the single most popular force. It hoped to reap the harvest of the three mass movements alone. In March 1947 Surendranath Dwivedy resigned from the Secretaryship of the PCC as even the criticisms by the Socialists was disliked, and any difference of opinion with Mahtab was interpreted as a revolt against the Congress.[100]

There were, of course, some problems which need to be spelt out. Here one can mention the polarisation of communal and caste identities in this phase. Although in many ways these can be traced back to the nineteenth century, these can also be associated with the politics of the anti-imperialist struggle itself as well as the 1943 famine.

Talking of specifics, we can mention the PCC's closeness to the Hindu Mahasabha[101], the growth of the Rashtriya Swayamsevak Sangh in 1946,[102] and the problem of rabid communalists within the PCC organisation itself.[103] One has to also refer to the way some Congressmen 'rallied round the cow' during their opposition to the 'grow more food' programme by labelling it the *'gorumara'* ('cow-killing') food programme.[104] Along with this was the communalised conception of the bureaucracy which looked upon Orissa as a 'Hindu province', if we go by Governor Trivedi's description.[105]

In such a context, the 1943 famine played a significant role. Bhadrak (in Balasore), which was badly hit by the famine, had a Muslim population composed of poor wage-earners; while the Hindus formed the landowning section.[106] In a context of crisis the sharpening of class relations took a communal turn with communalists playing their role. The happenings outside Orissa hardened communal identities. The colonial administration's inept handling of the situation triggered off a police firing on a 'Muslim' gathering which obstructed a 'Hindu' procession. The death of three people created a stir in Orissa.[107]

Another feature was the strained caste relations. Like communalism, it was associated with the tension between the rich and the poor which resulted from the 1943 famine situation. The attempts at assertion by outcastes, like the Pana labourers of Cuttack, who demanded higher wages were witnessed. What followed was a social boycott imposed on them by caste Hindus, and a subsequent clash. From Balasore we get a reference to the development of a class conflict, with the Harijans boycotting caste Hindus and not working in their fields since the latter had excommunicated their Brahmin priest. When the Brahmins employed labourers from neighbouring village a clash resulted. Fishermen in some neighbouring villages resolved not to carry the palanquins of high caste people.[108]

Another manifestation was the desire to go before the presence of the gods and goddesses 'stolen' by the upper castes. This concept was something rooted in the popular tradition and was also linked to the 'temple-entry' question focused upon by Congress and Gandhi in Orissa.[109] Given this background, Independence came to be associated with the advent of freedom for the outcastes to go the presence of the gods and goddesses. This explains the momentum gained by the temple-entry agitation.[110]

In this phase some castes like Khandayats and Sundhis organised themselves. The Khandayats attempted to get united and agitate in order to improve their conditions and enable themselves to meet the dominance sought to be exercised by the 'Brahmin-Karana' ministry. The Sundhis appealed to their caste people to take to professions other then their own caste profession —i.e. selling of liquor—and to give up 'ills' like child marriage. Consequently, we also witness a trend to try and emulate the dominant castes in several ways, including minor attempts at social reform. And in some cases this attempt led to inter-caste tension as in the case of Goudas (cowherds) and caste Hindus at Puri when the former sought upward caste mobility.[111]

Of course, the other problem was centred on differences with people form 'outside'—an ambiguous term used to describe Telugus and Bengalis. The striking thing is that in some cases Congress activists were directly behind these urban-based political trends. And, on occasions these took extremely crude forms.[112]

The threshold to freedom was also marked by an increase in crime. The following table[113] illustrates this phenomenon:

TABLE V

	Rise of crime in the first quarter of 1947	*Triennial average*
Murder	25	20.3
Dacoity	14	8.3
Robbery	25	20.3
Rioting	39	24.0

Besides, in the 1947-49 phase crime increased from about 60% (1947) to its peak in the 1939-49 period of about 84% (1949). Incidentally, the peak for the 1939-46 period was about 55% (1946).[114]

Although it is extremely difficult to establish links between this increase in crime and popular expectations of *swaraj*, 15 August 1947 was viewed as 'freedom from fear of the police and magistracy and in the zamindari areas, of estate officials'. Popular aspirations regarded Independence as an end of authority itself,[115] given its close association with colonialism. Strained relations between the landlords and peasants in all the districts of Orissa, including the estates, were witnessed in 1949.[116] Among the people there was also the hope of a future without landlords and moneylenders, and therefore without the zamindar-*sahukar*-sarkar nexus. One can cite here the perceptions of Ramchandra Barik, a domestic servant, originally from coastal Orissa but who at this time was working for his master, posted in East Pakistan. Barik asked his master's son if with Independence, his loans would be written off and his mortgaged lands returned to him by his village *sahukar*.[117]

This perhaps also explains the acts of some 'unimportant Congressmen' who 'instigated' people not to pay land revenue, asked *naikos* to report cases to them before going to the police, urged people not to go to the police and pronounced that in future *chaukidars* and union Presidents would be appointed only from among Congressmen.[118] And, given this perspective one can perhaps also explain the difficulty in comprehending why the price of rice should go up with the advent of freedom.[119]

It was in response to such trends that Mahtab's *Prajatantra*, funded by the landlords, carried a signed editorial by him 'advising ... (and) exhorting the public to realise the responsibilities of Independence and switch over from political agitation and an attitude of negation and obstruction to constructive activities'.[120]

III

The Mass Movements and the Dialectics of Retreat

This was the picture before the peasants and tribals of Orissa. The unresolved nature of the contradictions led to a spell of mass movements, especially in the coastal tract (including Ganjam) and some of the princely states. What appears impressive is that even in the face of certain definitely divisive trends, the politics of the Kisan Sangha as well as the Prajamandal movement united the peasants and tribals in a struggle against their oppressors. The strength as well as the role of these movements in 1947-48 normally goes unnoticed, unless one takes care to link them with the land reforms that were instituted (howsoever weak and limited they might have been),[121] the disappearance of certain feudal practices which were exploitative[122] and last, but not least, the integration of the princely states with the province of Orissa.

Let us begin by surveying the coastal tract. We find that the Kisan Sangha occupied the centre of Communist Party's activities in this phase of transition. The problem, of course, was the Congress' declaration of 'war' on the Communists in the early months of 1947, forcing some activists to go underground.[123] This trend intensified in the post-Independence context leading to the arrest of 70 activists by 1949 and prompting Nehru to write to Mahtab to stop these arrests and the banning of organisations as they earned a bad name for the Congress.[124]

However, in spite of these difficulties by the beginning of 1947 the Kisan Sangha focused forcefully on the abolition of the zamindari system which was being side-tracked by the Congress.[125] The activities of the Kisan Sangha were sought to be linked with the workers and students. On 18 March 1947 a Trade Union Day was organised at Cuttack. It passed resolutions asking for the abolition of the zamindari system along with demands of workers.[126] In May 1947 the Communists held a mass rally at Cuttack, which was attended by representatives from the different districts and also from the princely states, on the occasion of the first session of the Orissa Assembly. The basic objective of this rally was to demand the abolition of the zamindari system as well as the improvement of the condition of peasants.[127]

Besides this, the Kisan Sangha also tried to build a *bhagachasi* (share-cropper's) movement. The central theme of this was the demand to amend Tenancy laws in order to fix the share of the *dhulibhag* (produce rent) tenants at three-fifths of the gross produce and the grant of written leases to cultivators. Attention was also paid to the abolition of reserved forests and the distribution of essential commodities through village committees.[128] The demand for three-fifths share of the produce was a new demand of the Kisan Sangha and one can see the obvious parallel it had with the Tebhaga Movement in Bengal in this phase.

The 'Kisan March' to Cuttack (March 1947) was, of course, a massive attempt to mobilise the peasants and tribals of coastal Orissa. It originated from Ganjam on 20 March 1947, and the marchers reached Cuttack on 27 March. Numerous meetings were held on the way, which had an electrifying effect on the countryside of coastal Orissa. At these meetings the basic perspective of the Kisan Sangha was outlined and the people were urged to join the marchers. A systematic campaign was launched to abolish the zamindari system without compensation, for reduction of rent, tenancy rights over *inam* lands, prevention of encroachment by landlords on *heta* lands, exemption of rent of small peasants, confiscation of land from those who had more than thirty acres of land and its redistribution among the landless, subsidised sale of paddy to poor consumers, better irrigation facilities and more satisfactory procurement and distribution of controlled commodities.[129]

When the Kisan Sangha marchers met at Cuttack on 27 March 1947, a resolution was passed by 1,000 peasants present which called for the abolition of the zamindari system, forced labour and *bhag-chas*; restoration of ownership of lands to tenants; and amalgamation of the princely states with Orissa. Most of the speakers condemned the compromising character of the Congress and its sympathy with capitalists.[130] These activities paved the way for the share-croppers' movement.

The *bhagachasi* movement developed in Khurda (Puri) and we get a lot of references to it from the Puri district. In many areas the Kisan Sangha activists 'instigated' peasants not to pay rent in cash or kind for lands cultivated under the *bhag* system. On occasions share-croppers entered and cultivated lands of zamindars. There are references to such activities from Gop and Kakatpur.[131]

The Puri district Kisan conference held at Nimapara (12 May 1947) was attended by four thousand peasants. It reiterated the demand for abolishing the zamindari system without compensation and distribution of essential commodities through representative bodies. In an attempt to counter the *bhagachasi* movement a large number of its activists were arrested at Puri.[132]

Gradually the *bhagachasi* movement spread to other areas in the coastal tract. From Cuttack we get evidence of the rural rich being deprived of their grain stocks. On occasions lands of zamindars were 'forcibly' cultivated by peasants as in Kalantira and Ramkumarpur.[133]

What is indeed fascinating is the way the Kisan Sangha sought to link its activities to the nineteenth death anniversary of Gopabandhu Das to appeal to a wide section of the people (June 1947). Thus, at some of the meetings resolutions were passed urging the government to declare a date by which the abolition of the zamindari system would be accomplished.[134]

After Independence the *bhagachasi* movement spread to the entire coastal region, developing rapidly even under extremely repressive conditions. So much so that by November 1947 the pressure of the movement had forced the Congress Ministry to issue a communique which led to the enactment of the Share-croppers' Act. This gave three-fifths of the produce to the share-croppers and two-fifths to the landlords. However, the problem was of the actual implementation of this Act. In fact, the strength of the peasant movement was, ultimately, the only factor which could ensure its implementation. In areas where the peasant movement was weak the peasants were forced, through false cases and threats of eviction, to surrender fifty per cent of the produce.[135]

Consequently, the *bhagachasi* movement continued in 1948 in an attempt to assert the rights of the share-croppers in the face of brutal repression. From Brahmagiri (Puri) we get evidence of *mahajans* terrorising the *bhagachasis*. Kisan Sangha leaders were also to face repression in Khurda. From Cuttack district (especially Jajpur) a similar picture emerged. Meetings and conferences of the Kisan Sangha were banned.[136]

It was, however, Balasore which emerged as a storm-centre of the *bhagachasi* movement by 1948. The landlords terrorised peasants, and *mohunts* employed goondas in an attempt to smother the movement. The Congress government stood by the landlords and resorted to arrests of Kisan Sangha activists, most of whom were implicated in a host of false charges.[137]

The pressure of the Kisan Sangha and the movement of share-croppers forced the Congress government to accept that the Share-croppers' Act would remain valid till January 1949. Nevertheless, what needs to be pointed out is that Independence failed to solve the problems of Orissa's share-croppers.[138]

As for the princely states, this last phase saw a popular upsurge sweeping through them. What is noticeable is a close collaboration between these feudal chiefs and the retreating colonial power. The first indication of this was the restoration of the Chiefs of Nilgiri and Dhenkanal (1946). The feudal chiefs, pampered by the colonial bureaucracy, began to examine the possibilities of staying out of the Indian Union. This drive led to two meetings—one of the Orissan and Chattisgarh Chiefs at Puri (May, 1947) under the aegis of the Resident Eastern States and the Political Agent and the other, of Orissan Chiefs at Bhawanipatana (September 1947). In a national context, which was charged with communalism, these chiefs decided to raise an army of Muslims, Pathans and Gorkhas, with the obvious aim of splitting the Prajamandal movement.[139]

As the chiefs planned to ensure a transfer of power from the Resident of the Eastern States and the Political Agent to themselves, the Prajamandal got prepared to face the challenge. In August 1947 a conference of various Prajamandal activists was organised at Cuttack in which the Communists were actively involved. This called for a merger with Orissa and asked the people to resist the undemocratic rulers.[140]

In this context the uncertainties and ambiguities of the Congress also created confusion. Its initial response to the popular aspirations for the merger of the princely state was to drag its feet. Mahtab, the PCC chief spokesman, although known as a champion of the merger movement, initially talked about a mere administrative merger. This was turned down by the Congress High Command, and was followed by a policy of ambivalence.[141]

After Independence, the popular upsurge in the princely states assumed extremely militant forms. Realising the intensity of popular pressures the PCC began to shift its position.[142] And it is precisely at this juncture that we should turn to the spell of mass movements in the princely states which led to the integration of these bastions of feudal control with Orissa.

The most visible enclave of this was Nilgiri. With the restoration of the Raja, the *durbar* began to take steps to counter the Prajamandal. In its attempt to divide the people of the state the *durbar* turned to a section of the tribals, who were trained to oppose the Prajamandal. A conscious attempt was made to create an Oriya-tribal dichotomy harping on the theme that the Oriyas would grab the lands of the tribals and the only way of preventing this as to unite with the *durbar*. Given the fact that most of the tribals were agricultural labourers, the *durbar* could manage to project itself as their 'saviour'. The Raja linked his activity primarily to the Bathudi tribals whom the Communists had not been able to win over politically.

The Communists of Balasore met at Madapadia (Nilgiri) on 6 April 1946, where it was decided to counter the new offensive of the Raja. The Communists took the initiative to organise numerous meetings of the Prajamandal all over the state. They tried to emphasise how the *durbar* exploited the tribals as well as the non-tribals. There are references to the hectic activity of the Communists from certain areas of the state like Gohira, Kalakada, Garida, Kunchibania, Shyamsundarpur, Bhalukasuni, Nijgarh, Narsingpur, Bari, Dambarupal, Tinidesha and Baincha. Besides political propaganda, the Communists also started training their cadre to face the Raja. Funds were collected and a *bundh* was built by about eight hundred people, who got together at the call of the Communists, planted red flags and worked to complete the *bundh*. Although these activities helped in uniting the state people and made the *durbar* uneasy, the Communists failed to wean away the Bathudi tribals from the influence of the *durbar*.[143]

Around this time the Communist Party decided to mobilise the people to assert their fishing rights. According to the prevailing system waterways of the state were auctioned and everybody had to part with a portion of their catch to the auctioneer. Although this issue had surfaced during 1938, at this juncture a massive movement developed, with thousands of people fishing all over the state. The *durbar's* desperate attempt to smother the movement by arresting some of the leaders failed to achieve any success.[144]

The conference of the Balasore District Communist Party was held at Agasti Nagar (Nilgiri) where the prospects of a share-croppers' movement was discussed. The most important outcome of this conference was the expansion of the base of the Communists. Thousands of Communist sympathisers were recruited as members of the Communist Party and plans were made to increase the membership of the Kisan front.[145]

However, the elections for the Praja Sabha created differences between the Congress and the Communists. Things were complicated when the Praja Sabha had its first meeting (3 August 1947) since some tribals joined in demanding representation and raising anti-Oriya slogans. It was in this situation that on 15 August 1947, the Prajamandal organised a huge meeting which was attended by about twenty thousand people to celebrate Independence.[146]

After Independence, things took a serious turn when the Raja-backed loyalists began attacking non-tribals, derailing the plans to launch a share-croppers' movement. In some cases there tribals cut grain from the fields of non-tribals. The Communists made serious appeals for a united struggle to meet this new problem but failed to get any positive response from the Congress. The situation became extremely critical as the attacks mounted.[147] Initially, the Communists were in a dilemma since they had a strong base among the tribals. However, as the attacks continued they decided to retaliate, and drifted from their original plan of taking over the palace and surrendering it to the Orissa government. In fact this decision to retaliate was also influenced by Mahtab. Tragically, several tribal villages were burnt down by the Communists.[148]

The PCC, which had been observing everything sitting on the fence, at last decided to intervene.[149] Kailash Chandra Mohanty and Malati Choudhury met the Nilgiri Communists. Arms were distributed to a general gathering of people, including the Communists. At a time when the popular upsurge had thoroughly undermined its authority and credibility, the Orissa government sent in troops (November 1947) to merge the state with Orissa. This was the first princely state to be merged with the Indian Union and the PCC harped on it to tell the Rajas what awaited them in the future.[150]

After merger the defence of forest rights continued to occupy an important theme with the Prajamandal and the Kisan Sangha. In 1949, the Congress government sought to impose restrictions on the use of forests. Large-scale mass violations followed, forcing the government to abandon its policy.[151]

The merger of Nilgiri paved the way for the merger movement. When Patel and Menon discussed the issue with the Rajas of Orissa (December 1947),[152] they were speaking from a position of strength—the basis for which had been created by the popular Communist-led upsurge at Nilgiri, as well as the momentum gained by the merger movement in many other states. Faced with the popular movements the Rajas felt quite insecure. In such a context Patel's intervention made it clear to them that those Chiefs who did not agree to merge would be responsible for maintaining law and order in their state as the Congress government would not help them in any way.[153] On the one hand the Congress was not in favour of an offensive against the princely states; on the other it hoped to draw its strength from the popular upsurge sweeping the states.

As for Dhenkanal, we find that after Independence the merger movement gathered considerable momentum. The restored Raja (August

1946) decided to indulge in caste politics in order to salvage himself. He rallied Brahmins who were promised that their land grants (Brahmottar) would be made permanent and simultaneously, he promised lands to the landless outcastes. Besides, outcastes were mobilised to cut away standing crops from the fields of Prajamandal activists. Several dismissed officials were reinstated and a Praja Sammilani was established to campaign against amalgamation with Orissa. In order to terrorise the people the state recruited forty Gurkhas and procured arms and ammunition.[154] A rumour was circulated that if the state got merged with Orissa, then the price of rice would go up—the basis for which was there if one bears in mind that around the end of 1947 the price of rice did rise in the Orissa province.[155]

In this context the Prajamandal took a bold position for merger with Orissa.[156] The Communists established secret contacts with the Eastern State's police who agreed not to open fire if and when the palace was taken over.[157] The climax of the popular upsurge saw twenty thousand people marching to Dhenkanal town led by the Prajamandal and demanding responsible government.[158] This scared the Raja as well as the PCC. The latter, keen on toning down the popular upsurge and at the same time utilising it for amalgamating the state, carried out negotiations with the Chief.[159] The state *bandh* call of the Communists was opposed by the PCC leaders like Sarangadhar Das, who in fact, pressurised the administration to enforce Section 144 to counter the *bandh*.[160]

In the events that followed the Raja fled to Delhi. The Prajamandal occupied the palace and the administrative buildings. With this the ground was prepared for the merger of the state with Orissa. However, even in early 1948 the officials of the Raja resorted to arrests of Prajamandal activists.[161]

As for Talcher, Prajamandal activists like Pabitra Mohan Pradhan had refused to surrender, although from about 1945 they had been advised to do so, among others, by Gandhi.[162] In July 1947 all the warrants were cancelled. After Independence a massive demonstration was organised by the Prajamandal in which twenty thousand people joined in to demand amalgamation with Orissa.[163] Consequently, when the Raja of Talcher met Patel in December 1947, he was under considerable pressure.

At Ranpur, the arrests and repression following the death of Bazellgate had left the people in a demoralised state. This phase saw fresh initiatives by the Communists. This resulted in the organisation of meetings which, in turn, led to a lot of discussions and debates among the state people. In panic the *durbar* announced a ban on Prajamandal meetings which proved ineffective.

In an attempt to reach the state people the Prajamandal staged a play on Bazellgate, after every meeting, in which some leading Prajamandal activists acted. Besides, a song charged the atmosphere in favour of the Prajamandal. It went thus:

> Your Excellency listen to the cry of the poor.
> We the insignificant and the illiterate
> Are begging of you to listen to us.
> We are the illiterate *garjatias*
> Who from the time of our forefathers
> Have been your slaves
> And surviving upon your mercy.
> The temples, river ghats and fields
> Are all yours,
> Even after we pay the taxes and levies.
> We toil throughout the year in hunger
> But you have never given us
> Even rice-water to drink....
> We the hungry skeletons call out to you
> For the last time.
> Listen Oh! unconcerned Excellency
> Or else your chariot's wheel will crumble![164]

Very soon slogans like 'Victory to the Prajamandal' and 'Victory to Mahatma Gandhi' echoed from different parts of the state. People began to gather at the Ranpur garh. This set the ground for a massive gathering at Chandapur (4 November 1946). People joined in giving token food payments as membership. Among those present were Radhanath Rath (who presided over the meeting; he was also the editor of the *Samaj*, the organ of the PCC), leaders of the Orissa Prajamandal organisation, Congressmen like Banamali Pattnaik and Sarat Pattnaik (Secretary of the Communist Party of Orissa). Madan Mohan Pradhan (Secretary of the Orissa State People's Conference) called for a fight against the imperialists and the rajas and that only struggle could ensure freedom. Radhanath Rath appealed to the rulers 'to hear the call of their subjects' and expressed that 'we will not take away all the powers of the Rulers if they cooperate with us'.[165] This position reflected how the PCC was uncertain about its line *vis-a-vis* the states.

The Ranpur Prajamandal was finally reorganised with Ramchandra Ram as the President. A resolution was drafted which, among other things, demanded unconditional merger with Orissa, the abolishing of all princely states and the release of prisoners accused of Bazellgate's murder. Besides, there were a number of economic demands which related to the state people; these ranged from standardisation/reduction of land revenue, abolishing illegal dues, rights over forests and pastures, supply of essential commodities, a system of control over moneylenders to medical and educational benefits. The Communists pressed for abolishing *jagirs* and giving them over to the landless peasants.[166]

These developments led the *durbar* to set up a parallel Prajamandal. Interestingly, this was composed of oppressive state officials and unscrupulous businessmen who started wearing *khadi* caps. This organisation made no secret of its anti-Communist position. What is indeed fascinating is the way the Communists had been able to consolidate their position in the Prajamandal. Popular perceptions distinguished the real Prajamandal which was referred to as 'Ram Ram' Prajamandal, after Ramchandra Ram, the Secretary.[167] This shows the selectivity of popular consciousness and the way it distinguished between 'good' and 'evil'.

In an attempt to divide the state people the *durbar* set up a so-called representative body for which elections were held. The 'Ram Ram' Prajamandal swept the elections losing only one seat, despite the fact that the *durbar* spent lavishly, misused the administrative machinery and sought to secure promises of voters by serving *mahaprasad* to win the elections. The elected representatives boycotted the Raja at the first meeting itself. These activities prepared the ground for the merger of Ranpur with Orissa.[168]

In 1947 the Prajamandal of Gangpur was also revitalised by leaders like Nirod Goswami, Natabara Pandey, Sundarmani Patel and Natabara Naik. A charter of demands was submitted to the Raja which paved the way for its merger with Orissa.[169]

The state peoples' struggle climaxed with the merger of all the twenty-four princely states with Orissa. What needs to be emphasised is that a clear compromise was struck with these feudal chiefs. They were given a privy purse which was exempted from all taxes, besides various other concessions. The basic idea was that 'the government of India should not create as an aftermath of merger any social or economic problems for rulers or for their dependents',[170] which shows how a compromise was made, along with the landlords, with the feudal chiefs. Many ex-rajas thronged the Congress, some of them became its leaders and sought advice from Congress leaders about their business prospects.[171] As can be expected the merger movement had succeeded in uniting Orissa, but some tension persisted even in 1949 as some of the ex-rajas continued to champion divisive politics.[172]

This phase saw a militant Congress in the Jeypur zamindari. It appealed to the people not to do *bethi*. The 'Congressmen' criticised both the estate as well as the British and advised the people not to pay taxes or 'fines' for taking wood from the forests. Appeals were made against illicit distillation of liquor. On occasions 'Congressmen raided' liquor distillation units without informing either the excise or police authorities.[173] This reflects the links between PCC politics and a socio-reformist tendency.

This militancy was very often based on the argument that since *swaraj* had been already achieved, the police officials were powerless. The people had to obey only the Congress and should normally get their disputes settled by village committees. On occasions this also implied that the *naikos* should report all their cases to the Congressmen before going to the police. And, in some parts of the estate 'fines', 'contributions' and 'subscriptions' were collected in the name of the Congress.[174]

Considerable 'tension' and anxiety at Machkund, 'which had been chosen as a site to build a dam, was witnessed. Local leaders like Laikman Hontal (Khorsapada) and Mongal Hontal (Chicanput) gave expression to the fears of the tribals whose land was to be taken over for constructing the dam. It was obvious for these people to oppose all attempts to evacuate them until they were informed of the definite amount of compensation, the arrangements made for their future as well as the future benefits which they would secure from the scheme.[175]

IV

Conclusion

In conclusion we can say that the basic thrust of our study was to note the complexities of transition associated with the process of de-colonisation. We examined the formation of the new ruling class in this phase, along with its visions for the future. The electoral process (associated with the 1946 elections) was a watershed, which offers clues to understanding the future. It was marked by the Congress' shifting its position on the landlords (visible since the post-1937 elections, but assuming a more concrete shape now), and the officials, coupled with an alliance that was to emerge with the 'rich' peasants. The PCC steered away from its position of zamindari abolition. Besides, our discussion also helps one to grasp how the ruling class in the making, as well as the Congress, responded to various issues—

developmental projects, communalism, separatism and the princes. What is indeed paradoxical is the electoral success of the PCC and an increase in the Congress' influence, which co-existed with a substantial decline of its membership between 1938 and the 1945-46 phase. It also highlighted the popular construction/expectations of *swaraj*.

However, given the unresolved nature of the contradictions, this chapter focused on the peasant movements in this phase. The Kisan Sangha and the Communists staged a comeback through the share-croppers' struggle in the coastal tract. This movement pitted the Congress and the Kisan Sangha in a bitter struggle, which hardened after Independence, with the Congress aligning itself with the rural rich and strengthening the structure of power and control. We also saw how tribal/non-tribal differences derailed the plans to launch the share-croppers' movement at Nilgiri. Nevertheless, the *bhagachasi* movement led to certain land reforms and won some concession for the share-croppers and the rural poor.

This phase witnessed a major achievement of the Prajamandal movement—Nilgiri being the first princely state to merge with the Indian union. The response of the Congress to the Prajamandal struggle in this phase reflects how it prevaricated—shifting from uncertainty and a reluctance to alienate the princes, to harnessing the powerful anti-feudal struggles in order to integrate these feudal bastions with Orissa.[176] At the same time, the divisive trends (i.e. the tribal non-tribal conflict at Nilgiri,[177] caste politics at Dhenkanal and the separatist movement in western Orissa) indicate how the crumbling feudal chiefs, the retreating colonial power and the new stars in the horizon (i.e. the Congress) responded to a volatile situation, and even contributed to it.

And, finally, Jeypur reveals a rather interesting picture where the Congress had not been able to assert its complete hegemony and the Kisan Sangha had not been able to strike its roots. Our discussion illustrates the existence of a strong movement against immediate exploiters and plans for developments, coexisting with a socio-reformist current and the emergence of the Congress as an alternative order.

Notes

1. Interview: Damodar Samantarai (Jeypur, June 1981).
2. Linlithgow collection (NMML microfilm); from Lewis to Linlithgow, 30 January 1943 and 27 March 1943. It needs to be added that 25 political prisoners died in the district and the sub-jails of Koraput between 13 January 1943 and 19 November 1943 due to congestion and bad sanitation and 27 political prisoners died in the Koraput jail between 1943 and 1945 due to an epidemic of amoebic dysentery; cited by Mahtab in the Legislative Assembly, see *Orissa Legislative Assembly Proceedings, Vol.II, 1946* (Cuttack, 1946-1947) p. 693; and, *Vol III*, (Cuttack, 1947) p. 156.
3. HP 18/1/1943.
4. The poet's name was Hamid, and this booklet appeared around July 1943 in Cuttack; I got this evidence from my mother who had read the poem at that time.
5. Linlithgow Collection, *op.cit.*, from Lewis to Linlithgow, 7 August 1943; HP 18/7/1943.
6. HP 18/4/1944; the forecast was for the 1943 crops which were to be harvested in early 1944. This led peasants to withhold supplies.
7. Kalindi Charan Pannigrahi, *Granthabali, Part I* (Oriya; Cuttack, 1971), pp. 421-23. The author is thankful to Pragati Mahapatra for helping him translate this poem.
8. HP 18/8/1943; HP 18/5/1944; most of these demonstrations (1943) were inside jails; Acc. No.30 Who's Who Compilation Committee, Orissa State Archives (hereafter, WWCC) contains a number of references to secret pamphlets which called for millitant methods to fight the British, and looting the granaries of zamindars who hoarded paddy; help to the Quit India Movement victims centred primarily around the demand to release political prisoners and raising funds to help the affected people. The HP 18/2/1943, 18/5/1943, 18/6/1943 also throw light on the 'secret propaganda' carried out through leaflets. What needs to be emphasised is that some of these contained frontal attacks on the Communists who were described as the 'paid servants like the Ministry' and which exhorted Congressmen to arrange demonstrations against the Communists and to see that a 'peasant's government' was never established in India; WWCC, Acc.No.30.
9. The Raja of Khallikote bitterly criticised the Coalition Ministry as the Legislative Assembly had lost its representative character with the absence of 31 Congress Members. He expressed the opinion that it was indeed a rare thing to see how 'a minority is suddenly converted into a majority by the simple process of putting its opponents into jail'. See *Orissa Legislative Assembly Proceedings, Vol.VII*, 2 November, 1942, p. 77, cited by K.M. Patra *Orissa State Legislature and Freedom Struggle 1912-47*. (New Delhi, 1979), p. 200. In this context the leader of the Congress Legislature Party, in Orissa, Biswanath Das, sent a 'no-confidence' motion against the

Coalition Ministry from the Berhampur jail; *Indian Annual Register 1943*, 27 March, 1943.

10. This was based on a statement of the government in April 1942 that Orissa was a surplus province and it exported 48 lakh maunds of rice annually; mentioned by Patra, *op.cit.*, p. 208.

11. Linlithgow collection, *op.cit.*, Lewis to Linlithgow, 21 March, 1943; Lewis to Linlithgow, 22 September 1943, gave details for Koraput:
Export of rice from Koraput,
between 1 December 1942 and 19 August 1943

To;	Madras	279,536	maunds
	Ceylon	27,519	-do-
	Bengal	46,699	-do-

In an article, 'Kalahandi : From Rice Bowl to Starvation, *Statesman*, May 13, 14 1987, P.K. Deo, the former Maharaja of Kalahandi suggested that Kalahandi exported 50,000 tons of paddy to Bengal during the 1943 famine. What he, of course, does not mention is that huge profits were made by the *durbar*. Another feature that needs to be clarified is that rice was not the staple food in parts of western Orissa like these two areas, and instead of exporting all of it out of Orissa it could have been utilised to neutralise the effects of the famine in the coastal tract.

12. *Indian Annual Register*, 17 May, 1943.

13. Newspapers like *Samaj* (the organ of the Orissa Congress Party), *Muktijuddhya* and *People's War* (organs of the Orissa Communist Party and the Communist Party of India respectively) consistently focused attention to the wrong policies of the government in this phase. While discussing the Budget, Sarala Devi, a Congress member, raised the issue of exporting rice when there was deficiency in the Province; *Indian Annual Register* 1943, p. 248.

14. *Muktijuddhya*, 10/4/1943.

15. HP 18/9/1943, which quotes *Samaj*. According to an official estimate there were 50 starvation deaths in Balasore between May and August end, and there were 5000 beggars in the district, Linlithgow collection, *op.cit.*, Lewis to Linlithgow, 6 October 1943.

16. Balasore experienced a severe cyclone on 10 April 1943 as well.

17. *Muktijuddhya*, 10/4/1943 and 17/4/1943.

18. HP 33/17/1943; see especially the Report prepared by 6 persons including Bhagabati Charan Pannigrahi, who toured the famine affected areas in Balasore. This Report was published in the *Hindustan Times* of 2/5/1943.

19. Based on Mahtab's statement in the Orissa Assembly; see *Orissa Legislative Assembly Proceedings 1946 Vol.II* (Cuttack, 1946-47), p. 7.

20. The *Samaj*, the *Muktijuddhya* and the *People's War* of 1943 highlighted this phenomenon.

21. HP 18/5/1943.

22. HP 18/4/1943.

23. *Muktijuddhya* ?/3/1943.
24. HP 18/1/1943.
25. HP 33/17/1943, see the Report on the Famine, *op.cit.*.The author is thankful to his friend Kishore Chandra Das for helping him to grasp the agrarian structure of this area. His observation matched the basic points mentioned in the Report.
26. HP 18/11/1943 refers to the arrest of 16 Muslims by the Magistrate from a village in Bhadrak as they violated an order prohibiting cow slaughter during the Bakrid. Interestingly, there is a reference to how cow sacrifice 'had not been the custom...in this village'. HP 18/12/1943 informs us that the Magistrate was asked to explain his conduct as no cow slaughter had actually taken place.
27. Mansergh et.al (eds.), *Transfer of Power 1942-47 Vol. IV: The Bengal Famine and the New Viceroyalty 15 June 1943 to 31 August 1944* (London, 1973), Document no., 968. Viscount Wavell to Amery, 16 May 1944. C.M. Wright-Neville, *Report on the Administration of the Police in the State of Orissa for the Year 1949* (Cuttack, 1954), intro. chart no. 4 shows that 1943 recorded the highest number of dacoities (153) in Orissa between 1939 and 1949.
28. Mansergh *et.al* (eds.), *op.cit.*, Document no. 267, Wavell to Amery, 16 December 1943; the Fortnightly Reports in this phase always spoke of 'normalcy'.
29. See Patra, *op.cit.*, p. 220; the Premier resigned on 20 June 1944.
30. Based on *National Front,* 12/2/1939 and *Muktijuddhya* 24/4/1943. The *Muktijuddhya,* 8/5/1943 pointed to the treachery of the 'so-called' Kisan leaders which led to the decline of the powerful 1936-38 peasant movement, and how this led to the loss of certain privileges gained by the peasant movement.
31. *Muktijuddhya,* 27/3/1943; 8/5/1943; 5/6/1943, 19/6/1943; and *People's War,* 28/2/1943; 7/3/1943; 16/5/1943; 3/7/1943. Thus 'popular patriotism' was made into a serious theme with attempts to focus on Gopabandhu Das; *Muktijuddhya,* 26/6/1943.
32. HP 18/4/1943 refers to 'mass hunger' marches to the headquarters to demand relief (i.e. the opening of grain shops), stop export of rice and recognition of food committees. The marches stopped on the assurance that relief would be given, and the colonial administration made enquiries to find out who organised these marches.
33. *People's War,* 25/4/1943.
34. *People's War,* 18/7/1943; there were people among the marchers who had not eaten for three days. Around this time the price of rice had increased from Rs. 19.8 *annas* to Rs. 23.8 *annas* per bag, and the stocks had disappeared. It may be added here that the price of officially 'controlled' rice was Rs. 9 a bag; mentioned in *People's War,* 25/4/1943.
35. HP 18/4/1943; 18/6/1943; 18/6/1944; the Kisan Sangha prevented the

procurement of foodgrains as it grasped the links between the merchants and hoarders and the colonial administration.

36. HP 18/1/1943; the reference is to Bhubaneshwar where land had been taken over from the peasants to construct an aerodromme.
37. WWCC Acc. no. 30; 24/5/1943; WWCC Acc. no. 35, 14/2/1944; 7/4/1944.
38. HP 18/1/1943; 18/4/1944; *Muktijuddhya*, 25/9/1943; the Kisan Sangha opposed the 'war savings' drive; in 1943 there were 2,500 *Muktisenas;* the *Balasanghas* were aimed at recruiting the children of the peasants.
39. HP 18/9/1943; in several meetings the speakers demanded the release of political prisoners, protested against scarcity and high prices of paddy and demanded the opening of grain 'golas'.
40. Interview: Sarat Pattnaik (Cuttack, June 1983); the scattered evidence from the *Muktijuddhya* of 1943-44 also supports this formulation.
41. *Muktijuddhya*, 25/9/1943; besides there were 2,500 *muktisenas*, 1000 *mukticharas* and 500 women members in the women's front.
42. HP 18/10/1943; the references is to some 'Congressmen' of Cuttack district who joined the Communist Party. Our contention is that most probably they joined the activities of the Kisan Sangha on the food front.
43. Linlithgow collection, *op.cit.*, Lewis to Linlithgow, 24 August 1943 referred to the 'concern' posed to the colonial administration by the Communists.
44. *People's War*, 7/2/1943, 25/4/1943, 3/10/1943.
45. M.A. Rasul, *A History of the All India Kisan Sabha* (Calcutta, 1974), pp. 109-12.
46. *Muktijuddhya*, 6/5/1944.
47. WWCC Acc. no. 35, 14/2/1944; 7/4/1944.
48. *Ibid*, 7/7/1944, 21/7/1944.
49. HP 18/12/1944
50. *Muktijuddhya*, 13/12/1944.
51. *Muktijuddhya*, 8/5/1943.
52. All India State People's Conference (hereafter AISPC) file no.129 (Nehru Memorial Museum and Library, New Delhi); 'Schedule I: Allegations against the Raja of Dhenkanal during his twenty years rule' (undated).
53. Pabitra Mohan Pradhan *Mukti Pathe Sainika* (Oriya; Cuttack 1979) pp. 158-60; Sushil Chandra De, *Diary of Political Events in Orissa .1st April 1936-15th August 1947* (Cuttack, 1964), p. 49.
54. Nilgiri Praja Andolana Compilation Committee, *Nilgiri Praja Andolanara Itihas* (Oriya: Balasore, 1982), pp.125-26 (hereafter *NPARI*); HP 18/9/1943. We may add here that a number of Communists were arrested in July 1943; *NPARI*, *op.cit.*, p. 125.
55. HP 18/1/1944, 18/4/1944. We also get references to 'secret circulars' and 'rumours' which failed to evoke any response; HP, 18/8/1943; 18/9/1943.
56. Confidential File on Laxman Naik at Mathili Police Station.

57. Patra, *op.cit.*, pp. 223-24; *Indian Annual Register, 1945 Vol.I*, pp. 64, 67; HP 18/9/1945.
58. HP 18/8/1945; Patra, *op.cit.*, p. 225; Mahtab, *Sadhanara Pathe* (Oriya, Cuttack, 1972) p. 243 refers to the demoralised state of Congressmen in Orissa.
59. Durga Das (ed.), *Sardar Patel's Correspondence, Vol.2* (Ahmedabad, 1972), p.163; Mahtab to Patel, 21/11/1945.
60. See chapter 3, 'Of Movements, Compromises and Retreats: Orissa 1936-39'.
61. HP 18/10/1948; 18/12/1945.
62. All India Congress Committee, Private Papers, Nehru Memorial Museum and Library, New Delhi, file no. G-42/1947-48 (hereafter AICC papers) from Mathurananda Mohanty, Cuttack to Bapuji 12.4.1947. Mohanty wrote: 'Just before the elections I came to know that Moti Babu (Motilal Pandit) my Zamindar has turned a Congressman. I approached Naba Babu and Mahtabji with my case (eviction by Zamindar)'. Mohanty's grievances were enquired by the Cuttack District Congress Committee and found to be correct. 'Mahtabji wrote that Moti Babu is favourable and will return me my property'. However failing to get back his land Mohanty wrote about his experience in the *Muktijuddhya*, *Nava Bharat* and the *Janata —Samaj* did not print his statement. In the meanwhile his landlord 'spread the rumour in Congress circles that I am a Communist' and the Congressmen remained silent and refused to help this evicted tenant.
63. Acc.no. 50, WWCC, January 1946, mentioned that the Congress parliamentary board had adopted three basic principles to decide candidates; these included: (1) loyalty to Congress principles during the Quit India Movement; (2) their capacity to do legislative work; (3) their influence in their constituencies. As can be seen, Ranjit's selection violated the question of loyalty to the Congress' position during the Quit India Movement.
64. Durga Das (ed.) *Vol.2. op.cit.*, pp. 159-60; 325.
65. Mahtab, *op.cit.*, p. 253, mentions how he was accompanied by a Khurda businessman to Bombay. This person had made huge profits during the Wartime scarcities and wanted a Congress ticket for which he was willing to pay the amount. At Bombay, Patel accepted the amount but made it clear that this did not mean that he would be given a ticket; in fact, this businessman was refused the ticket but was requested to 'help' the Congress along with his friends during the 1946 elections. This is an indication that businessmen were perhaps even more eager to climb on the Congress bandwagon than *vice-versa*.
66. HP 18/10/1945, cited this news item in the *Niakhuntia*.
67. HP 18/9/1945.
68. HP 18/10/1945.
69. HP 18/11/1945; the observation was also made in this report that 'they (i.e. *chaukidari* Presidents) like many zamindars appear to believe in backing

the winning horse'.

70. HP 18/8/1945.
71. HP 18/11/1945.
72. HP reports of the period November 1945 to April 1946, especially, 18/4/1946.
73. HP 18/11/1945.
74. HP reports of the period November 1945 to April 1946 especially 18/8/1945; 18/9/1945.
75. HP 18/8/1945.
76. HP 18/10/1945; 18/11/1945; 18/3/1946; 18/4/1946.
77. This prompted the Superintendent of Police, Koraput to pass an order banning 'unlicensed' meetings; HP 18/2/1945.
78. Mahtab, *op.cit.*, p. 267, feels that Radhakrishna Biswasroi was selected to be a Minister because of the militancy exhibited by the people of Koraput and also because this was a very backward area.
79. AICC file. no. 3/1942-46; besides there were 4 non-elected members; whereas the Congress polled 66,281 votes, the Muslim League polled 4,336, the Independents polled 554 and the Communist candidate polled 2,234 votes. The victory of the Communist candidate was from the labour constituency and it was considerably creditable since he defeated the Congress rival from the constituency.
80. AICC file no. 3/1942-46.
81. AICC file no. EDI (KW-3)/1946-47, 'Orissa and the Congress Ministry 1946-47'.
82. HP 18/3/1947.
83. Mansergh *et.al* (eds.), *op.cit.*, Vol.7, document no.17, reports one meeting between Wavell, Cabinet delegation and Provincial Governors, 28/3/1946.
84. *Ibid*, document no. 62, Report of meeting between Wavell, Cabinet delegation and Mahtab etc., 6/4/1946. The question of centre: state relations was also expressed by Sarangadhar Das in the Orissa Legislature Assembly; as he put it: 'Being a poor province we did not ever have money. Now for 2-5 years we have the opportunity to get money from the Indian Government and if we do not take advantage of this now, when will we? (tr. from Oriya); *Orissa Legislature Assembly Proceedings Vol.3* (Cuttack, 1947-1948) p. 360. Mahtab, *Sadhanara Pathe*, *op.cit.*, p . 296, also hints at centre:state relations when he mentions that no one was bothered about Orissa in 1946.
85. AICC file no. ED1 (KW-3) 1946-47, *op.cit*, the Committee was expected to, among other things, make land revenue uniform, remove intermediaries, prevent fragmentation of holdings, make provisions for common land and improve agricultural production; the amendment of laws were planned to grant security of tenures, to simplify sale laws and introduce a rent ceiling; an agricultural income tax was planned; some steps were also planned to help small holders; and finally, laws were also contemplated to make it easier for government to acquire land for private companies 'in the

interests of planned economic development'.

86. Mahtab, *Sadhanara Pathe*, *op.cit.*, pp. 309-10; H.K. Mahtab, Private Papers (NMML) file 3;7;10. From what I gather, many people are yet to get compensation for their lands taken over during the construction of the Hirakud dam; from my childhood I have heard this point about water losing its properties if electricity is tapped from it.
87. Mahtab, Private Papers, file no. 11, Mahtab to Nehru 1/9/1949.
88. Mahtab, *Sadhanara Pathe, op.cit.*, p. 297.
89. S. Gopal (ed.), *Selected Works of Jawaharlal Nehru,* Vol. 6 (New Delhi, 1987), p. 489; speech at foundation-laying ceremony Bhubaneshwar, 3/4/1948. Here one is reminded of Sachidananda Routroy's 'Nisanga Pratima' (1972), *Granthabali Part II* (Oriya; Cuttack, 1976), pp. 325- 26; which gives a picture of Bhubaneshwar through the eyes of Bimalkrishna Babu, a freedom fighter. He saw how people involved in cement and permits scandals bought land and built palatial houses in Bhubaneshwar.
90. See Madhusudan Mohapatra's position in *Orissa Legislative Assembly Proceedings, 1946 Vol.II* (Cuttack, 1946-47), p. 361, while he debated the 'Orissa Military Police Bill, 1946'.
91. AICC file no. ED1 (KW-3)/1946-47; Mahtab, Private Papers, file no. 11.
92. Mahtab, *Sadhanara Pathe, op.cit.*, p. 271.
93. *Orissa Legislative Assembly Proceedings Vol.II; III* (Cuttack, 1946- 47; 1947-48), pp. 339;367.
94. HP 18/6/1946; 18/7/1946; 18/11/1946; 18/12/1946.
95. Mahtab, *Sadhanara Pathe, op.cit.*, p. 301, mentions how he got funds to set up the newspaper *Prajatantra,* around November 1947. This should be borne in mind while discussing how the landlords felt safe with the Congress in power and responded by patronising it.
96. HP 18/6/1947 mentions a zamindar of Puri who organised 30 scouts trained to wield *lathis* to counter peasants.
97. Board of Revenue, Cuttack file subject, 'Land Revenue Administration Report 1945 to 1948-49', the Report for 1947-48 mentioned how 'agriculturists', who had surplus for sale, profited from the prevailing high prices of foodgrains.
98. Mahtab Private Papers, file no. 7; Mahtab to Gandhi, 31/12/1947.
99. AICC file no. ED 1 (KW-3)/1946-47. This drive to strengthen the links with the 'rich' peasants also implied certain land reforms, and, in fact, the PCC's post -'47 moves to abolish the zamindari system should be seen in this light.
100. Surendranath Dwivedy, *Quest for Socialism: Fifty Years of Struggle in India* (New Delhi, 1984), pp. 139-40.
101. For example, HP 18/11/1944, mentioned how the *Muktijuddhya* advised the Congress to dissociate itself from the Hindu Mahasabha.
102. HP 18/11/1946; 18/12/1946; we get references to the circulation of rumours, leaflets and an increase in communal tension from November,

1946.

103. Mahtab Private Papers, file no. 11, wrote to Nehru thus : 'If I may say so, some of our Congressmen are more communal than the communalists themselves' 3/11/1947.

104. HP 18/7/1945.

105. Mansergh *et.al* (eds.), *op.cit.*, Vol.7, Document 235; C. Trivedi, Governor Orissa to Wavell; 9/5/1946.

106. HP 33/17/1943; discussion with K.C. Das, *op.cit.*

107. HP 5/6/47 refers to the intervention of Muslim and Hindu communalists of Bhadrak.

108. HP 18/4/1947; 18/5/1947.

109. This feature of popular tradition has been discussed in the first chapter. Although rooted in the nineteenth century as shown, it was championed both by Gandhi and the Congress in the 1920-47 period. Thus, Gandhi had never entered the temple of Jagannatha and the two Congress ministries of Orissa had attached considerable importance to this question; see for example Patra, *op.cit.*, pp.140-41; 255-58, for details. In fact the 1946 Congress ministry had formulated a bill to facilitate the entry of Harijans.

110. AICC file no. pp. 18/1946-49 mentions how Malati Choudhury led Harijans of Angul to enter a temple on 12 October 1947 which reflected a climax of the temple-entry movement.

111. HP 18/4/1947; we can add that the Khandayat conference in April 1947 was held at Bhubaneshwar, and was presided by Jadumani Mangaraj, an ex-Congress M.L.A, who had subsequently joined the Coalition Party in 1941.

112. See, for example, HP 18/2/1947; 18/4/1947. From HP 18/7/1947 we get evidence of how the issue of maltreatment of Oriyas at Calcutta was raised to rationalise misbehaviour with some Bengali women at Puri. Mahtab, the Premier, advised those indulging in such acts to restrain themselves through an appeal.

113. HP 18/5/1947.

114. C.M. Wright-Neville, *op.cit.*, intro chart no. 1.

115. HP 18/7/1947.

116. 'Land Revenue Administration, Report 1945 to 1948-49', *op.cit.*, mentioned the strained relations between peasants and landlords in all parts of Orissa.

117. The author is thankful of Professor Partha Sarathi Gupta for this reference. As he put it, Barik remained silent, perhaps not entirely convinced, when answered in the affirmative.

118. Mahtab Private Papers, File no. 3; from C.M. Trivedi to Mahtab 16/7/1946.

119. Mahtab Private Papers, File no. 7; from Mahtab to Gandhi, 31/12/1947. We can add here the mixed feelings of the Communists regarding independence and how this led them to speak of the 'farcical' nature of the freedom. They failed to grasp that an independent country had been born. Of course, our evidence suggests that in Orissa the Communists joined in the all-party

celebrations in all the districts; *Peoples' Age*, 31/8/47.

120. WWCC Acc. no. 97; 1st half of August 1947. One can add here the prediction of H.J. Todd in 1946 about the new rulers of Orissa. He expected them to be from the ruling families, 'the... Orissa Zamindars and ... the ... Congress'; cited by Mahtab, *The Beginning of the End* (Cuttack, 1972), p. 83.
121. See for example, Government of Orissa, *Report of the Land Reforms Committee Orissa 1958* (Cuttack, 1958), to get an idea of this dimension; perhaps the most significant recommendation was the suggestion to have a land ceiling, which was to be 7 acres; p. 15.
122. Here the author is referring to certain feudal obligations, including forced labour. However, the problem of bonded labourers remains in Orissa even today.
123. HP 18/2/1947; 18/2/1947 refers to *Muktijuddhya* where an article appeared about the government's 'declaration of war' on the Communists. The Socialists seem to have died out in this phase.
124. Mahtab Private Papers, File no. 11; Nehru to Mahtab, 8/6/1948; Mahtab to Nehru 1/7/1949. This is rather interesting since repression was the all-India policy of the Congress *vis-a-vis* Communists in this period.
125. HP 18/1/1947; 18/2/1947; 18/3/1947.
126. HP 18/3/1947.
127. WWCC Acc. no. 28; the rally also demanded improvement of the conditions of low paid workers.
128. HP 18/1/1947; we get some evidence to suggest an attempt by the Socialists to stage a comeback during this *bhagachasi* movement, which was peripheral to this movement; HP 18/4/1947; 18/7/1947.
129. HP 18/3/1947; the meetings also focused on the demands of workers and salaried employees.
130. HP 18/3/1947; most probably the abolition of the *bhag chas* implied granting of land rights to share-croppers; connected with the demand for the abolition of the zamindari system and ownership rights for tenants, this seems to be the logical corollary.
131. HP 18/4/1947; Biswanath Sahu, *Land Utilisation in Orissa* (Cuttack, 1951), p. 198.
132. HP 18/5/1947.
133. HP 18/4/1947; Bishwanath Sahu, *op.cit.*, p. 198.
134. HP 18/6/1947.
135. *Peoples' Age*, 6/6/1948.
136. *Ibid*; *Muktijuddhya*, 6/11//1948.
137. *Ibid*, gave some details; *Muktijuddhya*, 6/11/1948, referred to how the Congress government got Kisan leaders of Balasore like Nityananda Deb arrested, how certain zamindars like Jadunath Mahapatra and Radhanath Mahapatra terrorised peasants through middle-men and how in Rahanga village *mohunts* (Upendra Panda and his brother) used goondas to threaten

Abhimanyu Panda, a Kisan leader.

138. *Peoples' Age*, 6/6/1948.

139. WWCC Acc. no. 28, 99. *Peoples' Age*, 6/7/1947. The central points discussed included the establishment of a communication system (linking-up the different states telephonically) and raising a joint police force. The concept of a Mahakosal (i.e. Federation of States) was discussed.

140. WWCC Acc. no. 28.

141. AISPC file no. 129; P. Sitaramayya wrote to Mahtab: 'You contrast the scheme of amalgamation by which you describe your proposals....But how do you call your scheme a scheme of amalgamation when you retain the princes with their autocratic powers in their own states and offer them in addition the chances of becoming ministers with you.... Even now I say that so long you recognise the autocratic heads of individual States a scheme of amalgamation would be a misnomer' (21/7/1947).

142. See for example, Mahtab Private Papers, File no. 7. In response to a letter from Sarat Pattnaik, Secretary of the Communist Party of Orissa (18/9/1947) to Mahtab, seeking to work unitedly, Mahtab replied positively. As he put it '... I think the time has come when all political parties should frame a common policy towards the States problems'.

143. *NPARI* pp. 131-35; WWCC Acc. no. 99. It is worth mentioning how this bears some resemblance with Gandhian constructive work, *Ibid*, pp. 135-38; WWCC Acc. no. 100; the *durbar*'s uneasiness prompted it to arrest some Prajamandal activists.

144. *NPARI* p. 138. We do not have any clear evidence for Nilgiri but what needs to be mentioned here is that according to the available data, around this time, fishermen in some of the princely states asserted themselves *vis-a-vis* high caste people and refused to carry their palanquins; 18/5/1947.

145. *NPARI*, p. 139-142.

146. *Ibid*, pp. 145-48; *People's Age*, 31/8/1947; at these meetings the national flag was unfurled. People came in large numbers, carrying red flags as well as the Congress flags. We can add that on 15th August the *durbar* released many prisoners, including some criminals, with whom the Raja negotiated to counter the Prajamandal.

147. *NPARI*, pp. 152-62.

148. Interview: Banamali Das (Nilgiri, May 1982).

149. Mahtab had offered arms to the Communists which they had refused and had, instead, asked for some money which was never received; interview: Sarat Pattnaik. However, given the existing popular upsurge the PCC decided to intervene by November 1947.

150. *NPARI*, pp. 168-74; interview: Nanda Pattnaik (Cuttack, June 1987); WWCC Acc. no. 99; 47; after the merger of Nilgiri the *Samaj* and *Prajatantra* dropped hints that a similar fate awaited the other rajas; WWCC Acc. No. 47.

151. Interview : Banamali Das.

152. WWCC Acc. no. 99; two separate conferences were held—one with the rulers of 'B' and 'C' class states and one with those of 'A' class states.
153. Harekrushna Mahtab, *Beginning of the End* (Cuttack, 1972), p. 30.
154. AISPC file no. 129, 'Allegations Against Raja of Dhenkanal during his twenty years of Rule' (undated); Sarangadhar Das, 'A Review of the Political Situation in the Eastern States' (27/11/1947).
155. Interview: Sarat Pattnaik. The author has already referred to the increase in the price of rice in Orissa around the end of 1947.
156. AISPC file no. 129, Krutibas Mishra's (Secretary, Dhenkanal Prajamandal) statement articulated the popular feeling: "... the Dhenkanal Prajamandal requests the Government of India not to effect any compromise settlement with the Rajas, but to direct them to hand over all powers to the people' (undated).
157. Interview: Sarat Pattnaik; Baishnab Pattnaik (Dhenkanal, June 1985).
158. Sadasiv Pradhan, *Agrarian and Political Movements* (New Delhi, 1986), p. 148.
159. Interview: Baishnab Pattnaik; he told the author that Mahtab used to go to the palace to conduct negotiations which appeared strange.
160. Interview: Sarat Pattnaik.
161. AISPC file no. 129; Sarangdhar Das, 'Report on Orissa and C.P. States Merging with Orissa;' (2/2/1948).
162. Pabitra Mohan Pradhan, *Mukti Pathe Sainika* (Oriya; Cuttack, 1979), pp. 242-43; Pradhan also mentions Mahtab who on 8/4/1946 had advised him at Delhi to surrender to the Raja. The Talcher Raja made Pradhan's case a prestige issue and only in July 1947 was the warrant for his arrest cancelled; AISPC file no. 164.
163. Sadasiv Pradhan, *op.cit.*, p. 147; it seems Gandhi advised the Raja to merge.
164. Ramachandra Ram, *Sangramee* (Oriya; Cuttack, 1986), pp. 158-61; the leading Communist activists like Ram moved around the state, cycling 10 to 15 villages a day to mobilise the people.
165. *Ibid*, pp. 163-64; Mahtab Private Papers, File no. 13; Ramprasad Singh and Srivasta Naik, Secretary States Students Conference also expressed similar anger against the rajas.
166. Ram, *op.cit.*, pp. 164-71.
167. *Ibid*, p.172.
168. *Ibid*, pp. 175-77; we should add here that at the so-called democratic elections the *durbar* did not allow political prisoners and women to cast their vote.
169. Sadasiv Pradhan, *op.cit.*, p. 153.
170. V.P. Menon, *The Story of the Integration of the Indian States* (Madras, 1961), p. 154.
171. Mahtab's correspondence 141/44 with the Raja of Dhenkanal; the Raja wanted his advice for joining Bengal Breweries (20/8/1950) and Mahtab's Private Secretary replied to the Raja (22/8/1950) expressing Mahtab's

inability to advice him.

172. C.M. Wright-Neville, *op.cit.*, names the Rajas of Patana, Kalahandi, Sonepur and Bamra, p.10; we may add here that Rajendra Narayan Singh Deo, the Raja of Patana, became Chief Minister of Orissa later on.

173. HP 18/6/1946; 18/7/1946; 18/11/1946.

174. HP 18/11/1946, 18/1/1947; Mahtab Private Papers, File no. 3, from C.M. Trivedi, Governor to Mahtab, 3/7/46.

175. Mahtab Private Papers, File no.10, extract from Fortnightly Report of the Koraput district (March, 1947).

176. James Manor, 'The Demise of the Princely Order: A Reassessment', in Robin Jeffrey (ed.), *People, Princes and Paramount Power* (New Delhi, 1978), p. 319 argues similarly.

177. Jeffrey, *ibid.*, intro. p. 24, mentions how the Rajput rulers in the Balasore states sought to lead their tribal population to ward off the 'town dominated Hindu (but non-Rajput) Congress' movements. In case we assume that that he refers to Nilgiri (which is in the present-day Balasore district) this does not seem to be correct. First, the Raja of Nilgiri could win over only a section of the tribals, since the Communists had a reasonably strong base among the tribals from around 1939-40. Secondly, the Prajamandal movements included people from various castes/classes. And, finally, the Nilgiri Prjamandal was dominated by the Communists in this phase.

Epilogue

The present work sought to focus on the way peasants and tribals interacted with Indian nationalism in Orissa—an area that has hardly attracted scholarly attention.[1] An attempt has been made to delineate this process by associating it with popular perceptions—something that is riddled with complexities. The aim was to offer certain clues towards understanding how the peasants and tribals interacted with and related to the anti-imperialist struggle and how it altered their perceptions. A significant feature was to highlight the tribal/non-tribal interactions, through processes like Hinduisation. It also tried to explore the way the Congress related to the agrarian and the peasant question and how there were visible shifts and turns in its stand, given its interaction with mass movements in Orissa.

Certain general points emerge from our discussion of the anti-imperialist struggle in Orissa. This work questions the method of locating the centrality of the Congress—as a 'historic block'—as has been done by the nationalist historians.[2] Neither does it accept some of the basic premises of the subaltern historians like the 'duality of the nationalisms' (i.e. 'elite' and 'subaltern' nationalism) and 'popular autonomy'.[3] Thus although it accepts the specificity of the popular level and popular translations of *swaraj*, it illustrates the process of interaction, leading to the Congress and the national movement, both shaping and being shaped by the common people.

The three mass movements (i.e. Non-Cooperation, Civil Disobedience and Quit India) also throw light on the tensions and limits of this interaction and the historical evolution of the Kisan Sangha and the Prajamandal movement as well as the major movements they initiated, both by complementing and by attempting to enlarge the scope of these beyond what the Congress had envisaged. This implicitly made us look at shifts and turns in the social bases of the Congress and the anti—imperialist struggle in Orissa, as well as that of the militant movements of the Kisan Sangha and the Prajamandal.

A significant point that emerges is the location of the 1936-39 phase, especially 1938, as the high point of the consolidation of the national movement in Orissa. Although it is an obvious fact that the freedom struggle was an anti-colonial movement, the sweep of the anti-imperialist and anti-feudal currents in this phase question the validity of the method which harps on 'primary' (i.e. anti- imperialist) and 'secondary' (i.e. anti-feudal or class) contradictions as exclusive categories.[4] It also highlights a typical paradox—i.e. how the position of the Congress in Orissa, despite its limitations, ambiguities and compromises (and even its declining membership between 1938 and 1945-46) was inversely related to its mass appeal and, in fact, coexisted with the extension of Congress' influence.

It also focuses on how the involvement and mobilisation of women was geared to strengthen the national movement, and was channelised along a socially acceptable upper caste/male framework. As a result, gender related issues did not develop as sites of struggle.

This work also throws light on how the three mass movements weakened the political and ideological hold of the colonial and the feudal order, with the Congress seeking to replace them. Effort was directed at analysing the incompleteness of this process and the strain it was exposed to. At the same time the survival of certain internal contradictions—i.e. class/caste exploitation—and communal politics reflect the weakness of the anti-imperialist struggle in Orissa, and contradict assumptions regarding the unifying/integrating role of the national movement.

While concluding it would, perhaps, be apt to say something about the participants' present-day perception of their role in the anti-imperialist struggle and the state of the peasants and tribals of Orissa in contemporary times.

What was Orissa supposed to be for those who had struggled to build and strengthen the anti-imperialist struggle facing the combined terror of the British, the princely rulers and the zamindars? Baishnab Pattnaik of Dhenkanal breaks down saying how his expectations of *swaraj* were very different from the post-1947 developments. He shows a scar on his wrist left by a bullet in the course of a clash with the police during the Quit India Movement. 'Was this what we had struggled for?' he asks.[5]

One cannot forget the observations of Wasil Baksh of Kendrapada (Cuttack) who is no more. This old man of 78 had gone all the way to attend a public meeting addressed by Jayaprakash Narayan at Cuttack in 1973 to ask him just one question —'Why should we pay for salt after Independence? It should be available free, since, after all, we had courted arrest and had braved the *lathi* blows during the salt *satyagraha*'.[6]

Nor can one ignore the perception of those who had fought, suffered and lost their near and dear ones in remote parts of the Koraput district. They are still waiting for their *swaraj* when their miseries would end. The mining of bauxite and the several multi-purpose projects in this district have hardly changed the shape of their life, and, if anything, have only contributed to its shrinking even more.

'Laxman Naiko's statue', remarks Damodar Samantarai, 'hardly resembles him'.[7] As we have already mentioned Laxman Naiko was the only political prisoner in Orissa to be hanged for his involvement in the Quit India movement. For years the tribal folk of Malkangiri had refused to believe that Laxman was dead, and, in fact, when S. Sanganna, the victorious Congress candidate, toured this area after the 1952 elections a rumour had circulated that Laxman had come back 'successful' and 'rewarded' as a Minister for his role in the Quit India movement.[8]

Kausalya, Laxman Naiko's daughter, insists that she has always voted for the Mahatma's 'daughter' — Indira Gandhi—since, after all, she was a widow.[9] In fact, it is almost impossible to refute notions internalised over the years. If Kausalya is still alive today (she had complained about the stoppage of her freedom fighter's stipend in 1981) then she will perhaps continue to vote for the 'Mahatma's party' in the coming elections.

Those who were uprooted with the advent of *swaraj* during the construction of the Hirakud dam (early 1950's) are yet to receive the promised compensation. This is perhaps one component out of the many which have made people learn to protest against evacuations, even though promises of compensation are made by the government, like at Balliapal (Balasore).

The contradictions between the coastal areas and the western interior have become further sharpened after Independence. In most parts of western Orissa we see people gathering food and surviving on shifting cultivation, mango stone (the inner material used to be eaten but nowadays people prefer to sell them in Kalahandi and Phulbani as there is a growing demand for them to be used as noodle hardners) leaves, roots (sometimes poisonous) and ants. The thin balance between them and nature has been disturbed without the development of any alternative possibilities, leaving most of western Orissa in a near-famine situation over the last decade.

Of course, the problem of landlessness and migrations of peasant and tribal families is a common feature affecting both the coastal area and the interior.

In agriculture the situation is no better. Possibilities seemed to exist after Independence, especially in the merger of the princely states and the abolition of the zamindari system. These were the result of big struggles of the Kisan Sangha and the Prajamandal movement and partly due to the new ruling class' desire to consolidate its links with small landlords and 'rich' peasants. However, these possibilities have not been realised. The peasants and tribals have to depend on nature to survive even today. Progress is symbolised by the K.V. grid connections going above the fields without actually electrifying them or the tubewells that remain dry. Blood, sweat and tears have hardly yielded anything. Thirty per cent of the agricultural land is concentrated in the hands of about 4 per cent of the landlords and big farmers while the landless and marginal farmers constitute 87 per cent of the rural households.[10] The bonded labour system (which might be statistically absent), near-famine conditions over the last decade in most of western Orissa and migrations point to the deepening crisis.

What is more, although more than 40 years have passed since Independence, the ruling class of Orissa is yet to intervene effectively even today. The famine persisting in lush green Kalahandi illustrates this point. And its isolation from the peasants and tribals is perhaps epitomised by the folk song sung by a group of tribal girls to a gathering of journalists at Nagatundi village (Kalahandi):

We are strangers
We and you,
Tomorrow you will go away,
To places far away,
To Delhi and to Bhubaneshwar.
If you build bridges for us once again,
Please make sure that this time
We can cross the river without falling
Into the water and getting hurt.[11]

Yet this perhaps also indicates how amidst all this there is still hope. The peasants and tribals are making history even today at Gandhamardana and Balliapal. It is a well known fact that in the last few elections people have taken money from one and have voted for another. The double-edgedness of the system, given the literacy campaigns and media boom, coupled with the left and the democratic movement are evidently making people question things.

Notes

1. The main thrust of H.K. Mahtab, *History of the Freedom Movement in Orissa Vols. 1 to V* (Cuttack, 1957); K.M. Patra, *Orissa Legislature and Freedom Struggle 1912-47* (New Delhi, 1979); or, even Surendranath Dwivedy's *Quest for Socialism* (New Delhi, 1984), has been to focus on individuals, the dominant political trends and narrating events.
2. This seems to be the general tone of Bipan Chandra, 'Peasantry and National Integration in Contemporary India' in his *Nationalism and Colonialism in Modern India* (New Delhi, 1979); see, especially the third section of his paper. See also M.H. Siddqui, *Agrarian Unrest in North India: The United Provinces, 1918-1922* (New Delhi, 1979), who asserts that 'the patronage of politics from above helped agrarian discontent to get organised., p. ix (intro.).
3. One can perhaps cite a few examples to illustrate this point. Stephen Henningham, 'Quit India in Bihar and Eastern United Provinces', in Ranajit Guha (ed.), *Subaltern Studies II* (New Delhi, 1983), speaks of the 'duality of the insurrection (which)...consisted of an elite nationalist uprising combined with a subaltern revolt', p. 164. Similarly, Swapan Dasgupta, 'Adivasi Politics in Midnapur, 1760-1924' in Ranjit Guha (ed.) *Subaltern Studies IV* (New Delhi, 1985), asserts: 'Elite politics in Midnapur has only a very tenuous connection with the autonomous mobilisation of ... the subaltern. Adivasi insurgency belonged, on the whole, to another domain of politics'; p.135.
4. See, for example, Bipan Chandra, *et. al, India's Struggle for Independence* (New Delhi, 1988), where it is articulated thus: 'In the colonial situation anti-imperialist struggle was primary and the social—class and caste—struggles were secondary', p. 25.
5. Interview: Baishnab Pattnaik (Dhenkanal, June 1985).
6. Interview: S.B. Zaman, grandson of Wasil Baksh (Cuttack, June 1986).
7. Interview: Damodar Samantarai (Jeypur, June 1981).
8. Interview: Gopinath Pujari (Jeypur, June 1981).
9. Interview: Kausalya (Mathili, June 1981).
10. These statistics related to Orissa are based on *Times of India* 7 March 1989; statement of Godavari Parulekar, President All India Kisan Sabha.
11. Cited in 'Kalahandi: A Report' in *Economic and Political Weekly* 30 April, 1988; the author is thankful to Indrani Sen for translating this rather difficult song which we picked up while interviewing some tribals of Nagatundi (Kalahandi) in June 1987.

Glossary

abwab	illegal cess
amin	revenue official
amla	revenue official
andharuamulak	dark zone, term for a princely state
badadanda	big street in front of the Jagannatha (Puri) temple
Balijatra	a festival to mark the departure of maritime traders to Bali and south-east Asia
Bauri	an outcaste
bazyaftidar	a person holding a land which was originally rent-free but was subsequently assessed at full/half rates
begar	a form of forced labour
bethi	forced labour
bhadralok	the middle class which developed in the 19th century and had links with the feudal and the colonial order
bhagchasi	share-cropper
Bhattra	a tribe
bhogra	privileged land given in return of service rendered
Bhuyan	a tribe
Bonda	a tribe
brahmottar	land grant to a Brahmin
bundh	embankment
chandna	a non-agricultural homestead
Chandaluni	an outcaste woman
changu	tambourine
chalanta	mobile
Chamar	an outcaste
Chasa	agriculturist caste

chasi	peasant
cherapahara	the symbolic sweeping of the chariots on the annual Rathajatra day by the Puri Raja
cist	revenue
daffadar	a sub-officer of rural police in command of a number of chaukidars.
dahi	shifting cultivation
daktarakhana	hospital
debottar	dedicated to a god
dewan	top-most official of a princely state appointed by the colonial administration or the state chief
Dharmapinnu	smallpox goddess of the Kuttia, Kandhas.
dhulibhag	a system of payment of rent in kind by division of crop and all by-products between the tenant and the landlord
Didayi	a tribe
Domb	an outcaste
duma	ghost
Gadaba	a tribe
gajapati	the Puri Raja
gamcha	towel
ganda	village watchman
ganjhus	headman/revenue intermediaries
garzat	princely state
garzatia	a condemnatory term for a resident of a princely state
Gauda	milkman
Gauduni	milkmaid
gauni	a measure of grain
geeti	song
gherao	surrounding a figure of authority in protest
gomasta	agent/manager
Gond	a tribe
goti	a system whereby a poor person worked to repay a loan/interest
gountia	revenue farmer
gramya	village
Hadi	an outcaste
haliya	ploughman
handia	an intoxicating drink distilled from rice

harra	a tree
hata	weekly market
haspatal	hospital
hazat	police lock-up
heta	land tenure
hizrat	exodus
Ho	a tribe
hulahuli	ululation
inam	gift
Jagannatha	the chief deity at the Puri temple believed to be an incarnation of Vishnu, the Hindu god
jagir	land held on condition of rendering service
jagyan	sacrifical rites
jama	rent
Jatapu	a tribe
jatra	popular theatre
jhum	shifting cultivation
jogi	a singing mendicant
kamtuni	a femine agricultural labourer
Kandha	a tribe
katuri	a small scythe-like implement
Keuta	a fisherman
kendu	a plant
khalsa	area brought directly under the Mughal land revenue system
Khandayat	agriculturist caste drawing legitimacy from the Rajput caste (viz. khanda means sword)
Karana	a caste of writers/accountants
khanja	land grant
kirtan	a singing party normally associated with religious songs
Kittung	Savara god
Kols	a tribe
Koya	a tribe
kunchum	a measuring unit for grain (1 kunchum=3 1/2 kilograms)
lakhiraj	exempt from revenue
Lodha	a tribe
mahajan	moneylender
mahant	head of a Hindu religious foundation

Mahaprabhu	God
mahaprasad	sacred food offered to Jagannatha
Mahima cult	a popular religious form which evolved around the 1840's and was initially popular in some of the princely states
mana	a measuring unit for grain
Mapru	God
Mata	Didayi goddess
math	a religious foundation, monastry
maund	a measure of weight (1 maund=25 to 85 pounds)
Mehtar	a sweeper (an outcaste)
meli	rebellion
mohwa	an intoxicating drink distilled from the mohwa tree
mudhi	puffed rice
Muktisena	Liberation squad
muliya	agricultural labourer
Munda	a tribe
mustagir	revenue farmer
mustajar	revenue farmer
namak haram	traitor
naiko	headman
navakalevara	the rituals associated with the disposal and recreation of the deities at the Puri temple
nijchas	cultivated land held directly
padajatra	march on foot
pradhan	village headman
pagree	head gear
pahi	non-resident
pala	sail of a ship/boat
pargana	a revenue division
parganadar	a revenue farmer
paik	feudal warrior
paikali	a land grant to a paik
parishad	council
Paroja	a tribe
peshkush	a small present or peppercorn rent
pitaru	a root
podu	shifting cultivation
Prajamandal	State People's organisation

prayaschita	repentance
raija	self-rule
raiyat	peasant
raja	king
Ramdhun	Gandhi's song 'Raghu Pati Raghava Raja Ram...'
Rana	an outcaste
rasad	forced supply of provisions
Ringesun	God of the wind of the Savaras
Rumrok	Didayi god
Sadhaba	a maritime trader of Orissa
Sahibosum	Sahib god of the Savaras
sahukar	moneylender
salapa	a tree from which liquor is brewed
Samyavadi	Socialist
sanja	produce rent
sankirtan	a singing party normally associated with religious songs
Santhal	a tribe
Sentisena	Peace squad
sarbarkar	rent collector
Satyabadi	a place near Puri associated with a system of national education introduced by people like Gopabandhu Das
Savara	a tribe
sena	squad
shikar	hunt
subahdar	revenue collector
suniya vethi	new year's gift
taccavi	a loan from the government to a cultivator
Tanti	weaver caste
tar	telegraph
tari	toddy; also a Kandha goddess
tekauli	rent
Teli	oilman caste
tendu	a plant, the leaves of which are used to make Beeri
thakurani	goddess
thani	a resident cultivator
tikkus	tax

tola	a weight (1 tola=11.66 grammes)
Utkal	a traditional name of Orissa
varna	caste
Vishnu	Hindu god (the 'preserver')
zabardust	forcible

Select Bibliography

Primary Sources

Unpublished Sources

Koraput Collectorate (Koraput) — 'Judgement in Late Laxman Naik Case'.

Mathili Police Station (Mathili, Koraput) — 'Confidential File on Laxman Naik.

National Archives (New Delhi) — Home Political Reports, 1920-1947.

Nehru Memorial Museum and Library (New Delhi) — Private Papers — Institutional — All India Congress Committee; All India State People's Conference.

Individuals — H.K. Mahtab; Indulal Yajnik; Linlithgow; N.G. Ranga; Rajendra Prasad; Sarangadhar Das.

Orissa State Archives (Bhubaneshwar) — Who's Who Compilation Committee Records (Based on Confidential Police Reports); District Records.

West Bengal State Archives (Calcutta) — Confidential Reports on Native Newspapers, 1900-1905.

Interviews

Bisoi, Krushna Chandra, Jeypur, June 1981.

Das, Banamali, Nilgiri, May 1982.

Devi, Bina, Cuttack, December 1988.

Gomango, Gundu, Kuchindi (Koraput) December 1981.

Gomango, Nirakantha, Kuchindi (Koraput) December 1981.

Kausalya, Mathili, June 1981.

Misra, Krupasindhu, Ranpur, June 1984.

Pannigrahi, Kalindi Charan, Cuttack, June 1985.

Pattnaik, Baishnab, Dhenkanal, June 1985.
Pattnaik, Gurucharan, Cuttack, June 1983.
Pattnaik, Nanda, Cuttack, June 1987.
Pattnaik, Sarat, Cuttack, December 1980 and June 1983.
Pujari, Gopinath, Jeypur, June 1981.
Samantarai, Damodar, Jeypur, June 1981.
Zaman, S.B., Cuttack, June 1986.

Correspondence

Prafulla Das, Rajkanika, 13.3.1981.

Published Sources

Newspapers

Amrita Bazar Patrika, 1938.
Congress Socialist, 1936-1937.
Congress Socialist, 1936-1937.
Hindustan Times, 1943.
Krushak (Oriya), 1938,.
Leader, 1938.
Muktijuddhya (Oriya), 1942-1943; 1948.
National Front, 1938-1943.
Peoples' Age, 1947-1948.
Peoples' War, 1942-1943.
Prajatantra (Oriya), 1947-1948.
Samaj (Oriya), 1920-1938.
Sàmyavada (Oriya), 1295 Pausa (Oriya year)
Satyasamachar (Oriya), 1930-1934.
Searchlight, 1920-1922.
Utkala Dipika, (Oriya), 1869-1933.
Utkala Putra (Oriya), 1870-1873.

Official Publications

Behuria, N.C., *Final Report on the Major Settlement Operation in Koraput District 1938-64* (Cuttack, ?).
Completion Report of the Talcher State Revision Settlement Season 1928-29 (Cuttack, ?).

Dalziel, W.W., *Final Report on the Revision Settlement of Orissa 1922- 1932* (Patna, 1934).
Final Report on the Nilgiri Settlement 1917-1922 (Berhampur, 1922).
Final Report on the Re-settlement Operation of Banki Government Estate (Cuttack, ?).
Final Report on the Settlement of the Dhenkanal Feudatory State (Orissa) 1921-1924 (Berhampur, 1966).
Hossien, S.S., *The Completion of Report and Settlement for Kanika Ward's Estate (District Cuttack) 1889-94* (Cuttack, 1895).
Maddox, S.L., *Final Report on the Survey and Settlement of the Province of Orissa (Temporarily Settled Areas Vols.I; II* (Cuttack, ?).
Mukherjee, Indrabilas, *Final Report on the Land Revenue Settlement of the Gangpur State 1929-1936* (Berhampur, 1938),
Report on the Khurda Settlement of 1897-98 (Cuttack, ?).
Report on the Land Settlement 1911-1912 Talcher State (Cuttack, 1963).
Singh, G.N., *Final Report on the Original Survey and Settlement Operation of the Ranpur Ex-State Area in the District of Puri 1943- 1952* (Berhampur, 1963).

Bell, R.C.S., *Orissa District Gazetteers: Koraput* (Cuttack, 1945).
Cobden-Ramsay, L.E.B., *Bengal Gazetteers: Feudatory States of Orissa* (New Delhi, 1982; reprint).
Hunter, W.W., *A Statistical Account of Bengal Vol.XVIII: District of Cuttack and Balasore* (Delhi, 1976; reprint).
Hunter, W.W., *A Statistical Account of Puri and Orissa Tributary States' Vol.XIX* (Delhi, 1976; reprint).
O'Malley, L.S.S., *Bihar and Orissa District Gazetteers: Sambalpur* (Patna, 1932).
——, *Bihar and Orissa District Gazetteers: Cuttack* (Patna, 1933).
Senapati, N., and N.K., Sahu *Orissa District Gazetteers: Koraput* (Cuttack, 1966).
——, *Orissa District Gazetteers: Mayurbhanj* (Cuttack, 1967).
Senapati, N., and B. Mohanty,, *Orissa District Gazetteers: Sambalpur* (Cuttack, 1971).
Senapati, N., and P. Tripathy, *Orissa District Gazetteers: Dhenkanal* (Cuttack, 1972).
Senapati, N., and D.C. Kumar,, *Orissa District Gazetteers: Kalahandi* (Cuttack, 1980).

Bell, R.C.S., *Census of India, 1941, Vol.XI, Orissa Tables* (Simla, 1942).

Lacey, W.G., *Census of India 1931, Vol.VII, Bihar and Orissa Part I Report and Part II Tables* (Patna, 1933).

O'Donnel, C.J., *Census of the Lower Provinces of Bengal 1981: The Provincial Tables* (Calcutta, 1893).

O'Malley, L.S.S., *Census of India, 1911, Vol. V Bengal, Bihar and Orissa and Sikkim Part I Report* (Calcutta, 1913).

Bihar and Orissa Legislative Assembly Proceedings 1919; 1922 (Patna, 1919; 1922), Government of Orissa.

Government of Orissa at Work From 19 July 1938 to 31 March 1939 (Cuttack, 1939).

Indian Annual Register 1921-1947.

Mahapatra, J.N., *Orissa in 1936-37 to 1938-39* (Cuttack, 1941).

Memoranda on the Indian States: 1930-1940 (Calcutta, 1931-1941).

Misra, Godavaris, *et.al, Report of the Khurda Forest Enquiry Committee* (Cuttack, 1938).

Mozumdar, S.N., *Report on the General Elections in Orissa 1937* (Cuttack, 1937).

Orissa Elections Brochure (Cuttack, 1936).

Orissa Legislative Assembly Proceedings 1937-1947 (Cuttack, 1937-1948).

Ramdhyani R.K., *Report on the Land Tenures and the Revenue System of the Orissa and Chattisgarh Sates Vols. I-III* (Berhampur).

Report of the Joint Enquiry by the Revenue Commissioner Orissa and I.G. of Police Orissa into the Eram Firing on 28th September 42 (Cuttack, 1942).

Report of the Land Reforms Committee 1958 (Cuttack, 1958).

Report of the Partially Excluded Areas Enquiry Committee: Orissa 1940 (Cuttack, 1940).

Report on Administration of Police in the Province of Orissa Cuttack, 1949 (Cuttack, 1941; 1954).

Report on the Administration of Salt Department in Orissa 1927-1931; 1935-1941 (Cuttack, 1928-1932; 1936-1942).

Report of the Bihar and Orissa Provincial Banking Enquiry Committee 1929-30 Vol. I (Patna, 1930).

Report on Administration, Bihar and Orissa - 1920-21 (Patna, 1923).

Report on Land Administration in the Districts of Ganjam and Koraput 1936-1942 (Cuttack, 1937-1943).

Report on the Land Revenue Administration of the Districts of North Orissa for the Years 1936-1939 (Cuttack, 1937-1940).

Tottenham, R., *Congress Responsibility for the Disturbances: 1942-43* (New Delhi, 1943).

Unofficial Publications

Mahtab, H.K., *et.al, The Report of the Enquiry Committee Orissa States 1937* (Cuttack, 1939).

Report of the Congress Agrarian Reforms Committee AICC (Madras, 1945).

Utkala Brahmin Samitira Sastha Barshika Bibarani (Oriya; Puri, 1906).

Secondary Sources

Books

Bahadur, K.P., *Caste, Tribe and Culture of India Vol. III, Bengal, Bihar and Orissa* (Delhi, 1977).

Bak, J.M., and G. Beneck, (eds.), *Religion and Rural Revolt* (Manchester, 1984).

Beames, John, *Memoirs of a Bengal Civilian* (? 1896; New Delhi, 1984; reprint).

Biswasroi, Radhakrushna, *Orissa Rajaniti Ebon Eka Nua Pradeshara Parikalpana* (Oriya; Jeypur, 1973).

Bompas, C.H., *Folklore of the Santhal Parganas* (London, 1909).

Boulton, J.V., *Phakirmohan and His Times* (Bhubneshwar, 1976).

Burke, Peter, *Popular Culture in Early Modern Europe* (London, 1978).

Chatterji, Partha, *Nationalism and Colonialism: A Derivative Discourse* (Delhi, 1987).

Chattopadhayay, Harindranath and B. Sinha,, *The Boatman Boy and Forty Poems* (translations of Sachidananda Routroy's poems) (Calcutta, 1954).

Chaudhury, Valmiki (ed.), *Dr. Rajendra Prasad: Correspondence and Select Documents Vols. I, II* (New Delhi, 1984).

Chopra, P.N. (ed.), *Towards Freedom 1937-47* (New Delhi, 1985).

Dalton, E.T., *Descriptive Ethnology of Bengal* (Calcutta, 1872).
Das, B.S., *Studies in the Economic History of Orissa From Ancient Times to 1833* (Calcutta, 1978).
Das, Durga (ed.), *Sardar Patel's Correspondence Vol. II* (Ahmedabad, 1972).
Das, K.B. and L.K. Mohapatra, , *Folklore of Orissa* (New Delhi, 1979).
Das, M.N. (ed.), *Sidelights on the History and Culture of Orissa* (Cuttack, 1977).
Das, Prafulla, *Bharatara Sasastra Mukti Sangram* (Oriya; Raj Kanika, 1980).
Das, S.N., *Utkalamani Gopabandhu Das* (Oriya; Cuttack, 1975).
Das, Sudhakar, *Swadhinata Sangramara Bhumi Iram* (Oriya; Cuttack, 1977).

Datta Gupta, U.N., *Folktales of Orissa* (Calcutta, 1923).
De, S.C., *Diary of Political Events in Orissa 1st April 1936-15th August 1947* (Cuttack, 1964).
——, *Trend of Political Events in Orissa: 1882-1936* (Cuttack, 1966).
——, *Who's Who of Freedom Fighters in Orissa (Koraput, Ganjam and Baud-Phulbani Districts)* (Cuttack, 1969).
Desai, A.R., *Peasant Struggles in India* (Bombay, 1979).
Dhanagare, D.N., *Peasant Movements in India 1920-1950* (Delhi, 1983).
Dutt, R.P., *India Today* (Calcutta, 1970).
Dwivedy, Surendranath, *August Biplaba* (Oriya; Cuttack, 1972).
——, *Quest for Socialism* (New Delhi, 1984).
Elwin, Verrier, *Bondo Highlender* (Bombay, 1950).
——, *Tribal Myths of Orissa* (Bombay, 1954).
——, *The Religion of an Indian Tribe* (Bombay, 1955).
Eschmann, A., *et.al* (eds.), *The Cult of Jagannath and the Regional Tradition of Orissa* (New Delhi, 1978).
Foucault, Michel, *Discipline and Punish: The Birth of the Prison* (Paris, 1975).
——, *Power/Knowledge* (New York, 1980).
Freeman, J.M., *Untouchable: An Indian Life History* (London, 1979).
Fuchs, Stephen, *Rebellious Prophets: A Study of Messianic Movements in Indian Religions* (Bombay, 1965).
Ginzburg, Carla, *The Cheese and the Worms: The Cosmos of a 16th Century Miller* (Johns Hopkins, 1980).

Gopal. S., *Selected Works of Jawaharlal Nehru Vol. 6* (New Delhi, 1987).

Gramsci, Antonio, *Selections From Prison Note Books* (New York, 1971).

——, *Selections From Cultural Writings* (Cambridge, 1985).

Guha, Amalendu, *Planter Raj to Swaraj: Freedom Struggle and Electoral Politics in Assam, 1826-1947* (New Delhi, 1977).

Guha, Ranajit (ed.) *Subaltern Studies Vols. I-VI* (New Delhi, 1982; 1983; 1984; 1985; 1987; 1989).

Guha, Ranajit, *Elementary Aspects of Peasant Insurgency in Colonial India* (New Delhi, 1983).

Guha, Uma *et.al* (eds.) *The Didayi: A Forgotten Tribe of Orissa* (Delhi. 1968).

Habib, Irfan, *Agrarian System of Mughal India* (Bombay, 1963).

Hardiman, David, *Peasant Nationalists of Gujarat: Kheda District 1917- 1934* (New Delhi, 1981).

Hennigham, Stephen, *Peasant Movements in Colonial India: North Bihar 1917-1942* (Canberra, 1982).

Hill, Christopher, *The World Turned Upside Down* (Harmondsworth, 1975).

Hilton, Rodney, *Bondmen Made Free: Medieval Peasant Movements and the English Rising of 1381* (London, 1977).

Hobsbawm , E. J., Primitive Rebels (Manchester, 1959).

——, *Bandits* (Harmondsworth, 1972).

Hobsbawm *et.al* (eds.), *Peasants in History* (Calcutta, 1980).

Hobsbawm, E.J. and G. Rude, *Captain Swing* (Harmondsworth, 1985).

Hutchins, F., *Spontaneous Revolution* (Delhi, 1971).

Jena, K.C., *Land Revenue Administration in Orissa During the Nineteenth Century* (New Delhi, 1968).

——, *Socio-Economic Condition of Orissa During the Nineteenth Century* (New Delhi, 1978).

Kanungo, Binode, *Utkalamani Gopabandhu* (Oriya; Cuttack, 1976).

Kaplan, Steven (ed.), *Understanding Popular Culture* (Moulton, 1984).

Kumar, Kapil, *Peasants in Revolt: Tenants, Landlords, Congress and the Raj in Oudh 1886-1922* (New Delhi, 1984).

—— (ed.), *Congress and Classes: Nationalism, Workers and Peasants* (New Delhi, 1988).

Ladurie, E.L.R., *Carnival in Romans: A People's Uprising at Romans*

1579-1580 (Harmondsworth, 1981).
——, *Love, Death and Money in the Pays Doc* (Harmondsworth, 1984).
Lefebvre, G., *The Great Fear of 1789: Rural Panic in Revolutionary France* (London, 1973).
Low, D.A. (ed.), *Congress and the Raj* (London, 1977).
Mahapatra, Sitakanta, *The Awakened Wind: The Oral Poetry of the Indian Tribes* (New Delhi, 1983).
Mahtab, H.K., *et.al* (eds.), *History of the Freedom Movement in Orissa Vols I-V* (Cuttack, 1957).
——, *History of Orissa Vols I-II* (Cuttack, 1959; 1960).
——, *Gandhiji O Orissa* (Oriya; Cuttack, 1971).
——, *The Beginning of the End* (Cuttack, 1972).
——, *Sadhanara Pathe* (Oriya; Cuttack, 1972).
——, *Dasabarsara Orissa* (Oriya; Cuttack, 1977).
Mansergh, N., *Transfer of Power 1942-1947 Vols. IV; VII* (London, 1973; New Delhi, 1976).
Mansingh, Mayadhar, *A History of Oriya Literature* (New Delhi, 1962).
Margadant, T.W., *French Peasants in Revolt: The Insurrection of 1851* (Princeton, 1979).
Marx, K., and Engels, F., *On Colonialism* (Moscow ?).
——, *On Religion* (Moscow, 1975).
Menon, V.P., *The Story of the Integration of the Indian States* (Madras, 1961).
Misra, P.K., *The Political History of Orissa: 1900-1936* (Delhi, 1979).
Misra, Sadasiv (ed.), *Gopabandhu the Legislator* (Cuttack, 1977).
Misra, Manmohan (ed.) *Nabina Biswa* (Oriya; Cuttack, 1983).
Mohanty, Gopinath, *Paraja* (Oriya; Cuttack 1983; tr. into English, New Delhi, 1987).
Mohanty, Manindra, *Jatiya Kabi Banchanidhi* (Oriya; Balasore, 1987).
Mohanty, Prafulla, *Indian Village Tales* (London, 1975).
Mohanty, Surendranath, *Satabdira Surjya* (Oriya; Cuttack, 1970).
Mullick, Muralidher, *Biplabi Chakradhar* (Oriya; Cuttack, 1977).
Nanda, Dasarathi, *Saheed Laxman Naik* (Oriya; Berhampur, 1977).
Nilgiri Praja Andolana Compilation Committee, *Nilgiri Praja Andolanara Itihas* (Oriya; Balasore, 1982).
O'Malley, L.S.S., *Popular Hinduism: Religion of the Masses* (New

York, 1970).

Pandey, Gyanendra, *Ascendency of the Congress in Uttar Pradesh: A Study in Imperfect Mobilisation* (Delhi, 1978).

Pannigrahi, Kalindi Charan, *Matira Manisha* (Oriya; Cuttack, 1952).

——, *Granthabali Part I* (Oriya; Cuttack, 1971).

Pannigrahi, Kalindi Charan *et.al*, *Basanti* (Oriya; Cuttack, 1969).

Parulekar, Godavari, *Adivasis Revolt* (Calcutta, 1975).

Patra, K.M., *Orissa Under the East India Company* (New Delhi, 1971).

——, *Orissa Legislature and Freedom Struggle 1912-47* (New Delhi, 1979).

Patra, S.C., *Formation of the Province of Orissa: The Success of the First Linguistic Movement in India* (Calcutta, 1980).

Pattnaik, Gorachand, *The Famine and Some Aspects of British Economic Policy in Orissa* (Cuttack, 1980).

Pattnaik, Gurucharan, *Ganjam Re Rakta Kanda* (Oriya; Cuttack, 1953).

Pattnaik, Gurucharan (ed.), *Bhagabati Sanchayana* (Oriya; Cuttack, 1985).

Pattnaik, N.K., *Social History of 19th Century Orissa* (Allahabad, 1984).

Pattnaik, Sudhakar, *Sambada Patraru Orissara Katha* (Oriya; Cuttack, 1972).

Pradhan, P.M., *Mukti Pathe Sainika* (Oriya; Cuttack, 1979).

Pradhan, S., *Agrarian and Political Movements : States of Orissa 1931- 1949* (New Delhi, 1986).

Pradhan Sudhi (ed.), *Marxist Cultural Movement on India: Chronicles and Documents (1936-1947)* (Calcutta, 1979).

Praharaj, G., *Utkala Kahani* (Oriya; Cuttack ?).

Pujari, B., *Saheed Bira Laxman Naik* (Oriya; Bhubneshwar, ?).

Raichudamani, G., *Itihasara Padakshepa* (Oriya; Cuttack, 1977).

Ram, Ramchandra, *Sangramee* (Oriya; Cuttack, 1986).

Rasul M.A., *A History of the All India Kisan Sabha* (Calcutta, 1974).

Rath, Radhanath, *The Story of Freedom Struggle in Orissa States* (Cuttack, 1969).

Routroy, Sachidananda, *Granthabali Part II* (Oriya; Cuttack, 1979).

Roy, S.C. *The Mundas and their Country* (Bombay, 1970).

Rude, G., *The Crowd in the French Revolution* (London, 1959).

——, *The Crowd in History: A Study of Popular Disturbances in France and England 1730-1848* (New York, 1964).

——, *Paris and London in the Eighteenth Century: Studies in Protest* (London, 1974).

Sahai, Govind, *42 Rebellion* (Delhi, 1947).

Sahu, Biswanath, *Land Utilisation in Orissa* (Cuttack, 1951).

Sahu, L.N., *The Hill Tribes of Jeypur* (? 1942).

Samal, J.K., *Orissa Under the British Crown* (New Delhi, 1977).

Sarkar, Sumit, *Swadeshi Movement in Bengal 1903-1908* (New Delhi, 1973).

——, *Modern India: 1885-1947* (New Delhi, 1983).

——, *Popular Movements and Middle Class Leadership in Late Colonial India: Perspectives and Problems of a "History from Below"* (Calcutta, 1983).

——, *A Critique of Colonial India* (Calcutta 1985).

Sarkar, Tanika, *Bengal 1928-1934: The Politics of Protest* (New Delhi, 1987).

Satpathy, Nityananda, *Adhunika Oriya Sahitya* (Oriya; Cuttack, 1977).

Senapati, Phakirmohan, *Autobiography* (Oriya; Cuttack, 1969).

——, *Granthabali* (Oriya; Cuttack, 1963).

Shanin, T., *The Awkward Class: Political Sociology of Peasantry in a Developing Society: Russia 1910-1925* (Oxford, 1972).

Siddiqui, Majid, *Agrarian Unrest in North India: United Provinces, 1918-1922* (New Delhi, 1978).

Singh Deo, B., *The Goti System in Jeypur Agency Orissa* (Jeypur, 1939).

Singh, K.S., *The Dust Storm and the Hanging Mist: A Study of Birsa Munda and his Movement in Chotanagpur 1874-1901* (Calcutta, 1966).

Singh, Ramprasad, *Homasikha* (Oriya; Cuttack, 1950).

——, *Pratihinsa* (Oriya, Cuttack, 1954).

Sundarayya, P., *The Telengana People's Struggle and its Lessons* (Calcutta, 1950).

Talcher Prajamandal Compilation Committee, *Talcher Prajamandalara Itihas* (Calcutta, 1950).

Thompson, E.P., *Whigs and Hunters* (Harmondsworth, 1975).

Thusu, K.N., *Pengo Parojas of Koraput* (Calcutta, 1977).

Tilly, Charles, *The Vendee* (London, 1964).

Tilly, L.A., and C. Tilly, *Class Conflict and Collective Action* (London, 1981).

Venkatarangaiya, M.(ed.), *The Freedom Struggle in Andhra Pradesh Vol.III (1921-1931)* (Hyderabad, 1965).

Articles

Arnold, David, 'Dacoity and Rural Crime in Madras, 1860-1940', in *The Journal of Peasants Studies,* January, 1979.

————, 'Looting, Grain Riots and Government Policy in South India, 1918', in *Past and Present,* August, 1979.

Atlury, Murali, 'Allury Sitaram Raju and the Mamjam Rebellion of 1922- 24', in *Social Scientist,* April 1984.

————, 'Non-Cooperation in Andhra in 1920-22: Nationalist Intelligentsia and the Mobilisation of Peasantry', in *Indian Historical Review,* July 1985-January 1986.

Bailey, F.G. 'The Peasant View of the Bad Life' in Shanin, T. (ed.), *Peasants and Peasant Societies* (London, 1984).

Barik, R.K., Gopabandhu and the National Movement in Orissa, in *Social Scientist,* May, 1978.

————, 'Subaltern Politics and the Unrecognised Intelligentsia in Orissa', in *Social Science Probings,* September, 1987.

Bhattacharya, N., 'Colonial State and Agrarian Society, in Bhattacharya *et.al* (eds.), *Situating Indian History For Sarvapalli Gopal* (New Delhi, 1986).

Chandra, Bipan, 'Jawaharlal Nehru and the Indian Capitalist Class 1936', *The Economic and Political Weekly,* Vol. X, August, 1975.

————, 'Peasantry and National Integration' in his *Nationalism and Colonialism in Modern India* (New Delhi, 1979).

Chaudhuri, B.B., 'Land Market in Eastern India', in *Indian Economic and Social History Review Vol.12, 1975* (in two parts)

————, 'Eastern India', in Kumar, D. (ed.), *The Cambridge Economic History of India Vol.II c.1757-c.1970* (New Delhi, 1984).

Clarke, R., 'Panas of Orissa' in M. Kennedy, *The Criminal Castes in India* (? 1907; reprinted, Delhi, 1985).

Das, B.S. 'Decline of Balasore and Textile Industry in Orissa' in *Quarterly Review of Historical Studies* no. I, 1978-79.

Das, Hemanta, 'Adivasi Samajare Madyapanara Bhumika' (Oriya), in *Adivasi,* October, 1977-January, 1978.

Das, Nityananda, 'Martyr Laxman Naik: A Hero of the Freedom Movement', in *Adivasi,* 1967-1968.

——, 'Tribal Situation in Orissa' in Singh, K.S. (ed.) *Tribal Situation in India* (Simla, 1972).

Hobsbawm, E.J., 'Peasants and Politics', in *The Journal of Peasant Studies*, October, 1973.

Lefebvre, G., 'Revolutionary Crowds', in Kaplow (ed.), *New Perspectives on the French Revolution* (New York, 1965).

Mahapatra, K., and K. Debi, 'Shifting Cultivation in Orissa' in *Adivasi* Vol.XIV, no. 4.

Mahapatra, L.K., 'Social Movements Among Tribes in Eastern India with Special Reference to Orissa', in *Sociologus* Vol.18, no. 1. 1968.

Mahapatra, P.K., 'Handbook on Koya' , in *Adivasi* , Vol. XI no. 4, 1970-1971.

Mahapatra, S., 'The Insider Diku: Boundary Rules and Marginal Man in Santhal Society', in P.C Mahapatra, ., *et.al* (eds.), *Tribal Problems of Tomorrow* (Bhubneshwar, 1980).

Mahtab, H.K., Presidential Address Local History Section, *Proceedings of the Indian History Congress* 1949.

Marx, K., 'Debates on the Law on the Thefts of Wood', in *Rheinische Zeitung*, October-November 1942.

——, 'The Eighteenth Brummaire of Louis Bonaparte', in *Selected Works Vol .I* (Moscow, 1977).

May, J.A., 'Notes on the Bondas, of Jaipur' , in *Indian Antiquary* Vol.2, 1873.

Mittal, S.K. and K. Kumar, 'Baba Ramchandra and the Peasant Upsurge in Oudh', in *Social Scientist* no., 71, 1978.

Mohanty, K.K., 'A Weekly Market in Rural Orissa' in *The Journal of Social Research* , Vol. XI, no. 1, 1968.

Mohanty, Manoranjan, 'Social Roots of Backwardness in Orissa (A Study of Class, Caste and Power)', in *Social Science Probings*, June, 1984.

Mohanty, U.C., 'Bond Friendship among the Gadba', in *Society*, 1973-74 (inaugural volume).

Panda, B., 'The Prajamandal Movement of Nilgiri', *The Eastern Times*, 23 May, 1981.

Pati, Biswamoy, 'Reviewing the Emergence of the Orissa Province', in *The Quartely Review of Historical Studies*, October-December, 1984.

——, 'Complex Fabric of Tribal Life', in *The Economic and Political Weekly*, 12 December, 1987.

——, Storm Over Malkangiri: A Note on Laxman Naiko's Revolt, 1942' in G. Panday, (ed.)., *The Indian Nation in 1942* (Calcutta, 1988).

——, 'Perceptions in a Changing Society: A Note on Koraput (Orissa)', paper presented at an ICSSR Seminar, 'Peasants in History', Sri Venkateswara College, Delhi University, 7-8 December, 1984; published subsequently in *Economic and Political Weekly*' 5 May 1990.

Patra, K.M., 'Growth of National Consciousness and Freedom Movement in Orissa', in *The Indian Historical Review*, July,1985-January,1986.

Raut, S., 'Rural Stratification in Coastal Orissa (1866-1900)', in *Social Science Probings*, March, 1986.

Roy, S.C., 'An Indian Riddle Book - Orissa: Bhuya', in *Man in India* Vol. 23, 1943.

Roy, S.N., 'The Savaras of Orissa', in *Man in India*, Vol.7, 1927.

Sanganna, S., 'Revolts in Orissa - Martyr Laxman Naik: A Hero of the Freedom Movement', in V. Rangavaih, (ed.) *Tribal Revolts* (Nellore, 1971).

Somasundaram, A.M., 'A Note on the Gadbas of Koraput District' in *Man in India* Vol. 29, 1949.

Thompson, E.P., 'The Moral Economy of the English Crowd in the Eighteenth Century', *Past and Present*, February, 1971.

Yunus, S.A., 'Orissa', in S.N. Dubey, , and R.Murdra, (eds.), *Land Alienation and Restoration in Tribal Communities in India* (Bombay, 1977).

Theses and Unpublished Articles

Raul, Nathan, 'Intellectual Origins of Nationalism in Orissa: c.1870-1930', (M.Phil. thesis, Delhi University, 1981; unpublished).

Satpathy, Renubala, 'Utkalia Jana Jagarana Re Oriya Sahitya Ra Abadana' (Oriya; Ph.D thesis, Utkala University, 1984; unpublished).

Padhi, S.P., 'Property in Land, Land Market and Tenancy Relations in the Colonial Period: A Review of Theoretical Categories', paper presented at the Seminar on 'Commercialisation in Indian Agriculture', Trivandrum, 23-25 November, 1981 (unpublished).

Pandey, G., 'Peasant Unrest', paper presented at the History Congress, Bombay 1980 (unpublished).

Sahu, B.P., 'Orissa Society: Past Trends and Present Manifestations', paper presented at a Seminar on 'State Specific Caste-Class Situations in India', TDSS, Pune, 27-30 December, 1987 (unpublished).

Index

All India Kisan Sabha - delegates from Orissa for the
-Lucknow Session (1936) 88
-Palasa Session (1940) 147
-Vizayawada Session (1944) 212-13

Bhagachasi movement - 224-26

Caste - conflicts 221
-Kutchery 18
-and money relationship 17
Christianity and tribals 22
Civil Disobedience Movement 70-6
-attacks on chaukidars during 72
-collective protest during 72
-in the princely states 75
-rumours during 77
-violation of forest laws during 73
-and salt laws 71-2
Coalition ministry during '42 Movement 157,161,209
Congress - communalists within 220
-development projects visualised by in 1946-50 218, 232
-membership of between 1929-46 217
-and between 1938-40 153
-ministry of 1937 95-100
-and of 1946 217-20
-separatists within 220
-tenancy bills introduced by the '37 ministry 98-9
corruption during 1946-50 219
crime under colonialism 35

Didayi folk tale on the origin of trees 29
disease in popular perception 30-3

election of - 1937 89-93
-Kisan Sangha during '37 campaign 90
- 1946 212-15

Famine -1866 17-8, 35, 46
- 1943 209-11, 221
folk tales associated with liquor 26-7
formation of serfs 24

Gandhi - and 'non-interference' in the princely states 108
- in Orissa 62,69,76,102

Hinduisation of tribals 18-22
hoodwinking of spirits 31-2

indebtedness 15
interest rates on loans 15
internal exploiters within tribal society 18
imposition of restrictions on
- forests 29-30
- hatas 28-9
-intoxicants 2608
-pastures 29-30
-salt manufacture 25-6

Jagannatha cult 38-9
-folk tales associated with 39-41

Kandhas - turmeric sacrifice of 34
Khadal 26
Kisan Sangha membership - 1938-43 209

land market 15
liquor - folk tales associated with 26-7

Mahima cult 23-4
migration 37-8
minority ministry of 1937 93,95

Non-cooperation Movement 62-9
-in Kanika 62-7
-in the princely states 68-9

Orissa State Peoples' Conference - founded in 1931 109
Orissa States Enquiry Committee Report 1939 129
Oriya intellectual - at the turn of the 19th century 45-8
-responses to the Quit India Movement 186-7, 208
outcastes - dependence on forests 29-30
-perception of high castes 22-4

podu 2,29
princely states - Non-Cooperation Movement in 68-9
-Civil Disobedience Movement in 75
-Quit India Movement in 173-8

Quit India Movement - background 144-61
-chasi-mulia raj at Talcher during 176-8
-and Communists 174-5, 185
-and the intellectual during 186-7, 208
-in the Jeypore estate 178-85
-and Laxman Naiko 181-2
-the mass upsurge during 161-85
-in the princely states 173-8
-social composition of the participants 165-6,171-2,183-5
-the Swadhin Banchanidhi chakla during 169-72

Rajendra Prasad - the saviour of Orissa's Landlords 100
rebellions during the 19th century 36-7
regional chauvinism during 1946-7 221-2

Satnami cult 23
Sundhi 28

tar tax 24-5
temple-entry movement during 1947-8 218,221
traditional industries 25-6

Utkala Kisan Sangha - founded in 1935 88
Utkala Sabha 47
Utkala Sammilani 61-2
Utkala Union Conference 47-8
Utkala Samyavadi Karmi Sangha 87

Women - problems faced in the 19th century 33-4
-in the Civil Disobedience Movement 75, 77-8
-in the 1936-9 phase 130